HORRENDOUS DEATH
AND HEALTH

SERIES IN DEATH EDUCATION, AGING, AND HEALTH CARE

HANNELORE WASS, CONSULTING EDITOR

ADVISORY BOARD

Herman Feifel, Ph.D.
Jeanne Quint Benoliel, R.N., Ph.D.
Balfour Mount, M.D.

HORRENDOUS DEATH
AND HEALTH:
TOWARD ACTION

Edited by
Daniel Leviton
University of Maryland

⬤HEMISPHERE PUBLISHING CORPORATION
A member of the Taylor & Francis Group
New York   Washington   Philadelphia   London

HORRENDOUS DEATH AND HEALTH: Toward Action

1 2 3 4 5 6 7 8 9 0   B R B R   9 8 7 6 5 4 3 2 1

This book was set in Times Roman by Hemisphere Publishing Corporation.
The editors were Amy Lyles Wilson and Em Turner Yates; the production supervisor was Peggy M. Rote; and the typesetters were Lori Knoernschild, Darrell D. Larsen, Jr., and Laurie Strickland.
Cover design by Debra Eubanks Riffe.
Printing and binding by Braun-Brumfield, Inc.

A CIP catalog record for this book is available from the British Library.

Library of Congress Cataloging-in-Publication Data

Horrendous death and health: toward action / edited by Daniel Leviton
*   p.   cm.—(Series in death education, aging, and health care)*
*   Includes bibliographical references and index.*
*   1. Death—Psychological aspects.   2. Disasters—Psychological aspects.   3. Nuclear warfare—Psychological aspects.   4. Peace-Psychological aspects.   I. Leviton, Daniel.   II. Series.*
BF789.D4H67 1991
306.9—dc20   90-23324
                                                   CIP

ISBN 1-56032-186-5
ISSN 0275-3510

Contents

III
CONCLUSION

Contributors

NANCY H. ALLEN, M.P.H., is a Health Education Specialist at the Neuropsychiatric Institute and Hospital, University of California at Los Angeles. She is the author of *Homicide: Perspectives on Prevention*. In addition to her teaching and research, she is an M.F.C.C. and specializes in counseling the survivor-victims of horrendous deaths.

MAIRE A. DUGAN, Ph.D., has served as Executive Director of the Consortium on Peace Research, Education, and Development (COPRED) since 1987. She also holds an affiliated faculty position with the Center for Conflict Analysis and Resolution at George Mason University in Virginia. Prior to that she held positions on the faculty of the Center for Peaceful Change at Kent State University, and was a mediation and arbitration trainer for the Better Business Bureau system. She received her doctorate in peace studies and conflict resolution from Syracuse University in 1979, and has written and edited several works in the field, including a special issue of the journal *Peace and Change* entitled "Conflict Resolution: Theory and Practice."

EVA FOGELMAN, Ph.D., is a Senior Research Fellow at the Center for Social Research of the Graduate Center of City University of New York. She is a pioneer, along with Bella Savran, in developing groups for children of Holocaust survivors. Fogelman founded and is Co-Director of the training of mental health professionals in Counseling with Holocaust Survivors and Second Generation at the Training Institute for Mental Health. In addition, she is Founding Director of the Jewish Foundation for Christian Rescuers of the Anti-Defamation League of B'nai B'rith and a board member and research associate for Jerome Riker International Study of Organized Persecution of Children of Child Development Research.

PERRIN FRENCH, M.D., is a Clinical Associate Professor of Psychiatry and the Behavioral Sciences at Stanford University. He is a graduate of Harvard College and received his M.D. degree from Johns Hopkins University. He returned to Harvard for a 4-year fellowship in psychiatry and was awarded the Paul M. Howard Prize for skill in humane and comprehensive psychiatric treatment. In 1980, with three medical students, he founded the Stanford Mid-Peninsula and South Bay

Chapter of Physicians for Social Responsibility (PSR). He was appointed in 1987 to the American Psychiatric Association's Committee on Psychological Aspects of Nuclear Issues. His particular area of interest has been in the attitude of the public toward nuclear weapons and nuclear war, and how public attitude is affected by education.

DANIEL LEVITON, Ph.D., is a Professor of Health Education, an Adjunct Professor of Family Medicine, and the Director and Founder of the Adult Health and Development Program at the University of Maryland, College Park. He was one of the founders and first president of the Association for Death Education and Counseling.

JUDITH EVE LIPTON, M.D., is a Psychiatrist in private practice in Redmond, Washington. She founded the Washington state chapter of Physicians for Social Responsibility in 1979 and was president of that chapter until 1983. Currently, Lipton is chairperson of the American Psychiatric Association's Committee on the Psychological Aspects of Nuclear Issues, as well as chair of the American Woman Psychiatrist's Committee on Nuclear Issues. She has co-authored two books with her husband, David Barash, a Professor of Psychology and Zoology at the University of Washington: *Stop Nuclear War! A Handbook,* a complete guide to citizens' action to stop the nuclear arms race; and *The Caveman and the Bomb: Human Nature, Evolution, and Nuclear War,* an exploration of the psychological causes of the arms race from an evolutionary and sociobiological point of view.

EARL A. MOLANDER, Ph.D., is an Associate Professor of Management at Portland (Oregon) State University. He teaches and publishes in the area of the social and political environment of business. His articles have appeared in the *Harvard Business Review, Perspectives in Defense Management,* and other journals. He is the author of *Responsive Capitalism: Case Studies in Corporate Social Conduct* (New York: Pocket Books, 1983), and the coauthor of *Nuclear War: What's In It for You* (New York: Pocket Books, 1982). Dr. Molander is currently the executive director of the Ground Zero Pairing Project and Ground Zero.

ART NEWMAN, Ph.D., is Professor of Foundations of Education at the University of Florida in Gainesville. He could be speaking for all of the contributors when he writes, "So that my teenage children, Sean and Erica, and their millions of counterparts might inherit a somewhat less imperiled planet, I am committed to making a modest contribution to the process of helping raise consciousness of the threat of nuclear war. With eager anticipation, I look forward to participating in ongoing scholarly inquiry into educating others about the nuclear threat . . . and am committed to joining like-minded people engaged in this enterprise."

RICHARD A. PACHOLSKI, Ph.D., is the Warren F. Hardy Distinguished Professor of English at Millikin University in Decatur, Illinois. He teaches such courses as literature of the Holocaust, nuclear issues in literature, death and dying, and to lighten things up a bit, courses in sports and values as well as contemporary magazines.

MICHAEL H. SHUMAN is a Co-Founder and the President of the Center for Innovative Diplomacy, a 6,000-member nonprofit organization dedicated to preventing war by promoting citizen and city participation in foreign policy. Shuman graduated with distinction from Stanford University in economics and with a J.D. from Stanford Law School. He is now a member of the State Bar of California. In 1980 he won the *Bulletin of Atomic Scientists'* Rabinowitch Award for his essay, "How to Eliminate the Threat of Nuclear War." In 1987, he received a MacArthur Foundation Fellowship for International Security Writing and a Kellogg Foundation National Leadership Fellowship.

JOHN F. TUOHEY, Ph.D. is an Assistant Professor of Bioethics, Department of Theology, Catholic University of America, Washington, DC. He obtained his Ph.D. from the Katholieke Universiteit Leuven, Belgium, 1986. His dissertation focused on care for the terminally ill. He is also the author of *Caring for Persons with AIDS and Cancer: Ethical Reflections on Palliative Care for the Terminally Ill.*

Preface

There was a certain hopefulness in editing this book and its sister volume, *Horrendous Death, Health, and Well-Being* (Leviton, 1991, Hemisphere). The first book described the increasing types of people-caused, premature deaths affecting and threatening the global population with special reference to our children and grandchildren. It attempted to show that the study of death (thanatology) could serve as a stimulus to improving the quality of global health and well-being by removing the denial that your child and mine could die at any moment as a result of horrendous type deaths.

The key was *health protective action* by all of us. A means to action was universal health education of people of all ages where the goal was the improvement of global health and well-being for present and future generations. That universal, unique form of health education emphasized the humanities, and integrated death education as a means to valuing life and living by removing the denial of personal immortality.

Horrendous Death, Health, and Well-Being also described concepts and ideas to eliminate horrendous deaths as examples of what can be done. The larger message was that the global community needed to organize its intellectual and financial resources to eliminate causes of horrendous deaths similar to the coordinated efforts that occur during times of war or other national and international emergencies.

This volume carries on where the earlier volume left off. Its theme is *health protective action* using thanatology as a stimulus. Again, I feel strongly that the outcome of health education (as the term is used here) is action. Obviously the primary goal of action is to prevent horrendous death from occurring, that is preventive intervention. Another is to restore to health the survivor-victims of horrendous deaths. Here we are concerned with postvention or therapy.

So, on the one hand, the book is positive and hopeful because it describes individual and group action to eliminate forms of horrendous death, treat survivor-victims, and thus improve the quality of global health and well-being. On the other hand local and world events haven't improved too much since the first volume was published. Where I live, in the metropolitan Washington, DC, area, homicide rates are increasing. War in the Middle East is a distinct threat. Economic depression, unemployment, and hostilities between ethnic/racial groups and economic classes are increasing in actuality or probability.

Yet, people are becoming less passive. We are beginning to act in our best health interests. The theme, "I've had enough," is growing louder, and subsequent efforts more organized. For example, after a recent series of homicides in our community, citizens organized to take preventive action. Declaring war on Iraq, rather than seeking peaceful means to resolve the conflict, was challenged by our own U.S. Congress and the global community resulting in an open debate, and a delay of killing. People wanted to give the United Nations, economic sanctions, and other means of conflict resolution a chance.

This book provides models of health protective action. My hope is they will stimulate you to act in your best health and well-being interest. Do you wish your children and grandchildren to live long *and* well? Then act.

Daniel Leviton

Introduction

This book is the sequel to *Horrendous Death, Health and Well-Being* (Leviton, 1991) referred to her hereafter as Volume I. Its task was to *health-educate* the intelligent reader to the present, imminent dangers of *horrendous death* (or horrendous-type deaths to be more specific). You will notice the emphasis on *health education.* The contributors to this book and I are concerned with health in the broadest sense of not only being free from illness and disease, but also feeling good about the present and prospects for the future for oneself and others. Such health education is difficult because the topics are usually so threatening that they elicit defense mechanisms such as psychological evidence and reactionalization. For example, how many people think of the possibility (future orientation) that they or their loved ones will die in the next few months, hours, or weeks as a result of murder, suffocation from chemical and biological weapons, radiation from nuclear explosion, or burns from napalm as an enemy attacks with flame-throwers?

Because these causes of death are man-made they can be prevented and eliminated by people if we would put our collective minds to it. We would *health-educate* the reader toward action to influence (even better, demand) of our political, corporate, and military leaders, the gatekeepers of power, the elimination of the causes of horrendous-type deaths. On the other hand, we must act ourselves. The purpose of this volume is to provide examples of preventive and postventive intervention by individuals and small groups that will prompt you to act to improve the quality of global health by eliminating horrendous-type death. Actions, which by definition, are in your and your loved one's best interests. Jean Mayer, writing in the foreword to a Sivard volume, feels similarly. "There is little hope of official agreements to end the insanity of this arms race until enough of the world's citizens are *given the facts* and can *act collectively* to bring informed pressure to bear on their governments" (Sivard, 1987, p. 3).

The ultimate goal of both volumes, then, is to stimulate the reader to *action* to eliminate horrendous-type death. Horrendous-type death must become a salient concern for as many individuals, worldwide, as possible. But salience without action is meaningless.

In the Introduction to Volume I, I wrote that the contributors to that volume and I were scared. We felt that the probability of man killing his fellow humans in unheard-of numbers, and destroying the globe in the near future, was increasing dramatically. Keeping that from happening is the greatest health priority of this century, as great or greater than preventing death due to diseases such as AIDS, coronary heart disease, stroke, and cancer. So the authors and I need to do what we can to increase the probability that everyone's children and grandchildren (certainly including our own) will live both long and well. That is the bottom line—to improve the quality of global health and well-being so that our children and grandchildren live both long and well.

The threat has increased in the space of a few years. During the writing of Volume I, the threat of nuclear war with the Soviet Union was followed by the threat of war with Iran as a result of their taking American hostages during President Carter's administration. That crisis lay bilious and unresolved in the craw of the American public. Added to the soup of global horrendous-type death threats were a host of killings in South Africa and military excursions such as the Falkland Islands, Grenada, Panama, South Africa, and El Salvador, to mention a few. Almost simultaneously the industrialized countries were awakened, startled, and almost rendered impotent to the threat of other forms of horrendous-type death such as the significant lowering of the quality of the environment, the spread of AIDS, the misuse of drugs such as cocaine, and racism. In this country, racism, a form of horrendous death, and its correlates such as poverty, undernutrition, and homicide are increasing. Worse, the races are suspicious and hateful of one another, making it difficult to improve the quality of global health and well-being. To my way of thinking the Horses of the Modern Apocalypse are the forms of horrendous-type death that are the focus of Volume I and this book as well.

As we near the end of 1990 and *Horrendous Death and Health: Toward Action* prepares for the presses, this father, and other fathers and mothers the world over, watch as military posturing between Iraq, the United States, and their respective allies gallops toward the point of no return. In that war of words by political leaders little is said of the huge cost in *horrendous deaths* to be suffered by all innocent people (Arab and non-Arab) caught in the cross fire of chemical and biological warfare, and other forms of conventional and nuclear war.

One theme articulated in Volume I was a variation of the ecological dictum, "If any child dies due to horrendous-type death my (and your) child can die!" In August 1990 as events between Iraq and the United States heated, my beautiful 14-year-old boy asked me if he was going to die as a result of the Iraqi invasion of Kuwait. I said that the odds had increased that we all would unless we did something to prevent war. He was terrified! I don't care to see my boy terrified for no good reason. My task as a parent is to prevent such terrors. The good and great work for leaders of countries, the father-mother figure, is to do the same for their "children."

My neighbor's roots are in Palestine. Our children are the best of friends. My daughter knows more Arabic than Hebrew. She dines and sleeps so frequently at their house I have suggested to Mr. M. that he use Leslie as an income tax deduction. They are good and decent people. When the Iraqi invasion of Kuwait occurred, Mr. and Mrs. M. told us of a family of their relatives, including children, who were vacationing. They are prevented by the Iraqi government from returning to their home in Kuwait. Without access to their property and funds in Kuwait, this family was reduced from middle-class professionals to impoverished refugees. The effect on their children must be horrendous: One day happy, the next, refugees separated from those symbols and things representing security with the imminent threat of horrendous-type death hanging overhead. If this scenario can happen to their children and family it can happen to yours and mine.

I don't want to see any child—Arab, European, American, Black, Hispanic, Asian, White—terrified when the cause can be eliminated. There are ways of resolving conflict other than by war. Personally, I don't object to defensive military actions. It is the offensive kind that can eliminate the world as we know it that unnerves me. Thus war, as we approach the 21st century, is an anachronism.

I have several questions to be answered before I would even consider being supportive of an offensive war, say, in the Middle East.

• How did the industrialized countries become so dependent upon imported oil, especially after the oil embargo during the 1980s? Why weren't alternative sources of energy and conservation developed? Why should people die for "King Oil" when the multinational oil corporations have a history of exploiting consumers at every chance?

• How did Iraq and other developing countries obtain such sophisticated weaponry? Who sold it to them? How did they and other developing countries gain their technological expertise and materials to produce nuclear, chemical, and other modern weapons? Is it possible that soldiers, including Americans, will be killed by weapons sold to the enemy by America or its allies?

• Why do the children and grandchildren of political and corporate leaders rarely serve as lieutenants, sergeants, and privates of platoons of soldiers in combat? Put them on the front lines and the fervor for combat might be mitigated in favor of negotiations at the United Nations level.

Again, as this is being written, only a few world-class leaders and organizations like King Hussein of Jordan, President Mikhail Gorbachev of the Soviet Union, and the United Nations are seeking a peaceful settlement in a "world gone mad" as Hussein well put it. More power to them and others who seek peaceful ways to resolve conflicts that can destroy the globe.

Recently I read a review of *Kids Who Kill,* a book by Charles Patrick Ewing, who predicted that killings by children will quadruple by the end of the decade (Gentry, 1990). Ewing noted the relationship between this form of horrendous-type death and child abuse, poverty, drugs, and increasing access to guns, and decried the cuts in antipoverty programs such as Head Start and the school lunch program. "When you make life less livable for human beings, you pay for it," (Gentry, 1990, p. 2). Your child and mine could be killed by another child. The odds increase as the economy falters even more due to the buildup of war.

So the need for action to prevent horrendous-type death is even more relevant now. In order to achieve that grandiloquent goal, people of every country need to health-educate themselves to the threat of imminent, irreversible danger. As you are aware, we focus on a particular danger that has been labeled *horrendous-type deaths.*

HORRENDOUS-TYPE DEATHS

Horrendous-type deaths are characterized by being

• man-made (the sexist terminology is used intentionally because men, more than women, have perpetuated such deaths);

- motivated by the desire to kill, maim, injure, torture, or otherwise destroy another;
  - torturous in quality;
  - premature;
  - deadly to large numbers of people.

This genre of deaths is called horrendous death, type I (HD-I) (Table 1).

Our second focus is upon horrendous death, type II (HD-II) (Table 2). HD-II differs from the first in that it is caused by people but the deadly *motivation* to kill another is missing, and the quality of dying may or may not be torturous.

Examples of HD-I are conventional and nuclear war, homicide, torture, terrorism, genocide, death as a result of racism and the like.

Death by means of vehicular accident, suicide, starvation caused by people, destruction of or poisoning of the environment, abuse of drugs such as alcohol, tobacco, cocaine, heroin, and so forth are examples of HD-II. An illustration might be helpful. Say what you will of the tobacco industry, it cannot be accused of wishing to kill any group or individual. In fact, it wishes you alive. It is difficult to sell cigarettes to corpses. That particular industry is undoubtedly interested in profit. The motivation differs from that which governs HD-I.

A third category is labelled Other, and includes death as a result of cancer, coronary heart disease, Alzheimer's disease, and so forth, where the characteristics are

- May or may not be caused by people;
- Style of dying may or may not be torturous;
- Affects large numbers of people globally.

All causes of death might be termed *deathogenic*. Thus, HD-I, HD-II, and "other" causes of death fall under the broader category of deathogenic factors.

CONCEPTUAL FRAMEWORK
CONCERNING ACTION

In Volume I, a conceptual framework was developed with the outcome of increasing the probability of health protective action to eliminate horrendous-type death. Since then I have incorporated the theme of *grieving the future, premature horrendous death of one's own child* as an additional factor. First, a review of what was introduced in the earlier volume.

Denial of Death

The psychological denial of death is crucial to our concept of eliciting action to reduce the probability of horrendous-type deaths.

As Freud and others (Lifton, 1979; Segal, 1988; Meissner, 1988) have suggested, denial is an universal adaptation to the threat of personal death, that is, annihilation. World War I disillusioned Freud. He was horrified by the eradication of the rules of civilized moral and social conduct and the brutality with which men could inflict death and suffering upon people, whether soldiers or civilians (Freud, 1968). How could man be so barbaric? His answer was psychological denial of

Table 1 Horrendous death, type I

Characteristics
1. Man-made
2. Motivation is to kill, maim, injure, or destroy another
3. Style of dying or death is torturous
4. Affects large numbers of people globally

Examples
1. Nuclear and conventional war
2. Homicide
3. Terrorism
4. Assassination
5. Genocide
6. Man-made hunger and starvation
7. Racism

Approach: Prevention, intervention, postvention

---

personal death. "Our own death is indeed unimaginable," he wrote, " . . . at bottom no one believes in his own death, or to put the same thing in another way, in the unconscious every one of us is convinced of his own immortality" (Freud, as quoted in Rickman, 1968, p. 15)

Ernest Becker agreed when he wrote, "This narcissim is what keeps men marching into point-blank fire in wars: at heart one doesn't feel he will die, he only feels sorry for the man next to him" (Becker, 1973, p. 2).

Yet, Lifton is correct when he observes, "And our resistance to that knowledge, our denial of death, is indeed formidable. . . . But the denial can never be total; we are never fully ignorant of the fact that we die. Rather we go about life with a kind of 'middle knowledge' of death, a partial awareness of it side by side with expressions and actions that belie that awareness" (Lifton, 1979, p. 17).

Governments, like people, tend to deny the fact that horrendous-type death is inimical to health and well-being. *Health, United States, 1986 and Prevention Profile* and other publications of the U.S. Public Health Service and National Center for Health Statistics say little of the health costs of horrendous death, especially type I. Some mention is made of violent behaviors such as homicide and legal intervention, suicide, accidents, and child and spouse abuse (National Center for Health Statistics, 1986). It is not known whether this omission is intentional, but the result is the same. Generally, horrendous deaths (especially HD-I) are

Table 2 Horrendous death, type II

Characteristics
1. Man-made
2. Style of dying or death may be torturous
3. Affects large numbers of people globally

Examples
1. Accidents
2. Suicide
3. Substance abuse
4. Contamination of the physical environment and ecosystem
5. Man-made hunger and starvation where the motivation is not to kill another

Approach: Prevention, intervention, postvention

---

treated by the governmental health establishment as an aberration, unmentionable. It is only when one reads such mind-boggling, but objective, gems as *The State of the World Atlas* (Kidron & Segal, 1981) and two annual publications, *World Military and Social Expenditures* (Sivard, 1985) and *State of the World, 1987* (Brown, Chandler, Flavin, Jacobson, Pollock, Postel, Starke, & Wolfe, 1987) that the enormous economic and health costs of horrendous-type deaths for present and future generations are realized.

Removal of denial of horrendous-type deaths is central to my plan to motivate people to act to eliminate those forms of preventable deaths.

Grieving the Future, Premature Horrendous Death of One's Own Child

Once denial of horrendous death of the child is removed and the imagery of the torturous but preventable death confronted, the probability of action is increased. The next stage is one of anticipatory grief resulting from the imagery of the killed child or grandchild before the event occurs. Once denial is removed grief can occur.

Dennis Klass's *Parental Grief: Solace and Resolution* (1988) describes and explains the process of grieving for one's dead child. The death of one's child is one of life's most profound and strongest stressors. For many parents such a death supersedes the stress of one's own dying and death. It is no wonder that research indicates that suffering the death of a loved one is a health risk factor that increases the probability of the survivor's premature death and morbidity. In 1984 the Institute of Medicine published the results of its study of the health consequences of bereavement. It concluded that bereavement was associated with significant distress in practically everyone. Secondly, "some bereaved persons are at increased risk for illness and even death" (Osterweis, Solomon, & Green, p. 283).

The death of a child is a psychological indictment concerning parental competence. Are not parents supposed to protect their children from harm? Are they not viewed by the child as omnipotent and omniscient? "The child is a part of the parent's self," writes Klass (1988, p. 12), indicating that we identify with our child during its development. The identification is part of the parent-child bond. When the child dies it is often likened to an amputation. Not only has a part of the self been killed, but the psychological and physical pain also are excruciating. The death of a child destroys plans and expectations for the future. In a real sense, the future dies with the child.

But the horrendous death of a child is different than, say, death by means of childhood cancer. Besides identification with the dead child, that is, incorporating the dead child as part of the parent's ego, the parent internalizes the dead child's pain and suffering. The parent of a killed child cries out for vengeance and retribution, and rest does not come easily until such retaliation is achieved (Klass, 1988). For our purposes, the difference between anticipatory grieving of the fantasized and actual horrendous death of one's child lies in the modification and channeling of vengeance. If the child was literally killed, the odds are good that vengeance will be directed toward the killer or a killer-substitute (e.g., country, flag, etc.). It is possible that the vengeance of the parent might be channeled toward constructive outcomes, but most humans have yet to achieve control over such primal drives.

On the other hand, anticipatory, fantasized grieving over the death of the beloved child in the future elicits screams, fear, and trembling of what might be. Themes of hatred and vengeance toward the fantasized killer (individual, group, or state) are subordinate to the need to prevent such a death and to survive. *Anticipatory grieving has survival value.*

It became apparent in writing this book that anticipatory grieving concerning the future horrendous death of *my* children was both a stressor and a motivating force. As the horrendous death clock ticks closer to midnight vis-à-vis the Iraq-United States and Allies scenario, my own anticipatory grieving becomes more intense. I feel no hatred toward the Iraqis or Arabs. Instead, there is an overwhelming need to bring sane people together to prevent a war that surely will be long and deadly to large populations—including my children and yours.

Thus, in the conceptual framework presented here, the probability of personal action is hypothesized to increase if the individual is forced to experience the anticipatory grieving that results from the imagery of the child being killed by forms of horrendous death. Obviously action arousal is increased (at least in me) if the real-life situation (imminent war, homicide, etc.) reinforces the imagery.

THE TYPE OF DEATH-FEAR
OF DEATH-DENIAL-ACTION HYPOTHESIS

The question is what process would increase the probability that people would act to remove the causes of horrendous deaths, types I and II? Originally it was thought that one only had to remove the denial that our loved ones could die prematurely and horribly. I thought that once denial was removed people would act to protect their best interests. I now know that other factors are involved such as anticipatory grief and response efficacy, that is, the sense that one's responses will have an effect.

I also hypothesize that the perception of the quality, circumstances, and type of death are related to the level of denial or awareness (Table 3). For example, when my parents were alive I feared their death in old age as a result of cancer, heart disease, or other chronic diseases associated with old age, that is, the category of deaths labelled "Other." That fear was related to a certain level of psychological denial. I knew they, like anyone else, could die at any moment due to a host of causes but, at the same time, I denied it (that middle knowledge of which Lifton wrote). The prevention of my parents' inevitable death was important to me, and we did what we could to prevent the inevitable: Countless visits to physicians, tests, medications, and the like. I took some action to prevent their deaths (Table 3).

Now take the threat of death of my children. How? Say, in excruciating pain by means of *burning to death* (napalm), *bayonet, suffocation* (chemical weapons), *nuclear blast* (not an immediate death in the nanosecond of the nuclear flash but prolonged suffering), *torture, rape/murder,* or *lynching* (that is, HD-I). That specter is too maddening for most parents to contemplate even for a second. The fear of HD-I happening to our children and grandchildren is of the greatest magnitude. Consequently, the accompanying denial is highest, and the probability of action to

Table 3 Type of death-fear of death-denial-action hypothesis (future orientation)

Type and style of dying/death	Level of fear	Level of denial	Level of action
Death by cancer in old age of parents	High	High	Low
HD-II of children/grandchildren	Higher	Higher	Lower
HD-I of children/grandchildren	Highest	Highest	Lowest

Approach:	Remove denial; focus on quality of life on earth now and in future; stress self-interest, internal locus of control, and action.
Hypothesis:	Removal of denial of HD-I increases the probability of action to minimize or eliminate HD-I.
Mediating variables:	Religious beliefs, fear, apathy and learned helplessness, "true believer" personality, "Groupthink" and conformity, etc.

prevent such a death is very low. Thus a linear relationship is hypothesized: *The more horrible, and otherwise inappropriate, the type or style of dying and death is perceived, the greater the fear. The greater the fear, the greater the denial; and the greater the denial, the less chance of action to eliminate the very causes of those torturous deaths.* Thus to think of one's most beloved dying most horribly whether it is by burning as a result of napalm, nuclear fire, starvation, rape/murder, or torture with fire or knife is impossible for most of us. An example: At a conference on death at King's College in London, Ontario, I asked the president of Parents of Murdered Children whether, in her wildest imagination, she would have imagined her child ever being murdered. Her response was, "Never!" After her child was murdered she became involved with the organization. Murder had become most salient for her. Do our children have to be murdered before we act to prevent murder?

Another reason that the death of a child, more than that of a parent, arouses greater fear, hence denial, is that with advanced age death is expected. The death of a child is always an abomination, "unnatural," and an aberration. Another is that parents see themselves, and are seen by young children, as omnipotent and able to "fix anything." This fact, that we are not God-like in preventing death of fellow mortals, especially our loved ones, is terrifying, and adds to the denial of the preventable HD-I. Is a key to action, then, the removal of avoidance or denial of the horrendous-type death threat? I think it is part of the answer. Anticipatory grieving and response efficacy are others. The most efficacious but painful motivation seems to be the horrendous death experience itself.

Horrendous Death Imagery: The Holocaust

Since 1970 I have been teaching a course in death education at the University of Maryland. Each semester the issue of horrendous-type death is covered, usually using the Holocaust as the example. I am amazed how few students are aware that it happened and of its profound implications concerning the potential for evil in people. The exceptions are most Jewish students and others who lost loved ones in the Holocaust. I've had students come up to me after class with tears in their eyes asking what could be done to prevent such carnage from happening again. One young lady, a Christian, could not believe that Christians participated in state-sponsored genocide while others like the United States or the Catholic Church were apathetic or made no effort to prevent the persecution of non-Aryans prior to December 7, 1941. She, too, wanted to know what to do. It was important to point out to her that many Christians and countries (such as Holland) went to great lengths, often jeopardizing themselves, to save the victims of Naziism.

Lest we forget such a hideous event, the film *Genocide*,[1] or a discussion of genocide, is included every semester in my classes. The film has stimulated some students, not all, to act and become involved. A videotaped interview with Helen Caldicott, M.D., on the medical consequence of nuclear war had a similar result with students.

I have learned that while denial, anticipatory grief, and response efficacy might explain some of the variance predicting action or no action, other mediating variables are involved. Perrin French's chapters in this book discuss some of those factors.

Toward Action: The Stress Model

HD-I and HD-II are stressors affecting our health and well-being. In recent years the entire domain of psychosocial stress has gained prominence as a health risk.

Individuals and groups under stress tend to act to restore a state of homeostatis or equilibrium that enables them to function effectively. Two classic means of coping with stress are to take flight or to fight. Denial is a variation of "flight." Our task is to change that coping mechanism to one of "fight"; that is, action to remove the source of distress.

The stress model indicates that the meaning and perception given to psychosocial-physical events or environment affect behavior. You've heard of the mind-body duality? It *should* be the environment-mind-body triad. Perception, meaning, and attitudes ascribed to a situation are crucial for understanding contingent individual and group health-related behavior.

Distress may be defined as the actuality or threat of an event or situation that is perceived to cause or have the potential to cause harm to the individual or others who are valued. The ultimate "threat" or "harm" is perception or imagery of horrendous death, dying, and/or mutilation. The outcome of distress, in our context, is "unhealthy"; that is, it increases the probability of premature death, morbidity, anxiety, and the like.

The report, *Health, United States, 1986,* acknowledged that "Unless suitably managed, stress may contribute to physiological and psychological dysfunctions such as depression, fatigue, obesity, coronary heart disease, suicide or violence. In 1985 one-half of adults 18 years of age and over reported experiencing at least moderate amounts of stress during the 2 weeks preceding being interviewed in the National Health Interview Survey" (National Center for Health Statistics, 1986, p. 62).

Rarely discussed by members of the health professions, including medicine and health education, are ways of eliminating the causes of social stress such as unemployment, hunger, conventional and thermonuclear war, etc. Their emphasis is

---

[1]For information write to the Simon Wiesenthal Center, 9760 West Pico Blvd, Los Angeles, CA 90035. Telephone (213) 553-9036. Also see Grobman, A. & Landes, D. (1983). *Genocide: Critical Issues of the Holocaust.* Los Angeles: Simon Wiesenthal Center.

more on reduction of symptoms such as anxiety, depression, overeating, test anxiety and the like, by means of biofeedback, meditation, and other relaxation techniques. In contrast, our emphasis is on causation and prevention.

A simplistic two-factor psychosocial stress model may be represented by the following:

$$S_{HD} \longrightarrow SR^-$$

or

$$S_L \longrightarrow SR^+$$

On the left side of the paradigm, S_{HD} and S_L represent horrendous-death and lifegenic psychosocial stresses or factors, respectively. Examples of S_L are meaningful love and friendly relationships, education, employment, etc. (see p. xxvi for a complete listing). The former distress elicits an "unhealthy" stress response, SR^-, such as premature death, morbidity, poor mental health, etc. S_L elicits a "healthy" response, S^+, such as health, life satisfaction, happiness, sense of self-actualization, etc.

S_{HD} should be eliminated while simultaneously increasing S_L as the means to improving the quality of global health.

The research on coping with distress indicates that people generally cope best when they have:

1. Knowledge concerning the distressing situation
2. Forewarning
3. Independence and autonomy in selecting alternatives to deal with the distress
4. A sense of control or empowerment over the situation

A goal of this book is to provide the above to the reader with the hope of eliminating horrendous-type deaths. The first task is to remove the denial, allowing the individual to be health-educated to the distress of horrendous death.

Let us now talk of regaining control of our lives—a task always requiring action.

Toward Action: The Public Health Model

The Public Health Model has three aspects: prevention, intervention, and postvention. The emphasis in this volume is to prevent horrendous deaths before they occur by removing the causes of such deaths. Efforts toward prevention may be accelerated by individual and social awareness of the increasing probability of horrendous death with special reference to one's own children or other loved ones. "Prevention" is future-oriented. Prevention requires analysis, education, and development of policy and action *before* S_{HD} occurs. It is the strategy of choice when taking action to eliminate HD-I and HD-II.

Intervention is present oriented. The purpose is to intervene to stop or reduce the debilitating effects of S_{HD} as they are occurring, say, when hostilities are ongoing or when people are starving.

Individuals and society may intervene after S_{HD} has occurred. It is present- and future-oriented and is a form of rehabilitation. After war, for example, nations often try to help one another return to the social equilibrium of peace.

Again, the most rational path is preventive intervention.

ORGANIZATION OF THE BOOK

Three sections make up this book. Part I is concerned with the treatment and therapy of actual and potential survivor-victims of horrendous-type deaths. It makes the point that horrendous-type deaths affect not only the dead but also survivors as well. It elicits the most profound grieving: Life is death. An example? Think of surviving your most beloved's horrendous death, say, your child, as you watched him or her roast to death in an automobile accident or die of torture at the hands of a reactionary government. Action, then, includes rehabilitation after horrendous death as well as action to prevent it from occurring.

Part II brings us to the desired, ultimate outcome—preventive action. It discusses theory as well as grass roots initiatives that might serve as models to the reader. Its basic point is that action is necessary, but we need to act in ways best suited to us as individuals and groups. For those who need further guidance on what to do, Perrin French's contributions in this volume make realistic suggestions based on one's motivation and perceived efficacy. Part III serves as the book's conclusion.

WEAKNESSES OF THE BOOK

There are weaknesses in the volume that should be acknowledged. This book took two years to complete. Although some of the information may be outdated, the essential message of the book remains timely.

Unfortunately, this volume does not address in depth the complex problem of how to eliminate horrendous-type death, although most of the contributors to both volumes have thoughts on the matter. Our primary tasks were to present the danger as the ultimate health risk and to prompt people to act to eliminate horrendous-type death. There are knowledgeable and trained individuals who know how to improve the quality of global health and well-being. These include skilled health educators, physicians, politicians, concerned industrialists, military people, theologians, and ethicists, media specialists, scientists, engineers, and people trained in conflict resolution and the art and science of peace. They need to be marshalled together in a war against the various forms of horrendous death. My own feeling is that any answer to eliminating horrendous-type death must include the basic concepts of all religions: Love thy neighbor and Do unto others as you would have them do unto you. As a Jewish agnostic (don't ask me to explain) I have come to realize that theology long ago provided the ethical and moral basis for resolving the great question that we pose: How can the world come to live in love and brotherhood? (Chapter 8, this volume) Make no mistake. In a jungle one has to be prepared to deal with tigers. I see the value of military preparedness but its basic philosophy should be defensive rather than offensive.

I would have liked to have had more on post horrendous death sequelae, that is, counseling the survivor-victim so that life is seen as worth living once again. How does counseling the victim of the Holocaust or his or her children and grandchildren differ from counseling those who have suffered other types of loss? How does one counsel the survivor-victim of lynching or other deadly forms of racism?

ACTION

In times of war people who ordinarily are distant and distrusting of one another will come together to fight a common enemy. Why not band together globally to destroy the common enemy of horrendous-type deaths?

In any case, the reader should get the idea that something is fouled up in our globe and we had better do something about it—now. "We" means the public more than government leaders, corporate executives, the media, and others who make profit from horrendous death (including those who despoil the environment). My own feeling is that they have failed miserably in their role as stewards to protect the health and well-being of present and future generations. Yet, in a democracy, the government is "us." Ultimately we are to blame.

DEATH AS A STIMULUS TO IMPROVE THE QUALITY OF GLOBAL HEALTH PROJECT (DASIQGH)

Quality of Global Health

With an understanding of the concept of horrendous death, quality of global health (QGH) may be defined in the form of an equation:

$$QGH = LF_{max}/HD_{min} \text{ or elim}$$

where horrendous death (HD) is minimized or eliminated and lifegenic factors (LF) are maximized. Lifegenic factors are those factors that increase the probability of living long and well. Examples are:

1. Meaningful education
2. Meaningful employment
3. Meaningful love relationships and friendships
4. Financial security
5. Access to quality health care
6. Opportunity for self-actualization
7. Opportunity for enjoyable recreation and play
8. Purpose and meaning in life
9. Opportunity to achieve spiritual fulfillment
10. Opportunity to maximize health
11. Opportunity for artistic and creative expression

Thus a high value would indicate a high QGH Index. In this book we focus on minimizing or eliminating horrendous death and not lifegenic factors. Ideally, a global society would pursue both the elimination of HD and maximization of LF.

Motivation

A primary motivation is to insure *our* future health and the health of the future as represented by our children, grandchildren, works, loves, and other forms of what Lifton calls "symbolic immortality." My emphasis is our children and grandchildren. Why? Because for most parents and grandparents they are loved and valued even beyond ourself. Some have similar attachments to a pet. The crucial reason I focus on children is that they elicit an altruistic, protective, responsible, and nurturing response in most adults. Again, we wish our children to live long and well.

This concept reinforces or transcends other motivations. For example, if one is *altruistic,* that is, wishes to improve the world for future generations, one would have no trouble accepting our concepts. If an individual is motivated by the acquisition of material goods, ask: "For what purpose do you collect your fortune?". Usually the answer includes, "Why, for my children and grandchildren, of course." What if one is simply self-serving and hedonistic? One has to be alive in order to enjoy pleasure. Suppose one fears death? Then removal of one set of premature, torturous deaths should offer some surcease from death-related fear.

Consider an individual who literally contributes to the probability of horrendous death—a trader in arms and munitions, a horrendous death profiteer. Ironically, that person, too, needs to be alive, to have a future in which to enjoy the fruits of his unique labor. I imagine that most arms dealers have children for whom they wish health and longevity. The arms dealer needs to recognize his children's vulnerability and act to prevent their horrendous deaths . . . perhaps by turning to another trade. Farfetched? Who knows?

In days gone by the privileged could escape horrendous-type death. Today, no one can escape. Assassination and assassination attempts on presidents, the pope, multinational corporation executives, and civil rights leaders are not unusual. Terrorism is part of the world scene. The probability of escape by influential gatekeepers of power decreases as angry and aggressive people become more sophisticated in the sociology, psychology, and technology of power and death. Should we fail to improve the quality of civilized life (or global health, the two terms are used interchangeably) one can expect targets of horrendous death increasingly to include children.

Thus, the Death as a Stimulus to Improve the Quality of Global Health Project is seen as appealing to the motivation of nearly all people. The exceptions would be the "death lovers"—those who love war, death, and the dead.

The *necrophilous character*—the lover of death and the dead—was discussed at length by Fromm in his *Anatomy of Human Destructiveness* (1973). It is exemplified by the military general who proclaimed, "Long live death!". It was defined as "the passionate attraction to all that is dead, decayed, putrid, sickly; it is the passion to transform that which is alive into something unalive; to destroy for the sake of destruction; the exclusive interest in all that is purely mechanical. It is the passion to tear apart living structures" (H. van Hentig cited in Fromm, 1973, p. 332). On the other hand, it is possible that the death-lover and necrophilous character would be moved to positive, health-enhancing action. The former may be unconcerned with his own demise but concerned about the quality of life for his or her children. The latter may have little concern for others but may very much wish to live in order to enjoy death. In any case, my hope is that they, too, are in the minority with minimal influence in the world.

Domains of Power

How would the DASIQGH be implemented? The original plan conceptualized the bringing together of influential social policymakers from various domains to work cooperatively at the international level to improve the quality of life. Again, if one is not alive, or if one's children die, what good is power, acquisition of material goods, and so forth?

It was assumed that the domains and the gatekeepers within the domains exert and/or have tremendous influence over world events. For our purposes seven domains were identified:

1. Government-politics-law
2. Commerce
3. Labor
4. The military
5. Science and medicine
6. Religion
7. The media

One assumption of the model was that the individual domains cannot in themselves bring about the envisioned global change. Thus, the domain of government-politics-law in itself was seen as inefficient. Similarly, the other individual domains were seen as incapable of instituting, planning, and implementing the desired change on a global basis. However, in *collaboration* the product of the domains interacting with one another was greater than each individual domain.

The domain model may be diagrammed, where the seven circles represent the domains of power (Fig. 1).

Here, each domain is independent of one another. If they cooperate it is to attain mutually agreed-upon objectives. A model appearing like Venn circles is now suggested (Fig. 2):

The shared space represents the common effort to improve the quality of civilized life. Again, the motivation of the representatives of the domains may be one of altruism to improve the quality of civilized life for future generations, self-interest in a narrower sense (e.g., to survive to make profits), or fear of personal death. The motivation makes little difference for our purposes.

The charge of the various domains would be to develop and implement worldwide policy initiatives both within their domain and in cooperation with other domains in which the product was an integrated, systematic world plan to improve the quality of civilized life.

The "Treatment" Effect

How does one make horrendous death salient to these gatekeepers of power? Must everyone subject their children to homicide such as the mother who founded Parents of Murdered Children? Perhaps not. In order to keep those leaders focused on the task and to prevent preoccupation with personal agendas, the notion of HD-

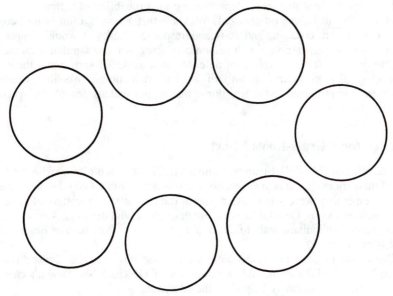

Figure 1 Domains of global influence.

I would be reinforced by flashing pictures of their loved one's face superimposed on the body of someone who died a horrendous-type death, that is, by burning, starvation, or war. If a leader had a beloved child or grandchild, a picture of that child would be used as starkly as possible to force the focus on the specific agenda. It is a means to remove the denial of personal mortality. Bizarre? Unfair? Perhaps.

To internalize the horrendous death the individual must grieve. The participants would literally observe whatever mourning ritual is appropriate for their dead child or grandchild (e.g., Mass for the Catholic, Shiva for the Jewish, etc.)

Figure 2 Domains of global influence
            interacting to meet common
            needs.

It is hypothesized that these steps increase the probability of action.

How is this technique rationalized? We know that action is a function of cognition, emotion, motivation, and self- and response-efficacy. I would couple the emotive-motivation response with response-efficacy. Anyone familiar with the literature on the effect of removal of defenses such as denial knows that there is a psychological risk in exposing an individual to such stimuli. Wouldn't vicarious experience be preferred to the real thing, that is, horrendous death? The outcome requires the risk.

Need for a Grass-Roots Effort

The original DASIQGH plan was unrealistic. First, I don't know who the leaders of the various domains are. Second, there was doubt that I could gain access to them even if they were known. Can you introduce me to the leaders of corporations such as Exxon, General Motors, Toyota, Pfizer, and the like? A more realistic approach is simultaneously to develop a grass-roots effort such as described in Part II of this book.

Organizations such as Global Education Associates[2] and the Consortium on Peace Research, Education, and Development[3] (COPRED) (see Dugan's chapter, this volume) are extremely helpful to the educator.

Each of us can do something. Certainly, the layperson or professional concerned with health is obligated to act in his or her own way. The means vary. Hopefully, this book will serve to stimulate all of us to action.

REFERENCES

Becker, E. (1973). *The denial of death*. New York: Free Press.

Brown, L., Durning, A., Flavin, C., Jacobson, J., Postel, S., Renner, M., Shea, C., & Starke, L. (1987). *State of the world: 1989*. New York: W. W. Norton.

Brown, L., Flavin, C., & Postel, S. (1989). Outlining a global action plan. In L. Brown, A. Durning, C. Flavin, L. Heise, J. Jacobson, S. Postel, M. Renner, C. Shea, & L. Starke (Eds.), *State of the World, 1989* (pp. 174–194). New York: W. W. Norton.

Chemical arms ban still uncertain. (1989). *Science, 243,* 301–302.

Freud, S. (1968). Thoughts for the times on war and death. In J. Rickman (Ed.), *Civilisation, war and death: Sigmund Freud* (pp. 1–25). London: Hogarth Press.

Fromm, E. (1973). *The anatomy of human destructiveness*. New York: Holt, Rinehart, and Winston.

Gentry, C. (1990, August 22). Juvenile homicide increasing. *The Prince George's Journal,* p. 2.

Kidron, M., & Segal, R. 1981. *The state of the world atlas*. New York: Simon & Schuster.

Klass, D. (1988), *Parental grief: Solace and resolution*. New York: Springer.

Leviton, D. (Ed.) (1991). *Horrendous death, health, and well-being*. Washington, DC: Hemisphere.

Lifton, R. (1979). *The broken connection*. New York: Simon & Schuster.

Meissner, W. (1988). Impending nuclear disaster: Psychoanalytic perspectives. In H. Levine, D. Jacobs, & L. Rubins (Eds.), *Psychoanalysis and the nuclear threat* (pp. 89–110). Hillsdale, NJ: Analytic Press.

National Center for Health Statistics. (1986). *Health, United States, 1986.* DHHS Pub. No. (PHS) 87-1232. Public Health Service. Washington, DC: U.S. Government Printing Office.

[2]Global Education Associates, Suite 570, 475 Riverside Drive, New York, NY 10015. The interested peace educator is referred to its valuable publication, *Educating for a global future, 8*(3–4), 1987.

[3]COPRED is located c/o Center for Conflict Resolution, The George Mason University, Fairfax, VA 22030. It provides national and local conferences, a valuable newsletter, *Peace Chronicle,* a scholarly journal, *Peace and Change,* a means of networking, course outlines, book and film reviews, and a directory of members.

Osterweis, M., Solomon, F., & Green, M. (Eds.). (1984). *Bereavement: Reactions, consequences, and care.* Washington, DC: National Academy Press.

Rickman, J. (1968). *Civilisation, war and death: Sigmund Freud.* London: Hogarth Press.

Rowan, H. (1989, March 12). Food may be future's next shock. *Washington Post,* pp. H1, H18.

Schneider, S. (1989). The greenhouse effect: Science and policy. *Science, 243,* 771–780.

Segal, H. (1988). Silence is the real crime. In H. Levine, D. Jacobs, & L. Rubin (Eds.), *Psychoanalysis and the nuclear threat* (pp. 35–58). Hillsdale, NJ: Analytic Press.

Sivard, R. (1985). *World military and social expenditures, 1985.* Washington, DC: World Priorities (Box 25140, Washington, DC 20007).

Sivard, R. (1987). *World military and social expenditures, 1987-88.* Washington, DC: World Priorities (Box 25140, Washington, DC, 20007).

World Development report. (1988). New York: Oxford University Press.

I

Treating the Survivors of Horrendous Death

Introduction to Part I

Living in the aftermath of horrendous death is, in a sense, often more painful than death itself. Survivor-victims of homicide, for example, often experience interminable grief and accompanying feelings of anger, despair, and guilt. Nancy Allen, a public-health educator and a specialist in counseling victims of homicide, writes in her chapter, "It may take a long commitment [on the part of the therapist], as it is not uncommon for physical and emotional flurries to occur the rest of the patient's life." She provides guidelines for the therapist as well as insights into the suffering of the victim by means of several case histories.

Judith Lipton, a physician, distinguishes between "plain old death," for example painful death from cancer or in childbirth, from horrendous death. She notes that if death from cancer or in childbirth is horrible, "full of pain, losses, and sorrow, with an inevitable final outcome . . . it is simply atrocious to add, in any way, to the existing burden of pain, waste, and misery in the world; moreover, murder, by any means and for any reason, is horrendous. Nuclear war is the ultimate murder, not only of the human species, but of life as we know it on earth."

The United States government periodically suggests that nuclear war is winnable, that construction and use of bomb shelters and the expertise of medicine will save a significant number of citizens. Lipton dismisses that assumption. In a nuclear holocaust, those who survived the blast effects would need also to survive smoke, burns, radiation, and nuclear-winter effects such as global famine. Quite categorically, Lipton says that medicine will be unable to treat or save any significant number of people.

Again, the only answer is prevention, especially when one realizes that the number of nations possessing a nuclear bomb is increasing. The five declared nuclear powers are the United States, the USSR, France, Great Britain, and China. Israel has not formally announced its capability but it probably has 100 to 200 nuclear weapons (Sivard, 1987, p. 18). According to Sivard, other countries engaged in the clandestine production of nuclear weapons include South Africa and Pakistan. Nation-states that may soon have the capability include Brazil, Argentina, Iran, Iraq, and Libya.

Eva Fogelman is a pioneer in developing groups for the children of Holocaust survivors. Her chapter looks at the "aftereffects of gradual degradation, torture, and massive extermination;" her goal is to provide effective therapy to survivor victims of war and Holocaust. Her chapter complements that of Charny, which also concerns the Holocaust.

One penetrating question asked by all the contributors to this section—and underscored by Fogelman—is whether the traditional goal and process of therapy is different for the survivor-victims of horrendous death. Generally, therapy has the goal of restoring the patient to a state of health. The process is one of accepting and coming to terms with the cause or causes of the trauma. Perhaps, in the case of the Holocaust or other examples of horrendous death, "restoration to health" may not be totally possible. Instead, restoration may fall on a continuum, from merely functioning, to living for revenge on the perpetrators of such deaths, to living "normally" at the conscious level but tortuously at a different psychic state of functioning. The process may involve coming or never coming to terms with the Holocaust events, which included massive suffering, loss, and degradation. Perhaps never accepting the Holocaust, hatred toward the Nazis and others, and unresolved grief are untraditional ways of coping with massive stress.

What Allen's and Fogelman's chapters strongly suggest is that the perception of the quality of the losses, deaths, and suffering can affect the therapeutic process and outcome. This agrees with the paradigm noted in the Introduction, where the type and quality of death—the relative horribleness of the death—is seen as related to the level of denial and ultimate probability of action to eliminate horrendous deaths. Thus, grief therapy and expected outcomes might be different for the person grieving over a more traditional death, say the death of a grandparent, compared to the Holocaust survivor or the survivor-victim of the homicide of a beloved child, mate, or the death of a pet.

If, indeed, horrendous death has a ripple effect, that is, the death deleteriously affects survivors and not merely the one who dies, and if the numbers of such survivor-victims are growing, what is the health and mental-health status of the world's population? Is the social contract—so necessary to the conduct of civilized behavior—less viable, as distrust and hatred increase and the value of life decreases? Certainly this topic needs to be discussed and addressed by the framers of global health and political policy. Just as certainly, this is an issue for the health-educated person.

1

Survivor-Victims of Homicide: Murder is Only the Beginning

Nancy H. Allen
University of California at Los Angeles, School of Medicine

Murder is the most burdensome and stigmatizing of all deaths. Bereavement for the survivor-victim is a difficult, uphill journey. The horrendous memories surrounding the homicide a loved one live in the mind of the survivor forever. Issues the counselor of therapist will confront during the mourning process are discussed and illustrated by using a variety of case histories. The counselor's responsibility is to respond to a wide spectrum of needs, and the facilitate and ease the stormy course of treatment. Besides the uniqueness of grief and bereavement therapy, the counselor should be familiar with and use appropriate community resources and victim-assistance programs. The value of the survivor-victim making an impact statement at the time of the murderer's sentencing is also explored, and examples are given.

INTRODUCTION

Homicide is perhaps the worst of all violations. The loss is uncompromisingly devastating, and the survivor-victim's sense of injustice is exacerbated during the aftermath of the murder; feelings of outrage are compounded without much relief.

When a death is due to natural causes, most bereaved persons are able to cope with their grief through the loving support of family and friends. But "the homicide death is stigmatizing, unnatural, especially burdensome, unexpected and unusually unwarranted. Survivors cannot grieve the usual way" (Allen, 1980, p. 58). Resolution comes slowly, if at all, when a loved one is murdered. Unexpected problems enter the survivor-victims' lives, such as police insensitivity, the coroner's misdiagnosis of mode and cause of death, the attorney's appearing to show more concern for the accused than for the victim, the judge's permitting multiple postponements of the trial, and the law itself, which allows murderers to be released from what was supposed to be a life sentence without the possibility of parole.

Grieving persons experience feelings of hopelessness, depersonalization, disorientation, and unreality, as well as a lack of interest in things and an inability to concentrate or remember (these symptoms are seen regardless of the cause or mode of death). Differences in the intensity and duration of the bereavement process are a function of multiple variables, including age, sex, personality, sociocultural details, relationship of the murderer to the deceased, and the extent to which the death is expected. "When the death occurs suddenly or unexpectedly and the survivors have had no opportunity to prepare psychologically, the loss is especially shocking" (Aiken, 1985, p. 240). There is a combination of distressing emotions expressed (and sometimes, sadly, withheld) by the surviving family; those emotions include hopelessness, guilt, fear, anger, overwhelming sadness, and self-pity. The feelings are so intense they cannot be faced all at once.

The survivor-victim feels an impotent rage directed toward the murderer of the loved one. The natural wish for retaliation is frequently fantasized and verbalized, and this can be an important and helpful outlet in reducing anger. The anger lessens when the offender is brought to justice and given an appropriate prison sentence, but there is rarely resolution and closure to the loss.

Unfortunately, the survivor-victim's wish for the offender to be swiftly brought to justice is often frustrated by any number of people, such as the police, coroners, lawyers, judges, victims' assistance programs, and employers. One of my patients recently told me about her boss who, a few months after her husband's murder, told her that it was time she put the murder behind her and got on with her life. The point was, she could not do that so easily.

In this chapter, I shall share my experiences in giving therapeutic assistance in order to explore differences in the grief process and its consequences on the family. Case histories will demonstrate various points and different types of outcomes. Community resources, such as victims' assistance programs and support groups, will be discussed.

SUGGESTIONS FOR HELPING THE SURVIVORS

The grief and bereavement process simply cannot be reduced to a formula or a simple set of stages. Survivor-victims are more depressed, reacting differently and more deeply. There are multiple variables in each special case.

When counseling the grieving survivor-victim of homicide, it is important to know the issues the therapist will be confronting in order to guide the bereavement through its often stormy course.

Initially, the bereaved are disorganized, forgetful, vulnerable, numb, erratic, and have difficulty in making decisions. Their concentration is limited and there is heightened emotional sensitivity to persons and environment. There is denial and disbelief. "No, it is impossible—my child is not dead." This is followed by disbelief regarding the insensitivity of the police, coroner, district attorney, and the criminal-justice process in general.

Mental-health counselors should know themselves well enough to assess whether they can help a survivor-victim of homicide. It may take a long commitment, as it is not uncommon for physical and emotional flurries to occur for the rest of the patient's life. The family may accept the fact that the loved one is dead, but frequently it is not possible to have closure or resolution regarding the loss (this is true especially when the survivor-victim is a mother). There are several reasons for the bereavement wounds not healing, such as when the murderer is known but is not brought to justice, when there is no clue as to the murderer's identity, or when the murderer goes on trial but receives a light sentence or no sentence. One of my patients explained it this way: "It is easier on the survivors if the murderer is caught and sentenced. There doesn't appear to be closure unless the murderer is found, tried, sentenced, and has served time, and the time served is not enough."

Besides the long commitment on the part of the counselor, there needs to be a familiarity with the grieving and bereavement process and what is special to survivor-victims of homicide. The counselor needs to be actively involved with the patient-survivors. The counselor guides the patient, helps him or her express a range of feelings, and acts as a facilitator to additional information and understanding. As a facilitator, the therapist must be familiar with the survivor-victim's rights as they relate to community resources, such as victims' assistance programs, self-help groups, disability insurance, and the criminal-justice system from prosecution to sentencing.

It is important that the counselor listen, really listen, and respond to what he or she is hearing and seeing as the patient's needs. The counselor should validate survivor-victims' feelings and not try to dissuade them from expressing grief. Friends and even family often find it difficult to understand that in the aftermath of a violent crime, prolonged bereavement is normal. It is not uncommon for these needed support people to turn their backs on the survivor-victim, as family and friends often find it easier not to talk about the homicide and the loss. But some survivor-victims need to talk about the range of emotions and problems they are experiencing, and the counselor can help. Patients want to have acknowledgment that what they are feeling is normal. They do not want to be patronized.

Perhaps the following case histories will give insight into the patients' feelings, pain, and frustration. The names of the homicide victims and their survivors have been changed. However, the circumstances of the murders have not been altered.

CASE HISTORIES

Case History A

Mrs. A.'s son was murdered in 1974. He was a prominent physician in the community. He was in the process of ending a troubled 2-year marriage and was about to cancel a large insurance policy made out to his wife. His death was recorded initially by the police and coroner as "suicide." The mother had a difficult time both accepting the death of her son and, more specifically, understanding why he would commit suicide. She stated, "It was like a bomb exploded in my life." She became obsessed with the death, feeling that too many questions were unanswered. She began what was to be years of uncovering the details of Dr. A.'s death. A series of private investigations were conducted and private lawyers were retained. Dozens of potential witnesses were discovered and the probable murderers were identified, as information began slowly to unfold.

Dr. A.'s death was recorded as death due to carbon-monoxide poisoning; mode of death, suicide. The coroner based his findings on the police report, which included a purported suicide note. No blood sample was taken, nor was an autopsy performed.

Mrs. A.'s intensive investigation produced the following information:

Her son had gone out for a haircut in the morning, returned home for lunch, watched a sports event on television, and spoken to a friend on the telephone. A maid was present cleaning and ironing. The wife returned about 2:30 p.m. and staged an argument with her husband. She then went to the maid's home because, as it turned out later, she was setting up an alibi for the period during which her husband was being murdered. She told the maid she was afraid to go back. Later that night the wife called the police to meet her at her residence. She asked them to escort her through selected areas of her home. Then she asked the police to look in the garage, where they found the doctor's body in his car. A copy of *Time* magazine was in his lap. It is interesting to note the garage was almost never used; storage boxes filled the garage, and the iron gate that enabled passage to the garage was too heavy for one person to open. The wife sent a friend upstairs to look for a suicide note, and one was found. One of the court witnesses later said that the wife had shown him the note 2 years previously, saying she planned to keep it, as she would have use for it later. At the time the dead body was found, the same friend was asked to go into the den for the doctor's eyeglasses and to place them on his face as if he had been reading. The investigating officers believed the wife and her story about the doctor's history of suicide attempts. The police did not note that the doctor's coloring was gray and not the cherry-red seen in carbon monoxide poisoning. The medical examiner went along with the police report, so there was no autopsy and no blood testing. The wife was anxious to have the body cremated, but the family wanted a funeral in the Jewish tradition and the doctor was duly buried. The wife collected the insurance, sold whatever she could, and moved to another part of the country, where she remarried.

Two years later, when some of the homicide information became known, Mrs. A. had her first heart attack, in part precipitated by the stress of her crusade to find the truth regarding her son's death. The identity of the maid was revealed to Mrs. A. They met and had many talks. More parts of the puzzle began to fit together.

Four years later, Mrs. A. made the painful decision to have her son's body exhumed. A forensic pathologist from another county performed the autopsy. The pathologist concluded: "It is my opinion that the most probable cause of death is death due to cyanide poisoning, the cyanide having been taken elsewhere other than in the car, and the dead body having been moved from the place of death and placed into the car by unknown persons." This was substantiated by other pathologists. This new report was so emotionally overwhelming to Mrs. A. that she felt she was going to explode. She phoned the University of California of Los Angeles and said she needed help and did not know where to go.

The University put her in contact with me. During our many counseling sessions, she expressed her feelings of anger regarding how the case had been mismanaged and the fact that most of her life savings (over $100,000) had been spent on what should have been the responsibilities of the police, coroner, and district attorney. Eight years after the murder of her son, a coroner's inquest ruled the doctor's death " . . . to have been at the hands of another person." I accompanied her to the deputy district attorney's office to have the case opened and reinvestigated. I wanted to be with her to help present the 9 years of findings in an organized and convincing fashion. Substantiating written materials were left with the Deputy District Attorney. The case was reopened. The new police investigators were protective of their "brotherhood" and did not want to listen to the many details Mrs. A. had uncovered that would help their investigation. The wife, in the meantime, had died from alcoholism. A new deputy district attorney was assigned the case.

It has now been well over 13 years since Dr. A.'s homicide. The significant survivor, his mother, has realized she is a victim of "the system." She feels the known suspects will never be brought to justice. Over the years, she has kept elaborate notes that have helped in releasing her feelings. Counseling opened the door to a coroner's inquest and opening the case again—this needed to be done in order for her to know she had done everything she could. (Parents still feel themselves to be in the role of the omnipotent protector even after the death of their child.) She joined the support groups Parents of Murdered Children (POMC) and Justice for Homicide Victims.

Mrs. A. has given much more than she has received. Other survivor-victims now turn to her for help. Recently she had her second heart attack, resulting this time in surgery. On numerous occasions she has told me that she could not have survived without counseling, illustrating the importance of a positive transference. Now Mrs. A. has begun the task of writing a book. "I think I'll be able to close the door on my son's death by exposing what happens to a mother when her son is murdered—the murder is only the beginning," she says.

As seen here, it is especially hard to have any resolution of the murder of a loved one when the murderers are known and it appears that nothing can be done about it. The survivor-victim keeps hoping that something will happen to bring the culprits to account and to expose the incompetence of the police and coroner so that other survivor-victims might be spared the same horrendous, prolonged bereavement.

Case History B

Mr. B. was referred to me 5 months after attending his first Parents of Murdered Children meeting. When he telephoned, he made it clear he did not wish to have marital therapy. He said he had gone to a marriage counselor and the therapist was taking his wife's side. Mr. B. needed help in dealing with the death of his 16-year-old daughter, Susan. He sounded very needy, very confused. When he arrived at my office, he carried a list of several items he wished to discuss. Number one was that he resented his wife deeply.

He started the session by describing what had happened to his daughter. Susan was having car trouble and was waiting at a bus stop when a car with several men in it stopped and offered her a ride. She accepted after being told they were friends of some people she knew. One of the men raped, bludgeoned, and stabbed her. She was found in an alley, alive, and transported to the hospital. Although she'd had a tracheotomy, she was able to respond to questions by nodding her head. A short time later, Susan died. The accused was arrested a few days later. He was 28 years old and rather hefty in stature. He confessed to killing the girl, although his story was radically different from hers. He reported that Susan had voluntarily had sex, attacked him, and that he killed her in "self-defense."

The second item on Mr. B.'s list of concerns was his resentment of gangs and males belonging to the race of the accused. We discussed his fantasies of revenge. I assured him that revenge fantasies are common as long as they are not acted out.

When Mr. B. first saw me, his memory and concentration were impaired. He was unable to work full time and lacked any motivation. During the past few months there has been an improvement. He is now self-employed, has a crew of men working for him, and is better able to initiate jobs. He goes to court for hearings and continuances, although no trial date has been set. At present he is working on an impact statement—the impact the death of his daughter has had on him—to be presented to the court during the sentencing phase of the trial. We have discussed its contents during several sessions.

The primary topic of discussion and frustration in his life was his wife. Every session has been dominated by stories of her behavior and how it has reduced the quality of his life. There were marital problems before Susan's death, but her murder exacerbated feelings of anger and blame. I pointed this out, telling Mr. B. that he and his wife needed to be in marriage therapy. Both his wife and her counselor have seen this need for some time. I suggested they see someone else and made a referral.

During a recent session, Mr. B. stated that his wife has started procedures to sue the hospital where Susan died. The family feels the case was mismanaged by the hospital staff. I advised him to think about such a suit carefully as it would add another dimension to prolonging the bereavement and resolution of their daughter's murder.

Mr. B. feels he is doing much better than his wife. "There are longer gaps between my anguish and depression," he has said. He added that counseling has helped him " . . . to understand the different emotions I was going through and to have a chance to talk it out and eventually go through the healing process." He continued that counseling "softens the harsh reality and maintains the needed focus." He has appreciated the practical preparation for what is ahead and the help in learning to work through the court process.

Case History C

Dr. C. told the story of her husband's murder through a stunning six-page impact statement that she read to the court in June 1985. Part of the statement describes what happened to her as follows:

1. I left my job for 4 months. I was in such a stupor that I didn't hear anyone. I retreated to my family and spent 3 months rearranging Christmas ribbons and doing nonsensical things; my mind was in such a state of shock. I slept with my husband's coat in my arms for months and cried when I realized I would never see him again. I did nothing. There was no reason to live and nothing to do. I cannot even remember these months. I try to, but the pain is so great they do not come back to me well.

2. I live in constant fear of people. Every night I tell anyone I am with, my nieces, my father, my mother, my sister, "Lock the door, someone could come in and kill us. Lock all three locks, you cannot be too safe. They did it to my husband and they'll do it to us." I still say this each and every night.

3. I went into therapy for 2 years, trying to deal with this tragic death. For months, I just couldn't believe he was dead. I lived with the reality that he never called me and I never saw him, but the realization was difficult to come to terms with. And even now as I prepared for this day, I have been back in therapy because the pain and fear of being around this man [the murderer] has renewed many nightmares and depression.

4. Months after he was killed, I was out walking the streets of Los Angeles in my nightclothes; I had been unable to sleep due to nightmares of my husband swimming around in a pool without a brain and telling me that he could not be with me "because I have no brain now. I had to die." By shooting him in the head, this man took my husband's brain. My parents were called and told to take me to safe territory. Their home is SAFE to me, and for months during the second half of my first year without him, it was the only place I could sleep.

5. Twelve months after the murder, I started becoming very physically ill. Shooting pains in my legs, pain in my stomach, bleeding problems, headaches, backaches, etc. After a work-up, the physician decided it was "stress, severe depression, and grief as a result of loss of husband." He recommended more therapy and I remained in therapy for another year as I started to cope with the depression that engulfs you once the shock has really worn off.

6. I lost weight and then put it on again. I still have not recovered the slender self I used to be. My anger and grief are expressed in eating.

7. I work 14-hour days because there is nothing to come home to at night. I used to love to cook, sew, read the paper, watch the news, etc. Now, with an empty home, I just stay and work. I have built a cocoon of no interaction with people who could be suddenly taken from me.

8. I am always afraid of any noise or anyone near me in the dark, especially on Saturdays. I feel an intense need for protection, having lights on at night when I sleep, extra bolts on all doors, even in someone else's home. I do not sleep, even now. Nightmares return and I miss him.

9. I worry about this man's release. I worry that he will come and get me like the other woman who once threatened him. This statement may threaten him. I am a living victim. I have lost my life too, and my security for eternity. I continue to be victimized for life as a result of this crime. If this man is ever paroled, my agony returns again.

I wonder what kind of man it is who would willingly take his son (15 years old) to an armed robbery—to teach him how to steal, assault, and murder. This same man took his son to dinner afterwards and then they showered and retired—as if nothing of any consequence had occurred. This court must make the consequence HARSHLY known. What crime is more serious than murder? Cold-blooded murder of an innocent, law-abiding citizen in his own home.

The San Francisco Chronicle, Friday, May 25, 1985, reported that a man who waited in the car while his two companions murdered three people in a house was sentenced to "life without possibility of parole." All he did was sit in the car. That man terrorized my family with guns, assaulted my mother-in-law, watched as my husband was shot in the face without ever being spoken to or given a chance to "stop" his walk toward the scene of his mother's assault, and then instructed his son to "take the carpets."

All of these details were part of the preliminary hearing.

Dr. C. was able to have some resolution regarding her husband's murder. The murderer was arrested 2 years after the death. The trial and sentencing were rapid. The murderer will be eligible for parole in 6 years.

The patient needs to be advised of times when another emotional flurry may occur. She came to me several weeks before the sentencing and asked about the impact statement. She already had plans to attend a conference at the same time, where she was to be the keynote speaker. I explained how her appearance and statement at court would help in the bereavement resolution. She faced the murderer on her own behalf (and her murdered husband's), told him what the killing had done to her, and asked the judge for the maximum sentence.

Case History D

Mr. D. was a patient in a local hospital when his son and daughter-in-law came to his room late at night to inform him that his youngest son, 19-year-old Jim, was dead. He was taken home to be with his family and learned the circumstances of the death from the homicide detectives who were waiting with Mrs. D.

Jim had gone to the neighborhood supermarket. He had just parked his motorcycle when he saw an elderly woman screaming and struggling with a young man. Jim went to the woman to help her retrieve her purse. The man shot Jim in the stomach. He died instantly. There were several witnesses.

Mr. D. came to see me 18 months after the killing. He had been referred by another parent of a murdered child because of his multiple problems and the emotional pain he shared with the group during the Parents of Murdered Children (POMC) meetings he had been attending.

Mr. D. was reaching out to every resource he felt could help him. He had been seeing a psychiatrist for 3 years; he'd been attending POMC meetings for almost a year. Mr. and Mrs. D. had started marriage counseling also.

Mr. D. was visibly shaking when he entered my office. He told me he was a disabled veteran and was unemployable. He eulogized his son Jim as a caring man. "My son was a hero—he got involved and it cost him his life." The family was presented with several posthumous gratitude plaques by city and county officials. Mr. D. had been proud of the plaques at the time they were presented, but over the years they became painful reminders of the slow-moving criminal justice system and his months of going to court only to be told there was another case postponement. During the year I saw Mr. D. he was able to ventilate his numerous frustrations. He cried and agonized over his son's murder. The family did not want to talk about Jim's death or Mr. D's raw emotional pain. He needed a place to talk and to help him sort out his life and feelings. His health was deteriorating and he had had several hospitalizations. The marriage had been shaky before Jim's death, and marital problems became exacerbated. Within two years, Mrs. D. filed papers for divorce.

After 2½ years the offender was brought to trial. He pleaded guilty to second-degree murder. Mr. D. told me he had been urged to write an impact statement, but he felt helpless about writing. I suggested that he make an audiotape of the many painful experiences the family has encountered as a result of Jim's murder, and volunteered to draft a statement using his words. The impact statement was read by Mr. D. at the sentencing of the murderer. Mr. D. told me later that reading it and facing the offender enabled him to feel that he did what he could to help his dead son. Mr. D. was then able to move on, both figuratively and literally, with his life. The family house was sold. He bought a mobile home and has moved to another community.

Case History E

A member of a support group, Loved Ones of Victims of Homicide, referred Mrs. E. to me. She had attended two meetings of this struggling group of survivor-victims and was able to express herself only through tears.

She arrived with Andy, her 26-year-old son, and together they told me the story of her daughter Debbie's murder. Debbie was 21, unmarried, and the mother of a 3-year-old child. On a fall evening in 1985, she was driving around the neighborhood with some girlfriends. They were throwing eggs from the car for laughs. One of the targets was a gang of young men standing on a street corner. One of the men told the other gang members to watch him, then he pulled a gun and shot Debbie in the head. She was taken to the nearest hospital emergency room, put on a life-support system, and the family was notified. Mrs. E. was at work when she was told her daughter had been in an accident. When Mrs. E. and her family arrived at the hospital, they realized the seriousness of the wound.

Debbie was brain-dead. Mrs. E. was numb, she later told me; "This nightmare can't be happening to me." She said the hospital kept Debbie alive "in order to get the family to donate her organs, but it was too much of a decision to make." Debbie died 2 days later.

Initially the police were unable to get any of the witnesses to testify—they were frightened for their lives. The offender was a drug dealer and intimidated the gang members and the girls in the car. Two months later two witnesses were willing to testify; within the year the perpetrator was sentenced to prison.

I counseled Mrs. E. for 6 months. She sought help throughout the sentencing period. She was surrounded by strong support systems, especially her family. Her husband, son, mother, father, and siblings pulled closer together. She is a religious person and welcomed the assistance of her minister and caring church members. She found comfort from the survivor-victims of homicide group meetings, telling me, "We experience the same thing, we talk and we cry there. I am not able to express myself when I go—I'm too full to express myself, words don't come."

When Mrs. E. started counseling with me, she wanted to know if she was normal. The tears just did not stop; she had difficulty making decisions and concentrating. She was depressed. She needed reassurance that the many feelings she was experiencing were normal. I suggested she go to her family physician and ask for a mild medication that would elevate her mood and reduce her depression. Following this, there was marked improvement.

Mrs. E. also needed help in understanding the criminal-justice process once the offender was arrested. We discussed the preliminary hearing and the trial. She had not heard of the impact statement. Once she understood its importance, she was eager to participate in that part of the sentencing. During one session I gave her some paper and a pencil and encouraged her to start writing about the impact Debbie's homicide had had on the family. I relayed statements she had made to me and she started writing, but she could not continue; her hand was trembling. I asked her just to talk to me about the impact, so she talked and I wrote. The statement was read at the sentencing.

Case History F

Mrs. F. could not accept the coroner's report stating as the cause of her husband's death, "occlusive coronary artery disease," or death due to natural causes. Her 52-year-old husband Dr. F. had been in "perfect health" when he was found by coworkers in the mental-health center where he worked. His body was wedged partly beneath his desk, the top of his head was cut, and his eyes were bruised. Blood was on the wall, a chair, a telephone, and on his desk. His shirt was bloodstained and torn, his tie was missing, his money clip was empty, and his wallet was gone.

Thus Mrs. F. began a long battle to uncover the truth of her husband's death. She believed he had been murdered. She had lengthy talks with the police, who also felt this was a homicide, but the coroner's report inhibited further investigation. Mrs. F. suspected a coworker of Dr. F.'s. Several weeks later he was arrested for stealing a car and Dr. F.'s credit cards were found on his person. He served 36 days in jail for stolen credit cards and forging a check. The district attorney did not have enough evidence to indict him for murder.

Mrs. F. started seeing a psychiatrist and was hospitalized for depression. She felt helpless against the system, but was determined to go further with the investigation of her husband's death.

She came to my office and discussed openly the circumstances of her husband's death. It appeared the only way she could move forward was to exhume his body. She did not know whom she could trust. I gave her the name and telephone number of Dr. Z., a forensic pathologist and medical examiner from northern California. An autopsy revealed that Dr. F. died "by strangulation or a blow to the head." His heart was normal; there was no evidence to support the diagnosis of heart disease. This was substantiated by two cardiologists. The effect of the blow to the brain could not be determined inasmuch as the brain was missing. It took 4 more years to have a coroner's inquest review the evidence. The coroner's jury unanimously agreed that Dr. F. had died at the hands of another. Six years after his death, murder charges were filed by the district attorney. Mrs. F. dreaded the trial, knowing she would "relive everything," but she felt the trial and sentencing would help to resolve her husband's death. After 8 difficult years, she faced the murderer at the time of his sentencing and stated, in part:

"I received a life sentence the day you killed my husband. I will receive no time off for good behavior, no parole, no probation. You took him away from me permanently. It was a shattering loss, to lose the man I dearly loved." The verdict had been second-degree murder, the sentence was 15 years to life in prison. I accompanied Mrs. F. to court one day. I wanted to sense what she was experiencing in the courtroom. I wanted to see the man who murdered her husband. Mrs. F. was reflective. "I think this is finishing my grief work. I do not think I could have ever finished what you call 'grief work' until this happened."

The final outcome of this case was that the perpetrator served 2 years in prison. The court reversed his conviction on the grounds that the district attorney's delay of 8 years in charging the offender with murder "illegally prejudiced his right to due process." The irony is that Mrs. F. spent over 6 years of private investigation and most of her resources before a district attorney would even acknowledge the case as a homicide.

It has now been 11 years since Mrs. F. started her struggle to resolve the murder of her husband. She has been on an emotional roller-coaster. During some of the dips she required hospitalization. She feels she has gone the distance with the criminal-justice system to clear up the mystery of her husband's death. She has become active in victim's assistance groups and an advocate for changes in legislation. She enjoys public speaking; her audiences now marvel at her courage and ability to channel her energy into constructive change.

Case History G

Alan was a 17-year-old senior honors student, a top athlete, and had scholarship offers envied by many pursuing a higher education with aspirations for a better future. Alan left school that day in early 1984 with his good friend Mark, who was going to give him a ride home. Alan was waiting for his friend to unlock his car door when he heard shots being fired. He was caught in crossfire between gang juveniles and was shot in the back. Mark helped his friend to some bushes across the street. Paramedics transported him to an emergency hospital. Alan did not respond to treatment and was pronounced dead at 4:30 that afternoon. There were some 200 witnesses to the shooting. Several of them recognized the gang members and gave names and descriptions. Three months later, when the case was in the preliminary hearing stage, only one witness would testify. Two years later the witness, a young woman, was with a friend when the accused bragged about his shooting Alan. Others were intimidated by the murderer and feared for their lives. A $35,000 reward for information and testimony that would lead to the conviction of the known offender has apparently not been enough to bring witnesses forward.

Alan's mother came to see me about 2 years after her son's death. She had begun psychotherapy a month after the murder, but she felt she could not afford to continue. During our first session she told me about the murder and her own difficult life.

Her father was murdered when she was 5 years old. She described the wake at their family home, her first experience with death and sorrow. She resented her strict home life and left home to marry at age 14. Later she married again at 17 and had four children. Her last was Alan, her only son.

During the past 18 months of therapy with me, Mrs. G. has spent time eulogizing her dead son. Although her family has been supportive in many other ways, they have stopped their bereavement. "They are getting on with their lives and feel Mom should do the same," Mrs. G. says. I told her that we all grieve differently, at a different pace and style. Especially important are such factors as one's relationship to the deceased, the age of the deceased, and how the deceased died. I suggested she should try to be understanding of her family and explain her feelings to them.

An approach to looking at feelings at a deeper level and helping patients to gain greater insights about themselves is the Make-a-Picture-Story (MAPS) test (Shneidman, 1951). The materials for the MAPS test consist of several background pictures—street, medical office, bedroom, forest, etc,—and separate figures (male, female, children, legendary, animals, silhouettes). The subject is asked to select one or more figures, put them on the background picture, and tell a story about the situation he or she has created. The choice and placement of the figures are recorded on a Figure Location Sheet. The MAPS Test is interpreted in ways similar to the Thematic Apperception Test (TAT). During a recent counseling session, Mrs. G. participated in this psychological projective technique with poignant results.

Mrs. G.'s response to the street scene was as follows (See Figure 1):

> *A man has been hit by this car. This man is lying down in the street and he's wounded. Here are people standing around. They may as well have no faces, because they're not willing to tell this policeman about this car hitting this man and they're not willing to help him at all. And they deliberately do not have faces. They are not going to be helpful. I'll put another policeman there too. He has seen it, but he's arrogant and he's not going to even tell his coworker that he saw the car hitting this man.*

When asked to give the story a title, Mrs. G. said, "No witnesses."

Mrs. G.'s responses to the street scene are reflective of her feelings of hopelessness and helplessness, and her anger at citizens and officials who will not step forward to help her bring the murderer of her son to justice.

Therapy offers a time when Mrs. G. can talk more about her feelings about Alan's death. Frequently she arrives with a button pinned to her blouse bearing a photo of the handsome, smiling face of her son—a clear clue that she wants to talk about him. There are times when she arrives so depressed she could barely get out of bed. There are times she overextends herself. Earlier in therapy, she was working full time, going to school, going to support group meetings, and helping her husband at his business. We discussed putting priorities on her activities and looking to the future. She has cut back on some activities and accelerated with others that give her pleasure.

During our sessions she questions herself as a mother, telling me how powerless she feels in relation to "at least bringing the murderer of my son to justice." She says, "I couldn't protect him from being murdered. I failed as a mother because I could not keep him alive." I asked her recently whether on a scale of 1 to 10 she felt she would have any resolution regarding Alan's murder. She said she would feel a 4 or a 5 if the offender were sentenced for the murder, and a 6 or 7 if he were dead.

Figure 1   "The Street Scene," from the Make a Picture Story (MAPS) Test, developed by Edwin S. Shneidman. Printed with permission of Edwin S. Shneidman.

Mrs. G. needs to feel better about herself. Her low self-esteem started early in life. Counseling, encouragement, and interpretation have helped build her feelings about herself and develop her coping skills, but more important are her other support systems.

Mrs. G. met her husband at an Alcoholics Anonymous (AA) meeting over 8 years ago. They were married soon after that. They love one another deeply, although they do have some arguments and disagreements. The basic love and commitment are there. Therapy has helped with their communication and with identifying issues that contribute to disharmony. The point is to identify, nurture, and encourage the use of her positive support systems. In addition to her husband, Mrs. G. gains support from her other daughters and other parents she meets in support groups. The greatest joys of her life are her grandchildren. She lights up as she talks about them; they are her connection with the future. She has become an active victims' advocate. She is on the board of directors of Justice for Homicide Victims and she is an articulate speaker/participant at meetings such as the Governor's Conference on Violence. She is a very nurturing person, reaching out to help other parents who have lost a child by murder. Her future goal is to operate a halfway house for young women with multiple problems.

FAMILIES

The surviving family of a homicide victim experiences a wide range of reactions and emotions in their bereavement. For some families, the homicide pulls them closer together; for others the family is torn apart. Divorce is common.

Families of murdered children undergo trauma that is in many cases insurmountable and has been, on the whole, ignored. They are truly the living victims. Marriages break up, children become unmanageable. Many who are unable to openly express their anger, resentment, and sorrow become physically ill with ulcers, strokes, and other related diseases. Families experience guilt, shame, anger, and a desire for revenge. Lives collapse and the survivor-victims are often powerless to prevent it.

The death of a child from any circumstance brings the most excruciating pain a parent will ever endure. We expect our children to outlive us. The death of a child upsets the balance of nature. One parent whose only child was murdered told me she had lost her future. She saw no reason for living. A surviving mother whose son was murdered in a New York subway writes, "The victim's song is a song of unadulterated hell. To lose someone you love at the hands of a murderer is to begin a life of unremitting suffering and unremitting hatred" (Kaminsky, 1985, p. 155). More often than not the murderer is not caught, or even if he is known to the police, the evidence is not sufficient for the district attorney to prosecute. This knowledge exacerbates the family's pain.

Families expect more from the criminal justice system than they receive. They want a greater expression of concern and regret. The families frequently are not advised of what is going on and what their rights are. The protection seems to go to the suspect. There are appalling deficiencies in the system, and families are not prepared for the feelings of injustice, helplessness, vulnerability, and anger that come forward as they try to handle the aftermath of victimization as best they can.

If the accused is brought to trial, the family is often subjected to even more trauma. The dead victim is frequently defamed by the defense attorney. One finds an outpouring of sympathy for the defendant, and the victim's life is made to seem insignificant in comparison.

Going to court, as painful as it can be for the family, has some healing benefits, however. The family is able to face the accused and, at the time of sentencing, give an impact statement that will become part of the murderer's permanent record.

The loving support of family and friends is critical to the healing process. At first the support system is there: family, friends, and church members rally around. Sympathy and comfort are offered, but they soon fade and disappear. Especially with the survivors of murder, the pain remains. This is when counseling directed to the very special needs of the patient is indicated.

Impact Statement

Most states now provide an opportunity for the survivor-victim to make an impact statement at the time of the convicted criminal's sentencing. The impact statement is a written description of the medical, financial, and emotional injury caused by the killer. The statement can be read on behalf of the surviving family or by a surviving member of the family. The statement is usually read by the survivor-victim to the presiding judge, members of the court, and the murderer.

Participating in this way helps the healing process and gives the survivor a sense of being able to speak his or her mind while also having the statement entered into the court record—all of which provide a moment of closure for those grieving the death of a loved one.

There are times when the survivor is so numb and depressed that writing the impact statement seems impossible. The counselor can help facilitate the process by taking notes about the patient's feelings and what has gone on within the family since the tragedy. These often serve to get the writer started. The following are excerpts from a few of my patients' impact statements, with names protected.

1. My son was a decent, law-abiding citizen who had honorably served in Vietnam to protect our country's interest. He had a full life ahead of him until this killer brutally murdered him. Our lives will always bear the terrible scars of this tragic loss. My dead son cannot bring justice to his murderer; that responsibility is left to his peers. Our society demands justice, and law-abiding citizens must be free from criminal attacks.

Until this incident happened to us, I never realized the deceptions in our laws and how they protect the criminal instead of the decent, law-abiding citizen. I do not want this person back in our society to further inflict violence on other innocent people and placing [sic] undue hardship on other families.

Your Honor, it is your responsibility to see that justice is done and I hope that you sentence this man to life in prison without the possibility of parole. This will reflect my family's wishes and protect our society from such criminal acts in the future. . . .

2. I speak to the court in behalf of my family, especially in behalf of my daughter's young son who cannot speak for himself. . . . Our lives have changed because of this terrible act of murder. We have lost our only daughter and our grandson—age 3—has lost his mother . . . he has a hard time understanding why his mommy is not coming home. What happens to a close family when a member is murdered is hard to describe. No matter where we go or what we are doing, something always reminds us of our daughter and we feel the anguish of her loss as if it just happened.

I am receiving professional counseling and it seems like my tears and depression will never stop.

_____ (name of offender), you gave our daughter the death penalty and you gave our family a life sentence of pain, grief and violation. Your Honor, our family sincerely requests (name of offender) is given the maximum sentence permitted by law. He is an evil man and should never be given the opportunity to kill again. We further request notification when he becomes eligible for parole, and that this statement becomes part of his permanent record. (This enables the family to go to the parole board hearing and request that the offender be kept in prison.)

3. I ask the court, why should the charges be manslaughter? Are you ready to take the responsibility for the offender on the street in 3 years or less . . . to return to the life of crime and more murders? . . . I feel great frustration in learning about this sentencing date at the last minute. I have never been contacted by the detectives or attorneys to give information that would make a stronger case in my son's behalf. Perhaps you can explain why victimization does not stop with the death of my son, but continues through the way our family is ignored, lied to, and made to feel foolish. Most of the time I feel so depressed no one wants to be around me. My family is broken . . . all living in different places. I am able to work sometimes, part time. I am not sure how I am going to survive this, the worst of all human tragedies.

4. Since the murder of our son, I keep going back to the courtroom after receiving subpoenas for my appearance, just to listen to the defense attorney asking for continuance after continuance—one excuse after the other. I would leave the courtroom hurt, angry, and confused. At the time of our son's murder, we were told by the presiding judge that the defendant was allowed two continuances and any more would be obstructing justice. Confusing, isn't it? Adding to this confusion were letters from the governor and the district attorney assuring my family of a quick and speedy trial—so far it has been 31 months! These delays extend our anguish. I have become so emotionally and physically incapacitated that I am no longer employable. I have had a series of illnesses since my son's murder. I have been hospitalized at least seven or eight times. I die over and over every day when I get up. Our once happy home has become a place of sadness and tragedy. After 38 years of marriage, we are now separated. . . .

The above are just part of the impact statements given at the sentencing. They are presented to sensitize the reader to the range of emotion, pain, exploitation, and family disruption experienced by the survivor-victims of homicide.

COMMUNITY RESOURCES

The 1980s were a decade of increased awareness and growing advocacy for the survivor-victims of murder. Now, in the 1990s, one of their most important and continuing needs is for information. First of all, survivors need to know what is happening to them emotionally and in their relationships as a result of the murder. Knowledge about the resources that are available is a first step. Professional intervention and help from victim's assistance programs is usually the best course of therapy for the survivor. The need for family and friend support systems cannot be underestimated, but it is not uncommon for some members of the family and many friends not to want to discuss the overwhelming and complex range of emotions some of the survivors are experiencing. This is where the mental-health counselor can help. In California alone there are over 400 victims' assistance groups.

Since 1965, when the State of California launched the first statewide victim-compensation program, most of the states and the federal government have enacted such programs (Bard & Sangrey, 1985). These programs vary in the services and amount of compensation offered. Support is usually limited to victims of violent crime; documentation of expenses is usually required.

"The 1982 President's Task Force on Victims of Crime recommended that victims be heard at every step of the justice process, from bail hearings to parole reviews" (Castleman, 1984, p. 169). This is a right granted in many states.

Victim-Witness Assistance Program

During the late 1980s California legislation improved. For example, 1986 changes in the law provided:

1. Reimbursement of up to $10,000 in medical expenses and/or mental-health counseling expenses to any member of the family of a person who sustains injury or death as a direct result of a crime, when that family member has incurred emotional injury as a result of the crime.
2. Reimbursement of mental-health counseling services provided by a licensed clinical social worker; a marriage, family, and child counselor; or a psychologist or psychiatrist.
3. Independent examination and report from any provider of psychological or psychiatric treatment, or mental-health counseling services if the Board determines a need for additional evaluation.

The survivor-victims have other rights such as payment (in part) of funeral expenses and compensation for salary lost. Staff from the Victim-Witness Assistance Program can be helpful in facilitating the reimbursement process.

The range of services and the amount of reimbursement given by victims' assistance programs vary from state to state.

Self-Help Groups

Self-help groups such as Parents of Murdered Children (POMC) include persons who share the same problem and unite for the purpose of mutual aid. Some of the benefits that self-help groups provide are as follows:

1. *Person-to-person exchange based on identification and reciprocity.*
2. *Access to a body of specialized information.*
3. *An opportunity to share coping techniques based on realistic expectation for optimal functioning.*
4. *An increased sense of person-worth, by focusing on how similar members are to others confronting the same situation.*
5. *Reinforcement for positive change and maintenance of effort toward change through feedback on performance.*
6. *An arena for advocacy and social change.*
7. *An opportunity for education, not only of other persons with similar problems, but also professionals and the public.*
8. *An opportunity to help others by giving concrete aid and providing a role model.*
9. Help for the helpers who themselves are aided by assisting others and by activism toward shared goals. (Osterweis, 1984, p. 241. From *Bereavement: Reactions, Consequences, and Care.* © 1984 by National Academy of Sciences, National Academy Press, Washington, DC.)

I have been asked to attend several POMC meetings. I was told, "We are members of a group that nobody wants to belong to." One of my patients explained how it feels to attend a POMC meeting: "When you can go to a group where everybody is suffering from the same symptoms, they know what you are talking about. Death is an everlasting thing and when one family member is murdered, it's not just that one person. That kid killed my family. He murdered a part of me."

Parents of Murdered Children, Inc., was founded in 1978 by Bob and Charlotte Hullinger after the killing of their 19-year-old daughter, Lisa. The group was formed in response to a need to talk and to break "the conspiracy of silence" that inhibited their bereavement (Magee, 1983, p. xii). In the 1980s, POMC grew from one Cincinnati group to a national organization with chapters in many states.

Parents of Murdered Children is primarily a self-help group and secondarily an educational force. Most mental-health professionals do not know how to handle the survivors of a homicide death—a good place to start would be by attending a POMC meeting. This self-help group has developed a brochure that gives the following information:

Parents of Murdered Children offers help to families cruelly bereaved. No one should have to endure the horror of a child's murder. But if you have endured it, or are enduring it; if you still are troubled about any aspects of your child's murder, we may be able to help each other.

We are a self-help group of parents that has discovered the truth in two principles of all such groups. First, a person who has recovered from a problem can be far more helpful than a professional using only theoretical knowledge. Second, when an individual helps another without charge, they both benefit.

As much as you want to do it, don't build a wall around yourself. It will help your recovery to be involved with people in some way, especially if you can channel your strong emotions into some kind of constructive action.

What survivor-victims experience was reflected in the theme of the first National

Conference of Parents of Murdered Children, "Healing After Murder: A Life-Long Process," held in August 1987.

Justice for Homicide Victims, Inc., also serves the family survivors of homicide, but members have gone a step further in the healing process; they also look toward rebalancing the scales of justice. Justice for Homicide Victims is the action arm of the California Center for Family Survivors of Homicide. Membership is mixed, comprising survivors of homicide as well as those who support the goals and services of the group. Their brochure includes this statement:

> *The scale of justice has gradually become weighted in favor of the accused, leaving the victim with no rights nor representation. We must re-establish the idea that homicide is the ultimate offense against humanity. Its punishment must reflect the gravity of the crime. Fortunately, the majority of our membership has not had to suffer the personal effect of a homicide in their family, but they support our goals. We seek to educate the public as to the injustices in the present system of criminal justice in California. Only when people are aware of the facts can change and reform be accomplished.*

The Sunny von Bülow National Advocacy Center (was known as the *National Victim Center*) was formed in 1985 by Alexander von Auersperg, the son of Sunny von Bülow, in response to his desire to make a difference. The Center works to enlighten the public about victims by conducting educational programs for victims and their advocates. The Center serves as a national resource data bank to provide information on victims' rights, legislation, and the social, psychological, and medical implications of victimization.

There are other self-help groups—especially in the large metropolitan areas—such as The Compassionate Friends of Los Angeles and Parents Who Have Lost a Child. Their purposes are to promote and aid parents in the positive resolution of the grief experienced upon the death of a child and to foster the physical and emotional health of bereaved parents and siblings. Some persons who have lost loved ones from homicide do find comfort from the Compassionate Friends group, but most survivor-victims of homicide gain greater understanding and help from individual therapy coupled with a specialized support group.

"Each community should encourage existing social health and welfare agencies to develop programs to supply a support system for such [homicide] survivors. Not only should these programs focus on the survivors themselves, but also they should develop contact with the police, medical examiner personnel, court personnel, and trial lawyer associations" (Danto, 1982, p. 95).

CONCLUSION

The horrendous trauma of losing a loved one through homicide does not follow the same pattern of grief and bereavement as do other deaths. Mourning occurs at a different level, pace, and style.

Bereavement is like swimming a channel of rough waters with the counselor or therapist beside you in a rowboat. The patient is supported along by words of direction and encouragement, but the patient has to do the swimming alone. The therapist coaches, but the hard work of mourning is done by the survivor-victim.

Many therapists do not understand the ramifications of a homicide. One simply cannot go by the book and expect the bereavement to end in a year or so. With most survivor-victims, it takes years, and with some it takes a lifetime. The case histories were written to give a brief sense, a small glance at the extensive period of mourning and the broad range of experiences that intensify bereavement. Each story is more complex and devastating than can possibly be described in a short case history.

There is a variety of individual responses to losing a loved one to murder. The closer the survivor and the victim were, the more difficult the bereavement. The most difficult mourning of all is that of a parent for a child.

In prolonged mourning, psychological and physiological symptoms appear. The therapist must attend to the emotional pain and needs to be aware of the typically increased possibility of morbidity and mortality, and to encourage medical monitoring of the family.

In addition, the murder is only the beginning of a long struggle with the criminal-justice system. The therapist can help facilitate this process by being knowledgeable about community victims' assistance programs and other resources that may help survivor-victims. There are times when healing appears to be progressing, and then a phone call from a detective or district attorney will vividly awaken the painful memory of the homicide. Healing has many low points, and recovery is never complete. The therapist or counselor should be able to openly discuss the death with the survivor and acknowledge the unfairness of the untimely, unwarranted death. Reminiscing can facilitate the grieving. I have come to view the family and loved ones of a homicide victim as persons who are suffering as though from a chronic disease. Over a period of time there are occasional exacerbations of the mourning process, but most of the time the survivor is able to cope, though the numb pain of the loss is always there.

EXERCISES

1. Review the case histories and identify factors that should be considered when counseling the survivor-victims of homicide.

2. Describe the feelings and emotions experienced by survivor-victims. How is the mourning process different from that attending a natural death?

3. What are the resources in your community that are available to the survivors of a homicide death? Specify what services are provided (examples: victims' assistance programs and Parents of Murdered Children).

REFERENCES

Aiken, L. R. (1985). *Dying, death, and bereavement.* Newton, MA: Allyn & Bacon.
Allen, N. H. (1980). *Homicide: Perspectives on prevention.* New York: Human Sciences Press.
Bard, M., & Sangrey, D. (1985). *The crime victim's book* (2nd. ed.). New York: Brunner/Mazel.
Castleman, M. (1984). *Crime free.* New York: Simon & Schuster.
Danto, B. L., Bruhn, S. J., & Kutscher, A. H. (Eds.). (1982). *The human side of homicide.* New York: Columbia University Press.
Kaminsky, A. K. (1985). *The victim's song.* New York: Prometheus Books.
Magee, D. (1983). *What murder leaves behind: The victim's family.* New York: Dodd, Mead & Co.
Osterweis, M., Solomon, F., & Green, M. (Eds.). (1984). *Bereavement reactions, consequences, and care.* Washington, DC: National Academy Press.
Shneidman, E. S. (1951). *Thematic test analysis.* New York: Grune & Stratton.

APPENDIX A: RECOMMENDED RESOURCES

Victims of Crime: Silent No More, videocassette. A K.C.E.T. Production. For further information write to: Mr. Dick Cook, Director of Marketing, K.C.E.T., 4401 Sunset Blvd., Los Angeles, CA 90027, (213) 668-9540.

Harris, J., Sprang, G., & Komsak, K., *This Could Never Happen to Me.* A handbook for families of murder victims and people who assist them. Available for $1.00 from: Mental Health Association of Tarrant County, 3136 West Fourth Street, Fort Worth, TX 76107, (817) 335-5405.

APPENDIX B: ORGANIZATIONS FOR VICTIMS OF CRIME

The interested reader should contact the office of the state Attorney General for a listing of resources. Also, the district attorney's office in individual counties should be familiar with victims' assistance programs and survivor-victim support groups.

1. Victims of Crime
   Resource Center
   (800) VICTIMS
   1130 K Street, Suite 300
   Sacramento, CA 95814
   (916) 324-9140

2. County of Los Angeles
   Office of the District Attorney
   Victim-Witness Assistance Program
   210 West Temple Street
   Los Angeles, CA 90012
   (213) 974-7499
   (800) 522-8669

3. Justice for Homicide Victims, Inc.
   P.O. Box 256
   Beverly Hills, CA 90210
   (213) 457-0300

4. Loved Ones of Homicide Victims
   c/o The Martin Luther King Legacy
   Association
   4182 South Western Avenue
   Los Angeles, CA 90062
   (213) 295-8582

5. Office of Criminal Justice Planning
   (Victim's Assistance)

6. Parents of Murdered Children
   National Headquarters
   1739 Bella Vista
   Cincinnati, OH 45237
   (800) 442-9929

7. State Board of Control
   (Victims' Compensation)
   926 J Street, Suite 300
   Sacramento, CA 95814
   (916) 322-4426

8. National Victim Center
   Suite 1001
   307 West 7th Street
   Fort Worth, TX 76102
   (817) 877-3355

9. The Compassionate Friends
   P.O. Box 3696
   Oakbrook, IL 60522

When writing to any of the above resources, enclose a self-addressed stamped business-size envelope.

2

Nuclear War: Horrendous Death, Death, and More Death

Judith Eve Lipton
Redmond, Washington

Although "plain old death" has challenged human imagination since the dawn of consciousness, the concept of "horrendous death" is relatively new, and even more difficult. The ultimate form of horrendous death is nuclear war, which represents not only the death of the human species, but quite possibly the termination of life on earth. Nuclear war would be a cataclysm in stages, each one building upon and expanding from the earlier stages. Short-term effects of nuclear war would be primarily blast effects, thermal radiation, firestorms, and intense short-term nuclear radiation. Intermediate effects would be the result of the previous ones, and would include global darkening, cooling, bacteriological contamination of food and water resulting in plagues in both human and animals, and radiological contamination of the food chain, resulting in even more deaths. Long-range nuclear effects would include changes in the earth's climate, probable genetic and mutagenic effects in humans and animals, and further destruction of the biosphere as a result of all of the above. Social effects of nuclear war would include the destruction not only of populations but of civilizations as a result of the direct effects of bombing as well as economic collapse. Psychological effects, consisting of acute and chronic posttraumatic stress syndromes, would cripple survivors, who would probably ultimately perish anyway.

More than any other form of horrendous death, nuclear war highlights this basic concept: plain old death is inevitable, while horrendous death in general and nuclear war in particular can be prevented. Nuclear war is a man-made problem, with man- and woman-made solutions. It is not inevitable. All that is necessary to prevent nuclear war is the collective will and imagination to do so.

INTRODUCTION

The novelist Kurt Vonnegut called it "plain old death," and it is none too pretty. Regular old garden-variety death is common, indeed universal and unavoidable, but nonetheless upsetting, even terrifying. Glorious golden-plumed Waldeau—my 15-year-old golden retriever and the noblest, gentlest dog that ever lived—died in amorous pursuit, the entire top of his skull ripped off by the horny, competitive, half-mastiff, half-St. Bernard next door. A neighbor's pregnant mare developed colic; as she died the foal was ripped from her belly, a last-minute Caesarean section. We worked all night pumping fluids and antibiotics into the floppy baby, but to no avail. By morning, the soft, furry creature was stiff and still, dead in a wheelbarrow, eyes filmed over and tongue protruding, yet perfectly formed, born never to trot or gallop in the spring. After six surgeries, ten thousand venipunctures, and innumerable consultations, my father's body is rotting away from cancer, and although his eyes are still bright and his mind is clear, I know he's tired and ready to give up.

"Plain old death" is no picnic. What then differentiates "horrendous death" from the horrifics of commonplace misery? Why contemplate "horrendous death," when regular death boggles the mind, and is already the stuff of night-mares? Why write about the medical consequences of nuclear war, when everyone knows that the consequences are just death, death, and more death?

The answer to these questions, I believe, is embodied in the structure of this book: thinking about horrendous, man-made death is the only route to becoming empowered enough to do something about it. It seems to be a natural aspect of the human animal that we deny unpleasantness until it is too obvious to avoid any longer. In particular, we avoid and deny death in general, because of the feelings of helplessness, anxiety, and fear of loss, pain and abandonment that seem to accompany our perceptions of it. My husband and I have noted that an adaptive aspect of denial is rooted in the human evolutionary history: when an animal perceives that a problem is too big to solve, it is adaptive not to waste energy on it (Barash & Lipton, 1985). This opens the door, however, to a common mistake when human beings misperceive the magnitude of a threat, or its manageability.

This commonplace error is particularly exemplified by the current world situa-tion regarding nuclear weapons. Many people downgrade the magnitude of the risk, suggesting that because an all-out nuclear war hasn't happened yet, it never will. Others suggest that it would be survivable. However, I suggest that the most common misperception about the nuclear arms race—and perhaps one of the most pernicious—is that the problem is too big for any individual to solve, and therefore it is best not to bother about it. Even the current improvement in U.S.–Soviet relations, which reduces the threat of war, is balanced by conflict in the Persian Gulf, which highlights problems of proliferation. The U.S.–Soviet thaw has *not* ended the nuclear arms race.

The wisdom of differentiating "horrendous death" from "plain old death" is that the concept of horrendous death places the burden of responsibility for the death squarely on the shoulders of men and women who plan, prepare, and perpe-trate murder. "Plain old life" is hard enough, full of pain, losses, and sorrow, with an inevitably fatal outcome. "Plain old death" is scary, painful, and often extremely wasteful. In my opinion it is simply atrocious to add, in any way, to the existing burden of pain, waste, and misery in the world; moreover, murder, by any means and for any reason, is horrendous. Nuclear war is the ultimate murder, not only of the human species, but probably of life as we know it on earth. Ironically, it is also one of the most preventable forms of horrendous death, and thus it is incumbent on every thinking person to participate in its prevention.

Yet most people continue to drowse through the incipient crisis, lulled by illu-sions that some wise parental figure is in control, one who would not let a nuclear war happen. The Intermediate-range Nuclear Forces (INF) treaty, of 1988, signed by President Reagan and General Secretary Gorbachev, while contributing consid-erably to stabilizing tensions in Europe that might have resulted in nuclear war, may have also reduced the sense of tension in Europe, as well as in the Soviet Union and the United States, resulting in turn in a premature and misleading sense of security. A similar situation occurred in 1963, when a Partial Test-Ban Treaty was signed by President Kennedy and Premier Krushchev. Cold-war tensions, illuminated by atmospheric testing and brought to a head by the Cuban missile crisis, were relieved by the Partial Test Ban Treaty; but the testing and develop-ment of nuclear weapons were not stopped, merely put out of sight, and once out of sight, nuclear war was out of mind for most people (Barash, 1987).

Beyond discussing the horrendous death that would result from nuclear war, another purpose of this chapter is to remind the reader that the prospect of that death is all too real. There are still more than 50,000 nuclear weapons in the world, the vast majority owned by the Soviet Union and the United States, and even with political changes like *glasnost* and *perestroika* in the Soviet Union, and President Bush's campaign promises to make a "kinder, gentler nation," no one has seriously suggested that we cease targeting each other for horrendous nuclear death. In fact, further refinement and development of the MX and Trident D5 missiles, as well as stealth and strategic defense weapons on the part of the United States, and similar "improvements" in missile accuracy, survivability, and defensive technologies within the Soviet Union are continuing unabated, even as both countries groan under the economic consequences of their lethal dance, locked, as E. P. Thompson puts it, in each other's nuclear arms.

In the early 1980s it was easier to drum up concern for preventing nuclear war than it is today. This is because the Cold War was in a period of high rhetoric (i.e., warmer), and in the United States and Europe, cavalier talk by national leaders about the survivability of nuclear war, and a kind of "holy war" anticommunist rhetoric frightened, angered, and aroused many individuals who never before involved themselves in politics. It was a time of extreme responses.

In 1982, for example, my husband and I were on an extremely long backpacking trip in a very remote wilderness area. On the third morning out, about 30 miles from the nearest dirt road and more than 70 miles from any town, we encountered two men who appeared quite out of the ordinary for backpackers. Both were dressed in camouflage suits; both carried not only shotguns but pistols. The younger one wore a drab green T-shirt showing a man in a radiation suit, crossed by a rifle and a sickle; the shirt read Better Dead than Red. We asked what they were doing, and they replied, "survival maneuvers." They explained that the younger one was a survivalist trainer, the older a businessman from Detroit who had decided that because nuclear war and social chaos were inevitable, he had best take steps to protect himself and his family. Among other things, he had purchased several thousand rounds of .22 shells, because, as he said, "After the war, ammunition will be great for barter, 'cause everybody's got a .22."

Everybody's got a .22? Can one really prepare for nuclear war by hiking in the wilderness, shooting squirrels, or relying on stockpiles of ammunition for barter in the "post-attack period?" What were the underlying assumptions that these men made? First, that nuclear war is inevitable and therefore attempts to prevent it are a waste of time. Second, that nuclear war could be survived, with adequate preparation, equipment, and know-how. These men were an extreme example of "survivalism," a doctrine of individual survival. And they were not alone: the governments of the United States, the Soviet Union, China, England, Germany, Sweden, and Switzerland continue to pour billions of dollars into survivalism on a national scale, by attempting to make preparations for so-called "civil defense," based on the premise that nuclear war can be survived in some meaningful way.

Unfortunately, the nature of war has changed completely with the escape of the power of the sun and the stars to earth; the capacity of the human imagination to comprehend this danger has lagged behind a technology that grows ever more lethal. Therefore, a description of the medical consequences of nuclear war is most effectively an appeal to the imagination, because the effects of nuclear bombs are qualitatively different from anything in human experience. I can summarize and say again that the medical effects of nuclear war are gruesome deaths, everybody's death. One can purchase a circular slide rule from the Rand Corporation that automatically computes the temperatures, pressures, and radiation levels at any given distance from any given bomb. If numbers were all there were to understanding nuclear war, this chapter would be unnecessary; Dr. Leviton could simply include a few spreadsheets in his text. However, numbers are frequently numbing, serving only to obscure the horrible facts, which are that no one really knows what a nuclear war would be like, except that it would be by any accounts, horrendous.

In the rest of the chapter, I summarize the short-term, long-term, ecological, and psychological effects of nuclear war. Many of my conclusions will be speculative, and I will try to portray the situation imaginatively, in an effort to mobilize the reader both cognitively and emotionally, and through the integration of information and affect, to move toward an attitude of dedicated empowerment (see Barash & Lipton, 1982). My goal is to enable the reader to understand the realities of the medical consequences of nuclear war, to feel the horror and sense of personal threat, and to respond to that fear with dedication and a resolution to prevent it. I will not give a citation for every assertion, but I will provide general references for each topic.

IMMEDIATE EFFECTS OF NUCLEAR WEAPONS: BLASTS, BURNS, AND RADIATION

There are more than 50,000 nuclear weapons in the world's arsenals, representing some 20,000 megatons of TNT. These numbers are simply too big for the human imagination to comprehend, by factors of millions. Multiply anything in human experience by one million, and it changes qualitatively. With a dollar in your pocket, you can barely purchase a cup of coffee; multiply by a million, and you can buy almost anything. People walk about two miles an hour; multiply by a million, and you would be launched into outer space. Water boils at 100 C; the temperature in the very center of a thermonuclear bomb is one hundred million degrees C. It takes about a second to say "megaton"; it takes less than a millionth of a second for the nuclear reaction in a bomb to occur. All of the bombs exploded during the Second World War, including the two nuclear weapons exploded at Hiroshima and Nagasaki, represented a total explosive force of three million tons of TNT. Twenty million tons of TNT exploding within a few hours or days defies comprehension.

Yet this is the reality of nuclear war. There will be no fronts, no battle lines. The boys will not go off to war. Rather, the war will come quickly to all, and the effects will be everywhere. In past wars, soldiers were among the first victims, and represented the majority of casualties. Nuclear war will be a war first between automated weapons and weapons systems, and then against cities and civilians. Women, men, and children will be incidental victims, at first, while each side targets the weapons and weapons systems of the other side, in a doctrine known as a "counterforce strategy." As the war escalates, cities themselves will become targets of so called "countervalue" attacks. People, homes, and ordinary buildings are called "soft targets" by the U.S. military, because not being reinforced by structural concrete, they are easy to destroy. "Hard targets" are missile bases, underground command and control centers, and other targets that are specifically protected from the blast impact of nuclear weapons. This is because these weapons, systems, and personnel are the only ones deemed to be of strategic value in a so-called "nuclear exchange."

There are approximately the equivalent of 10,000 1-megaton bombs targeted at the United States, and an equal number targeted at the Soviet Union. Each country has only about 200 targets of strategic value. This is what is meant by "overkill"; there are so many bombs that Pentagon targeters compete for finding suitable targets in the Soviet Union, and, one assumes, vice versa. Every city with a population of 25,000 or more is targeted. Every airport, oil refinery, military base, military factory, key bridge, dam, and nuclear power plant is targeted. One school of thought holds that certain key industries in the Soviet Union, like steel, oil, pharmaceutical, and tool-and-die manufacturers should be targeted to "bottleneck" the economy of the opposing country (Office of Technology Assessment Report, 1979).

It is a sobering exercise to mark each of the above types of targets on a map of your own local region. Remember that many highly critical military installations are small, unassuming buildings with large radio towers or underground facilities, hidden far from urban centers. Remember to mark every military base, major industry, government center, airport, port, and power-generating facility. Now take a protractor and draw a circle of 20 miles' diameter with its center at each strategic facility. Locate your own house, place of work, school, and day-care center, and your recreational retreats.

Within that 20-mile region most buildings will be destroyed, and massive fire storms will crisscross the area. Notice that there are no exits.

Furthermore, no one is really certain where the bombs will actually fall, because no country has ever fired an ICBM across the North Pole, and no country has successfully test-fired large numbers of ICBMs simultaneously. Once the bombs begin to explode, they also produce enormous pulses of electromagnetic radiation, which may disrupt the targeting of other incoming missiles. Therefore, bombs destined for Chicago may well land in Ann Arbor, or bombs targeted for the major command and control center for the Air Force, at Cheyenne Mountain near Colorado Springs, may just as well land in Denver or deep within the Rocky Mountain wilderness.

It takes about 30 minutes for ICBMs to travel from the Soviet Union to the United States, or vice versa, and about 12 minutes for the Submarine Launched Intercontinental Ballistic Missiles (SLBMs) to hit coastal cities and installations on either side. The Emergency Broadcasting System, which triggers air-raid sirens and the annoying tone that we hear tested on radio and television, requires about 15 minutes for activation. Therefore, in the event of a surprise attack, people living in coastal cities will be vaporized 3 minutes before the sirens might have gone off, and the residents of inland cities will have some 10 to 15 minutes to panic before the bombs start to fall.

What about advance warning? Most likely, there will be none. But if there is, note that spy satellites on both sides can easily detect the movements of populations, and the massive traffic jams which would result from a call to evacuate cities would alert each side that one or the other country considered nuclear war to be imminent. Thus, in an era in which striking first can confer some strategic advantage, the initiation of an evacuation program could literally be the spark that ignites the holocaust. Each side might well consider that population evacuation signaled that the other side was planning a first strike, whereupon it would be tempting—perhaps irresistible—to initiate a so-called "preemptive first strike." Thus evacuation planning actually increases the likelihood of nuclear war by signalling to the opponent an anticipation of conflict (Leaning & Keyes, 1984).

The bombs explode with the heat and the force of the sun and the stars—and this is an accurate description, not a metaphor (Glasstone, 1977). Thirty-five percent of a bomb's energy is given off as pure heat, or infra-red radiation. The temperature at the center of a fireball is 20 to 50 million degrees C, while the outer edge is a mere 3000 degrees C. This means that whether the bombs explode on the ground or in the air, people, plants, and animals, as well as concrete, steel, and asphalt are vaporized, or turned into gas. Thousands of people were unaccounted for at Hiroshima, their bodies or bones never found, presumably because they were simply vaporized and blown away (Committee for the Compilation of Materials on Damage Caused by the Atomic Bombs at Hiroshima and Nagasaki, 1981).

Beyond the fireball, the infrared pulse travels outward at the speed of light, causing paper, fuels, plastics, and wood to ignite spontaneously, burning and melting living tissue. The bombs melt people, plants, and animals. The additional fires caused by the spontaneous ignition of combustible material can coalesce, forming a firestorm that increases the lethal radius of the bomb five-fold.

An additional 60% of a bomb's energy is given off as blast effect, resembling a conventional bomb, only on a massive scale. Two kinds of blast effects can be observed: the first is called static overpressure, measured in pounds per square inch (psi), really a giant pressure wave that moves out from the epicenter faster than the speed of sound. When Mt. St. Helens exploded in Washington State on May 18, 1980, it was a similar kind of pressure that blew the top off the mountain and turned the rocks into ash and dust. A missile silo can be hardened with layers of concrete to withstand up to 3000 psi, but a conventional frame or wooden house collapses at just 2 psi. Overpressure measurements sound deceptively low, unless you realize that we are talking about *additional* pounds per square inch, above the sea-level norm; moreover, our world consists of many square inches. Thus, at only 1 psi an average window measuring 2 square yards would be subjected to 2,592 pound of pressure.

Accompanying the pressure wave are winds that rush out from the center of the fireball at 300 to 500 miles per hour, and then reverse as the heated air rises and expands, leaving a vacuum at the epicenter. The winds add to the chaos by picking up pieces of debris, the remains of people, houses, buildings, and so forth, and churning the debris at high speeds. For example, the glass from windows that have been shattered by overpressure into thousands of shards become deadly miniature missiles, as the small sharp pieces are hurled about by hurricane winds.

Prompt radiation, that is, the radiation released by the bomb within 2 minutes of detonation, accounts for about 5% of the energy of the bomb. The radiation that appears later in the form of fallout may account for up to 15% of the power of the bomb, but it is released slowly, over a period of up to 250,000 years. Delayed radiation, however, is not even included in bomb force calculations, although it is persistently deadly. For bombs greater than 100 kilotons, the thermal and blast effects devastate an area much larger than the radius of immediate radiation danger. So if you live near ground zero, in an area of high strategic priority, you are much more likely to die of burns and blast injuries—in other words massive trauma—than of radiation sickness. However, in a lightly targeted or "lucky" area, you will probably die a few days later of radiation sickness.

Thus, the immediate effects of nuclear explosions, including blast, burns, and radiation sickness, would probably affect any person in the United States or the Soviet Union who lives in a city of more than 25,000 population, or near any other facility of economic or military value. To illustrate more concretely, imagine the effects of even one medium-sized weapon detonated over a major city. If a single 1-megaton bomb were air-burst over Seattle, Washington, about 440,000 people would die immediately, and approximately 360,000 people would be seriously injured. Some 10,000 people would suffer third-degree burns. The casualties from this explosion would overwhelm the entire medical capacity of the United States. For example, people with severe burns may sometimes recover functionally, if they are treated at a specialized burn center over a period of years at a cost of about $500,000 per patient. Even with marvelous care, such persons often die. There are only 200 hospital beds in the United States dedicated to caring for burn patients, and these are almost all in target areas. Most common among the victims would be those with multiple injuries, blinded and charred by the heat and the fires, crushed and broken by the collapsing buildings, and dazed and doomed by radiation (for a summary, see Adams & Cullens, 1981). Recall the devastation caused by the earthquake in Soviet Armenia in 1988, where 55,000 people died, and then multiply the casualties by ten. But remember that the Armenians did not have to contend with firestorms or radiation. And perhaps most important, for them there was an outside would willing to help with relief and efforts to rebuilding.

The most poignant psychological problem in the immediate nuclear aftermath would be that most families would die separated from one another. If the war starts on a working day, fathers, mothers, and children will most likely perish alone. Survivors will likely be isolated from family and unable to find or reach them. Acute posttraumatic psychological reactions, shock and numbing, will follow the initial panic, and normal bereavement reactions will be impossible, given the entire disruption of the social fabric.

DELAYED EFFECTS OF NUCLEAR WEAPONS: FALLOUT, STARVATION AND INFECTIONS

The most serious problem for all forms of life following the immediate barrage period will be fallout. Just as the force of a single nuclear explosion can be roughly compared to the explosive force of erupting Mt. St. Helens, roughly in the megaton range, so the radioactive fallout can be compared to the fallout from the volcano, in distribution and pattern, only instead of ash, the fallout from a bomb is deadly. Imagine ten, or a hundred, or several hundred explosions all at once: that would be the barrage period. Now imagine the sky darkening with ash, the birds becoming silent, and clouds approaching not just from one explosion but from many. Fallout is composed of a mixture of particles, some large and some small, some intensely radioactive for short periods and some emitting only large, slower particles—but for thousands of years. Fallout occurs when the nuclear fireball touches the ground, causing particles of dirt both to become radioactive and to be coated with radioactive debris. Larger particles settle to the ground first, while smaller ones may circle the globe for many years.

The effects of fallout are identical to the effects of acute radiation sickness, only the dosages may vary somewhat. At very high doses, death occurs within hours, from central-nervous-system damage, with symptoms progressing from lethargy to loss of coordination, convulsions, coma, and relentlessly, death. Mid-range doses kill within weeks, by causing the death of the cells that line the intestine. The result is death by infection, diarrhea, and dehydration. Even smaller doses are still lethal, killing the blood-forming cells in the bone marrow, resulting in death within about three weeks from hemorrhage, infections, and anemia.

About 50% of normal, healthy adults will die of a dose of 400 rads of radiation. But children, the aged, and the sick will succumb at much lower doses. Furthermore, exposures of "only" 100 to 200 rads will cause lethargy, confusion, and susceptibility to infection. If any physicians remain, at any hospitals, triage will be a very perplexing problem, because a patient presenting with nausea, vomiting, and exhaustion may recover completely, or may die, regardless of treatment modality, within days, weeks, or months. There is no treatment for acute radiation sickness. For this reason, civil-defense planners have stockpiled massive quantities of morphine, presumably both for pain relief and euthanasia.

Additional environmental effects of the explosion of nuclear weapons, unknown to the strategic planners of the first three decades of the nuclear arms race, are the atmospheric consequences of depositing millions of tons of debris into the upper levels of the atmosphere. The most renowned study of these hitherto unappreciated environmental effects of nuclear explosions was published in 1983, the so-called TTAPS report (Turco, Toon, Ackerman, Pollack, & Sagan, 1983). These authors coined the phrase "nuclear winter," referring to a prolonged period of cold and darkness following nuclear war, caused by the shading of the planet by smoke from the fires, and dust from the explosions. Black smoke and dust will absorb the sun's energy directly, rather than allowing solar radiation to penetrate the lower levels of the atmosphere and be absorbed by the earth as well as by atmospheric carbon dioxide upon re-radiation—the normal process by which the earth's temperature range is maintained.

Atmospheric effects of this sort have been noted even from the explosions of single volcanoes. In 1815, the volcano Tambura in Indonesia erupted, and the year 1816 was known as the "year without a summer" as crops failed throughout America and Europe. The TTAPS study analyzed various scenarios for nuclear attacks and concluded that there could be widespread and unpredictable changes in the earth's climate even from very limited "nuclear exchanges." While smoke, soot, and dust would likely lower the temperature of the earth's atmosphere, possibly by many degrees, airburst blasts would also damage the earth's ozone layer, which would theoretically permit more solar energy through to the earth's surface, in the form of ultraviolet radiation. The interaction of these conflicting effects is unpredictable (Ambio, 1983; Ehrlich, Sagan, Kennedy, & Roberts, 1984). It seems likely, however, that even regions not subjected to direct attack would suffer in the massive worldwide starvation that would result from disrupted agricultural production and the virtual cessation of international trade (Pollack et al., 1985). Although uncertainties remain—concerning the role of the oceans, the actual magnitude of the arsenals detonated, their precise targets, the exact amount of soot to be released by various kinds of fires—at this point the nuclear winter scenario appears to be quite robust.

LONG-TERM SURVIVAL?

For the sake of argument I shall now try to describe life as I imagine it for the very few who have prolonged their deaths by getting to shelters. Let us imagine, for example, the fate of Swiss citizens, whose government has prepared vast underground cities for people to take refuge in as Europe is decimated. Let us imagine that some people survive 3 weeks underground. Outside Switzerland, there are few programs that are designed to provide refuge for any persons other than military or political leaders, so that survivors in other countries will be mostly male adults who will have lived for 3 weeks with minimal food, water, sanitary facilities, medical care, or communication with the rest of the world. Let us imagine that these survivors fail to succumb to low-level radiation sickness, infections caused by crowding, and incapacitating post-traumatic stress disorders and despair. What will they find?

The social fabric of modern life will be gone, leaving our modern cavemen as alone as men on the moon. Massive food and water shortages will probably be their first concern, complicated by ubiquitous radiation and contamination. If war comes in the fall, food shortages may be less severe than if war comes in the spring, killing all of the young, radiation-sensitive plants. Livestock will generally be dead; no shelter plans exist for cows, chickens, or pigs. Certain crops—for example, rice and broccoli—are more radiation-resistant than others. However, while a world without Wheatena or oatmeal (let alone oat bran!) is not unimaginable, it will be difficult for any society to subsist on rice, lima beans, sugar beets, and broccoli alone. Moreover, it is quite possible that for the first year or so, surface temperatures will be too cool for even these crops to germinate, and solar intensity may well be too low to provide adequate light for growth. Infants and children who have not yet died of radiation will be particularly vulnerable to malnutrition, physical and mental retardation, stress disorders, and starvation.

Not only will crops die, but there will be no farm machinery, no fuel, no pesticides, fertilizers, or distribution systems. Natural methods of organic farming will be difficult without animal manures, and even more difficult since normal helpful garden predators like birds are less radiation-resistant than flies and maggots. Surface water as well as soils (once they thaw out) will be contaminated with various short- and long-lived radio-isotopes, which are readily taken up into plants and then pass up the food chain, concentrating as they go. A post-attack gardener would labor in the cold and dark, on contaminated land overrun by rats and flies, usually without even the benefit of machinery, irrigation systems, or modern agricultural chemicals. Ironically, would-be survivors would be making maximum demands on the "natural" environment precisely when it has just undergone the most overwhelming and horrendous trauma since the extinction of the dinosaurs. One can barely imagine the plight of modern executives, "rescued" only to emerge and confront less than Stone-Age agriculture.

Even drinking water will be a problem. There will be no sewage systems, which require fuel or electricity for operation. Billions of rotting human and animal corpses will contaminate existing water supplies. There will be no fuel to drill wells, or to pump water for irrigation, industry, or drinking.

Exposure will probably kill a significant number of survivors, because housing will be destroyed and most heating fuels will be unavailable. Even wood will be in scarce supply because massive forest fires are likely during the barrage period, with no fire fighters. The TTAPS report suggests that substantial quantities of the Northern Hemisphere's fresh water would be frozen, at least temporarily, and possibly covered by one or two meters of hard ice.

Trillions of flies will breed in the dead bodies of people and animals, once the cold relents. As the poet Norman Corwin put it, "Dogs will die, but not the flea; tubers die, but not TB; trees will die but not the blight; day will end, but not the night" (Corwin, 1963).

Most hospitals will be gone, along with most doctors, nurses, and staff. Modern medical equipment will be gone, as well as drugs and pharmaceutical and equipment factories, and workers will likely have been vaporized.

The cultural heritage will be gone. Most museums will be vaporized, along with most great paintings and sculpture. Music, from Bach to the Beatles, will be heard no more, because there will be no orchestras, instruments, recording studios, or audiences. Those who brought "personal listening devices" and tapes into the shelters will eventually run out of batteries, and there will be no battery factories. The great libraries of the world will burn, along with librarians, authors, and readers. Is it any consolation to know that the original Constitution and Declaration of Independence will be buried under 50 feet of concrete in Washington, DC, and that original tapes of *Gone with the Wind* and other movies are even now buried in salt caves outside Kansas City? (Along with Pizza Hut franchise records and updated VISA and MasterCard billings.)

Most schools, universities, faculties, and teachers will be dead, but then, there will be virtually no children or young people to educate because nuclear war is particularly hard on the very young.

Any projection of the effects of nuclear war must also include mention of the possibility of vastly increased incidence of cancers and long-term genetic effects. These projects presuppose that a certain number of individuals survive the barrage period and the immediate years following the war, which would be characterized by increasing social chaos and environmental degradation. In order for genetic effects to occur, some individuals would have to seek to reproduce. In the post-attack period, with society shattered and the globe contaminated, I have strong doubts that anyone would have the emotional capacity to fall in love, much less dare to have children. As Jonathan Schell has pointed out, nuclear war is an attack on the unborn, not only because of an increased incidence of spontaneous abortions and fetal malformations, but because few adults would be capable or inclined to become parents (Schell, 1982).

In other words, nuclear war will destroy the past along with the future. It is not really war at all, but rather the end of everything that has ever had meaning to human beings.

CONCLUSION

The purpose of this book is to remove the denial of human responsibility for man-made death (sexist reference intended) and to promote the implementation of man- and woman-made solutions to human and social problems, excluding murder as a desirable or tolerable option. There is no social problem that is more crucial than the prevention of nuclear war, because all other solutions are dependent upon it. Overpopulation, environmental degradation and pollution, global starvation, malnutrition, homelessness, and every other issue depends for humane resolution on the persistence of society, and the overall integrity of the biosphere, which would be destroyed almost instantaneously in a major nuclear war. The solution of the problem of nuclear war and the elimination of the threat of nuclear war, which in my opinion can only be effected by the total abolition of all nuclear weapons, weapons systems, and means of producing such systems, is necessary, if not sufficient, for the survival of life on earth.

However, there is a formidable emotional barrier which must be transcended for the reader even to grasp the immediacy and magnitude of the problem. The threat of nuclear war is so big, and individual humans feel so small.

Yet history is replete with stories and myths of ordinary individuals, transformed by historical pressure to fulfill extraordinary tasks. We must not wait for Flash Gordon, the Lone Ranger, or Popeye to eliminate nuclear weapons, yet in their stories lie inspiration. We can all change. We all grow. We can all do something. My favorite transformation myth is the story of Frodo, the hobbit, in Tolkien's trilogy, *The Lord of the Rings* (Tolkien, 1955).

Frodo was a small and peaceful little creature, suddenly thrust by fate into a direct struggle with the Dark Lord, an ultimate image of evil and destruction. Frodo is compelled to become the bearer of the One Ring of Power, on a quest against all odds to destroy the Ring, and thus to save the world. Nuclear weapons are the One Ring. They appear to promise unlimited power but in fact they are too powerful for fallible, corruptible, selfish human beings to control. Hence, we must agree with UN Secretary-General Javier Perez de Cuellar, who noted that "the question may justifiably be put to the leading nuclear weapon powers: By what right do they decide the fate of all humanity?" (cited in Johnson, 1988).

Like the Ring, nuclear weapons are wholly evil. They are horrendous, filled with the promise of horrendous death. They exist only to threaten and coerce other humans with death that is not personal, but planetary. Such enormous, absolute power corrupts all who try to control it, all individuals and governments that build, design, and possess it. Fortunately, nuclear weapons are man-made objects that can be created and destroyed. Like Frodo, we must not rest until they are unmade.

EXERCISES

1. Multiply something concrete by a million. For example, buy a million BBs. Now drop the BBs into a wastebasket and listen to the noise. Try to walk a million paces; at 2 feet per step, this would be 2 million feet, or 378 miles. Walk just one mile, and imagine with every step that you are counting a nuclear bomb, or ten thousand corpses. Try to imagine a million, by multiplying something concrete, and then meditate on the concept of nuclear war: a million degrees hot, a million people dead from a single airburst over a large city.

2. Imagine how you would feel if you heard that a nuclear attack was on its way. Draw a circle 20 miles in diameter on a map of your region, around the closest target of strategic value. What would happen to your house in an attack?

3. Read *On the Beach*, (Shute, 1974, Ballantine), or *A Canticle for Leibowitz* (Miller, 1961, Bantam). Both of these are excellent novels about World War III.

Now read *The Lord of the Rings* by J. R. R. Tolkien. Ask yourself, "How do I wish to respond to the threat of permanent darkness?"

4. Go to a crowded beach in the summer and sit in the surf, watching toddlers play with their buckets and shovels. Feel the threat of nuclear war pass over you and the children, like a dark cloud. Now ask yourself what you need to do to bring back the sunshine.

REFERENCES

Adams, A., & Cullen, S. (1981). *The final epidemic: Physicians and surgeons on nuclear war.* Chicago: Educational Foundation for Nuclear Science.

Barash, D. (1987). *The arms race and nuclear war.* Belmont, CA: Wadsworth.

Barash, D., & Lipton, J. E. (1985). *The caveman and the bomb: Human nature, evolution, and nuclear war.* New York: McGraw-Hill.

Barash, D., & Lipton, J. E. (1982). *Stop nuclear war! A handbook.* New York: Grove Press.

Committee for the Compilation of Materials on Damage Caused by the Atomic Bombs at Hiroshima and Nagasaki. (1981). *Hiroshima and Nagasaki: The physical, medical and social effects of the bombings.* New York: Basic Books.

Corwin, N. (1963). *Overkill and megalove.* Cleveland and New York: World.

Erlich, P. R., Sagan, C., Kennedy, D., & Roberts, W. O. (1984). *The cold and the dark.* New York: Norton.

Glasstone, S., & Dolan, P. J. (Eds.). (1977). *The effects of nuclear weapons.* Washington, DC: U.S. Department of Defense.

Johnson, K. D. (1988). *Realism and hope in a nuclear age.* Atlanta, GA: John Knox Press.

Leaning, J., & Keyes, L. (1984). *The counterfeit ark: Crisis relocation for nuclear war.* Cambridge, MA: Ballinger.

Office of Technology Assessment, Congress of the United States (1980). *The effects of nuclear war.* Monclair, NJ: Allanheld, Osmun, and Co.

Pollack, D. T., Ackerman, P., Crutzen, P., MacCracken, M., Shapiro, C., & Turco, R. (1985). *The environmental consequences of nuclear war: Volume I, physical and atmospheric effects.* New York: John Wiley.

Schell, J. (1982). *The fate of the earth.* New York: Knopf.

Tolkien, J. R. R. (1955). *The lord of the rings.* Boston: Houghton Mifflin.

Turco, R. P., Toon, O. B., Ackerman, T. P., Pollack, J. B., & Sagan, C. (TTAPS) (1983). Nuclear winter: Global consequences of multiple nuclear explosions. *Science, 222,* 1283–1292.

3

Survivor-Victims of War and Holocaust

Eva Fogelman
City University of New York

The persecution inflicted on innocent men, women, and children during the Nazi period represents an "evil so appalling" that facing it "brings with it a horror too large and intensely personal to confront safely." (Des Pres, 1976). This chapter addresses the long-range psychological aftereffects of massive psychic trauma, therapeutic alternatives, and implications for public policy.

Survivor-victims of war and holocaust exemplify both the resilience and adaptive ability in humans, and at the same time the arduous and ongoing task of mourning. The loss of one's identity, symbolic world, community, and family members takes a lifetime to grieve.

The trauma that survivors of the Nazi Holocaust endured reappears in fragments, even in the most well-adjusted individuals. It permeates associations in everyday life, dreams, social interactions, perceptions, attitudes, identity, and in coping mechanisms. The degree to which the victimization becomes an organizing factor in one's personality is a subject for further inquiry. In this chapter, the focus is on a heuristic model for mourning which clinicians and researchers agree is part of the healing process.

For the most part, survivors have resorted to self-healing mechanisms and have rarely sought out mental-health professionals. Only in recent years has the aging process among survivors necessitated more contacts with institutions. In order for the community to best serve this population, attention must be paid to the lingering memories and the pain that afflict its members. Furthermore, professionals need to understand their own reactions to the Holocaust before they can develop the proper care and empathy necessary for serving survivor-victims of war and holocaust.

INTRODUCTION

The passage of more than two generations since the destruction of European Jewry has allowed for a myriad of psychological conceptualizations of the aftereffects of gradual degradation, torture, and massive extermination. What has emerged are "competing psychological paradigms of the nature of survivorship" (Marcus & Rosenberg, 1988). Therapeutic intervention for the treatment of massive psychic trauma can best be understood by considering the process that survivor-victims of war and holocaust undergo in order to heal themselves.

In the psychological literature the term "Holocaust survivor" has been used in several ways. Those who survived concentration camps, or anyone who experienced persecution and losses under Nazi occupation is a Holocaust survivor (Kestenberg, 1972). This has meant that Jews who lived in Germany between 1933 and 1939, but managed to escape before the start of World War II, are included in this cohort. Naturally, the severity and duration of the trauma varies among different types of survivors. In this paper the broader definition of "holocaust survivor"— the survivor of any systematic genocide—will be used and interchanged with the term "survivor-victim."

THE IMPRINT OF DEATH

The survivor-victims of the Second World War and the Holocaust experienced physical and psychic traumas including degradation, restricted social interaction, confiscation of property, loss of civil rights, deportation, forced labor, exposure to epidemic diseases, starvation, extreme heat and cold, medical experimentation, physical torture and, finally, horrendous death. Lifton (1968) concludes that the "key to the survivor experience, the basis for all survivor themes, is the imprint of death" (p. 480). Survivors of the Nazi Holocaust experienced "more prolonged humiliation and terror, and more generalized psychic and bodily assault," and "grotesqueness surrounding the death imprint." In addition, genocide during the Nazi period imparted the "psychological sense that death was not only everywhere, but was bizarre, unnatural, indecent, absurd. . . . After any such exposure the survivor internalizes this grotesqueness as well as the deaths themselves, and feels it to be inseparable from his own body and mind." As Wiesel (1960) has written about his Nazi concentration-camp experience: "In every stiffened corpse I saw myself."

When it comes to the Nazi Holocaust, the word *death* seems too benign; it connotes a state of normalcy and naturalness. Rather, as Lifton noted, nothing was more unnatural, inhumane, bizarre, or severe. The threat of death was imminent, regardless of whether the survival was in concentration camps, ghettos, in hiding, escaping, in resistance activities, or in disguise as an Aryan.

The social reality of living under permanently tortured conditions and constant fear of annihilation represents a massive psychic trauma (Krystal, 1968). Trauma consists of the breakdown of the structure of the self and its representations of reality. The trauma to the individual was cumulative, but it was also intentional, a part of a general social process to break down the identity of an entire group of people. In 1933, racial laws against Jews were instituted and were governmentally sanctioned in Nazi-occupied countries. Systematic infliction of physical and mental torture lasted as long as 12 years for Jews living in Germany and less than 1 year for Jews in Hungary.

As stated earlier, the severity, duration, and circumstances of torture varied. For some it started with the loss of civil-service jobs or businesses. Others were brutally invaded by policemen or soldiers accompanied by dogs, and were ousted from their homes. The constant threat of being brutally murdered, or of dying from disease and starvation, together with multiple losses of community, family, and even one's own former self has left each and every survivor with the almost-impossible task of prolonged grief and mourning.

THE STRUGGLE TOWARD HEALTH
AND WELL-BEING

For Holocaust survivors, the struggles fall into three categories: coping with multiple losses; restoring oneself; and interacting with others in the family and outside world.

First, what are the psychological dynamics of coping with the loss of family members, community, and former self? How does one mourn the dead without graves? In many cases, the disappearance of a family member has never been verified with certainty. It is difficult to begin grief work without some concrete evidence that the person one is grieving for is indeed dead.

Second, Holocaust survivors have the additional problem of learning how to regain a sense of self that is not one of a victim, hero, or survivor. How does one develop a continuity with his or her former self, thereby integrating past and present?

Third, having been treated like a pariah, how does a survivor re-enter society and feel a sense of belonging to a new community and family? How do survivors communicate about their traumatic experiences with family members and with those in the outer world? What obstacles need to be overcome in personal relationships?

CONSEQUENCES OF WAR AND HOLOCAUST

We can best understand the impact of the war and the Holocaust on the survivor-victim from Jean Amery, an Austrian philosopher who was deported to Auschwitz:

> *Anyone who has been tortured remains tortured. . . . Anyone who has suffered torture never again will be able to be at ease in the world, the abomination of the annihilation is never extinguished. Faith in humanity, already cracked by the first slap in the face, then demolished by torture, is never acquired again. (As quoted in Levi, 1988, p. 25)*

The posttraumatic years for survivors are associated with another dynamic: that of prolonged grief and mourning. The severe traumatization, the suffering and losses remain part of the conscious and unconscious life of survivors. Regardless of how one has adjusted, the memory interferes with daily life to a lesser or greater degree. As Primo Levi (1988), author and survivor of Auschwitz, writes, "the memory of a trauma suffered . . . is itself traumatic because recalling it is painful or at least disturbing. A person who has been wounded tends to block out the memory so as not to renew the pain. . . . " Levi goes on to say that the survivor-victim continues to suffer "even at a distance of decades."

One survivor described his experience to a college audience this way: "Every morning when I shave, I see in front of the mirror a scorny face with a shaven head. I drive off to work in my Porsche and sit at my big desk and run a successful business." A day does not go by when this survivor does not remember his horrific past.

Forty-four years after liberation, there are different views of the way in which the survivor's lingering pain can best be alleviated. On the one hand, there are proponents of the survivor syndrome (Niederland, 1961; Krystal, 1968). Their clinical observations lead them to conclude that depressive features are pervasive in the character of survivors. This has to do with "an inability to mourn appropriately for dead relatives, a mourning that would have allowed for a gradual decathexis of the lost object and subsequent internalization" (Jucovy, 1986). Niederland (1961) describes a group of symptoms known as the "survivor syndrome":

> . . . *morose behavior and a tendency to withdrawal, general apathy alternating with occasional short-lived angry outbursts, feelings of helplessness and insecurity, lack of initiative and interest, prevalence of self-deprecatory attitudes and expressions.* . . .

[This state is exacerbated by a] severe and persevering guilt complex, a partial or full
somatization . . . usually accompanied by hypochondriacal symptoms. States of anxiety and
agitation resulting in insomnia, nightmares, motor unrest, inner tension, tremulousness, fear of
renewed persecution, often culminating in paranoid ideation and reactions. (p. 237)

Krystal (1984) emphasized the aftereffects that represent a continuation of the traumatic process: cognitive constriction, episodic emotional "freezing" when under stress, and the avoidance of dreaded memories. In essence, the survivor does not experience either pleasure or adverse feelings (anhedonia), and is unable to identify and express feelings and fantasies (alexithymia).

Other clinicians (Orenstein, 1981; Klein, 1984; Kestenberg, 1972) assert that the survivor syndrome theory does not take into account the pre-Holocaust personality, the severity of the persecution, the developmental stage of the occurrence of the trauma and the post-Holocaust conditions and adjustment. They do not describe the survivor as irreversibly damaged and pathological. Rather, Klein (1984) observed in Israel that "the majority of survivors have been able to recover ego capacities and have rejoined the paths their lives might have taken before the Holocaust." And Orenstein (1985) defined the survivors' recovery as "the capacity to maintain a sense of continuity, to anticipate the future with enthusiasm and vitality—not the absence of psychopathology."

In retrospect, coping with massive psychic trauma can be analyzed in a heuristic model parallel to the stages of mourning (Fogelman, 1988). Survivor-victims can be at any point along the continuum. At times they are fixated at one stage; at times they fluctuate. During the initial years after liberation, adaptation was accomplished by denial. By forming love relationships, starting new families, exerting energy into education and work, survivors did not allow themselves to feel the pain of all the losses. Survivors who emigrated to Israel used the rebuilding of the land as a form of denial. This is a coping mechanism, rather than a pathological denial that the Holocaust happened.

In the mid-1950s, many survivor-victims began a new stage of formulation. This stage of mourning evoked an outburst of emotions. Survivors experienced intense feelings of depression, anger, rage, helplessness, survivor guilt, lack of interest in their surroundings, and an emotional distancing from people. Recognizing the reality that family members were not coming back necessitated an emotive response. Grief reaction was painful and necessary, if survivors were to come to terms with replacing losses and identifying with the past that was destroyed, rather than with the suffering of the dead.

In the final phase, survivor-victims search for meaning. They struggle with attaining a sense of connection with everything they lost—family, community, familiar objects and their own self. They search for a way to integrate the self, to transmit the memory of those who are no longer here and to assure a continuity with the past. A Polish survivor of the Warsaw ghetto and several concentration camps, Luba Gurdus (1989), described the sentiments of this final phase:

What binds us, Holocaust survivors, is our Jewish identity, our solemn resolve to bear
witness to the painful past, our promise to keep and guard the sacred memory of our murdered
brethren, to perpetuate and rescue from oblivion every vestige of our obliterated legacy and to
restore the honor and dignity of the murdered six million. (p. 15)

Impaired mourning in any of these phases could result in dysfunctional behavior and somatization. For example, in the first phase a survivor-victim must acknowledge that a loved one is really dead. There are people who still search for missing relatives in telephone directories when they visit a new city or attend survivor meetings. Not having witnessed the death of a family member, along with the missing-grave phenomenon, makes it much more difficult for survivors to begin grieving. Some never do. There may be a fear that if they start, they will not be able to control their emotions. Such survivor-victims continue to cope by avoiding any reminders of the past. Others adjust to every-day life as if they are still living in a war/Holocaust situation. They resort to the coping mechanisms that helped them survive. For example, they acquiesce to authority figures, consider every decision as a life-and-death matter, hoard food, do not call too much attention to themselves, and participate in other behaviors they attributed to their survival during the Holocaust.

Survivor-victims who do allow themselves to grieve feel the pain and re-experience that grief periodically. Such states include irrational guilt: "Why didn't I do more to save others?"; survivor guilt: "Why did I survive while others were killed?" and helplessness at not being able to undo the pain that loved ones suffered. Holocaust survivors who cannot come to accept that they have a right to live, that under the circumstances they could not have done any more than they did, may not be able to enjoy their present lives and relationships.

Responsibility to the dead is not expressed through continued loyalty to the suffering, but rather through loyalty to the memory of values and heritage they represented. Continuity with the past is not continuity with the bestiality and inhumanity of the persecutors, but with the Jewish culture and traditions and the life-enhancing values that symbolize the victims' lives, rather than their deaths.

THERAPEUTIC ALTERNATIVES

Mental-health professionals have for the most part ignored or misunderstood the Holocaust survivor generation (Fogelman, 1988). Clinicians who have accepted the survivor syndrome as the aftereffect of the Holocaust on every survivor have serious doubts whether the survivor can benefit from psychotherapy or psychoanalysis (Krystal, 1984). On the other hand, those who theorize that survivors have the capacity to recover their ego strength believe in the therapeutic value of psychotherapy with this population (Klein, 1984; Orenstein, 1981; Kestenberg, 1972).

The ineffectiveness of psychotherapeutic work with survivors is attributed by Krystal (1984) to their fear of their emotions. Grieving requires an ability to tolerate intense feelings of anger, vengeance, sadness, and helplessness. Krystal therefore concludes that survivors are not capable of carrying out the process of mourning that would be a crucial element of their treatment. He feels that aging survivors are even more incapable of grieving their losses and hence benefiting from an analytic or psychotherapeutic relationship.

The therapeutic work of accepting what happened would mean that survivors would have to accept that Nazism and the persecution they experienced was justified by its causes. This leads Krystal to suggest that "self-healing" would be "antithetical to the only justification for their survival: to be angry witnesses against the outrage of the Holocaust."

This is further compounded by the limitations of mourning certain kinds of losses. Krystal compares the inability of parents to complete the mourning process of a lost child to the impossible task of mourning multiple losses during the Holocaust. Although Kestenberg (1989) would agree that it is impossible to complete the mourning process in one generation, she has a more favorable view of the possibility of engaging a survivor in a therapeutic relationship.

Survivors' reactions to psychological treatment are rather negative and pessimistic. The consensus among survivors is that no one will understand them, and that it is too painful to share their horrific memories. Talking about the past will not soothe the throbbing torment. We find that even those who were suffering from a survivor syndrome did not seek out mental-health professionals. What emerged was a self-help movement: Holocaust Remembrance Days, *Landsmannschaft* groups (organizations comprised of people from the same European community), "memorial books" about destroyed communities, and organizations based on common persecutory experiences during the Holocaust (for example, the Bergen Belsen Association).

One of the main therapeutic goals for Holocaust survivors is that of mourning. A communal trauma cannot be resolved by mental-health professionals in the traditional patient-therapist paradigm (Marcus, 1984). A communal commemoration, however, relieves the individual of personal anxieties by presenting survivors with an opportunity to share grief via a publicly sanctioned and legitimate avenue. The ritualization of mourning is a therapeutic alternative. As Klein noted:

> . . . [t]he importance of collective mourning [is] not only for the integration of the generations and the community, but also for the feedback which the individual receives that affirms his own feelings. This affirmation, the vital aspect of sharing, is continuously re-experienced by the survivor families. [These ceremonies provide the individual with] less of an opportunity to engage in denial and to overcome feelings of guilt and helplessness. (Klein, 1978, unpublished manuscript)

Policy Planning

For more than 40 years there has been a considerable lack of therapeutic alternatives for survivors. This can be attributed to the survivors' motivation to adjust to their new lives by working and establishing families, and the community's desire to avoid looking too closely at Nazi inhumanity while the world was silent.

As early as 1948, Friedman discussed the continued psychological plight of survivors. Incredible as it sounds, when the initial plans for the rehabilitation "of Europe's surviving Jews were outlined, the psychiatric aspect of the problem was overlooked entirely. Everyone engaged in directing the relief work thought solely in terms of material assistance. . . . We accepted the fact that the very fact of survival was evidence of physical and psychological superiority. . . . "

With some exceptions, both private and institutional, efforts were not made toward investing in the psychological well-being of survivors and their families. Paradoxically, when exceptions occurred, such efforts were often met with criticism for not understanding the survivor or for continuing to stigmatize a victim population.

In recent years, survivors have been aging and their emotional and social needs have increased. As their impending death is imminent, their prior closeness to horrendous death is reawakened. For some, the mere thought of being placed in an old-age home, or of having to be hospitalized for an illness, evokes nightmarish memories of incarceration during those traumatic years.

Social-service agencies, old-age homes, religious institutions, and hospitals have a responsibility to train their staffs and to be prepared to provide specific attention to the possibility of the recurrence of a "survivor syndrome." Nightmares, insomnia, depression, paranoia, anomie, and somatization are some of the symptoms that may develop in aging survivors. If a supportive environment is set up for survivors to be able to share their past, the symptoms may in time dissipate. This may include the opportunity to talk about one's losses and fears even though they may seem irrelevant to present-day life. (For example, patients may fear hospital attendants as if they were SS officers, and the nurses as if they were female guards.) Survivors also need to bear witness by giving oral or written testimony, by teaching others about what happened and by transmitting lessons they draw from their persecution. Such activities have a self-healing effect, and therefore need to be implemented in cities that have survivor populations. In locales where social structures do not exist, public-policy initiatives are necessary to institute survivor speakers' bureaus, oral-history projects, and writing workshops staffed by volunteer teachers and editors to assist survivors with their testimonies.

In areas where such activities are already ongoing, this approach must become known to the survivors themselves. Many are isolated and do not even know that Yad Vashem, Israel's National Holocaust Museum and Archives, collects testimonies of survivors and of non-Jews who rescued Jews during World War II. Grassroots efforts are the only way to find those in the community who need to avail themselves of such services. Educating the public about the existence of these facilities and projects will ultimately reach the appropriate people.

Today, in most major cities in North America, Europe, and Israel, one can notice the proliferation of Holocaust memorials in the form of monuments and museums. While building monuments creates the possibility for mourning, it is not enough without the opportunity for more personal expressions or grief (Lifton, 1968). The dearth of planning for rehabilitation centers for survivors, although a few major developments are currently taking place, primarily in Israel and Holland, limits the accomplishment of authentic grief work.

In Israel, some specific services exist for survivors: a mental-health center for Dutch survivors has served the needs of this specific population. More recently, a center has been established for survivors and their families from all Nazi-occupied countries (Amoha), an old-age home for survivors is in the process of being built, and, in addition, survivors can enjoy a resort for a subsidized fee.

In New York, several agencies are providing services for aged survivors with very limited funds. However, no uniform policy in the Jewish community or in its agencies exists for meeting the rehabilitation needs of survivors.

A recent major development is the new category in the *DSM-III-R* for diagnosing survivors for a post-traumatic stress disorder. This will enable some survivors to receive financial reimbursements for psychiatric care through insurance or workman's compensation (Spitzer et al., 1989).

CONCLUSION

The mental-health profession has come a long way in understanding the survivor of war and holocaust. The humiliation, degradation, and exposure to horrendous death have left indelible memories in each and every survivor. For the most part, survivors have adapted to their new environments while they continue the arduous process of grieving multiple losses. Over the years, social-services agencies and service-delivery policies have not been sufficiently receptive to the rehabilitation of this population, nor for that matter have other groups who have also experienced massive psychic trauma, political torture, and war. It is incumbent upon the helping professions to be aware of the long-range effects of war and holocaust, because the individuals themselves may not always be cognizant that an experience they had more than 40 years ago still has a profound effect on their daily lives.

EXERCISES

In order to understand the impact of Nazi persecution on its survivors, it is not enough to read the psychological literature. Ask yourself, "What books and films have I read and watched about the subject?" "Am I familiar with the historical facts about Nazi occupation from 1933–1945?" "Can I name three survivors, three rescuers, three Nazis whose life stories are familiar to me?" If you cannot answer these questions in the affirmative, ask yourself, "Why have I shied away from dealing with this period?"

When it comes to contemplating doing treatment or working on oral histories with this population, it will not be sufficient to learn about the Holocaust only through books and films. One must talk with people who lived in Europe during World War II. Ask them to share their experiences in their lives before, during, and after this period. If they themselves are not Jews, ask them if they were aware of their own imminent death? Did Nazi racial laws and their implementation present any conflict for them as human beings? How were they affected by the Nazi occupation?

REFERENCES

Des Pres, T. (1976). *The survivor.* New York: Oxford University Press.

Fogelman, E. (1988). Therapeutic alternatives for Holocaust survivors and second generation. In R. Braham (Ed.), *The psychological perspectives of the Holocaust and of its aftermath* (pp. 79–108). New York: Columbia University Press.

Friedman, P. (1948). The road back for the D.P.s: Healing the psychological scars of Nazism. *Commentary, 6*(6), 502–510.

Gurdus, L. (1989). What binds Holocaust survivors. *Together, 4*(1), 15. Reprinted by permission.

Jucovy, M. (1986). The Holocaust. In A. Rothstein (Ed.), *The reconstruction of trauma: Its significance in clinical work* (pp. 153–157). Madison: International Universities Press.

Kestenberg, J. (1972). Psychoanalytic contributions to the problem of children of survivors from Nazi persecution. *Israel Annals of Psychiatry and Related Disciplines, 10*(4), 311–325.

Kestenberg, J. (1989). Coping with losses and survival. In P. Sghabad and D. R. Dietrich (Eds.), *The problem of loss and mourning: New psychoanalytic perspectives.* New York: International Universities Press.

Klein, H. (1978). Holocaust survivors and their children on kibbutzim. Unpublished manuscript.

Klein, H. (1984). The survivor's search for meaning and identity in the Nazi concentration camps.

Proceedings of the Fourth Yad Vashem International Historical Society (pp. 543–554). Jerusalem: Yad Vashem.

Klein, H., Zellermayer, J., & Shanan, J. (1963). Former concentration camp inmates on a psychiatric ward. *Archives of General Psychiatry, 8,* 334–342.

Krystal, H. (Ed.) (1968). *Massive psychic trauma.* New York: International Universities Press.

Krystal, H. (1984). Integration and self-healing in post-traumatic states. In S. A. Luel & P. Marcus (Eds.), *Psychoanalytic reflections on the Holocaust: Selected essays* (pp. 113–133). New York: Ktav Publishing House.

Levi, P. (1988). *The drowned and the saved.* New York: Summit Books. Reprinted by permission.

Lifton, R. J. (1968). *Death in life: Survivors of Hiroshima.* New York: Simon and Schuster.

Marcus, P. (1984). Jewish consciousness after the Holocaust. In S. A. Luel and P. Marcus (Eds.), *Psychoanalytic reflections on the Holocaust: Selected essays* (pp. 179–195). New York: Ktav Publishing House.

Marcus, P., & Rosenberg, A. (1988). A philosophical critique of the "survivor syndrome" and some implications for treatment. In R. Braham (Ed.), *The psychological perspective of the Holocaust and of its aftermath* (pp. 53–78). New York: Columbia University Press.

Niederland, W. G. (1961). The problem of the survivor. *Journal of the Hillside Hospital, 10,* 233–247. Reprinted by permission.

Orenstein, A. (1981). The aging survivor of the Holocaust: The effects of the Holocaust on life cycle experiences: The creation and recreation of families. *Journal of Geriatric Psychiatry, 14*(2), 135–154.

Orenstein, A. (1985). Survival and recovery. *Psychoanalytic Inquiry, 5*(1), 99–130.

Spitzer, R. L., & Gibbon, M., et al. (Eds.). (1989). *DSM-III-R Case Book.* Washington, DC: American Psychiatric Press.

Wiesel, E. (1960). *Night.* New York: Hill and Wang.

II

Action Approaches from
the Grass Roots

Introduction to Part II

The factors predicting health-protective behavior have long been of interest to behavioral scientists like Muzafer Sherif, Irving Janis, and others. Questions of importance include these: What type of message increases the probability of people acting in their own best health interest? What distinguishes the health-oriented activist from the non-activist? Perrin French, a psychiatrist active at the international and national levels in reducing the threat of horrendous death, explores the issue of precursors to action in two magnificent chapters. He creatively combines theory and data into personal action.

The succeeding two chapters explore the role of education as an instrument to health-protective action. Art Newman reviews some of the existing educational measures useful to the teaching of children up to the age of 18 years.

Maire Dugan describes the history, role, and function of the Consortium on Peace Research, Education, and Development (COPRED). COPRED is a fine, multifaceted peace organization that regards peace studies as a rigorous social science requiring grass-roots participation.

John Tuohey, a Catholic theologian and bioethicist, writes on the question, "What is the response of religion to horrendous death?" Does religion offer insight to people concerning *action*? He writes, "Religious insights offer a place to start this reflection by describing the relationships each person shares with others, the meaning of horrendous death, and the link between the protection and promotion of life."

Michael Shuman and Earl Molander *acted* by developing grass-roots organizations involving citizen participation. Michael Shuman is the co-founder and president of the Center for Innovative Diplomacy, a 6000-member organization of people who believe that horrendous death can be eliminated by participatory democracy. The organization's emphasis is on the political control of leaders by the public at the national and international level. His view is consonant with French, Leviton, and others writing in this volume who feel that it is only the will of the populace to which the gatekeepers of power and influence will respond.

Earl Molander is Executive Director of the Ground Zero Pairing Project (GZPP), and one of the leaders in promoting citizen diplomacy. GZPP is one of the largest suppliers of educational materials concerning U.S.-Soviet relationships to schools; its goal is to promote friendships between children of the two countries. The organization is also involved in establishing other human linkages between the two countries. The purpose is obvious: Having knowledge and contact with "enemies" helps people come to see each other as individuals rather than in terms of stereotypes and labels.

In the last chapter, Daniel Leviton describes an 18-year-old intergenerational health program that pairs college students and others with older institutionalized and non-institutionalized adults. As both "staffers" and "members" exercise, play, and learn together, stereotypes are eliminated and people become friends. The implications of this Adult Health and Development Program in the elimination of horrendous death are discussed.

Also discussed is an academic course, "Theories of Children's Love and Peace Behaviors," which was designed for actual and potential teachers and parents. The goal is to learn the art and science of raising children so that they are loving and peaceful human beings.

Thus *action* to eliminate horrendous death can take many forms: political, parental, religious, international, educational, and the like. There is no lack of actions to take if the motivation is present.

As this was being written, additional resources valuable to the action-oriented individuals and groups became available. One is a monograph by Alan B. Durning, *Action at the Grass Roots: Fighting Poverty and Environmental Decline* (Worldwatch Institute, 1776 Massachusetts Ave., Washington, DC 20036, 1989). Besides describing examples of action and offering a fine bibliography, it also lists other volumes in the Worldwatch Paper Series. The Worldwatch Institute is an independent, nonprofit research organization created to analyze and focus attention on global problems.

In the area of audiovisuals, The Educational Film and Video Project (5332 College Ave., Suite 101, Oakland, CA 94618, (415) 655-9050) deserves commendation and attention. They specialize in video and film programs for a safe and sustainable world. Titles include *There are Alternatives*, an interview with Professor Johann Galtung (the father of peace research), who summarizes peace research and offers an alternative plan to military conflict and violence; *Economic Conversion*, which discusses the conversion from a military to a civilian economy, emphasizing the need to deal with the fear of job security; and *The Search for Common Ground*, a two-part program on conflict resolution.

A new journal, *Peace Review: The International Quarterly of World Peace* (2439 Birch Street, Suite 8, Palo Alto, CA 94306) should be added to the subscription list of the concerned individual.

There is much that a health-educated and health-concerned individual or group can do to eliminate horrendous death. Follow the examples described in this chapter or come up with your own. Above all—act!

4

The Psychology of Survival-Directed Action, Part I: The National Pathway to Survival

Perrin French
Stanford University, Stanford, California

There are diverse forms of horrendous (horrible, man-made) deaths, the prevention of which might be facilitated by psychological inquiry. The most urgent form is that which is most likely and most potentially destructive: nuclear war. This two-part analysis first explores responses to the threat of nuclear war at the national level (Part I), and then at the level of the individual (Part II).

In Part I, civil defense, military defense, and deterrence as a long-term venture are considered in turn as methods of national protection. Problems of both a psychological and practical nature inherent in these approaches are discussed. Nonviolent, nonthreatening methods of international conflict management appear to offer greater hope for long-term survival. To succeed, they will require efforts at education, cooperation, and negotiation beyond any currently in evidence. Specific examples of such requisite efforts are given.

Part II explores the social and psychological forces influencing individuals to attend or fail to attend to the nuclear threat, and to select one course over another as a pathway to survival. Psychological considerations which might persuade individuals to select the most promising path toward survival are discussed, as well as factors determining whether or not individuals take actions moving their nations or other individuals along that path.

INTRODUCTION

This book is concerned with the understanding and prevention of horrendous-type death, defined as forms of death that are at once both horrible and man-made. For it, I was asked to write a useful chapter, a chapter with some practical applicability, on the psychology of survival-directed action. I agreed to do so, and began by asking myself three preliminary questions to circumscribe the topic: (a) What kind of horrendous death should one choose to be most concerned about? (b) Given this choice, what constitutes survival-directed action? and (c) With a definition of survival-directed action in hand, what can the discipline of psychology tell us about people's comprehension of this situation and their support of the necessary action? Answering these questions proved sufficiently complicated to require expanding the project to two chapters.

This first chapter, Part I, starts with an answer to the first question by choosing a specific form of horrendous-type death as particularly worthy of attention. It goes on to offer answers to the other two questions, charting a course of survival-directed action and examining its psychology—but solely at the level of national behavior. Here it may seem as if we are concerned with political science rather than psychology. To any who find this confusing, I would suggest that political science may, to some extent, be viewed as the psychology of individuals when aggregated into nations. The following chapter, Part II, explores answers to the third question in the realm more typically thought of as "psychological"; in other words, at the level of the separate individual. It examines the forces impelling individuals to ignore or attend the threat of horrendous death we feel to be of most concern, and to support or reject those national actions that considerations in this chapter indicate may be survival-directed.

A MOST IMPORTANT TYPE
OF HORRENDOUS DEATH

There are many types of man-made death. Suicide, homicide, drug abuse, automobile accidents, conventional warfare, toxic pollution, starvation through misallocation of resources—the list is long and the role of psychological understanding in the prevention of each is central. The constraints of writing something practical and within the confines of a chapter or two, however, force a narrowing of scope. In the interest of maximal effectiveness, indeed, we would do well to restrict ourselves to a discussion of the single most significant form of man-made death.

A reasonable formula to use in selecting the most important type of man-made death would be to find the one that is both most destructive and most likely to occur. By this criterion, the logical choice would have to be nuclear war.

The immediate and eventual deaths of tens—or possibly hundreds—of millions human beings in a nuclear war would overshadow the loss of lives through such daily man-made events as auto accidents, drug abuse, and suicide. Nuclear war would be to those events as a redwood tree is to a pile of toothpicks. A single modern nuclear missile of the Titan II variety, detonated over a major metropolitan area, would generate a firestorm enveloping scores of square miles and would immediately kill two to four times as many people as the United States lost in the Civil War, World War I, World War II, the Korean War, and the Vietnam War put together (Trabalka, Eyman, & Auerbach, 1980).

As for the likelihood of nuclear war, while estimates vary, it's not much comfort to know that (a) it has already happened once, and (b) it has nearly occurred several times since.

Public estimates of the likelihood of nuclear war vary from year to year and from poll to poll (where exact wording of the questions constitutes a variable). Though mitigated by Eastern Europe's renunciation of communism and by the shift in Soviet/American relations, there has been general agreement about a significant level of likelihood. In 1987, 49% of U.S. adults surveyed in a Gallup poll rated the chances of a nuclear war within 10 years as 6 or higher on a scale from 0 (no chance) to 10 (certainty) (Gallup, 1987). A study of over 2,500 U.S. high school seniors in 1989 found 22% "mostly agree" or "agree" with the statement that "Nuclear or biological annihilation will probably be the fate of all mankind within my lifetime" (J. G. Bachman, personal communication, October 26, 1990). Even more alarming is the conclusion of Professor Martin Hellman, a world-renowned probability and statistics expert at Stanford University, who believes that a mathematical process known as the two-step Markov principle demonstrates the inevitability of nuclear war, if our reliance on nuclear weapons continues indefinitely. He compares our situation to a game of Russian roulette, wherein "Every 'small' war is pulling the trigger; each threat of the use of violence is pulling the trigger; each day that goes by in which a missile or computer can fail is pulling the trigger." As he puts it in summary, "If we keep taking low-probability chances, the probabilities of World War III is not low—it is certain" (Stokes, 1984, p. 9).

Beyond the importance of its own possible occurrence, the nuclear arms race, even without a bomb detonated in open warfare since 1945, contributes importantly to other forms of man-made death by blocking work on their solutions. It diverts funds, scientific and engineering resources (of both human and material nature), and social priorities into the creation of a culture increasingly uninterested in the idea of finding non-military solutions to our problems.

It has been estimated that approximately every two seconds, somewhere on earth a child is dying of frank starvation or other nutritional disorders which would be treatable at a cost of $100 per year. Instead of devoting any such expenditure to the prevention of these Type II (inadvertent) horrendous deaths, the nations of the earth lavish the equivalent of $60,000 per starving child per year on their military establishments (PSR, 1989). Approximately half of these monies (Kaldor, 1981) goes toward the production of weaponry, including nuclear: the irony is that these are nonconsumable items whose most desired outcome is that they never be used.

Any successful contribution toward ending the nuclear arms race thus has the potential to free up vast funds and human capacities to reduce other horrendous-type deaths.

Yet of equal or greater importance might be the ethical ramifications of a nuclear arms race halt. It seems likely that the evolution of human ethics in regard to the killing of people will be a 'top-down' movement, with nuclear war addressed first for the simple sake of survival, and lesser forms of homicide eradicated secondarily, as extensions of the moral and practical changes involved. Impossibly utopian as it may at first sound, the prevention of nuclear war over the long term not only requires but may eventually succeed in bringing about a complete reassessment of the role of violence in the management of human conflicts. Reflection on our nuclear-age options seems persuasive toward this conclusion.

NATIONAL OPTIONS IN THE NUCLEAR ERA: WHICH WAY TO SURVIVAL?

As a guide to determining what may constitute survival-directed action in the face of the threat of nuclear war, I would like to share an overview I have come to have of our current predicament.

Starting in the 1940s, a nuclear arms race began which has now reached the point where the potential exists to effectively destroy the human species—"omnicide," the death of all. Protection against the effects of nuclear weapons has thus unfortunately but unavoidably become a top human priority. Figure 1 is a flow chart showing the several courses of national response invoked by our need for protection, and indicating where, by the preponderance of available evidence, each will lead.

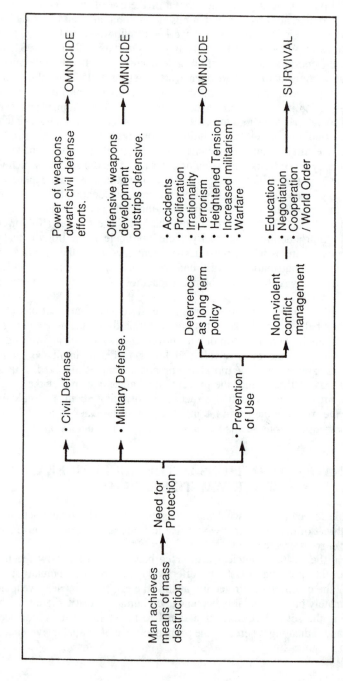

Figure 1 Flow chart of national options in the Nuclear Age, indicating where, by the preponderance of evidence, each one seems likely to lead.

Civil Defense

Civil defense—the notion of protective fortification via bomb shelters, or protective maneuvering through evacuation of target areas—still has appeal for at least a few Americans. The Federal Emergency Management Agency (FEMA), generates plans from year to year for updates of the "duck-and-cover" school education programs, as well as for the establishment of nationwide Emergency Operating Centers: hundreds of fallout shelters to protect state and local government officials and records in the event of a nuclear war. FEMA is aware of a general public resistance to such measures, and has responded to it by threatening to withhold all federal disaster funding from states or localities refusing to participate.

Attempts to force efforts at protection that appear at once both ineffective and undemocratic upon the public have tended to fail. The majority of Americans, educated in the early 1980s to the consequences of individual nuclear detonations, not to mention compounded effects of a nuclear winter, perceive the power of nuclear weapons as sufficient to swamp civil defense efforts. On this point, the public's opinion coincides with that of nuclear scholars, such as physicist and arms control expert Sidney Drell, who has written that he "cannot conceive of a civil defense system that could protect our society—or the Soviet society—from the unprecedented disaster and devastation of nuclear war" (Drell, 1983, p. 12). Seventy-one percent of the respondents in a 1984 national poll (82% of them under 30) agreed with the statement that "The idea of civil defense is a dangerous delusion because there is no defense in a nuclear war" (Public Agenda Foundation, 1984, p. 34).

Military Defense

If the shield is ineffectual, what of crossing swords? While moral revulsion and sufficiently invulnerable retaliatory forces may combine to rule out a pre-emptive first strike, might there not be a defensive use of military force with which we could protect ourselves? Can a military defense not be mounted against a military threat?

In the 1972 SALT I accords, Soviets and Americans together agreed to put aside this notion. They determined that their collective security was better served by acknowledging mutual vulnerability than by depleting their resources in a race to perfect the skill of "shooting down bullets with bullets," as the cross-targeting of missiles traveling 17,000 mph came to be called.

In 1983, however, new life was breathed into the idea of a military defense by President Reagan in his March 23 speech launching the Strategic Defense Initiative (SDI, dubbed "Star Wars"). "What if free people," he asked, "could live secure in the knowledge that . . . we could intercept and destroy strategic ballistic missiles before they reached our own soil or that of our allies?" He called on our scientists to "give us the means of rendering these nuclear weapons impotent and obsolete" (Herken, 1987, p. 20).

Coming as it did after several years of intense consciousness-raising by a coalition of groups and individuals concerned about nuclear devastation, President Reagan's message was a welcome suggestion to a public ill-informed about the actual details of our nuclear situation. Not only did it provide the reassuring notion that there was now a plan to take care of that particularly alarming problem, but it promised to do it through a means especially appealing to the American character. From de Tocqueville's observations in the first half of the last century to those of public communication campaign authors in the last half of this one, Americans have consistently been described as fascinated with technology (Paisley, 1981). Education, engineering, and enforcement have been dubbed the "three E's" of prevention campaigns in matters of public health. The order of preference of these options for Americans, with their anti-authoritarian social contract and their faith in technology, is engineering first, education second, and enforcement only as a last resort (Paisley, 1981). The desire for a "technological fix" rendered Star Wars as appealing to Americans in the 1980s as the snake-oil miracle cures of traveling salesmen were in the 1800s.

According to many authorities on the technologies involved, unfortunately, the analogy of Star Wars to snake oil is as apt in regard to its effectiveness as it is in regard to its appeal. SDI space weaponry, could it overcome the Herculean—many say impossible—problems of meeting its computational software requirements and actually be deployed, is described as readily susceptible to numerous countermeasures (Drell, 1983; Lebow, 1985a; Kogut & Weissman, 1986; Ris, 1987). SDI weaponry can reportedly be faked out by inexpensive sheet-metal decoys. It can be eluded by speedier missile boost phases or "air breathing" (low, intra-atmospheric) missile flights. Space-based portions of the system, many experts assert, can themselves be shot down much more easily and economically than they can shoot down their prey. Space-based "battle stations" can be blown up on command by pre-placed, adjacently orbiting "mine" satellites. The complexity and untestability of the software requirements for computerized battle coordination, plus the ease and economy of effective countermeasures, are the two principal failings cited by the Congressional Office of Technology Assessment report in its conclusion that any SDI-type defense against Soviet missiles would be prone to fail "catastrophically" should it ever be used (Lindley, 1988).

In sum, many experts believe that since human ingenuity at weapons delivery can now be combined with devices of mass destruction, military second-guessing by means that cannot be battle-tested is not the approach to security on which they wish to stake their children's lives. To cite Sidney Drell again, "The President's plans and his goals notwithstanding, there remains a physical reality of nature: owing to the very great destructive power of nuclear weapons, the offense has—and can maintain—a predominance over the defense" (Drell, 1983, p. 12). Nuclear devices, with their quantum leap in physical efficiency beyond prior explosives, obviate the notion of an "adequate defense." Such weapons demand a nearly perfect defense. And while some have argued for attempting this with the preamble "If we can land a man on the moon . . . ," the difficulties become more obvious when one considers that the moon was not attempting to fight back.

Prevention of Use

This brings us to the third and final avenue of response to our need for protection against devices of mass destruction: prevention of use. If we cannot fortify ourselves against the weapons, or knock out their means of delivery, there is no other course toward survival but the prevention of their use. Surveys of the public (Public Agenda Foundation, 1984; Los Angeles Times, 1982) and individual interviews with 80 of the top U.S. nuclear weapons policymakers (Kull, 1985) indicate that the overwhelming majority of both lay and expert Americans have settled on this third branch of our flow chart as the most likely route toward survival. As more and more light has been shed on the realities of such an event, those who at the start of the 1980s suggested America might fight and win a nuclear war have shifted over to join in the general agreement that, in the words of the joint communiqué of President Reagan and Secretary General Gorbachev at the 1985 Geneva summit, a nuclear war "cannot be won and must never be fought."

Where the major remaining difference of opinion lies is in how best to achieve this prevention of use. Should we rely on deterrence as a long-term policy, inclusive of developing Star Wars for this purpose? Or should we continue, as we have started with the Intermediate-Range Nuclear Force (INF) agreement, to move gradually toward significant (and eventually complete) nuclear disarmament via arms-control negotiations?

At various moments, statements and actions emanating from one or the other superpower—and occasionally both together, as in the recent rapprochement of Secretary General Gorbachev and President Bush—have seemed to favor nuclear disarmament. But until both sides have simultaneously ceased production and testing of nuclear weapons, as well as desisting from their enthusiastic efforts to develop and promote new generations of weapons, deterrence will remain the branch of the flow chart (Fig. 1) along which we are all traveling.

Deterrence

The essence of deterrence, in the parlance of gunfighting, consists of "keeping the other guy covered." It is based on an assumption of adversarial relations. The presumed aggressive intent of other nations is kept in check by an ever-present threat of devastating retaliation. With two nuclear powers "covering" each other with weapons of mass destruction deployed by such relatively invulnerable means as nuclear powered submarines, the script for our gunfighting standoff reads, "One false move and we both get it."

To make the situation more precarious, one commonly accepted formula for calculating the strength of deterrence (attributed to General Russell Dougherty) states that "the power of deterrence = military capability × the (perceived) will to use it." This formula is cited to justify the need for not merely a static nuclear stockpile, but a dynamic, ongoing, ever-changing nuclear weapons research and development program, based on changing notions of defensive and targeting strategies. Such a program is felt to indicate a greater degree of "will" in the matter.

The merits of this situation as a method of avoiding World War III for very long are debatable. Some see a good deal of stability in the distribution of nuclear weapons, crediting it fully for the lack of a world war since 1945 and generally referring to it as a desirable situation. Others, looking at the accidents, threats, near-uses, and proliferation over the last four to five decades, see our avoidance of world war more as a matter of blind luck, and view deterrence as a fundamentally unstable state we've stumbled into by historical accident and would do well to get out of as quickly as possible.

A number of factors render deterrence a precarious strategy to depend on for long-term security. They include the eventualities of accidents, proliferation of nuclear weaponry, irrational actions, terrorism, and escalating conventional warfare. They also include—even if the factors just mentioned should never result in nuclear war—the insidious fostering of a mental, social, and physical setting that may in itself predispose nations toward major war.

Accidents. The highly reputable Stockholm International Peace Research Institute estimates that there have been 125 major nuclear weapons accidents in the U.S. Armed Forces alone between 1945 and 1976 (Leitenberg, 1977). These include such events as a 24-megaton bomb (blast power equivalent to a freight train full of TNT 4800 miles long) falling from a distressed B-52 on Goldsboro, North Carolina in 1961, with five of its six interlocking safety devices failing in the fall (Lapp, 1962).

More recently, faulty computer parts or faulty computer loading and programming have been responsible for major mishaps. A good example of the latter was the 1979 episode in which three squadrons of nuclear-armed B-52s were launched during a six-minute false alarm when a War Games practice tape fed into a Pentagon computer was read as *reality* by mistake (Thiermann & Thiermann, 1981).

Most likely the worst nuclear accident to have occurred to date—probably worse than Chernobyl—involved the massive leakage of radioactive waste into bodies of water in the Southern part of the Ural mountains, near the town of Chelyabinsk, at the end of 1957. It may or may not have involved a lateral explosion of nuclear materials (whether of military or peaceful nature remains unclear), but in any event resulted in the disappearance of over a dozen small towns from the map of the Soviet Union (Trabalka, Eyman, & Auerbach, 1980). In my meetings with a number of eminent Soviet scientists between 1981 and 1987—including heads of major scientific institutions—only one of them had heard of this event. I don't believe the others were feigning ignorance; they had simply been kept in the dark about it, just as residents of New England were kept in the dark by the U.S. government regarding the crash of a nuclear-armed FB-111 off the coast in 1980 (Talbot, 1981). Nations developing and deploying devices of mass destruction have a stake in maintaining the ignorance of both adversary nations and their own citizens regarding major mishaps.

With deterrence—and notably the more "dynamic" conceptions of it, which call for constant, ongoing development of nuclear weaponry—more accidents are bound to happen, and in greater number and extent than the nuclear powers involved are likely to acknowledge. Whether a major nuclear accident could lead to nuclear war might depend on how destructive the accident was of any ability to communicate how it had occurred, as well as how much panic it caused in the minds of officials obliged to manage it.

Proliferation. The Iraqi research reactor destroyed by Israeli bomber jets in June, 1981, is one of over 170 research reactors abroad, some in unstable nations and many supplied for years by the United States with bomb-grade uranium and sophisticated nuclear technology (Diamond, 1981). It was from research reactors that India got its material for an atomic bomb explosion in 1974 (Diamond, 1981).

In 1968, 135 nations, including the United States and the Soviet Union, signed a non-proliferation treaty in which the nations not yet equipped with nuclear weapons agreed to stay so as long as the United States and the Soviet Union made efforts to reverse their "vertical proliferation" (in-house development) of nuclear weapons. A number of nations refused to sign the agreement, including, in addition to the then known nuclear nations of France and China, several which are now known or believed to have nuclear weapons (Israel, India, Pakistan, South Africa).

Those nonsignatory nations are free to sell nuclear technology abroad without the safeguards required of signatory nations to prevent conversion to military use.

Despite their coauthorship and participation in this treaty, the two superpowers have proceeded with the development and production of increasing quantities of new generation nuclear weapons. This puts them in an unstable moral stance as they urge abstinence on the not-already-nuclear nations. With the greater risks of triggering nuclear war in the next century arguably resting in countries other than the United States and the Soviet Union, it seems exceedingly unfortunate that the United States is pushing to extend the arms race through Star Wars, and stands out as the only nation in the entire United Nations opposed to a resolution for a nuclear test ban—probably the most effective device for arresting nuclear proliferation.

Irrationality. The "safety" of a nuclear force is dependent on the rationality and discipline of its personnel. Congressional hearings on the Department of Defense determined that over a 10-year period, 48,000 out of the 112,000 troops in the U.S. nuclear forces were decertified—about 5,000 per year. Over half of them suffered from major psychiatric difficulties and/or abuse of drugs or alcohol (Abrams, 1987). Initial screening for a soldier or sailor's admission into the nuclear forces is often based on his or her dossier alone, without reliance on individual interview; moreover, subsequent monitoring generally depends on observation by an individual's colleagues rather than any independent evaluation (Abrams, 1987).

A recent study of drug use among army personnel on duty estimated it to be as high as 43% (Abrams, 1986). While drug abuse is a widespread and increasing problem in United States armed services in general, conditions predisposing to it are notably present in nuclear-weapons areas, where boredom, social isolation, stress, absence of job satisfaction, peer pressure, and lack of positive group cohesion are great. One nuclear weapons expert (from whom I have not obtain permission for attribution) reported to a university seminar recently that while inspecting U.S. nuclear forces in Europe in the mid-1970s he found heroin in the urine of 30% of the troops at one base. He added wryly that there was a logical explanation: the French had been cracking down on marijuana trade, causing the "pot" supply to dry up.

This is not just an American problem: consider that in 1976, for every American dying of alcohol intoxication, over a hundred Soviets died of the same cause (Abrams, 1987). It has been estimated that alcohol dependence within the Soviet armed services may reach as high as one out of three individuals (Abrams, 1987). This is not a very reassuring consideration with prevention of nuclear war depending on stable Soviet—and American—nuclear control and command.

Terrorism. A number of recent novels and films have dealt with the theme of nuclear armed fanatical groups threatening to blow up major cities if their political or financial demands are not met. A nonfictional account of such occurrences appeared several years ago in a *New West* magazine article by D. E. Kaplan (1981) entitled "Where the Bombs Are." It contained descriptions of an extortion attempt on the city of Los Angeles via notes requesting payoffs in the millions; the demands were accompanied by blueprints of purportedly readied nuclear devices. The article describes the relative helplessness of the governmental body set up to deal with such events: a branch of the Treasury Department equipped with radiation-sensing search vehicles (Kaplan, 1981).

In terms of terrorism on the international scale, one can't help wondering exactly what Libya's General Ghadafi expects to get in return for the millions of dollars he has given for Pakistani nuclear research and development. One might equally wonder what various Iranian groups might attempt if armed with the latest nuclear technology.

As long as a state of deterrence continues, not only will nuclear technology continue to proliferate, but more weapons-grade uranium and plutonium will be produced and more will join the considerable quantity that is already "unaccounted for" (Calder, 1980).

Escalation of conventional warfare; aggravating effects of deterrence policy. Escalation of conflict from the level of conventional warfare is commonly thought of as the most likely scenario for getting the world into a nuclear war. It has already happened once, when the United States used nuclear weapons against Japan, and has come close to happening again on at least a dozen occasions (Ellsberg, 1981)—most notably during the Cuban missile crisis, when President Kennedy reportedly estimated the chances of nuclear holocaust as "between one out of three and even" (Sorensen, 1965, p. 705).

Robert Oppenheimer and other scientists involved in the development of nuclear bombs in the 1940s hoped that these devices, by making the possible outcome of a conventional war so horrific, would serve as a deterrent to the initiation of warfare in the future. To whatever extent this effect may have occurred to date, deterrent policies have also produced side-effects whose eventual consequences, paradoxically, may be to increase the likelihood of warfare being initiated.

Reliance on deterrence to prevent nuclear war, like reliance on sips of alcohol to prevent the withdrawal symptoms of alcoholism, may work in the short term, but in the long term, will serve to aggravate the underlying conditions and render ultimate disaster more likely. Even while the threat of mutual annihilation is arguably helping to stave off immediate catastrophe, economic and social consequences of the military nature of this approach may be altering the health of our political body and international relations in ways deleterious to long-term security. Long-term security, for nations no less than for individual citizens of nations, depends upon a state of internal strength combined with external cooperative—or at least nonhostile—relations. A dynamic military standoff (deterrence) could render warfare more likely for a nation, in the long run, through its internal effects on economic priorities and social structure, and through its external (foreign-relations) effects on the perceptions of other nations and relationships with them.

If a nation is engaged in a standing competition to invent, produce, and deploy expensive weaponry, it has less capital and manpower available for the invention, production, and marketing of useful, consumable items that could contribute to its economic strength. If funds are devoted to military research and development, those funds are unavailable for such security-related items as health, education, and social programs, or for nonmilitary-related research. To give a specific example of these considerations, the 1981 U.S. budget allocated more funds for research on a single weapons system—the MX missile—than were provided in the combined research and development budgets of the U.S. Department of Labor, the Department of Education, the Department of Transportation, the Environmental Protection Agency, the Federal Drug Administration, and the Centers for Disease Control (Rothschild, 1981).

When military expenditures become swollen to this extent, the effect can be self-augmenting. People who are deprived of goods and services become disgruntled; they may be more likely to look for enemies to blame for their misfortunes and to serve as targets for their anger. At the same time, citizens who have been deprived of the chance for a higher education because funds have been reallocated from education to the military might well be more supportive of simplistic military approaches to problems than if they had received more education. An extensive national survey by the Public Agenda Foundation found college graduates less likely than those with lower education levels to see the Soviets as "the cause of all the world's troubles," less likely to agree that "democracy and communism can't coexist," less likely to feel our best route to security lies through a build-up of military defenses, less likely to agree we should continue to develop new and better nuclear weapons, and less likely to agree that "the only language the Soviets understand is force" (Public Agenda Foundation, 1984, pp. 27, 31, 34–37).

Reliance on deterrence can also make war more likely through its promotion of an increasingly restrictive government. The military itself has a highly hierarchical authority structure, and such a structure tends to be fostered at all levels in a nation that becomes devoted to military pursuits. While unquestioning obedience to authority is a great source of strength within a military unit, it can be a weakness in the civilian context of a participatory democracy. It can, among other effects, destroy the oversight capacity citizens need to exercise over the military in order to maintain both a free democracy and a balanced perspective on what security entails.

With increasing militarization of physics research, for example, projects that were previously funded by the National Science Foundation are coming to be sponsored by grants from the Departments of Energy (in its military capacity of responsibility for nuclear weapons) or Defense. Indeed, for several years now, Pentagon spending at universities has exceeded spending by the National Science Foundation (Sanger, 1985). While such funding may initially have minimal strings attached, as work becomes more militarily interesting and projects become classified, researchers begin to need security clearances, and censorship and restrictions of access begin to set in. Through such shiftings the U.S. is beginning to look more like the pro-Glasnost Soviet Union, as the obtaining of clearances and the requirement of a "need to know" before information is disclosed lead to a decrease in openness (and speed and flexibility), and an increase in secrecy (and bureaucracy and obstructionism).

With the increasing Defense Department funding of research, the military more and more calls the tune, and those who do not choose to dance to it have less and less chance of dancing at all. As Will Karush, a mathematician who helped develop the atomic bomb in the Manhattan Project, pointed out, "It's a real problem for graduate students. It's almost impossible to get financial support for graduate work and a Ph.D. in physics unless you're willing to take money for Star Wars" (Karush, 1987, p. 4).

On the international front, deterrence becomes self-reinforcing through a decreased willingness and capacity to pursue nonmilitary approaches to crises, and through the need to constantly keep alive the image of an enemy to justify one's actions. In 1959, social psychologists Leon Festinger and Merrill Carlsmith carried out an experiment in which they had undergraduate students perform a tedious task, in return for which some of them received small, token payments, while others were given substantial sums. When asked to evaluate the task afterwards, those experimental subjects who were paid only a token amount to perform it consistently rated it as more interesting than it was rated by subjects whose reimbursement was large enough in itself to justify their participation. These findings were taken as evidence of peoples' need to reduce "cognitive dissonance," to come up with justifications that will make any illogical behavior in which they find themselves engaged appear logical to themselves and others (Freedman, Sears, & Carlsmith, 1978). When one finds one's nation engaged in a nuclear arms race, one's cognitive dissonance can be reduced through the (erroneous) perception of nuclear weapons as similar to previous weapons, where larger numbers and faster delivery means more security. It can also be reduced by a heightened perception of the other nation as an "enemy," with stereotypically evil attributes rendering at least some of its people deserving of a horrible fate; even further reduction can be achieved by perceiving oneself to be "in the white hat" with whatever one chooses to do being justified *a priori* by one's own inherent virtue. In general, cognitive dissonance in this situation is reduced through a loss of the appreciation of how complex international relations really are. The psychologist Philip Tetlock (1985) has dramatically demonstrated such a tendency toward reductive simplification by analyzing the political speeches of superpower leaders just before they were about to launch competitive policy initiatives.

Good guy/bad guy, win/lose relational perceptions and a fostering of military solutions are actively promoted by our military-industrial forces. It is not generally known, for example, that movies which fail to present the enemy (or us, or war) in a manner consonant with how the military and related industries would like them portrayed find themselves effectively censored. This is sometimes done in a direct manner, via refusal to lend military equipment for the filming of a movie. *Top Gun,* an enthusiastically pro-military film, got its equipment on loan from the Department of Defense; *Platoon,* with a significantly less heroic portrayal of war, did not, and had to make shift with expensively rented, nongovernment-issue props. The premise of *Amazing Grace and Chuck,* a film about how a Little League baseball pitcher inspired a national boycott against participation in the nuclear arms race, was so politically repugnant to the Department of Defense that the department refused to permit cooperation in its filming not only by an obliging SAC base (ready to lend a training silo and an F-15), but by a National Guard unit whose assistance had already been authorized by the governor of the state where it was to be shot (D. Field, personal communication, October 8, 1987). Deterrence-inspired censorship can also be indirect, via pressures on a studio. The made-for-television film *The Day After,* with its portrayal of a nuclear holocaust, ran into much political resistance to its production (Meyer, 1984); this occurred even though ABC-TV had scrupulously rendered this nuclear war film devoid of any attribution of causality or hint at any method of prevention.

In a deterrence-oriented political climate, the media will be subject to both internal and external pressure to foster a perception of the nations involved locked in a win-lose competition. To the extent it succumbs to this, media productions will heighten each nation's tendency to see the other as an enemy. Deterrence generates, as Carl Sagan has described it, "a kind of *de facto* conspiracy to prevent tensions from falling below a minimum level of bureaucratic acceptability" (Sagan, 1988). In this atmosphere, tension-reducing attempts at negotiation and at establishing cooperative enterprises between the nations become more difficult. Should a disarmament proposal be put forward by one side, "reactive perception" mandates that it be distrusted by the other ("if they came up with it, it's bad for us"). Indeed, research by social psychologists Constance Stillinger and Lee Ross (1987) demonstrates that the acceptance *even of one's own proposal* by someone perceived as an adversary immediately causes it to be reevaluated in a dimmer light—a phenomenon that would seem to have occurred several times in the course of the nuclear arms race. Through such processes, prophecies of inability to come to terms other than by military threat fulfill themselves in the "death to nonmilitary approaches" ambiance of deterrence.

Finally, in asking whether deterrence would tend to prevent or to promote the escalation of a conventional war to a nuclear one, it is important to see what the history of deterrent approaches can tell us. Professor Ned Lebow of Cornell University, a scholar who has looked closely at this question, has determined to his own satisfaction that while deterrence may have a certain intuitive appeal as a preventer of war, historical evidence points to its actual repeated failure. He decries deterrence as one of a number of shibboleths regarding human behavior people cling to despite contrary evidence (Lebow, 1985b). According to Lebow, deterrence, in regard to the nuclear armed superpowers, is a theory developed by company executives and economists, for whom its major appeal was that it allowed them primacy while not requiring that they know anything whatsoever about the Soviet Union. He describes it as merely a totem to keep away the fear of nuclear war, not a theory based on observable human behavior. According to history, Lebow states, citing examples from World War I to the attack on the Falkland Islands, wars are generally not the result of military weakness inviting challenge, and nations, when they do determine to challenge another nation, generally do not attend to the other side's possible response. Such challenges are most often a response to *internal* pressures. Because of different nations' inability to appreciate the values of other nations, the actual historical effect of attempts at deterrence has been, as often as not, to provoke the behavior they were intended to prevent (Lebow, 1985a). This conclusion is supported by the extensive historical research of anthropologists Naroll, Bullough, and Naroll. After reviewing the behavior of states over a 2,000-year period, they concluded that "military preparedness was typically practiced as a form of deterrence; but in the long run, the preparation for war through arms races made war *more* probable" (cited in Fisher, 1982, p. 494).

Our conflict with the Soviet Union, according to Lebow, arose from three sources: real hostility, clash of interests, and misunderstanding. Only if the inspiration for our conflict were hostility alone would the response of deterrence have been a correct one. In the case of misunderstanding, deterrent behavior is a clear provocation, while in clash-of-interest situations, the best tools are diplomatic. A more sophisticated theory of conflict management, less prone to escalation of warfare, would need to address all three sources of tension, starting with an attempt to reduce misunderstanding (Lebow, 1985b).

The need to move beyond deterrence in our nuclear policies is being recognized by more and more Americans, including, most promisingly, a number in positions of national leadership. At the same time, however, the military machinery and economic roots of deterrence continue to spread wider across, and deeper into, the commercial and academic fabric of our nation. The warning issued by the National Conference of Catholic Bishops in their 1983 pastoral letter on "The Challenge of Peace" is even more timely today, at the beginning of the 1990s, "Progress toward a world free of dependence on deterrence," the pastoral letter states, "must be carefully carried out. But it must not be delayed" (Drell, 1983, p. 15).

Nonviolent Conflict Management

With civil defense and military defense options quite capable of leading to omnicide, and prevention by deterrence headed in the same direction—via accidents, proliferation, irrationality, terrorism, escalation of conventional warfare, or escalation of tension and 'military will' brought on by the effects of deterrence on our society—what route is left for us to take toward survival?

As both critics and friends of the peace movement have been pointing out for years, a fundamental obstacle to the progress of those who decry the civil defense, military, and deterrent approaches is their lack of a clear-cut, easily defined alternative. While we may agree that the old methods of pursuing security are doomed in our new situation, they are familiar and hence easy to visualize and comprehend. Their continued use has the same appeal as looking for a lost object where the lighting happens to be good rather than in a darker area where it actually could be found.

Limiting our search to the old, well-lit, familiar area, we see a world of nation states vying for the advancement of their individual interests through a variety of methods, the ultimate trump card of which is brute military force. If we move away from this version of human society, as we must in order to survive our discovery of the scientific principles of mass destruction, what sort of area are we moving toward? No model of international cooperation has been devised yet to take the place of national military might as the ultimate arbiter of conflicts of interest between nations. Acknowledging our vulnerability to mass destruction forces us to seek new prescriptions for survival; but until we have such a prescription in hand, as Stephen Kull states, "[e]schewing the ineffective placebo of reflexive arms building may create some anxiety" (Kull, 1985, p. 52).

It is incumbent upon those of us who perceive our situation in the manner outlined above to reject the old placebo prescriptions, and not to hold our breath until our governments get around to writing real ones. We must write our own: medicine to counteract the insanity of the arms race and bring our governments to the "new way of thinking" spoken of in the 1955 Manifesto of Bertrand Russell and Albert Einstein (Kapitza & Hellman, 1988, p. xv).

While the exact prescription is unclear, certain ingredients can be recognized as essential. If we are to achieve long-term survival via nonviolent conflict management, progress by the world's nations is clearly required in the areas of education, cooperation, and negotiation. Progress in these areas is mutually reinforcing and must be pursued simultaneously. Although efforts are already underway to various extents in each area, if we are to keep moving toward survival they will have to be vastly expanded.

Education. A realistic prescription for survival in the nuclear era requires nations to develop education on several fronts.

Adults and children (at the level of their understanding) must first of all be educated to the realities of the nuclear age. These include, in addition to the nature of the nuclear threat, such problems with our military, civil defense, and deterrent responses to it as have been elaborated above. People around the world should, for example, be educated sufficiently about the realities of the arms race that if one nuclear power takes so significant a step as to cease testing nuclear arms for an extended period of time (as the Soviets did from 1985 to 1987) citizens of other nations will appreciate the importance of it. No spokesperson should be able (as President Reagan was during the self-imposed Soviet test ban) to dismiss this as "propaganda" and expect the characterization to be generally accepted. Americans should also be aware, as 81% of them are not (Public Agenda Foundation, 1984), that it is our stated national policy, but not that of the Soviet Union or China, to reserve the right to use nuclear weapons first against other nations, even in the absence of their using them against us. It is equally important that people be educated about the direct and indirect harmful effects of the production of nuclear weapons, from radon-caused cancer deaths in uranium mine workers, to preventable radiation exposure near uranium reprocessing plants.

Further, citizens in all nations must be educated both about their abilities and their responsibilities to participate in national policymaking. The need for this latter kind of education in the United States has been highlighted by the findings of Van Hoorn, LeVeck, and French (1989) in their longitudinal study of attitudes toward nuclear war in Northern California college students. A sense of helplessness, with a concomitant willingness to blindly leave matters to "leaders," was found over the last four years to have replaced an earlier intent within a previously surveyed cohort of young students to express views on nuclear issues and carry out activities related to them. Should such a trend toward fatalism prove broad-based and enduring, it would not bode well for the future of participatory democracy, let alone hopes of creative thinking on our nuclear predicament.

Another critical area of education for all the world's citizens is learning as much as possible about other nations. At least two of the three sources of tension identified by Lebow as feeding the arms race—hostility and misunderstanding—could be reduced by such education. This could begin with the elemental step of increasing support for learning foreign languages. Other education of an immediately helpful nature might involve opportunities for citizens of adversarial nations to hear of aspects of the other side they would be likely to applaud. Absent any special efforts to do this, a prejudiced media often filters out these positive images, producing negative, monolithic views of the other nation. During the height of the Cold War, for example, the stereotypical Soviet view of Americans emphasized greed, lawlessness, drug abuse, and AIDS; Soviets through American eyes, on the other hand, tended to be viewed as oppressed or oppressors, but in either case surly, joyless cogs in a malevolent, totalitarian machine.

It might have lessened Soviet misgivings to learn of America's Medicare system, our Veterans Administration, Social Security, and other subsidy benefits, and medical-care coverage systems for the disabled. It could have lessened Western images of antidemocratic totalitarianism to learn of elections with meaningful choices beginning to take place in the Soviet Union in the mid 1980s (Belchuk, 1988), or weakened images of a rigidly Communist economic system to know that Visa cards were preferred over travelers' checks as currency in Moscow,[1] or that a transition from an administered economy to one based on costs and profits was even then being encouraged by the Soviet leadership (Belchuk, 1988).

Two final areas of education requiring emphasis by nations seeking to survive the nuclear age are nonviolent conflict management and global citizenship. The

[1]Observation by author during visit to Moscow to participate in conference of International Physicians for the Prevention of Nuclear War, May–June, 1987.

former, in addition to teaching principles of negotiating strategy, should include education about the aspects of human psychology and behavior that push us toward warfare (see Part II, Chapter 5).

As for global citizenship, it should become as integral a part of the content and values learned in all schools as any information or values relating to national citizenship. From the very first grades, children must be taught a global human perspective that encourages a species-wide sense of identity: they must acquire knowledge and understanding of the lives of peoples throughout the world, together with a global perspective on resources and environmental issues. The teaching of this sort of perspective and understanding is at one and the same time both a moral matter and a pragmatic one. Robert Lifton (1987) speaks of an awareness of "species self," tentatively engendered in man by the common enemy of nuclear annihilation. It is a fragile new element of human identity, as yet easily intimidated by the older, habitual tendency toward nationalistic "pseudo-speciation" identified by Erik Erikson (1983). Nourished through adequate programs of education, however, as well as through people's various religious faiths, it could become both a major and a lifesaving part of everyone's sense of self.

Cooperation. Cooperation in mutually beneficial endeavors can build affinity and trust between nations just as surely as it can between individuals. An effective prescription for human survival will require increased cooperation between nations in at least three major areas: the promotion of greater mutual familiarity, mutual stewardship of the globe and global community, and the reduction of the dangers of nuclear war.

The enhancement of mutual familiarity and understanding could be facilitated at the governmental level by sponsorship of mutual exchange programs, as well as by the establishment of such entities as a U.S.-Soviet Center similar to the East-West Center developed in Hawaii—a mutually funded institution designed to foster understanding and respect between cultures through cooperative study, training, and research (Fisher, 1982). Such a center might well include within it a Peace Institute for the study of economic conversion from military dependence, as well as other problems inherent in ending the arms race.

The mutual exchange programs, for their part, might include not only sponsorship of a full spectrum of cultural, academic, and sporting interchanges, but opportunities for mutually productive cross-visiting of politicians, military leaders, business people, and professionals. Such cross-visits, in keeping with the social-psychological research of Brislin (cited in Fisher, 1982), should be set up according to certain guidelines to maximize their chances of success. For a cross-cultural trip to have a positive outcome, it should relate to the visitor's area of expertise; it should permit the visitor to make a positive contribution of some sort; it should involve a host with cross-cultural experience; it should provide the visitor a choice of activities to engage his interests; and it should offer opportunities for informal social contact.

The social psychologist Sherif, after creating bitter rivalry in a boys' summer camp by the simple means of dividing the campers into separately named residence cabins and arranging competitive activities between them, found the rivalry could be overcome by engineering common crises (e.g., a breakdown in the camp's water supply), requiring the combined resources of all to repair (Sherif, Harvey, White, Hood, & Sherif, 1961). Not all the world's crises are internationally threatening in a direct sense. Modern technology has nonetheless made the world small enough so that even distant crises may have their points of painful impingement. Awareness must be heightened of the danger of widespread international effects from such problems as malnutrition and disease in underdeveloped countries, pollution of our common seas and air, and festering conflicts in some of the world's chronic "hot spots." Experiencing these crises as common threats, nations with sufficient resources might be induced to cooperate in an attack upon them, which could in turn serve to lead us, as in Sherif's summer camp, out of any states of hostile competitiveness.

One model of such cooperation involves joint sponsorship by Soviet and American members of International Physicians for the Prevention of Nuclear War of a space satellite to assist in communications regarding medical care in Africa. Another good example is provided by the International Center for Development Policy, which convenes international policy specialists to focus on resolving regional conflicts through halting the spread of arms and encouraging superpower cooperation in economic development.

Examples of governmental cooperation in peaceful projects include such U.S./Soviet joint ventures as the Apollo-Soyuz manned space flight, the campaign to eliminate smallpox worldwide, and the joint Space Medicine program. There was also, during the Reagan Administration, the November 1985 Agreement on Contacts and Exchanges in Scientific, Educational, and Cultural Fields. Unfortunately, confrontation tends to prove more newsworthy than cooperation, due both to its greater innate interest (conflict being inherently more interesting than the lack of it, as any writer knows) and its scratching of the itch of chauvinistic nationalism. As a result, most East-West accords during the Cold War tended to receive little media or even official attention. For nations to derive the maximum benefit possible from their interrelationship, as political scientist N. Jamgotch, Jr. writes (1986, p. 39), ". . . politics must moderate, accommodate, and on select occasions assume a subordinate role in favor of expanding joint enterprises with transcendent values of their own."

The most obvious and important area for mutual international cooperation is in the reduction of the danger of nuclear war. The agreement to establish Crisis Control Centers in the two superpower nations, to aid in the prevention of accidental nuclear war, seems a positive step. It could be enhanced beyond what is currently planned by incorporating William Ury's (1985) notion of staffing each crisis center with both Soviets and Americans. In an earlier effort, superpower cooperation produced the 1968 nonproliferation treaty, with its promise of capping the nuclear arms race in exchange for other nations' abnegation of nuclear weapons development. In the INF proposal, the United States and the Soviet Union may finally be taking a step to live up to our end of the bargain. While this provides some basis for hope, it must be kept in mind that if negotiating an end to the threat to our planet from nuclear warheads were to be represented in football terms, as Jack Geiger (1987) put it, "we'd have to call this 'second down and 48,000 to go.'"

Finally, there is one area of cooperative effort that is of the greatest importance in eventually permitting more complete nuclear disarmament. The superpowers, working together with other nations either through or separately from the United Nations, must cooperate in the establishment of an international world order. This might be achieved most readily through increments in the power and role given the United Nations. Alternatively, it could be derived through the development of a different model, perhaps arrived at by an international commission of statesmen and scholars appointed for the purpose. The first step in this latter process, as suggested by Mendlowitz and Beer (cited in Fisher, 1982), would be international agreement on a set of underlying principles, of values that could serve as a starting point to such a commission. These values would need to include peace and ecological preservation, as well as maximum social justice, economic benefit, and participation for all. Only with the development of some form of world order based on such principles can war and intimidation be relinquished as a means of guaranteeing the rights of nations. Only through some form of world order can we begin to redress the worldwide social and material imbalances that foment warfare, or address the need for enlightened global stewardship of the world's resources.

Negotiation. Although education and increased cooperation can heighten the motivation and trust required to negotiate rather than fight, only negotiation can remove the actual weapons and can alter the specific policies putting us at risk of nuclear war. Negotiation toward these ends may be direct, such as attempts (mediated or not) to forge single, multilaterally approved versions of a treaty; or negotiation may be indirect, such as the series of unilateral but reciprocated, graduated, verifiable weapons reductions Charles Osgood suggested in 1962 under the acronym GRIT (Graduated Reciprocation in Tension Reduction, Osgood, 1962).

Be it direct or indirect, negotiation is more likely to succeed if preparatory steps have been taken. Examples of such steps include the setting up of Peace Academies—institutes for the study of methods and aspects of successful negotiation—and the beginning of the conversion of involved industry from weapons-making to the manufacture of consumable goods. The latter would help remove major economic stumbling blocks from the roadway of disarmament negotiations.

Goals for negotiation between East and West should include stopping the ongoing arms race, reducing current stockpiles of warheads (as well as the delivery systems we have started reducing in the INF accords), and developing confidence-building measures. A ban on the testing of nuclear weapons of over 1 kiloton (KT) in size is generally agreed to be the best first step in stopping the race. The 1 KT threshold is chosen because it is high enough to permit confident detection by current seismological methods potentially acceptable to both the United States and the Soviet Union (Evernden, Archambeau & Cranswick, 1986), while at the same time it is low enough to forestall the development of new-generation weapons (e.g., Star War's nuclear-pumped X-ray laser), since their manufacture generally requires a series of test blasts of well over 5 KT in magnitude. Beyond the test ban, as a second step—or replacing it as a more comprehensive first step—could be a freeze: a halting of the construction and deployment as well as the testing of any new nuclear weapons.

Further negotiated steps to reduce current stockpiles and build confidence in non-military approaches to security might be initiated following the curtailment of new weapons production. A bilateral 50% reduction in nuclear forces could be undertaken without any effect on the relative security of either side, and could produce a momentum leading to further cuts (Panofsky, 1988). Numbers and sizes of "nuclear weapons free zones" already agreed upon by both superpowers and other nations could be expanded, as could the sharing of military data such as already occurs between Soviet and American naval forces on a regular basis. Notifying the other side of military drills ahead of time reduces tension associated with unanticipated deployments, as could pre-arranged contingency plans in the event of training accidents, inadvertent overflights of militarily sensitive areas, and other accidental provocations.

The final goal of negotiation, as described under "Cooperation" above, should be to arrive at a model of some form of world order acceptable to as many nations as possible. The failure of attempts to achieve this following each of the two major wars of this century must not discourage us, for on the ultimate success of this venture hangs the survival of our species, or at the very least, of a great part of it.

CONCLUSION

The development of nuclear weapons has marked the beginning of a new human historical epoch, characterized by a capacity to produce means of mass destruction. Our burgeoning technology will surely produce other devices of similar potential, be it through the splicing of genes, the production of chain reactions in substances other than uranium and plutonium, or further methods not yet envisioned. The wedding of such technical sophistication with the level of aggression and competitiveness manifest in human society to date has the potential to beget the greatest forms of both Type I (intended) and Type II (inadvertent) horrendous death imaginable.

In this chapter I have charted various pathways of national response to the advent of weapons of mass destruction. Noting pitfalls in several of these pathways, I have indicated the route that seems most likely to lead to survival. Finally, I have sketched several features essential to this survival-directed course.

Having committed ourselves to the choice of a pathway toward survival at the level of national behavior, we are now positioned for a discussion of the psychology of survival-directed action on the part of individuals. What are the forces compelling individuals to (a) attend to this issue in the first place, and then (b) choose one pathway toward survival over another? To what extent and by what means may these forces be modified to induce more individuals to attend to the issue and to follow the pathway we believe to be survival-directed? What factors might induce individuals, persuaded to our choice of the survival-directed pathway, to take action to set their governments and/or the other peoples of the world along that path? And finally, what are some effective actions that might be taken toward that end?

REFERENCES

Abrams, H. (1986). Sources of human instability in the handling of nuclear weapons. In National Academy of Sciences (Ed.), *The medical implications of nuclear war* (pp. 490–528). Washington, DC: National Academy Press.

Abrams, H. (1987). The problem of accidental or inadvertent nuclear war. *Preventive Medicine, 16,* 319–333.

Belchuk, A. I. (1988). Restructuring of Soviet society. In A. Gromyko & M. Hellman (Eds.), *Breakthrough/POPbIB: Emerging new thinking* (pp. 229–239). New York: Walker & Co.

Calder, N. (1980). *Nuclear nightmares.* New York: Viking.

Diamond, S. (1981, August 5). Behind the fearsome spread of nuclear arms. *The San Francisco Chronicle,* p. C7.

Drell, S. D. (1983). *Facing the threat of nuclear weapons.* Seattle: University of Washington Press.

Ellsberg, D. (1981). Introduction: Call to mutiny. In E. P. Thompson & D. Smith (Eds.), *Protest and survive* (pp. i–xxviii). New York: Monthly Review Press.

Erikson, E. (1983). A developmental crisis of mankind. In Proceedings of *Prescription for prevention—Nuclear war: Our greatest health hazard* (pp. 112–120). Symposium organized by Physicians for Social Responsibility, Stanford/Mid-Peninsula Chapter, and sponsored by Stanford University School of Medicine, Stanford, CA.

Evernden, J. F., Archambeau, C. B., & Cranswick, E. (1986). An evaluation of seismic decoupling and underground nuclear test monitoring using high-frequency seismic data. *Reviews of Geophysics, 24*(2), 143–215.

Fisher, R. (1982). *Social psychology: Applied approach.* New York: St. Martens.

Freedman, J. L., Sears, D. O., & Carlsmith, J. M. (1978). Cognitive dissonance. In J. L. Freedman, D. O. Sears, & J. M. Carlsmith (Eds.), *Social psychology* (3rd ed., pp. 426–461). Englewood Cliffs, NJ: Prentice-Hall.

Gallup, G. (1987, January). War and peace (Survey No. 269-G). *The Gallup Poll.* Princeton, NJ: Gallup.

Geiger, H. J. (1987, December 12). It's second down and 48,000 to go. *The New York Times.*

Gollon, P. J. (1986). SDI funds costly for scientists. *Bulletin of the Atomic Scientists, 42*(1), 24–27.

Herken, G. (1987). The earthly origins of Star Wars. *Bulletin of the Atomic Scientists, 43*(8), 20–28.

Jamgotch, N., Jr. (1986). Superpower cooperation often overlooked. *Bulletin of the Atomic Scientists, 42*(2), 37–40.

Kaldor, M. (1981). Disarmament: The armament process in reverse. In E. P. Thompson & D. Smith (Eds.), *Protest and survive* (pp. 173–188). New York: Monthly Review Press.

Kapitza, S., & Hellman, M. (1988). Preface/A message to the scientific community. In A. Gromyko & M. Hellman (Eds.), *Breakthrough/POPbIB: Emerging new thinking* (pp. xi–xx). New York: Walker & Co.

Kaplan, D. (1981). Where the bombs are. *New West, 6*(4), 76–147.

Karush, W. (1987, September). *On beyond war.* (Available from Beyond War, 222 High Street, Palo Alto, CA 94301.)

Kogut, J., & Weissman, M. (1986). Taking the pledge against Star Wars. *Bulletin of the Atomic Scientists, 42*(1), 27–30.

Kull, S. (1985). Nuclear nonsense. *Foreign Policy, 58,* 28–52.

Lapp, R. (1962). *Kill and overkill.* New York: Basic Books.

Lebow, R. N. (1985a). Assured strategic stupidity: The quest for ballistic missile defense. *Journal of International Affairs, 39*(1), 57–80.

Lebow, R. N. (1985b, October). The psychological context of deterrence. In *Society, self, and nuclear conflict.* Symposium conducted by the Department of Psychiatry at the University of San Francisco Medical Center, San Francisco, CA.

Leitenberg, M. (1977). Accidents of nuclear weapons systems. In Stockholm International Peace Research Institute (Ed.), *SIPRI yearbook of world armaments and disarmament, 1977.* Cambridge, MA: Massachusetts Institute of Technology Press.

Lifton, R. (1987, May). Nuclear normality: Dubious assumptions. In P. French (Chair), *Psychosocial research on adaption to the nuclear age.* Symposium conducted at the annual meeting of the American Psychiatric Association, Chicago.

Lindley, D. (1988, April 28). Leaked report on Star Wars. *Nature, 332.*

Los Angeles Times. (1982, March 14–17). Nuclear weapons (Study No. 51). *Los Angeles Times poll.* Los Angeles: Author.

Meyer, N. (1984). "Day After" director hopes for raised consciousness. *Media & Values, 28*(2), 2.

Osgood, C. E. (1962). *An alternative to war or surrender.* Urbana, IL: University of Illinois Press.

Paisley, W. J. (1981). Public communication campaigns: The American experience. In R. E. Rice & W. J. Paisley (Eds.), *Public communication campaigns* (pp. 15–40). Beverly Hills, CA: Sage.

Panofsky, W. (1988). Limited success, limitless prospects. *Bulletin of the Atomic Scientists, 44*(2), 34–36.

PSR. (1989). Militarism's social costs. *Nuclear Times, 7*(3), 28–29.

Public Agenda Foundation. (1984). *Voter options on nuclear arms policy.* New York: Author. (The Public Agenda Foundation, 6 East 39th St., New York, NY 10016.)

Ris, H. (1987, September). Letter from Union of Concerned Scientists (Available from Union of Concerned Scientists, 26 Church St., Cambridge, MA 02238).

Rothschild, E. (1981). The American arms boom. In E. P. Thompson & D. Smith (Eds.), *Protest and survive* (pp. 108–121). New York: Monthly Review Press.

Sagan, C. (1988, February 7). The common enemy. *Parade Magazine,* p. 6.

Sanger, D. E. (1985, July 22). Campuses' role in arms debated as Star War funds are sought. *New York Times,* pp. A1, 12.

Sherif, M., Harvey, O., White, B., Hood, W., & Sherif, C. (1961). *Intergroup conflict and cooperation: The robbers' cave experiment.* Norman, OK: University Book Exchange.

Sorensen, T. (1965). *Kennedy.* New York: Harper & Row.

Stillinger, C., & Ross, L. D. (1987). *A cognitive barrier to conflict resolution.* Unpublished manuscript. Stanford University, Department of Psychology, Stanford, CA.

Stokes, D. (1984, September 9). Nuclear war inevitable, says probability expert Hellman. *Campus Report* (Stanford University), p. 9.

Talbot, S. (1981, February 7). The H bombs next door. *The Nation,* pp. 141–148.

Tetlock, P. E. (1985). Integrative complexity of American and Soviet foreign policy rhetoric: A time-series analysis. *Journal of Personality & Social Psychology, 49*(6), 1–21.

Thiermann, E., & Thiermann, I. (1981). *The last epidemic.* A 28-minute film available from the Educational Film & Video Project, 5332 College Ave., Suite 101, Oakland, CA 94618, (415) 655-9050.

Trabalka, J., Eyman, L., & Auerbach, S. (1980). Analysis of the 1957–8 Soviet Nuclear Accident. *Science, 209*(4454), 345.

Ury, W. (1985). *Beyond the hotline: How crisis control can prevent nuclear war.* Boston: Houghton Mifflin.

Van Hoorn, J., LeVeck, P., & French, P. (1989). Transitions in the nuclear age: Late adolescence to early adulthood. *Journal of Adolescence, 12,* 41–53.

5

The Psychology of Survival-Directed Action, Part II: The Citizens' Pathway to Survival

Perrin French
Stanford University, Stanford, California

THE KEY ROLE OF U.S. CITIZENS IN ENDING THE NUCLEAR ARMS RACE

In the previous chapter we developed a map of national options in the nuclear age. We found survival to lie along a course involving arms control and increasing degrees of disarmament, based on international cooperation and negotiation. We shall now consider the options of individual citizens in the nuclear age. We shall examine with particular attention the forces moving individuals to support or reject the survival-directed national pathway we have already identified.

Top-Down vs. Bottom-Up

Progress along the survival-directed path requires that we bring an end to the nuclear arms race. Two basic mechanisms suggest themselves. One, which could be referred to as "top-down," involves leaders, on their own initiative or with high-level advice, making important decisions and taking important actions to end the race. The other, which might be called "bottom-up," involves people becoming sufficiently concerned about the situation that they oblige their leaders to take action to end it. In actuality, the two approaches are necessarily interwoven—especially in the United States, where the "leaders" lay claim to no greater authority than to be the elected representatives of the people.

In an article despairing of both approaches, but particularly of the "bottom-up" one, psychologist James Blight (1987) points out the ephemeral nature of public concern, the virtual language barrier between policymakers and citizens (or at least psychologists), and what he reads as the lack of any historical foundation for hope of public interest influencing national policy on the arms race. He speaks instead of a biological imperative towards violence in man, with the only hope of psychology impinging on the arms race lying in the area of contributions to crisis management—"top-down" territory. With skepticism almost to the point of derision, Blight writes "[t]he more we learn about our mammalian ancestors, the less optimistic we ought to become about expunging human aggression. . . . And the bulwark of our contemporary international security regime, the sovereign nation-state, shows no sign of dissolving into a pacific world federation" (Blight, 1987,

p. 2). I disagree with Professor Blight's contentions. As they represent serious counter-arguments to my point of view, however, I shall address Blight's points now before proceeding with my own prescription.

My rebuttal to Blight takes several forms. Firstly, his half-empty glasses are my half-full ones. Negligible as the effect has been so far on the arms race, I would contend that the success of public opinion in the early 1960s in driving nuclear testing underground is significant proof of its capacity to affect major policy decisions on arms issues. Likewise, the transformation of Congress' previous rubber-stamp approach to defense spending into legislative support for a freeze and other stringent arms-control measures in (1986) was another glass half full—even though then President Reagan short-circuited the process by his plea not to "tie his hands" at Reykjavik. I might also butt heads with Blight on the ultimates in human nature, contesting his evidence of a biological imperative for human aggression (along the lines of the scientific conference at Seville, May, 1986, wherein scholars of relevant sciences from around the world issued a Statement on Violence protesting the notion of an inescapable, genetically inherited human tendency to make war (APA, 1990)).

I would not be able to present these arguments without a certain self-consciousness, however. As a psychiatrist, I would have to acknowledge that the differing views of Blight and myself on human nature, for all their scientific support, are at least in part reflections of our personal psyches, with their particular genetic and formative-experience vicissitudes. Ultimately, with or without scientific bases, we are all "free" to believe what we may about our species, with our most important beliefs formed by a number of other elements in addition to a dispassionate appraisal of facts. What we believe is nonetheless terribly important, for regardless of what physic levels it may be rooted in, it will affect which national pathway to survival we subscribe to in the nuclear age, which in turn may determine whether our species (among others) lives or dies.

Underlying the long-term choice of deterrence versus active endorsement of arms control and disarmament, are two opposing views of the relationship between the major powers. These views, reflecting two opposing viewpoints on human nature, consist of an "aggressive enemy" perception of the "other" as opposed to a perception of international conflict as simply an unfortunate action-reaction spiral. Each of these views has its sophisticated, "deluxe" model, as well as its standard, pedestrian model.

Aggressive enemy. The standard model of the "aggressive enemy" view has other nations perceived as evil (or evilly led) empires. Throughout the Cold War, the Soviet Union was thus often portrayed as a bully nation, uninhibited from aggressive actions that would never be contemplated by our well-intentioned nation. The sophisticated model, on the other hand, paints neither nation as devil or angel, but has seen them as nonetheless implacable mutual enemies by virtue of their opposed religious, political, or economic belief systems, coupled with innate human aggressiveness. In this view, nations are seen as tending to do whatever they can get away with—these drives putting them in natural conflict with each other. One might consider this the "Darwinian" (as opposed to the standard "creationist") aggressive enemy model.

Action-reaction spiral. For subscribers to the "action-reaction spiral" view, the unsophisticated version sees other nations as "just like us," only regrettably misunderstood, so that if one nation in conflict with another simply stopped its aggressive posturing and increased communication, it would learn that both were peace-loving nations, frightened by the mask the other had donned out of *its* misplaced fear. The sophisticated action-reaction model, like its sophisticated opposite, sees nations as multi-hued in regard to who's in the white or black hat. It differs from its opposite in being able to imagine a live-and-let-live relationship between different political systems, however, perhaps even seeing each as standing in need of benefits the other offers (individual human rights and freedoms, on one hand, for example, versus freedom from want, on the other). It has, concomitantly, a less imperative view of innate human aggression.

We would argue that it is not a question of which point of view most accurately describes our situation *as it really is*. We would assert, rather, that it is a question of which we are going to *choose* to be our belief about ourselves. In the realm of social behavior, it is beliefs that determine reality.

But what if, one might ask (mindful of Hitler and the Munich accords) there really *is* an enemy (i.e. hostilely aggressive other power) and one chooses to think otherwise? Mightn't that be risky? Not intolerably so, when one considers that (a) not viewing the other as an enemy doesn't mean one should leave everything in the other's hands, and (b) there may be a greater risk, in the nuclear age, in regarding the other as an enemy, hostile as he may be, than in not doing so, in view of the self-fulfilling nature of human thought. When Hamlet declared that "nothing is but thinking makes it so," his thrust was double-edged. On the one hand, his statement may be taken as a philosophic comment on the site and role of human conscious-ness in the universe. On the other, it could be taken as a reflection on the power of thoughts to attain realistic fulfillment. Thinking of another as an enemy gets trans-lated into treating the other as an enemy. Treated like an enemy, the other responds in ways more enemy-like than they might have otherwise, in turn increasing one's perception of hostility and likeliness to reciprocate with hostility, and so on, in a destructively bent spiral.

Similar doubts might be raised, at the level of the sophisticated hypotheses, about the dangers of misconstruing human nature. What if, as Blight cites in the writings of Thucydides, there *is* "a hard core of inherited, unalterable aggressive-ness down deep in all of us," obliging the powerful to "exact what they can and the weak [to] grant what they must" (Blight, 1987, p. 23). Even if the other weren't an enemy in the sense or to the degree Hitler was, mightn't there be danger in failing to take such a human verity into account? In counter to such thoughts as these, we would suggest that there is a distinct limit to sociobiology's ability to blueprint human conduct. Women may be biologically less adapted to hunting and fighting, but this doesn't mean women can't be leaders of nations, or that they don't get to vote in most democracies in the world today. (And think how they got that right—it wasn't from leaders handing it to them!). Men have always had and continue to have the physical and social ability to enslave other men, but this hasn't kept most nations in the world today from deciding slavery is not in keeping with human nature as it *ought* to be, with erstwhile slave-holding nations altering the "reality" of their cultures accordingly.

We are headed toward an abolition of warfare at this time as surely as we were toward an abolition of slavery during the 19th century. And hope for this lies not alone in the power of ideas on what human nature ought to be, but in a fortunately allied, equally powerful determinant of human behavior: economic imperative. Technology is helping make war obsolete, just as it helped make slavery obsolete.

Technology brought about the obsolescence of slavery by making it economically unnecessary. It is now rendering war obsolete by making its outcome—and even its preparation—economically unfeasible. As technological and economic conditions change, so do human beings' beliefs about human nature. Abhorrent aspects were always present in slavery, and when it lost its economic advantageousness, people were free to allow those abhorrent aspects to determine their response to it. The economically too-destructive nature of nuclear war is similarly freeing human beings to let abhorrent aspects of warfare determine their response to it.

With powerful forces already moving us in the right direction, from whence comes the need to write a prescription for ending the arms race? The need arises from one problem: there is a serious question of whether our rate of progress on this issue will suffice to outdistance disaster.

Why It Is Up to U.S. Citizens and Not Their Leaders

The prescription we endorse for moving us along the pathway towards survival falls into the "bottom up" category. This is not because we doubt the ability of leaders to make all the difference in the world through choices taken on their own initiative, but rather because I am skeptical of the direction those choices tend to take in the absence of powerful public constraint. The primary reason for selection of an approach that starts with the people is that people, but not their leaders, tend *a priori* to favor the pathway we feel to be most promising.

In his latest assessment of what constitutes the fundamental psychological impetus for the nuclear arms race, Jerome Frank identifies the drive of national leaders for power (Frank, 1987). He makes the case for how a strong drive to accumulate and exercise power often dominates leaders' lives. He then goes on to enumerate personality traits often found in leaders that have particular relevance to their roles in the nuclear arms race. These traits include fearlessness, optimism, competitiveness, willingness to sacrifice, and above all, the love of power.

Leaders are politicians whose own careers, by definition, have succeeded: they have reached the top circles of their nation's power hierarchy. Such individuals are bound to have a strong will to prevail, and this may be accompanied by a correspondingly weak need for affiliation. Also flowing from the fact of being a winner may be a positive view of risk-taking, an enjoyment of competition (with an attendant competitive image of the nature of man), and a conviction that sacrifice will be rewarded. In the context of nuclear weapons, this means that whereas the general public might tend toward caution out of fearfulness, a leader might not be afraid; whereas the public might be swayed by compassion for thousands or millions of potential victims, a leader might condone the sacrifice of lives; and whereas others might think in terms of mutual cooperation for purposes of avoiding war, a leader might operate from competitive assumptions. It may mean that the declared goal of the leaders of both superpowers, the elimination of all nuclear weapons, "is merely a sop to the public's fear of these weapons," and that the goal of true arms control and nuclear arsenal reduction may have a hard time competing with the determination of leaders to improve their nation's power positions (Frank, 1987, p. 340).

In 1984, the Public Agenda Foundation undertook what is probably the most extensive survey ever done of American citizens' ideas on nuclear war and the arms race. At the same time, the group interviewed 40 individuals recognized as "spokespeople in the nuclear defense field." These "experts" were spread as far across the political spectrum as the hundreds of randomly chosen subjects were in the public survey. Their main difference from the public subjects lay in their political rank as leaders or advisors to leaders. What the Public Agenda Foundation found was directly supportive of Frank's perception of leaders' personality traits. They found the "experts" fearless where the public was afraid—i.e. confident that the barriers to nuclear war were substantial and reliable and nuclear war's likelihood minimal—and they found them content to take risks where the public was not. The "experts" were more accepting than the public of continued dependence on nuclear weapons as an ongoing deterrent.

In the early 1980s, I conducted surveys of various groups, both captive and self-selected, on their beliefs and attitudes regarding nuclear weapons and nuclear war. The 60 separate groups surveyed belonged to seven different larger groupings: school classes, church forums, medical conferences, corporation seminars, public gatherings, activist group meetings, and men's service club lunches. Of these seven different categories, comments from discussion during the meetings where the surveys took place led me to believe the group with the highest representation of "leaders"—for example, holders of political office, or advisors thereto—was the men's service clubs. And it was this single category that stood out as having the highest percentage of positive responses to the statement that there are causes worth fighting a nuclear war for, and the lowest estimate of the likelihood of nuclear war occurring (French, 1983).

Such a division between views of leaders and the public are behind the conclusion of psychologist Otto Klineberg that "nowhere can governments be looked to for leadership in disarmament," and his attendant conviction that "organizing public opinion rather than attempting to lobby officials" would offer the best chance of success in ending the arms race (Klineberg, 1984, p. 1251). This public/leader divergence in thinking is behind physicist Freeman Dyson's dichotomy of "victim" and "warrior" responses to nuclear arms, and his conclusion that the means to reach a non-nuclear world "must be firstly moral, secondly political, and thirdly technical," where "[m]oral means are peace movements and public campaigns arousing the conscience of mankind against weapons of mass destruction . . . " (Dyson, 1985, p. 84). It was an awareness of the inherent bias of government leaders toward power and competition that caused President Eisenhower to speak in 1959 of how " . . . people in the long run are going to do more to promote peace than our governments," and to add, "indeed, I think that people want peace so much that one of these days governments had better get out of their way and let them have it" (Eisenhower, 1960, p. 625).

Can "The People" Do It?

If public opinion, because of its greater chance of supporting what I see as the most promising path to survival, is to be the vehicle for our prescription, what evidence is there of its promise in this regard? "[P]ublic opinion rarely influences foreign policy," and "ranks far behind perceived geopolitical realities in influencing government leaders' decisions in this realm," according to psychologist Susan Fiske's research on the matter (1987, p. 215)—not to mention the dour views of

Professor Blight already cited. While this is doubtless true the majority of the time, it may be pointed out as a counter to discouragement that (a) the nuclear arms race is not just a matter of "foreign policy," and (b) the first and last of the six major instances of popular movements producing great changes in the American scene *did* involve matters of foreign policy. These instances, separated as they may have been by long periods of public apathy or ineffectiveness, do testify to the power of popular movements once they get going. They consisted, in historical order, of our initial rebellion against British domination, the abolition of slavery, the establishment of women's rights, the obtaining of a better life for American workers, the ending of racial discriminatory laws and practices, and the withdrawal of American armies from Vietnam. To bring such instancing up to date, it might be pointed out that it was "not until polls showed a strong aversion to the Nicaraguan *contra* operation that Congress dared to forbid military aid and to investigate Administration conspiracies" (*The Washington Spectator*, 1987d). Public opinion, although perhaps not the usual force in American politics that one imagines it should be in a democracy, is potentially the ultimate force.

Looking specifically at the record to date of the effect of public concern on the nuclear arms race, we are inclined to reach conclusions totally opposite to the pessimism in the cited passages of psychologists Fiske and Blight. We would agree, instead, with arms control negotiator L. D. Weiler's assessment that it has *only* been when public concern has been effectively aroused that progress has been realized in curbing the nuclear arms race (Weiler, 1983). The "glasses" of public input, half-full or half-empty as one may choose to see them, are virtually the only glasses on the table—at least in the United States. A public concerned about strontium 90 in children's teeth in 1963 brought world leaders who a year before had been on the brink of war during the Cuban missile crisis to conclude the Limited Test Ban Treaty. Secretary of State Robert McNamara's push to avoid large-scale anti-ballistic missile deployment, culminating in the SALT I accords in 1972, succeeded in large part because of the support of public opinion (Ground Zero, 1982). President Nixon's memoirs reveal that public opinion, in the form of giant protest marches in October and November of 1969, persuaded him not to proceed with a plan to escalate the Vietnam war massively, including—according to aide Haldeman's memoirs—the possible use of nuclear weapons (Ellsberg, 1981). And it was massive public resistance in Europe to NATO's installation of Tomahawk and Pershing II Missiles that caused NATO governments to insist the deployment decision be accompanied by a "parallel track" of U.S.-Soviet negotiations on limitations on European nuclear missiles (Ground Zero, 1982, p. 217).

With its recent foray into democracy so shaky and untried, "bottom up" may not yet be an effective approach in the Soviet Union to influencing government policy. Serendipitously, however, the leadership in the Soviet Union now sees its best hope of retaining national power as residing in stopping the economic drain imposed by the arms race. The United States, on the other hand, a country where public opinion's power is constitutionally guaranteed and historically demonstrated, has largely been leading the arms race, and continues to be driven by a "commanding perspective within U.S. foreign and defense policies" that "the best defense against nuclear war is achieved through vigorous development of nuclear weapons" (Markey, 1985, p. 557). American public opinion, then, both in regard to its propensities (versus those of leaders) its positioning (versus the need and importance of similar public opinion in the Soviet Union), and its historically proven capacities, offers the most hopeful fulcrum for leveraging a brake on the nuclear arms race. The understanding and influencing of American public opinion in this matter is thus what constitutes the psychology of survival-directed action.

INDIVIDUAL OPTIONS IN THE NUCLEAR AGE

Many people have studied and theorized about the responses of individuals to the nuclear threat, deriving theses that may be relevant to a citizen-driven approach to end the arms race. John Mack (1981) has dichotomized us into "thinkables" and 'unthinkables" in our attitudes on the purpose and survivability of nuclear war. Erik Erikson (1983), using the term "pseudospeciation," has described a malfunctional human trait predisposing us to nuclear war. Robert Lifton (Lifton & Falk, 1982; Lifton, 1987) has described our unfortunate tendency towards "psychic numbing," as well as a potentially positive response in the form of an evolving "species self." Jerome Frank (1982a) has explored a number of highly relevant areas, from the perceptual distance of the issue, to the development of enemy images. Tyler and McGraw (1983) have studied characteristics of "survivalists" and contrasted them with "activists." Fiske, Pratto, and Pavelchak (1983) have found heightened concreteness of imagery of nuclear destruction among activists. Solantaus (1986) found a peaking of reported nuclear worry occurring in early adolescence. French (1984) correlated factual knowledge of the nuclear situation with reluctance to countenance nuclear war. Roger Fisher (1981) has pointed out three major mistakes people make in their thinking about the nuclear situation. Sandman and Valenti (1986) have contrasted the anti-nuclear motivating potential of fear with that of anger, hope, love, and action. Eric Chivian and others (Chivian et al., 1985) have studied children's attitudes toward nuclear weapons and nuclear war in both Eastern and Western nations. Greenwald and Zeitlin (1897) and others have studied how families confront "the nuclear taboo." The list is extensive and could be continued. It should definitely include the pollsters (Bachman, Doble, & Yankelovich, *The Los Angeles Times*, Gallup, etc.), whose categorizations of attitudes towards nuclear war are derived empirically and on a large scale.

With all of these disparate contributions shedding light on particular, discrete areas of human response to the nuclear threat, what seems called for at this point is an overall, unifying framework. Such a framework could illuminate the different studies' relationships to each other. This is exactly what I have attempted to construct in this chapter.

I have formulated, albeit tentatively, an overarching flow chart of where different individuals may be found at different times in their beliefs, thoughts, and actions regarding the nuclear arms race. I have done so for heuristic purposes. While I have confidence that the elements I identified in individuals' responses exist as described, two caveats are in order. The first is that these elements are doubtless not all-inclusive. The second is that the sequencing chosen is not the only order in which these elements might occur. To the extent this effort is successful, however, it should provide a synthesizing framework for all the separate observations of the many scholars whose attentions have focused on one or another aspect of individuals' responses to nuclear weapons. What is more important, such a framework may provide help in mobilizing a sufficient number of U.S. citizens to apply a brake to an omnicidal nuclear arms race.

The Status Quo and an Overview of the Pathway

The flow chart begins with "Business as Usual." Business as usual for the nation means the ongoing design, production, and deployment of ever newer nuclear weapons, augmented by the export of technologies useful in their manufacture.

Business as usual for *individuals* means not thinking about nuclear weapons or nuclear war most of the time. There is generally no immediate stimulus to think about it. It is uncomfortable to think about. Such thoughts are unpleasant, demanding as they do either an acknowledgment of helplessness or an assumption of responsibility. Hence one "adapts" to the nuclear reality by repressing thoughts about it, assisted by an active "gate-keeping" process of selective inattention to any incoming information regarding it. Robert Lifton (Lifton & Falk, 1982) catalogued the psychoanalytic terms for some of the defense mechanisms involved in this process—repression, suppression, isolation, denial, undoing, reaction formation, and projection—and offered a categorical term to encompass them all: psychic numbing.

Business as usual is where most of us live, most of the time. Business as usual is engagement in both the obligatory (urgent) and optional (cultural) Maslovian need categories. That is, it includes providing the next meal, as well as straightening our children's teeth. It does not include thinking about where this nation is drifting with its nuclear policies. It takes an extraordinary event to force our attention upon our nuclear predicament. Once such an event occurs, there are half a dozen routes by which we may rapidly return to Business as Usual, with hardly a shiver in the veil of inattention and denial with which we shroud the nuclear issue, to indicate it had been disturbed.

There exists for individuals, nonetheless, a route from Business as Usual to action in the prevention of nuclear war (per the national pathway favored in Chapter 4). For most of us, to get there is an upstream effort against a constant current of habituation, denial, moral disengagement, and isolation of our thoughts from our feelings.

Overview of the Pathway

Three major requirements are necessary for individuals to reach a point of effective action in the prevention of nuclear war. First, they must overcome selective inattention to the problem. This is often referred to as denial, or psychic numbing per Lifton, but more of the time, perhaps, it simply reflects the absence of any significant manifestation of the issue in our daily lives. Second, individuals must select the most appropriate approach to the problem (see Part I). Finally, individuals must overcome inertia—the failure on the part of most persons to take any action even after their denial has been overcome and they are persuaded that true national and international security lies in stopping the arms race. As others have pointed out (Fiske, 1987), it is the rule rather than the exception for most people to be politically inert on most issues much of the time.

Rule or no rule, we can ill afford inertia in this area, and efforts to overcome it must start with an understanding of what makes it up. My own and others' research indicates this inertia to be made up of three major components, the presence of any of which suffices to produce it. These three components are (a) a belief in one's own helplessness, (b) a lack of sufficient motivation, and (c) a lack of opportunity for action.

Figure 1 is a chart representing the pathways of thought and action an individual may follow, starting from "business as usual," once some planned or inadvertent event occurs of the necessary type and magnitude to overcome one's usual inattention to the problem. The chart illustrates how selecting a nonproductive approach to the problem, or foundering on one of the three components of inertia, results in a side-tracking reversion to "business as usual." As with attempts to thread the most difficult but rewarding path through a pinball-machine maze, most plays for most players most of the time result in the ball being sent back to the beginning. Also as in pinball, excursions ending up back at the beginning may have nonetheless scored some points, and have prepared the player for a further excursion at a subsequent time. This chapter is about how to enhance the chances of more individuals successfully making progress through the maze, with a significant number of them threading the maze to its endpoint of activity.

In Chapter 4 we argued for a particular pathway to survival at the national level. We believe our chances of survival can be enhanced by enough U.S. citizens actively supporting this most promising approach to the issue. In view of the aforementioned rule of general political inertia, the number of individuals becoming active in the appropriate path need only be a small percentage of the total population. With the inactive majority of the population experiencing sufficient discomfort with the status quo to be at least passively supportive, U.S. policy may be caused by the active minority to shift direction and come about on a new course. The people make up the inertial guidance system of the U.S. ship of state, and a captain (elected from among them) would have a hard time trying to aim the ship in a direction different from those encompassed by their tolerance. Thus the problem reduces to a consideration of (a) how the inactive majority of people may be sufficiently alerted and oriented to the issue to make the status quo unacceptable to them, and (b) how to get the politically active minority motivated to select *this* issue as the one to be active about. In terms of Figure 1, this means moving the bulk of the people to the arms control/disarmament approach at point D, and a significant minority on beyond this juncture to point H.

Comprehending the Threat

Failure to comprehend the magnitude of the threat prevented many victims slated for Nazi death camps from making efforts to escape when it might still have been possible. People speak of denial being involved, and this was doubtless true for some who heard rumors of terrible events and ignored them. But part of the ignoring by that group and all of the inactivity on the part of the others is explainable in terms of the perfectly human, normal, conscious phenomenon of not being able to take in that which one has not yet experienced. Events are certainly more difficult to comprehend if they are so horrible in nature the mind naturally shies away from their contemplation. But what makes events even harder to comprehend is having them lie on a plane different from that of our daily lives and experience. Say, a level of inhumanity never before encountered, or a level of physical energy never before produced by man. That which is beyond the realm of our experience does not come readily to mind, so that there is no natural inclination to take steps against it.

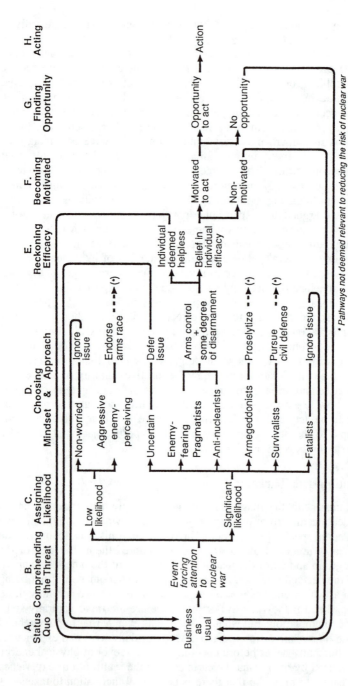

Figure 1 A flow chart of individual options in response to the nuclear threat, indicating a pathway toward action likely to reduce the risk of nuclear war.

* *Pathways not deemed relevant to reducing the risk of nuclear war*

Realistic contemplation of nuclear war, as Lifton (1987) points out, goes far beyond thoughts of individual or even collective death, to involve the possible renunciation of a more ultimate concern: the flow of life that has throughout civilization provided a meaningful context for our individual human lives. To look on nuclear war with open eyes is to call in question all possible notions of posterity, from the concept of living on through one's children or one's influence or creations, to the previously safe enough fall-back position of at least imagining a posterity in terms of the contribution to the carbon cycle by one's physical remains. But it is not simply that the human spirit is unwilling to contemplate the end of posterity. Major factors further increasing the difficulty of thinking about a nuclear holocaust are that such a threat (a) has never existed before, and (b) is of disproportionate enormity. It is so out of scale with the size of our daily experiences as to be invisible to us.

A final stumbling block to perceiving the threat of nuclear war is the remoteness of its manifestations. The material involved with the nuclear arms race is well removed from the sphere of day to day living for most of us. The processes involved in planning for nuclear war are similarly distant. They have their own built-in distancing mechanisms, even for those taking part in them directly. Finally, the American press, which might otherwise be expected to serve as at least a secondary stimulus for thought about nuclear war, "like the American people, has had neither direct experience of the facts nor the kind of freedom necessary to compensate for the absence of direct experience" (Manoff, 1983, p. 208).

The Matériel

Should you or I actually behold a nuclear warhead, no terror of an automatic, instinctive, energizing sort would possess us. We are "hard-wired" to respond with fear only to objects of danger in primitive environments: slithering forms, deep growls, gaping tooth-lined maws. Behavioral psychologists have found it harder to condition humans or animals to be fearful at the sight of flowers or guns than at the sight of snakes or bears. But even non-instinctual, cognitive awareness of danger is denied to us. Nuclear weapons are removed, via secrecy, entirely from our field of vision. People have been inclined to reject out of hand "good" Germans' claims of not knowing what their crematoria were burning during World War II. Yet consider anti-nuclear activist Bishop Leroy Matthiessen. He states that he had served for nine years as a parish priest two miles from the Pantex plant at Amarillo, Texas, without realizing that its output was nuclear bombs. Pantex covers 10,000 acres and employs 2,400 people; it does final assembly of the entire nuclear arsenal (d'Heurle, 1987).

The remoteness of nuclear weapons from our field of perception renders them less likely to be objects we would respond to in any way. Not only do we not see the weapons as we drive by the docked ships, air fields, or Army bases, or as they are transported by us in trucks or vans that look like oversized Winnebegos on the highway (Kaplan, 1981), but when we inquire as to their existence in a given spot, their presence is "neither confirmed nor denied," relegating them to a concern-extinguishing oubliette of perceptual limbo.

The Process

Even for individuals directly involved in work relating to the design, production, or deployment of nuclear weapons, "distance" is a major factor. First there is the sheer vastness of the organization of the Pentagon and the complicated nature of its structure. Beyond this, there is the requirement for "clearance," in order to deal with information of "classified access." This distances workers from the product of their work in a number of ways. For one thing, it may keep workers from thinking about their work as profoundly as they might were it subject to public scrutiny. Public scrutiny introduces the opportunity for criticism on moral, technological, and economic grounds. "Clearance" effectively blocks such scrutiny. Instead, it encourages compartmentalization (which, incidentally, often works to the economic detriment of projects, whose secret classifications render them unable to pool secretarial or other ancillary help, or even to know if the project next door may be duplicating their work). Moreover, clearance creates a preoccupation with one's rank in the hierarchy, analogous to concern over acceptance by a fraternity or country club. Concern over this kind of acceptance then has the unfortunate tendency to overshadow and render of secondary importance concerns about the actual end product of the work (Nash, 1981).

When those among us who are direct participants in the arms race are able to talk of their work, say with members of the same classified project, it is in "technostrategic language" (Cohn, 1987): a discourse preoccupied with playing numbers games, where the relationship of weapons to human lives becomes "an incidental consideration," and "almost irresponsible pursuit" (Nash, 1981). "Bean counting" abstractions permit isolation of thoughts from feelings, while inappropriate metaphors alter reality in reassuring directions (is a "surgical strike," painful as it may be, not perhaps for the enemy's own good? and might it not be covered by Blue Cross?).

In her book, *Eichmann in Jerusalem*, Hannah Arendt seeks an explanation for the lack of a sense of guilt experienced by the Nazis in carrying out the monstrous crimes committed in "the final solution to the Jewish question." Her conclusions seem directly relevant to participation in the arms race. Arendt's explanation was that the Nazi bureaucracy provided mechanisms for establishing distance between the individual and the reality of genocide. Those who did the actual killing were not the ones who had done the planning. Those who planned were never required to kill. "The Nazi state was administered by ordinary men and women performing routine acts no one of which seemed, in itself, unacceptably sinister. This aspect of the Holocaust is suggested by Arendt's statement that her study of Adolf Eichmann is a 'report on the *banality* of evil.'" (Nash, 1981, p. 159)

It should be kept in mind that when we talk of the bureaucracy involved in potential genocide from U.S. nuclear weaponry, it is not just targeters, designers, or manufacturers who are implicated. All of us, through our tax payments, are the bankrollers, the financiers of these weapons. We are the electing body that chooses a number of the key decision-makers in the arms race as our representatives. They serve in a government whose policies are ultimately to be determined by the people, for the people.

In social psychologist Stanley Milgram's well-known experiments on obedience to authority (Milgram, 1974), a surprising number of people proved willing to deliver what they believed to be potentially lethal electric shocks to "students" in a supposed "experiment on the effects of punishment on learning," just because a man with a clipboard standing by in a white lab coat told them they "must continue." Among other variations on his experiments, Milgram tested for the effects of distance between his subjects and their "student victims." In the "distant" case, he had subjects "deliver shocks" from a different room, without hearing the cries of the "students," while in the closer condition, he had them "deliver the shocks" directly within sight and sound of the "suffering" accomplices. Milgram found a dropoff from 65% compliance to 30% with the reduction of the distance factor. As we continue to be financially complicitous in an arms race which the majority of us believe to be both unnecessary and dangerous, surely the remoteness of the connection between writing an annual check to the IRS and the first nuclear flash of World War III (or the flash of pain across the face of a starving child) is a critical factor permitting us to continue. To paraphrase the remark Arthur Koestler made in regard to statistics, "1040 forms don't bleed."

The Media

Barring such conditions as living in proximity to Three Mile Island, the media is the only way by which nuclear issues have so far found any place on the agenda of the daily lives of most of us.

Daily film clips from the front kept the United States on a constant diet of the carnage of the Vietnam War, until the whole effort was regurgitated in repudiation. The American nuclear experience, by contrast, has been "the experience of limited knowledge and constrained inquiry" (Manoff, 1983, p. 209), a not inconsequential reason for it still sitting, undealt with, in the pits of our stomachs. This has been true from the dawn of the nuclear age, when General MacArthur placed Hiroshima off limits to American civilian journalists. "Everything the American people learned about the bombing from its newspapers on August 7th and for days and weeks to come, had been prepared for it by the War Department, which set and controlled the journalistic agenda during those first crucial moments of the atomic age" (Manoff, 1983, pp. 206-7). When a Western journalist had the temerity to report on continued deaths 30 days after the bombing from a mysterious "atomic plague" (radiation poisoning), he was ordered expelled from Japan by MacArthur's army. The only aspect of the situation fed to the U.S. press was the "success" of the weapon in demonstrating to the Japanese the impossibility of resistance.

Robert Karl Manoff, managing editor of *Harper's* magazine, described as "the central political fact of American life" the observation that "the epistemological structure of the nuclear regime is incompatible with the epistemological structure of democracy itself." Nuclearism and democracy, he points out, "embody antagonistic ideals of knowledge. They foresee different patterns for its dissemination. They contemplate entirely different consequences for social action and political participation" (Manoff, 1983, p. 210). Detecting in nuclear weapons a threat to our political fabric as great as the weapons' threat to our nation's material existence, he states "The United States cannot long endure as both nuclear and democratic. . . . For one system requires secrecy, the other, in the finest sense of the word, publicity. One system must concentrate control, the other exists in order to diffuse it" (op. cit., p. 210). The press, media, and entire communications industry have proved "exceedingly pliant" in yielding to the requirements of the nuclear regime. In addition to dismissing the radiation effects story at Hiroshima, as the government told it to do, "[i]t faithfully bought the idea there was a single atomic secret to be guarded . . . that the super bomb should be built, that the bomber gap existed, that the missile gap existed . . . that MIRVs were a good thing . . . that the MX was a necessary weapon . . . " (op. cit., pp. 210-11).

In a nation founded on an anti-authoritarian social contract, one needs to ask what factors have served to keep the press so well in line. Has it been simply a combination of informal pressures from the Administration and formal threats to prosecute alleged breaches of "security"? What keeps the press so well in line today on matters of foreign policy, so that stories generated by the White House-cued "Office of Public Diplomacy" are too often simply repeated by bright and hard-working reporters who fail to dig deeper (Coffin, 1988d).

According to Walter Lippmann, who was surely in a position to know, "The most important forms of corruption in the modern journalist's world are the many guises and disguises of social climbing on the pyramids of power" (Coffin, 1988d). On the one hand, journalists, no less than politicians, wish to avoid being labeled "leftist" or "soft on communism." On the other, they have a desire to keep their sources friendly by using stories leaked to them and asking few questions. Reporters who ask too many questions get shut out, become no longer privy to "exclusives" with which to win front-page bylines, don't get their telephone calls answered, find office bosses called away when they go to visit, are cut off social lists and denied perks. The *Washington Spectator* editor-in-chief, Coffin (1988d, p. 1), feels this may be more true in recent times because the press is "no longer made up of staunchly independent editors, but suffers from monopoly control, as the TV networks do." The net effect of all this, columnist Alexander Cockburn writes, was to give the Reagan administration "a virtually free ride" during its first term, glossing over the President's "repeated misstatements of elementary fact," and repeating without comment such "absurd claims" as "that he wanted a balanced budget, even though his military spending (plus the tax cut) was causing deficits to soar" (Coffin, 1988d, p. 2). Just how rigorously, for example, might one have expected NBC-TV to take Reagan and high military spending to task when NBC is owned by General Electric, a major nuclear and other military contractor and a corporation for whom Reagan spent a number of years as a public-relations figurehead?

The Slippery Slope Away From Attention to a Nuclear Threat

Manoff states that the press responds "above all to government and elite opinion," but this does not preclude grassroots movements from receiving press coverage. This will occur "primarily when they begin to throw their weight around and when those with real power begin to take notice. On that day the grassroots story moves from the category of human interest to that of politics, and out of obscurity and onto page one" (Manoff, 1983, p. 211). Such a movement of nonleaders, concerned about a nuclear threat, did occur in the early 1980s. But, as the study of attitudes and actions in a group of California college students over the subsequent years by Dr. Van Hoorn, Paula LeVeck and myself (1989) attests, sustaining attention to nuclear threat is extremely difficult. The media, like a nerve ending repeatedly stimulated, fatigues on addressing the same issue; and without media attention, the issue falls off the agenda of most individuals.

A rejuvenation occurred in 1979–81 in America's dormant awareness of the hazards of nuclear forces and the dangers of the nuclear arms race. Helen Caldicott, Bernard Lown, Jack Geiger, Eric Chivian, and a small group of other physicians helped to get it started. They were aided mightily by the accident at Three Mile Island occurring at that time, combined with such Administrative loose talk as Secretary of State Haig's "nuclear shot across the bow" and Vice-President Bush's "winnable nuclear wars." Many months of more-than-usual news coverage of nuclear arms developments and opposition to them culminated in the made-for-TV ratings-buster *The Day After*. For several years, the concept of nuclear war was *salient*. It had been made so by a combination of concerned individuals and political and accidental circumstances, and by the media's attention to the subject.

Before-and-after surveys done in the fall of 1983 (French & Van Hoorn, 1986; Schofield & Pavelchak, 1984) found that individuals reported thinking about nuclear war significantly more often shortly after viewing *The Day After* than they had before. This was particularly true of those who learned the most about the actual effects of a nuclear war by watching the film (Schofield & Pavelchak, 1985)—a group which tended to be under 20 years old (French & Van Hoorn, 1986). Hollywood, with modern-day special effects, had joined Physicians for Social Responsibility (with footage from Hiroshima) to provide concrete images of nuclear devastation sufficient for a number of people, for a period of time, to overcome the customary remoteness of the issue and have it seem real to them.

Even surveys conducted in the early 1980s, however, which served to reveal the breadth of people's concern, also revealed the tremendous effort necessary for people to attend to the topic at all, and certainly to do so in a sustained manner. Goldenring and Doctor (1986) conducted a two-pronged study of teenagers' worries about nuclear war. In it, they first asked their student subjects to list their three biggest fears. They then asked them to pick the five top fears they had out of a list of 20 possible choices (with nuclear war tucked away in the middle). Only 7% listed nuclear war among the fears they were to come up with spontaneously. On the other hand, nuclear war was the second choice (after death of parents) from the list of 20 suggested fears. In their desire to emphasize young people's concern about the issue, Goldenring and Doctor failed to highlight this interesting discrepancy. *Only when reminded of it would students acknowledge nuclear war to be one of their greatest fears.* Should one set about to do it, it would be hard to design a better study to illustrate selective inattention to (or "denial" of) the nuclear issue.

In our long-term follow-up study of attitudes towards nuclear weapons and nuclear war during the period 1983–1986, Judith Van Hoorn, Paula LeVeck and I (1989) found a significant falling off of attention to these issues, accompanied by a decreased estimate of the likelihood of nuclear war. This was a period of time during which the "warning clock" on the face of the *Bulletin of the Atomic Scientists* went from 4 minutes before midnight to 3, indicating that in the opinion of weapons and arms control experts, the situation had, if anything, become more precarious. Asked to explain the change in their attention to this issue, the students attributed it chiefly to a fall-off in media coverage. This explanation was in keeping with the students' identification of mass media (primarily TV) as the most significant source of influence on their attitudes, thoughts, and feelings regarding nuclear weapons and nuclear war.

Comments of the students we studied in follow-up also illustrate a further denial-facilitating phenomenon: a rebound effect of efforts like *The Day After* or the INF Accords. It seems as if the urge to escape the issue is so great that events like these run the risk of being used by our psyches as tickets out of the uncomfortable realm of concern over nuclear war. Our students' decreased tendency to attend to nuclear war, they told us, was based in part on the reassuring thought that films like *The Day After* and other media attention had resulted in other people, including superpower leaders, becoming more educated on these matters. This, then, provided a basis for decreasing their estimations of the likelihood of nuclear war occurring.

Behavioral scientists have long noted this tendency of individuals to remain inactive upon perceiving others to be aware of a problem. One of the most glaring examples of this involved the protracted murder by repeated stabbings of a woman named Kitty Genovese on a street in New York City under the witnessing eyes of 38 separate onlookers. Not one of the witnesses called the police. Each, it has been speculated (with experimental support—Latané & Darley, 1968), was certain that others must have done so. It seems we must beware of "nuclear Kitty Genovese phenomena," wherein eye-opening media events like *The Day After* can produce unfortunate paradoxical results in regard to public attention. The strength of our denial is such that efforts at overcoming it are prone to backfire.

Achieving Salience

In order to be surmounted, a nuclear threat must be comprehended. In order to be comprehended, the issue must become salient to the public and remain so over an extended period of time. Such salience is not easy to achieve. Nuclear weapons do not impinge on our daily lives. We have no immediate motivation to attend to the issue. The issue has difficulty in attracting the attention of a media compliant with governmental priorities and constraints. If these obstacles can be overcome and salience achieved, the overall result might well be to promote our choice of a national pathway to survival. This would occur not because such a choice is guaranteed once one considers the problem, but simply because our favored path is in keeping with the preferences of the majority of the public (see below). As Fiske (1987, p. 213) points out, "Salience exaggerates people's propensity to act in whatever direction they already would tend to act." When the message of the dangers of nuclear war is accompanied by a message stating the futility of seeking technological solutions, such approaches as SDI fail to co-opt or nullify public concern. Then, as Fiske asserts, "[k]eeping the issue salient is likely to accentuate people's existing worry and their preference for a mutual nuclear freeze" (p. 215).

The single event most likely to overcome remoteness, denial, and media inattention, bringing the need for action into immediate salience, would be the occurrence of a nuclear blast somewhere on earth, killing, blinding, burning, maiming and poisoning many hundreds of thousands of people. When two such blasts, albeit very tiny by today's standards, were visited on the Japanese by the United States in the 1940s, it made Japan into an instant, outspoken, and durable opponent of nuclear weaponry. A similar denial-evaporating event today, however, would not only in itself constitute one of the greatest tragedies ever to hit the human race, it would very likely either intentionally signal or accidentally trigger the onset of a nuclear World War III.

Have lesser events, either unforeseen (e.g., Chernobyl, Three Mile Island) or willed (e.g., *The Day After*) combined spontaneously or been combined through the media to inspire the prevention of nuclear war? Possibly. If so, effective means must be found of enhancing the salience of the nuclear threat for the American public, whose arousal is the key to prevention.

Content of the message. The physicians' movement in the United States, starting with two papers on the effects of a nuclear blast on Boston in the New England Journal of Medicine in 1962 and progressing through the winning of the Nobel Peace Prize by the International Physicians for the Prevention of Nuclear War in 1985, did not revive concern about the dangers of nuclear war by *convincing* people of its destructiveness, but rather by *reminding* them of it. Moreover, it did so *repeatedly* and *graphically.* Polls indicate Americans have been convinced of the uselessness and destructiveness of nuclear war since the 1950s. In a 1956 Gallup poll inquiring how many Americans out of every 10 would die in a nuclear war, the median response was seven (Gallup, 1956). What was arresting about the physicians' message was its *authority*, its *disinterested nature*, and its *concreteness of imagery.* Following a Physicians for Social Responsibility (PSR) presentations throughout the 1980s, people could imagine themselves and their loved ones not so much as dead, but rather in an even more compelling state: severely, critically, horribly wounded, living in an environment hostile to life, and without hope of medical care.

For the PSR message to be heard, however, it was essential that the physicians also offer a remedying prescription. Janis and Feshbach (1953) and, later, Leventhal (1970) demonstrated that arousing fear without offering hope of a method of risk reduction tends to produce only denial and rejection of the message. PSR stressed the need for a ban on further weapons testing and a halt to the development of new generations of nuclear forces, as well as the need for everyone to educate themselves and others on the issue. It is possible, however, that more might have been accomplished in the direction of arms control and multilateral disarmament in the first half of the '80s had the physicians been as singlemindedly clear in their prescription as they were in their diagnostic description of the problem. (It is also possible that they did the best they could, since the public could perceive them as experts on the medical consequences of nuclear war, but perhaps not as experts on the political means of its prevention.)

To truly comprehend our nuclear situation in a manner that could lead to survival, the American public must get the rest of the message, too. They must, in addition to hearing of the danger, hear of the problems with deterrence and the pursuit of technological advantage discussed in Part I, as well as of the economic and psychological causes of the arms race.

Form of the message. Psychological studies in persuasion (the "Attitude Change" literature in Social Psychology) indicate the value of having "experts" as the bearers of messages to the American public—but it is essential that the experts be regarded as trustworthy. If a messenger is to be perceived as trustworthy, he or she must have no self-interest in the information being presented. (In this regard it was helpful that a key film used by PSR portrayed individuals addressing a conference of physicians, so that the public audience viewing the film was "overhearing" the message rather than being spoken to directly, as by someone intent on persuading them.)

In his book *Influence: Science and Practice*, Robert Cialdini (1985) lists several procedures that can make an idea easier to picture. They include analogy and metaphor, repetition, prior imagining of an event, and reference to prior concrete experience. All of these have had direct application to the overcoming of distance and denial in getting people to comprehend the threat of nuclear war.

• *Metaphor.* Members of the audience at a number of PSR lectures heard the sound of a BB dropped into an empty 50-gallon oil drum and were asked to imagine that it represented the detonation of all the explosives used in World War II. They were then told that what they were about to hear would, on the same scale, represent the explosive force of the nuclear weapons currently available for use in a war by the two superpowers. At this point a stream of many hundreds of BBs was poured into the oil drum in an ear-jarring continuous flow over a protracted period. The metaphor was so effective as to have been dubbed "Caldicott in a can" (alluding to the power of activist Dr. Helen Caldicott's talks). It went a long way toward overcoming the "remoteness" factor. It produced a mental image of nuclear war which may have been only metaphorical but which, without the metaphor, might have been unavailable altogether. The experience made nuclear war seem both more credible and likely.

• *Reference to the familiar.* Another effective analogy drawn by PSR speakers combined metaphor with reference to actual experience. They pointed out the equivalence between the potential explosive force of the single nuclear bomb dropped by accident (fortunately without detonation) on Goldsboro, North Carolina, in 1961, and the explosive force of a 5,000-mile long freight train packed to the roof with TNT. By analogy to experienced forces and distances, the unimaginable strength of nuclear forces becomes imaginable and thereby enters the realm of things which may be thought about and must be dealt with.

In a typical speech, Dr. Caldicott describes how children, victims of radiation, are "put in an isolated ward all by themselves . . . and their parents suddenly appear in a gown and mask. Nobody tells them what's the matter. They have some strange drugs which make them feel funny. They live in a state of abject terror and ignorance for two weeks, and suddenly they die from a hemorrhage from their nose or mouth." Speaking for the millions of victims following a nuclear attack, which she can see so clearly and which her audience by now can picture as well, she completes her message, as the audience is pulled along with her by the power of her concrete and familiar images. "These politicians have never seen the grief of the parents, with their beautiful children dying. Have they ever seen or witnessed anything like that? Because if they had, they wouldn't be doing this unless they were psychotic" [excerpts from speech heard in San Jose, CA, in early 1980s]. Caldicott's moving description may be more than an image when one knows that a certain number of leukemic deaths are already inevitable byproducts of the arms race. People for whom the medical consequences of nuclear war have remained uncontemplated abstractions are taken along step by step.

• *Concrete imagery.* The most directly relevant concrete images, those of our only experience of actual nuclear war to date, are fading with time. Their impact can still be powerful, however, when they come from the mouths of people present at the time. It can help a person begin to comprehend the threat of nuclear war to read or hear the words of Gene Fugita, a Hiroshima survivor interviewed on CBS news with Walter Cronkite (1/29/81). "There was one scene that I . . . I . . . I still remember very well. That this little girl just kept on screaming, 'Please kill me! Please kill me! I can't stand the pain!' And I really did want to go over there and . . . and . . . and kill that child. And there were thousands of people like that, just . . . just all over. No matter which way you turn, they were just . . . And that's when I thought, 'Gee, if this is mankind, I came in the wrong era.'"

Fortunately for our species and others, the years from World War II to date have spared us further detonations of nuclear weapons as part of open hostilities. It is nonetheless possible to cull concrete images from the arms race itself. Doing so can make an effective statement where words may fail. The atmospheric test ban of 1963 came about in part because of public concern based on early efforts of this sort by Physicians for Social Responsibility. In Philadelphia and other areas throughout the country, PSR supervised the collection of children's deciduous teeth and announced to a duly alarmed public their finding of significant amounts of potentially mutagenic strontium 90 incorporated into them. The teeth differed in this regard from deciduous teeth collected from milk-fed children prior to the era of atmospheric nuclear testing. Where denial may dissolve words of warning without a trace, it is harder to dispose of the evidence in baby teeth.

• *Repetition.* If persons are exposed repeatedly to an idea, "it springs to mind more easily and seems more likely" (Cialdini, p. 7). As mentioned above, many college students in the longitudinal survey of Van Hoorn and myself explained their falling-off of attention to the topic of nuclear weapons/war as due to no longer hearing reports of it or seeing films featuring it repeatedly on television. In addition to being authoritative, metaphorical and/or concrete, messages aimed at alerting the public to the threat of nuclear war must be *repeated* so that exposure to them occurs at different times and in different contexts.

• *Prior imagining.* Actively imagining an event that has not happened yet has been demonstrated to speed a person's grasp of an idea, cause people to believe more strongly that the event could actually occur, and then increase the likelihood of people acting on that expectancy (Gregory, Cialdini, & Carpenter, 1982). This has been explained in terms of the "availability principle," where the imagining serves in much the way an actual experience might to render relevant mental images about it more available. To the extent this is effective, it could serve to promote thinking about the nuclear predicament in both a positive and a negative fashion. This power of imagining in a negative sense may be what makes a film like *The Last Epidemic* (Thiermann & Thiermann, 1981) so effective. The film audiovisually guides viewers to imagine the consequences of a nuclear detonation on a major American city today. When an undesirable event becomes more "real" through the imagination, people feel a greater need to avoid it. Groups stressing a positive image of the future, on the other hand, such as the very effective Beyond War movement (with its invitation to "Picture a world beyond war . . . "), would seem to be tapping into the positive application of the principle. Imagining the desired future helps it "become more likely," with the individual in turn more likely to work to bring it about.

Media for the message. Different media reach different audiences and are suitable for different sorts of messages. For the more straightforward sorts of information about the arms race, mass-media audiovisual presentations (TV or films) suggest themselves as preferable to written or oral presentations. Social-psychology literature points to the greater ability of the audiovisual medium to transmit simple ideas than written or unaided oral presentations can (Chaiken & Eagly, 1976; Fransden, 1963). Moreover, television is ubiquitous, and, as our own researches have indicated, already the established principal source of information in this area for the young. It should be kept in mind, however, that passive exposure to information without opportunity for interpersonal contact, while effective at agenda-setting (bringing matters to conscious attention), is unlikely to produce attitude change (Flay & Cook, 1981). Methods for producing attitude change will be addressed in the section below entitled "Choosing Mindset and Approach," as well as in the sections on motivation and action.

Audience for the message. Research into effects of *The Day After* (French & Van Hoorn, 1986), found that individuals under 20 years of age who had just seen the film reported increased thinking about nuclear war four times more than did individuals who had just seen the film who were over 20. Younger subjects have long been noted in studies on persuasion to be more of a *tabula rasa* than older ones. For younger people, whether or not they get exposed to information is a more important consideration than how the information fares in competition with already held attitudes. Wherever choice of audience age is a factor, it should be born in mind that youths are the group that will reap the most from educational efforts.

The Task is Critical

Despite recent advances in disarmament between the U.S. and Soviet Union, attention to the foregoing factors and generally arousing public concern about the danger and inappropriateness of the world's nuclear situation remains critical. Such efforts should be pursued with the enlistment of the press (reluctant though it may be) whenever possible. Should the press balk altogether, one should not wait upon them. Like the politicians, they will eventually follow the people. It is essential to keep the issue salient, as that is the first step in the pathway of individuals toward survival-directed action. As Harvard psychologist Susan Fiske (1987, p. 215) states, "Keeping the issue alive may indeed help to keep us all alive."

Assigning Likelihood

The Chicken or the Egg?

At what point in thinking about nuclear war do we estimate its likelihood? For many of us, it seems as if we trouble ourselves about the topic at all only because we have become convinced it has some possibility of occurring. My own and others' researches indicate that people's likelihood estimates are related to their ideas about how the nuclear threat should be handled, with militarily aggressive approaches being associated with lower likelihood estimates (Hamilton, Chavez, & Keilin, 1986; French, 1983). Whether estimations of likelihood precede choices of approach and help determine them, or whether they follow them and are consequences of them, is not clear. It could be that choosing an approach to the nuclear threat that involves building more bombs may oblige one to secondarily lower one's estimate of nuclear war's likelihood, precisely in order to avoid "cognitive dissonance"—the uncomfortable mental state of supporting something unsupportable. To put this possibility in a more positive light, people who experience themselves as "warriors" (to use Dyson's term) may, as part of that persona, see themselves as not being at risk. They may feel that they and others of their ilk have the "right stuff" to stay in control and prevent war from actually erupting, or at least going nuclear.

Despite the uncertainty involved, I felt it important, for heuristic purposes, to determine a specific locus for "Assigning Likelihood" within the flow chart of the individual's options in the nuclear age. The preponderance of logic dictated that it precede "Choice of Mindset and Approach." It would seem logical that individuals who favor arms control and disarmament efforts do so out of concern about nuclear war's having a significant likelihood. Someone starting out with a high estimate of nuclear war's likelihood would seem logically more inclined to methods of prevention that reduced the number of bombs. Even for those of a militant approach, Doble and Yankelovich (Public Agenca Foundation, 1984) felt this to be the logical sequence. Of the most militantly aggressive segment of the population they surveyed, the pollsters write " . . . unlike most other Americans, they don't think there is any real chance [nuclear war] will happen. Consequently, they are prepared to take far greater risks than are the rest of the public. They are less interested in negotiation than in building up our military strength" (pp. 38–39).

With these considerations in mind, we have placed the assignment of nuclear war's likelihood as the event immediately following comprehension of the nuclear threat. We see it having a determining role in whether one falls into the camps of the militant "aggressive enemy-perceiving" or non-worried, on the one hand, or whether one chooses instead from among the larger group of approaches based on estimating a significant likelihood of nuclear war's occurrence—the fatalists, the survivalists, the Armageddonists, the anti-nuclearists, the "energy-fearing pragmatists," or those concerned about the risks but uncertain of what approach to take.

Salience Effects

In the cohort of California college students followed by Van Hoorn, LeVeck, and myself (1989) from 1983 to 1986, there was no change during the 3-year interval in their estimations of the likelihood of a nuclear blast occurring by accident, and no change in their estimates of the destructiveness of a nuclear war. There was, however, a distinct fall-off in their estimates of the likelihood of a nuclear war occurring between the superpowers, and it was accompanied by a distinct decrease in the reported frequency with which they found themselves thinking about nuclear war. Ignoring for the moment the question of what may account for these drop-offs (diminished press coverage? changes in life priorities between freshman and senior years of college? world events? The Iron Curtain had not yet fallen and Cold War rhetoric was still abundant.), it seems clear there is a connection between nuclear war's estimated likelihood and nuclear war's salience for these individuals.

In the early 1980s I showed a large number of different audiences the film *The Last Epidemic* (Thiermann & Thiermann, 1981). In order to measure attitude changes produced by it, I used a before-and-after survey I called the Nuclear War Attitude Survey (NWAS, French, 1983; French & Van Hoorn, 1986). Opinion items in the NWAS dealt with such issues as the value, likelihood, dangerousness, limitability and preventability of nuclear war. The film and accompanying discussion addressed all of these issues, but the single item that registered the most change from before to after on the survey was the estimation of likelihood of one's own death resulting from nuclear war (versus other causes). The film guided the audiences through an imagined nuclear destruction of San Francisco (the nearest major metropolis); the main effect of viewing it seemed to be to make such an event appear a more likely cause of one's death.

Enhanced salience of the nuclear issue, then, whether as a short-term effect of viewing a single film or the cumulative effect of exposure to ongoing multimedia attention, seems to result in a higher estimate of nuclear war's likelihood. This likelihood estimate may, in turn, function as an important determinant of one's response to the issue.

Characteristics Associated with Likelihood Estimates

Local, national, and international surveys have uniformly found women to give a higher estimate to the likelihood of nuclear war occurring than men. To give an example from my own research (French, 1986), in a survey of 132 Stanford University psychology students (59 males, 73 females, mean age 21), 67% of the females rated nuclear war as "somewhat likely" to "very likely" to occur within the next 50 years, versus 44% of the males ($p < .005$). Social class differences are not associated with any variation in likelihood estimations, but age differences are, with younger subjects (peaking at ages 12–15) attributing higher likelihood to nuclear war's occurrence (Van Hoorn & French, 1986; Solantaus, 1986). Bachman, Mack, Chivian, and others have found that young people who do find nuclear war likely and worry about it are not simply anxiety-ridden. They tend, instead, to be constructive worriers, politically aware and active individuals, on the average better adjusted and better students than their peers (see Diamond & Bachman, 1986). Their higher levels of estimated likelihood are accompanied by a greater knowledge of the nuclear situation compared to their fellow students (French, 1986). Among the adult groups surveyed on both knowledge and attitude by the author in the early 1980s, the group with the lowest estimate of likelihood (men's service clubs) was also the group with the lowest scores on the knowledge test (French, 1986; Van Hoorn & French, 1986).

Tyler and McGraw (1983) found, for all but the statistically small group of "survivalists," a high correlation between increased estimates of nuclear war's likelihood and increased reported levels of worry regarding nuclear war ($r = .47$, $p < .001$). They also found a high correlation between estimates of nuclear war's likelihood and antinuclear activism, with higher estimates of likelihood being a key factor in distinguishing activists from the nonactive public. One might posit a logical connection between high estimates of nuclear war's likelihood and low faith in national leaders' abilities to prevent such an occurrence, with a concomitantly greater assumption of responsibility on one's own part to do so.

In the author's surveys of seven different types of audiences (school classes, doctors' grand rounds, business seminars, church forums, public meetings, activist group meetings, and men's service clubs), the men's service clubs were made up of individuals closest to the category of political leaders. In the section asking for estimates of the likelihood of various nuclear events happening within the next 50 years, the responses of the men's service clubs were comparable to those of the other groups regarding "a nuclear blast occurring somewhere on earth" and "terrorists planting a nuclear device in a populated area." But in regard to the likelihood of nuclear war between two or more nations, this single group gave estimates far lower than the rest. And the most divergent response of all for the group was the minimal likelihood they gave to the possibility that they themselves would die in a nuclear war.

The Importance of Likelihood Estimates

What's so important about people's estimates of the likelihood of nuclear war? Its importance lies in its role as a prime determinant of both people's endorsed approach to the nuclear threat, and their ultimate willingness to act on that approach. Beck and Frankel (1981) concluded from a review of literature on protective health behavior that three cognitions determine people's willingness to act in response to a health risk: (a) Do they think the danger is real? (b) Do they think the recommended plan will decrease the danger? and (c) Do they think they can carry out the plan? The lower the estimate of nuclear war's likelihood, the less real its threat appears. The less real the danger, the less likely one is to take any preventive action.

This is part of the reason "leaders" (governments) must not be counted on to take the initiative in reducing the risk of nuclear war. "Leaders" assign a lower likelihood estimate to the possibility of nuclear war occurring than do most of the rest of the population. To this extent, they have a relative lack of motivation to alter the status quo through any moves towards prevention. Fiske, Pratto, and Pavelchak (1983) noted the correlation between anti-nuclear activism and the availability of concrete images of nuclear war's destructiveness. Likelihood estimates would seem to be the bridge between the images and the activism. The availability of the concrete images make the event seem more likely, according to Tversky and Kahneman (1973), with the likelihood then making people more prone to action, according to Beck and Frankel (1981). Where ordinary citizens, identifying with the "victims," have concrete images of nuclear war's destructiveness, the "warriors" (to use Dyson's category) or "leaders" (in Frank's categorization) tend to have concrete images only of "hardware" and/or statistics.

For women, at least, an increased estimate of nuclear war's likelihood correlates positively with belief in the benefits of arms control (Nelson & Slem, 1984). (In men, attitudes towards arms control are more closely tied to notions of relative military superiority [op. cit.].)

Thus whatever can be done to enhance our notions of nuclear war's likelihood should, more of the time than not, help to move us down what we believe to be the path toward survival. Regarding concerns about the remoteness of the issue, as well as Fiske et al.'s findings on the benefits of the concrete imagery of destruction, it would seem films like *The Day After*, *Threads Testament*, or *Letters From a Dead Man* (a powerfully moving Soviet post-nuclear war film) offer the most hope in this regard. In the words of Locatelli and Holt (1986), they "make real for us the empty abstractions or sanitized phrases ('nuclear exchange,' 'countervalue targeting,' etc.) by which we designate allegedly possible events in which it is otherwise difficult to believe. The unavailable becomes available and hence subjectively more probable. . . . " (p. 155).

Mindset and Approach

Once people's attention has been forced to the topic of nuclear war and they have ascribed a level of likelihood to it, they develop (or strengthen or change) an attitude about it. This attitude includes both an assessment of its preventability, survivability, and likely role in the overall scheme of things, and also includes an approach towards its prevention. The assessment, which we have chosen to call a "mindset," and the approach go hand in hand, the approach being dictated by the mindset. It seems appropriate, therefore, for us to consider them together at this point in our flow chart.

Just as the sequence of items in the flow chart is arranged for heuristic purposes

and is ultimately arbitrary to a certain degree, the division into discriminate mindsets must also be appreciated as somewhat arbitrary and for heuristic purposes.
First of all, four of the major mindsets that we shall discuss were derived through
cluster analysis, a process that categorizes on a probabilistic rather than a taxo-
nomic basis. Thus while a trait may be characteristic of one mindset, it may be
present as well in individuals of a predominantly different mindset. Secondly,
maintenance of anything like a pure type of one or another mindset is probably less
common than having an attitude that shifts between mindsets over time, or that
entertains all or parts of different mindsets simultaneously. These caveats in mind,
it is none the less useful to think and speak of these mindsets as distinct categories,
both because of the ease it imparts to our considerations and because the various
trait attitudes do cluster in these modes.

The Major Mindsets

The Public Agenda Foundation (PAF), in collaboration with The Center for
Foreign Policy Development at Brown University, performed a computer-based
analysis on their survey sample of the American public interviewed on nuclear
arms-related issues prior to the 1984 elections—a time when many Americans still
viewed the Soviets with great suspicion. On a purely mathematical basis, they
sorted out four like-minded groups of people according to how their attitudes
clustered together. Their cluster analysis showed the public to be most sharply
divided by four variables: (a) the tendency to minimize or to stress the threat of
nuclear war, (b) the presence or absence, at that time, of ideological animosity
toward the Soviet Union, (c) the favoring of an assertive or a conciliatory policy
towards the Soviets, and (d) the inclination to see the conflict between the United
States and the Soviet Union in religious or in pragmatic terms. While the factors
are potentially independent of one another, the Public Agenda Foundation (1984,
pp. 38–42) found them to combine and divide in particular ways among the sampled portion of the U.S. population. Despite the renunciation of Communism in
Eastern Europe, the data remain of interest to us because the tendency to perceive
our situation in terms of competition with an aggressive enemy goes beyond the
specific issue of communism. This is the best study of popular attitudes toward
nuclear weapons that I am aware of, and perception of any new international
threats are likely to divide us along the same lines of schism.

A quick grasp of the relative size and relationship of the different clusters
derived by the Public Agenda Foundation can be conveyed by mapping them on a
grid. I have taken the liberty of doing this in figure 2; the first variable, perception
of the nuclear threat, is on the horizontal axis, and the second variable, perception
of an enemy threat, is on the vertical. I have, moreover, taken the further liberty of
labeling the groups in a manner differing from and unauthorized by the Public
Agenda Foundation, which specifically warned against such attempts on the basis
that the clusters' interests are "too distinctive and revealing to be reduced to
descriptive labels."

With apologies, then, to the Public Agenda Foundation, and at the acknowledged risk of distorting and oversimplifying their data (but with the intent of
rendering it in as broadly applicable a form as possible), I have engaged in the
following renamings, in accordance with key traits of the groups. The cluster they
refer to as "nuclear threat minimal" I have called "aggressive enemy-perceiving,"
that which they call "Soviet threat minimal" I call "antinuclear," their "war-

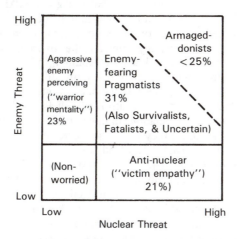

Figure 2 A grid-map of U.S. public opinion regarding nuclear war and the perception of enemy threat. (Derived from survey data contained in *Voter Options on Nuclear Arms Policy*, a publication of the Public Agenda Foundation, [6 East 39th St., New York, NY 10011], in collaboration with the Center for Foreign Policy at Brown University).

conscious pragmatists" I call "enemy-fearing pragmatists," and a portion of those they describe as seeing the "communist and nuclear threat maximal" I am calling "Armageddonists." I have also indicated on the grid (in parentheses) the relative positions of some additional groups. These groups, unclusterable as they may have been from the Public Agenda Foundation data, round out a more complete, though doubtless not exhaustive, list of possible "mindsets." They consist of the "uncertain," the "fatalists," the "non-worried," and the "survivalists."

Aggressive enemy-perceiving. The group I refer to as aggressive enemy-perceiving (approximating PAF's "nuclear threat minimal") believed that the "Munich" lesson warned us against Chamberlain-like accommodation of adversarial "aggressive enemy-perceiving" leaders. They favor continued testing and building of more nuclear weapons while downplaying the risks of such a course. Most of them, like virtually all other Americans, believed nuclear war would be unwinnable. But unlike most other Americans, they didn't think there was any real chance it could happen. They rejected conciliatory gestures in favor of weakening the other nation in every way possible, including outspending them in the arms race. PAF data indicates their "nuclear threat minimal" group to be older, predominantly male (69%), conservative, moderately well-educated, and with good incomes.

Many of the architects of the U.S. role in the nuclear arms race in recent years seem to fall into this camp. Indeed, the attitudinal profile corresponds to that of Jerome Frank's "leaders," demonstrating such traits as optimism, suspiciousness, competitiveness, fearlessness, and willingness to sacrifice (others). In Dysan's terms, this group shares a "warrior" mentality. At 23%, they constitute a distinct minority of the Public Agenda sample, yet their approach to national security—continuing the nuclear arms race—is the determining voice in current U.S. policy.

Antinuclear. The category I refer to as "antinuclear" generally corresponds to PAF's "Soviet threat minimal" cluster, which they describe as the youngest and best educated of their four groups. Like the first group, PAF found them more male than female (56% to 44%), but they tended to be liberal rather than conservative. They believed the possibility of nuclear disaster to be significant and urgent. They saw the real "Munich" analogy being a matter of unthinking accommodation not of the other nation's leaders, but of the buildup of nuclear weapons. They harbored a freedom from ideological hostility toward the other nation that was unique among PAF's four groups, seeing the international threat almost completely in military terms. They favored arms control, as well as variable degrees of mutual disarmament, rather than confrontation. In this regard, combined with their lack of "enemizing" the other nation, they came the closest of all the mindsets we shall discuss to following the pathway I feel leads to survival.

Enemy-fearing pragmatists. The largest cluster (31%) in the PAF survey was made up of Americans ideologically opposed to the other nation's form of government but peaceful and non-assertive in their thinking about how to deal with the threat. They didn't trust the other nation, but they thought a lot about the possibility of nuclear war and didn't feel the U.S. had done enough to reach serious arms-control agreements. They felt we should aim for a peaceful accommodation on a live-and-let-live basis. This was the most female of the PAF groups (60%), and tended to be made up of individuals who were fairly young, of average education, and politically middle-of-the-road. They, along with the "antinuclear" group and with part of the "Armageddonist" group favored arms control and at least partial mutual disarmament as the best hopes for survival.

Armageddonists. The Public Agenda Foundation found 25% of its sample population to be persons who saw the other nation not just as a political and military adversary with a poor record of respect for individual rights, but as a full-blown "Evil Empire," threatening our moral and religious values. Viewing the conflict in religious terms, they deemed it a certainty that someday the U.S. would have to fight them to keep their form of government from taking over the world. Such a war, they feel, will be the fulfilling of Biblical prophecy, and a majority of them believe that in the event of a nuclear holocaust, their faith in God would ensure their survival' (Public Agenda Foundation, 1984, p. 39). They were the least well-educated of the groups, and the only one of the clusters to agree with the suggestion that the subject of nuclear weapons was too complex for them to think about and should be "left to the President and to the experts" (op. cit., p. 42).

This "Armageddonist" group divided into two segments when it came to endorsing an approach to the nuclear threat. For some, its religious opposition to the other form of government predisposed them to endorse the utmost in nuclear military strength for the United States. But for others, its greater apprehension of imminent nuclear danger mandated relenting in our efforts to weaken the other nation too much, lest they respond "like cornered rats" (op. cit., p. 39). Thus there was majority concern that we had not done enough in negotiating with the other nation, and while some favored building up arms and a number were fatalistic, there was even a large minority favoring unilateral reductions in our nuclear stockpiles.

The "Armageddonist" group that I am including under "Mindset" in Figure 1 does not correspond to the PAF group ("communist and nuclear threat maximal") we have been discussing in its entirety, but only to that portion of it whose approach to the nuclear threat was limited to proselytizing. According to research at the Christic Institute, a Washington D.C.-based ecumenical public policy center, 8 million Americans believe in survival by being "raptured"—taken to Heaven—in the event of a nuclear holocaust. Viewing the holocaust as the inevitable work of a "higher power," they renounce any responsibility to work towards its avoidance and bend their efforts solely toward the conversion of others to their way of thought. This is the group that hands me *The Watchtower* at the door of my home, with headlines reading "The End of the World—Something to Fear or to Hope For?" or the *Kingdom News* with the headline "Are We Nearing Armageddon?" Inside the latter we read that "Armageddon is God's war to cleanse the earth of all wickedness, paving the way for a bright, prosperous new order! . . . the righteous will possess the earth." Above this text we see a colored drawing of white people, black people, oriental people, lambs, tigers, deer, all in a lovely meadow together with beautiful flowers and abundant fruit. Above the picture are the words "After Armageddon—a marvelous new order of peace and security" (*Kingdom News*, No. 31).

Such a message must have tremendous appeal to the naive and uneducated. In the face of a major threat to our existence, it offers at once a positive context of meaning, a translation of destruction into restitution, and a route of survival that substitutes rapture for death from third-degree burns and radiation poisoning. The Reverend Jerry Falwell, who has written widely on "rapture," publicly stated that President Reagan agreed with him on "the whole question of prophecy" (Fryszman, 1984, p. 10). James Mills, one-time president *pro tem* of the California State Senate, recalled Governor Reagan during a lunch in 1971 as quoting to him with "firelit intensity," Biblical scripture he regarded as proof that Libya's communist takeover signaled an imminent Armageddon involving nuclear weapons (Coffin, 1987b). And those who think such beliefs are limited to an unsophisticated President and a few of his like-minded friends should be aware that on the *Voters Options* survey (Public Agenda Foundation, 1984, p. 40), 39% of the American public sampled (28% of the category "college graduates," 48% of the category "those earning less than $20,000 per year") agreed with the item "When the Bible predicts that the earth will be destroyed by fire, it's telling us about a nuclear war."

The uncertain. Polls like the 1984 Public Agenda Foundation one have a tendency to pressure people into forced choices between strongly worded alternatives. This happens as a result of the demand character of the situation, even when a "not sure" or "undecided" option is offered. It is possible that a number of items upon which the cluster analysis is based might, in reality, have had a larger "uncertain" response than the results would indicate. It seems likely, in particular, that a large category of persons exists who assign significant likelihood to nuclear war, but remain effectively immobilized in terms of choosing an approach to dealing with the problem. These would be persons paralyzed by an awareness of the militarily useless nature of nuclear weapons, on the one hand, but, on the other, equally aware that such weapons' very existence demands that we reevaluate the use of force in general (Kull, 1985). To get rid of nuclear weapons, such people may reason, calls for international constraints not yet in place and in any event unwelcome to a nation used to getting what it wants. They may not see the other nation as "evil" and ourselves as "good," but both rather as entities of dubious trustworthiness who need to be held in check by something other than a quixotic "international order."

Ignorant of what specific actions might decrease the risk of nuclear war, they do what many do when uncertain: nothing. The need for belief in a plan that will reduce the risk, as Beck and Frankel (1981) point out, is an essential cognitive determinant of whether people will act in response to a health risk. Instead of facing the existential dilemma and making a choice in the absence of any certainties, this group puts off deciding. And with its choice to defer the issue, the attention of the "uncertain" group drifts back to business as usual. This seems to be a large group, for one meets many who are members of it. Its size as a percentage of the U.S. population is likely to remain obscure, however, because ordinary polling methods have difficulty capturing and describing it.

The Minor Mindsets

Rounding out the cast of possible mindsets/approaches are three categories with relatively small populations. For two of these, the "non-worried" and the "fatalists," being at opposite extremes on their estimates of nuclear war's likelihood leads them, ironically, to an identical approach. They *ignore* the issue: the "non-worried" do so because their faith in human nature, in leaders, in the benignity of the universe and/or the mercy of God, convinces them that the likelihood of nuclear war is nil. The "fatalists" do so because their pessimism convinces them that nuclear war is inevitable and inescapable, so that time spent either in preparation for it or in efforts to prevent it is time wasted. Only members of the third minor mindset, the "survivalists," endorse an approach to the problem, but it is one which we do not deem relevant to reducing the risk of nuclear war.

The non-worried. Hamilton, Chavez, and Keilin (1986) conducted a survey of 308 undergraduates in psychology courses at Colorado State University, offering them a menu of described attitudes towards nuclear war and asking them to choose the one best representing their personal perspective. Five and a half percent of them chose the category that read as follows: "Because human beings are basically good (i.e., rational, caring, desiring self-preservation for all people), nuclear war will never occur. In a nuclear crisis, political leaders will act rationally for the good of all humanity, and nuclear war will be prevented." For such individuals, their Panglossian optimism spares them any obligation to endorse approaches or engage in behavior aimed at reducing the risk of nuclear war, and they are free to return to "business as usual" the moment the event forcing their attention to nuclear war is over.

Fatalists. The category of "fatalists" in Figure 1 was conceived as containing those who, like the "Armageddonists," believe nuclear war to be inevitable and unpreventable by human effort, but unlike the Armageddonists, have no reassuring set of beliefs offering meaning or blissful survival. Instead, unable to support the inutility and pain of contemplating a horrible inevitability, members of this group make a conscious effort to put it out of their minds and return in short order to "business as usual."

In the survey by Hamilton et al. (1986), two items on their menu of attitudes involve a somewhat different form of fatalism: personal helplessness through inefficacy. Fatalism in this sense is actually a large category. The survey of Hamilton et al. divides it into a "Hedonist" faction (12% — " . . . getting what I want out of life in the time remaining") and an "Altruistic Fatalist" faction (40.9% — " . . . unable to lessen the threat, so why worry about it? The best I can do is . . . contribute to humanity in the best way that I can"). These two factions together constitute the majority of their respondents. Defining fatalism as a conviction of inefficacy would remove the category from column D to "helpless" in column E (where the individual is "reckoning efficacy"). In reality, convictions regarding efficacy *do* in many instances affect people's choice of an approach to the nuclear threat. Unfortunately, our model becomes excessively complex if we try to factor this in. For the sake of clarity, then, we shall restrict ourselves here to the limited definition of "fatalist" as a non-fundamentalist believer in nuclear war's inevitability. The key question of efficacy we shall explore below.

Survivalists. Survivalists share with Armageddonists and Fatalists a low estimate of nuclear war's preventability and a high estimate of its likelihood. They differ, however, from these groups (from *all* other groups, for that matter) on the question of its physical survivability. Tyler and McGraw (1983) distributed an attitude and opinion survey to members of a survivalist group and compared their responses to those from an activist group, as well as to those from a control group of the general public. They found the survivalists to have a high estimate of nuclear war's survivability (higher than that of the general public), and a low estimate of nuclear war's preventability (lower than that of the general public). The contrary was found to be true of the activists. They conclude that "it is the view that war is preventable but not survivable that drives anti-nuclear activism, while it is the belief that war is survivable but not preventable that drives survival behaviors" (ibid., p. 36).

Tyler and McGraw's observations on survivalists suffer a partial hemmorhaging of significance upon the realization that those with a "survivable but not preventable" attitude towards nuclear war make up an extremely small group—so small a group that to talk about them seriously at all may be to set up a straw man. There were evidently 6 individuals (2%) among Hamilton et al.'s sample of 308 undergraduates who agreed that survival precautions were the most appropriate response to the threat of nuclear war.

Survivalists are a colorful group, as one sees them on TV news documentaries with their plaid shirts and pistol practice. They are something of an American traditional type. They are a group also, perhaps, destined for some increase (together with the Armageddonists) as we approach the end of the millennium. But with their pursuit of preparations instead of prevention, they are a group removed from the path of approach we contend will reduce the risk of nuclear war.

Changing Mindsets Through Education

An important point to realize is that people's choice of mindset or approach is not necessarily based on much information. To a large extent, people's mindsets on nuclear war and the arms race reflect their general outlook on life, rather than representing conclusions reached after consideration of facts. For the most part, U.S. citizens are quite ignorant of the facts about our nuclear situation. Reliable national surveys taken over the past few years indicate that only 36% of Americans are aware of the existence of the ABM treaty between the superpowers, only 32% are aware the U.S. has no ballistic missile defense, only 19% have a sense of the approximate percentage of the defense budget spent on nuclear weapons, only 15% are aware that SDI as currently conceived would protect less than 10% of the U.S. population, only 11% know it is U.S. policy to use nuclear weapons first (i.e., without being attacked) if we or our allies deem ourselves sufficiently threatened, and only 10% are aware that both the Soviet Union and the United States signed the SALT II accords (Rosen, 1987, p. 3).

My own research (French, 1984) and that of others (e.g., Feshback, Kandel, &

Haist, 1985) has found high correlations between test scores of knowledge about nuclear issues, and the attitudes aligned with our path towards survival. Those who were most reluctant to approve nuclear war scored the highest on a nuclear facts quiz in my researches, while in Feshbach et al.'s studies (1985), a favorable attitude toward a nuclear moratorium correlated with greater nuclear knowledge. Of the six adult audience types I studied in the early 1980s, the Activists had the highest average knowledge scores and the greatest reluctance to countenance nuclear war, while the Men's Service Clubs (those closest to Jerome Frank's "leader" category) had the lowest knowledge scores and the greatest willingness to countenance nuclear war (French, 1983).

Such correlations do not in themselves mean greater knowledge of our nuclear situation will produce attitudes favorable to arms control and mutual disarmament. It could be that they are causally related in the reverse direction, with those predisposed towards arms control being more inclined to educate themselves. Or it could be that knowledge and attitude regarding these matters are both reflections of other factors and not causally related to each other. Some indication that increases in knowledge can *result* in attitude change is offered by the surveys I conducted before and after lectures by Physicians for Social Responsibility speakers (French, 1984), and by the before-and-after surveys Van Hoorn and I conducted at the time of the showing of *The Day After* on television (French & Van Hoorn, 1986). The survey results of PSR audiences showed a modest but statistically significant reduction, following the educational presentations, in the already low percentage of audience members prepared to countenance nuclear war. Although finding no change on a variety of other items (including the item about the countenancing of nuclear war), the survey of *The Day After* viewers showed a statistically significant ($p < .01$) increase in support for arms control following viewing of the film. [Interestingly, this turned out on segmentation of the responses to be due almost entirely to a change in appreciation of arms control by males. Females already had (and maintained without change) the higher level of appreciation that the males achieved only after seeing the film.]

If many current mindsets/approaches are uninformed ones and are susceptible to change through education, what sort of education is required? What sort of learning is liable to move people toward the approach we have argued is the only one leading to survival: endorsement of halting the arms race through arms control and disarmament? Referring to Figure 2, changes in this favorable direction involve movement toward the right and downwards—in other words, toward greater appreciation of the nuclear threat and less preoccupation with other nations as "enemies."

Education regarding the nuclear threat. Education of the public regarding the medical consequences of nuclear war has been extremely useful in moving people towards a higher appreciation of the nuclear threat. Many people are now aware that there would be at the most some 2,000 hospital beds in the United States (should they miraculously go undestroyed) capable of treating the sorts of massive burns that would afflict millions of Americans if they survived the immediate death toll of a full-scale nuclear war. This and a host of other nuclear medical verities, including the occurrence of a global "nuclear winter," tend to have a tempering effect on persons who might otherwise imagine "going nuclear" as a feasible military option.

Education regarding the potential for disasters from the ongoing arms race as detailed in Chapter 4—accidents, proliferation, human instability, increasing terrorist access to plutonium, the escalation of conventional conflicts—helps sensitize the public to the benefits of reducing the numbers of nuclear arms and curtailing their processes of production.

Education about the technical, economic, political, and psychological forces and realities in the nuclear arms race may cause people to think twice before committing the vast expenditures involved. If leaders are locked by their own personality traits into unrealistic positions on the deployment and use of nuclear arms (Frank, 1987), if, as investigative reporting has revealed, key parts of the guidance systems of our mightiest nuclear weapons are bought at Radio Shack to make a quick buck for Northrop (ABC-TV, 1988); if, as sources in the scientific and political communities attest, international arms-control negotiations are hostage to the weapons designers' desire to design weapons (Blum, 1988; Herken, 1987)—just how serious are the people in charge of this whole thing about it? And if they're not serious, or not serious for reasons having anything to do with true national security, why exactly should we keep pouring a hundred billion of our hard-earned, taxpayer dollars down this nuclear rathole every 18 months?

Education about the current costs of the arms race helps people consider another side of the nuclear threat: what the nuclear weapons are doing to us now, without being detonated—just by existing and by draining our resources. Children grow up "in a nuclear shadow"; academic openness and scientific debate gets stifled; people involved and uninvolved in weapons processing—from uranium miners to neighbors of weapons plants—die of cancer; educational, nutritional, health, child-care and other social needs go unmet as we watch a national debt mount up whose interest consumes (with nothing to show for it) alarming percentages of our tax dollars.

In point of fact, education *in general* seems useful, even beyond education specifically devoted to nuclear-related issues. In a February 1986 Gallup Poll wherein the public was noted to favor cuts in "defense" spending by a margin of 2:1, college graduates favored such a cut 3.3:1. When Gallup segmented its population sample to determine which factors correlated the most with favoring less "defense" spending, college education constituted the lead category out of 14 (Gallup, 1986a). College graduates, together with the young (18–24 years old) and the affluent (income over $50,000), were the lead supporters of a bilateral test ban, according to a June 1986 Gallup poll. And college graduates, with the exception of "non-whites" and "mid-westerners," were the only group which did not agree that there was greater risk in falling behind the other superpower in nuclear weaponry than there was in having an ongoing arms buildup (Gallup, May 1986b). The opinion that matters of "balance" or "superiority" are irrelevant at this point in the arms race seems to be the "educated" one.

Education regarding the "other." While it is necessary to have movement on our gridmap in Figure 2 toward the right side, the side of higher nuclear threat perception, in order to steer people onto the pathway toward survival, it is not sufficient. Alarmed about the arms race and the nuclear threat, but convinced of aggressive antagonism—if not inherent evil—in another nation or nations, people are more likely to become religiously fatalistic than they are to become convinced the prevention of nuclear war lies through demands for meaningful arms control and bilateral disarmament. There must be movement downwards on the grid-map, as well as toward the right. Education on various fronts is called for to create as realistic and mature a response to the people and leadership of other nations as we must have towards nuclear weapons.

To decide what sort of education is required along these lines, let us briefly review some of the forces already discussed that tended to promote exaggerated fear or enemy stereotyping of the Soviets during the Cold War.

First, there was the effect of "keeping our distance" from each other. The United States and the Soviet Union have been doing this, with the exception of a brief period during World War II, from early in the century until very recently. Lacking images of each other as human beings, fully clothed with human emotions, needs, and vulnerabilities, each side found it easy to project onto the other a stereotyped enemy image. Added to this was indulgence in the "fundamental attribution error": the tendency to always see our own behavior as understandably attributable to circumstances, while *their* behavior is seen as emanating from their (evil) nature. (If it's bad behavior, it is a direct reflection of that nature. If it's desirable behavior, it's either a trick or the coerced reward of our "hanging tough" and being strong.) Then there have been the effects of Administration efforts, from the distorting but conventional use of "worst-case" planning in estimating enemy capabilities, to out-and-out instances of apparently intentional deception, such as former under-secretary of Defense Richard Perle's assertions of Soviet test ban cheating in the face of contrary evidence (McTigue, 1986), or former Secretary of Defense Caspar Weinberger's frequent assertions of the Soviet's being ahead of us in Star Wars research. Finally, there has been the belief of many that the nature of human beings is inescapably warlike, as well as the sociohistorical factor of a generation being in power on both sides whose political diet during its formative years consisted of World War II and the Nazis.

In view of these forces pushing upwards on our grid-map toward greater perception of "evil" in the other, a set of specifically countervailing forces and educational efforts suggests itself as useful in moving individuals in the opposite direction toward a more objective and perhaps even affiliative view. Firstly, education aimed at "humanizing" the other nation's people would seem helpful. *People Weekly* made such an effort, for example, in its 4/6/87 issue entitled *"People Weekly* goes to Russia." The entire magazine consisted of articles on a "slice of life" of Soviet citizens, with none of the usual Western journalistic emphases on overall social or economic difficulties or human-rights failings. The more such efforts as this, or, for another example, the coffee-table photo book *A Day in the Life of the Soviet Union*, circulated about, the more the Soviets tended to become humanized in our eyes. According to social psychologist Albert Bandura, humanization has considerable power in counteracting cruel conduct. "Studies examining this process reveal that it is difficult for individuals to behave cruelly toward others when they are humanized or even personalized a bit" (Bandura, Underwood, & Fromson, 1975). Material from 'real life' supportive of these research findings includes the difficulty abductors have in harming hostages after having gotten to know them personally, or the fall-off in support of the death penalty from "high" by people considering it in the abstract to less favoring of it when there is more knowledge about specific individuals who might be put to death under it (Bandura, 1988).

Mutually cooperative activities, such as the public and private enterprises discussed earlier, serve to humanize the peoples of other nations through familiarity. What's more, they offer the potential for forming active bonds of friendship and/or respect around shared activities, shared profits, or shared altruism (e.g., in the assisting of Third World countries, or in the resolution of international pollution problems). Additional factors promoting greater familiarity and interconnectedness, with a concomitant increase in "humanization," include the increased availability of audiovisual and computer-based communication world-wide, and the increased ease and speed of international travel.

A sociohistorial factor likely to favor rapprochement over armed conflict between the United States and other nations is the attitudinal watershed occurring in the late 1960s. Prior to the Vietnam war, young people in the United States were more enthusiastic generally about military confrontation than those over 40 years of age. Subsequent to the Vietnam era the situation has reversed, and those youths in the late '60s and early '70s who are now assuming power as they come into middle age, tend to be less warlike than their elders (Jeffries, 1974).

Finally and most promisingly, the actual changes occurring in the Soviet Union and education of the American people about them have moved individuals downward on our grid-map, away from "enemizing" the Soviets, demonstrating the speed with which such enmity can be eradicated. Trust can be based on belief that the other is a trustworthy entity, but it can equally well, and perhaps more securely, be based on knowledge of the other's *situation*—for example, knowledge of how cooperation is in the other's self-interest. Even where there is deep-seated distrust of the other as a person (or nation), one may succeed in convincing people of auspicious circumstances obliging the other to be less hostile or to adhere to agreements. Education regarding the mutual benefits of ending the arms race for both superpowers would seem to have persuaded many Americans not to be excessively fearful of the Soviets. Neither side desires to end its children's futures, nor to bankrupt its human and financial resources. A most important function of *glasnost*, openness, is the new candor under Gorbachev about the Soviet Union's economic weaknesses. It lends great credibility to the idea that the Soviet Union wants to turn its attention from political and military expansionism to matters of internal economy.

Education about other aspects of the new Soviet shifts under Gorbachev can be reassuring to Americans as well. Though still limited and crude, there are increasing degrees of private enterprise in a number of areas. Though rife with dictatorial habits and clouded with suspicion, there is increasing use of democratic election processes at all levels of government. There are increasing degrees of freedom of the press and of speech.

Mindset Not the Biggest Problem

The wrong mindset is not the biggest obstacle to movement along our path toward survival. Although education about the nuclear threat and about other nations can shift more people to favorable mindsets, there is already a majority in favor of our endorsed approach. Just looking at the Public Agenda Foundation's 1984 data, the enemy-fearing pragmatists (31%) and anti-nuclearists (21%) together make up a majority, without even adding that subsegment of the Public Agenda's communist-and-nuclear-threat-maximal group whose sense of the imminence of the world's end propels them toward arms-control and disarmament.

Ample survey data indicate that current baseline attitudes among the majority of the United States population are not far off from where they need to be to favor our route toward survival. Most believe there to be "no causes worth fighting a nuclear war for" (though this is subject to reversal on surveys by posing loss of all freedoms, etc., as the alternative). Over 75% of U.S. citizens favor a mutual freeze on the testing, construction, and deployment of new nuclear weapons. Over 70% favor arms-control processes. And almost 100% have an appreciation of the widespread if not total destructiveness of nuclear war. Moreover, the younger the group surveyed, the more "anti-nuclear" they are. Research of Judith Van Hoorn and myself (1986) comparing high school, college, and adult populations on identical survey items, found less favoring of civil defense, more favoring of arms control, and less willingness to countenance nuclear war in the younger population. Earlier work of my own (1983) had found the highest willingness to countenance nuclear war among those in the decade of 50 to 60 years of age—a corroboration of Vincent Jeffries' (1974) researches on political generations. Such data seem to hold out the hope of even larger majorities in favor of our steps toward survival as time goes on.

So what *is* the problem? Put as simply as possible, difficulties include the following: First, these peacemaking attitudes are not so pronounced among our national decision makers. Their age (Jeffries, 1974), gender (French, 1983; Nelson & Slem, 1984; all major polls), and personality traits (Frank, 1987) all induce leaders toward what the flowchart in Chapter 4 would indicate are the wrong decisions and attitudes. Second, people have immediate countervailing concerns that keep them locked into behavior continuing the arms race (e.g., Kotz [1988] consistently found the power of self-interest to overwhelm military considerations in the B1 bomber story). Third, we—people and leaders—seem to have a capacity for double-bookkeeping. Alongside our realistic awareness of nuclear war's devastation and the mutual vulnerability of both sides, the old memories of schoolyard bullying and win-lose competition, where more muscle means more security, continue to exist. And from moment to moment, according to the stimulus, we draw from whichever memories we feel inspired to, as if the other mindset were nonexistent. Fourth, even when their concerns are focused on our endorsed path to survival, people are not easily moved from attitude to *action*.

The first point, the mismatch between the task of ending the arms race and the personality traits often found in leaders, is addressed through our advocacy of a bottom-up approach. The second point, the lubricating power of immediate rewards in perpetuating the arms race, is addressed by a number of strategies considered in the Action section below. The third point, our capacity for "doublethink," is best dealt with through heightened awareness of when and to what extent we do it—a task adroitly handled by Steven Kull in his book, *Minds at War*. It is now time to address the fourth, the inertia factor, the friction that slows progress from attitude to action. How may it be overcome? As noted before, the process of overcoming inertia divides up into separable (albeit interconnected and overlapping) steps of reckoning one's efficacy, becoming motivated, and, finally, finding opportunities for action.

Progressing along on our map of individual options in the nuclear age (Figure 1), we have now reached the point where an individual has decided upon an approach. What we are faced with from here on is a chain of causality: a series of three necessary links leading from the choice of our endorsed approach to actual survival-directed action. The first two of these links are attitudinal, the third situational. At each link there is a potential for stepping back from the process. Each link represents a fork in the road, with one path leading back to business as usual, and the other leading on to the next link. A certain percentage of those favoring participation in survival-directed action is lost at each juncture on the way. As we examine each link, we shall try to find out what determines whether an individual progresses through that link or returns to business as usual.

Crude as this current chain may be, I offer it as an initial model, open to further refinement, which can be tested "in the marketplace." It can be used as a source of hypotheses about the effects of particular interventions on people's tendency to take survival-directed action. Reference to the chain may help pinpoint ways in which survival-directed action can be made more effective.

Reckoning Efficacy

Once one's attention has been forced upon the nuclear threat, and once one has developed a sense of the national approach most likely to lead to survival, the first question likely to come to mind is, "Is it possible for me to help promote this approach?" Such questions of efficacy are generally thought of as having two parts. The first is, "Do I have the personal qualities, skills, and knowledge to be effective?" This is referred to as "instrumental efficacy." The second, called "response efficacy," is, "How effective are the proposed strategies, the political actions of which my efforts would be a part?" Efficacy on the nuclear issue, however, seems to blend aspects of both instrumental and response efficacy in a manner that renders this distinction of little import. Most people who believe in the potential responsiveness of the American political system believe they personally can make at least a slight difference, while virtually all who believe in their own ability to make a difference believe it will be mediated through effective actions within a politically responsive system. Conversely, those who despair of their own votes or actions making a difference perceive the system as nonresponsive.

Many American character traits (e.g., a "can-do" attitude) and political ideals (e.g., the importance of everyone's vote) favor a sense of individual as well as collective political efficacy. The value attached to independence and to questioning authority might be expected to foster such a sense, as would our constitutional rights to freedom of speech and assembly, supportive of our general right to protest. Indeed, the whole concept of a government of the people, by the people, and for the people would seem an inherent antidote to the sort of learned helplessness expectable in, say, a nation ruled by despotism. Yet somehow in spite of these propitious circumstances, as Susan Fiske (1987, p. 215) reminds us, "The average person . . . has a low sense of political efficacy." To quote a U.S. college student explaining his lack of political involvement in response to a survey by Van Hoorn, LeVeck and myself (1989), "There's so many people above me that would make a decision before it would get to me that my opinion wouldn't have much influence." Attempts to reverse this in regard to the nuclear issue demand a close scrutiny of this initial fork in the road toward survival. Here is where the effective persevere, while the helpless separate from them and return home. What can be done to reduce the size of this latter group?

We shall examine, first, some general social and demographic factors associated with a greater or lesser sense of political efficacy. Having done this, we shall describe a survey we conducted of a socially and demographically homogeneous group (a group likely to have a sense of efficacy), to determine differences between individuals who felt themselves to be potentially effective in doing something about this issue and individuals who did not. Finally, we shall discuss the implications of our findings with a view to inspiring a sense of efficacy in preventing nuclear war.

Efficacy: General Truths

What can be said in general about the sense of political efficacy required to take survival-directed action in the nuclear age? For one thing, it does not tend to exist in isolation. It is to be found more often than not in individuals with a strong sense of political effectiveness and a history of prior political activity on other fronts (Tyler & McGraw, 1983; Fiske, Pratto, & Pavelchak, 1983; Fiske, 1987). Secondly, it makes no distinctions regarding gender, being distributed equally among males and females (French, 1986). Thirdly, belief in one's capacity to contribute to the prevention of nuclear war is more prevalent in the young and decreases with age. Van Hoorn and I (1986) found 60% of high school age subjects, 56% of college age subjects, and 47% of adults (over 22 years of age) in a 1983 survey of 1,239 Northern Californians to concur with an item indicating that they, personally, could contribute toward the prevention of nuclear war.

A final general correlate of a sense of personal efficacy on this issue was dramatically highlighted in a finding from the survey just referred to. Among the eight schools we surveyed, the extremes of response to the item on personal efficacy ("You, yourself, could do something that might aid in the prevention of nuclear war") came from two high schools in the same city. The major distinction between the school with 74% of those surveyed responding "True" and the school with 38% responding "True" was that the families of the students were from "opposite sides of the track." The students at both schools saw eye-to-eye on virtually every other opinion item on the survey, including concurring (approximately 90%) on the general issue of nuclear war being preventable. But when it came to their personal ability to contribute toward that prevention, the children of factory workers and welfare families indicated a drastically lower estimate of their effectiveness than did the sons and daughters of predominantly business and professional families (French & Van Hoorn, 1986). This exemplifies the general finding in social psychology of greater "field dependence" (less tendency to function from an "internal locus of control") among less advantaged people. It may also relate to the studies of Seligman (1975) on "learned helplessness" (wherein rats, conditioned to expect frustration, give up trying to escape, even when circumstances permit it). And it doubtless relates to the findings of a poll conducted by Doyle Graf Mabley and the Roper Organization that "high-income [over $100,000 per year] people were five times as likely to participate in political activities than were average Americans" (UPI, 1987).

Socioeconomic class differences correlate with different levels of political activity for reasons relating to motivation, of course, as well as efficacy. But the contrast in the surveys of the two San Joaquin Valley high schools noted above speaks purely to class differences in perceived efficacy. This finding seems to indicate that the more numerous the "middle class," the more "franchised" individuals—or politically active in matters beyond their immediate concern—our society will have (even the homeless can organize to protest for something as pressing as shelter).

Efficacy: Individual Determinants

Significant economic improvement for America's poorest people, should we be wise and fortunate enough to bring it about, will be some time in coming. We cannot wait for such a major class shift, but must continue to work on the prevention of nuclear war and addressing our most pressing social and ecological needs through the reduction of nuclear arms. Public engagement of an immediate sort, to whatever extent possible, seems called for. With this in mind, I reexamined survey data collected from a fairly homogeneous group of same-aged, for the most part "advantaged," individuals (Stanford University undergraduates), individuals who might be expected to have a higher sense of self-efficacy than disadvantaged people, or even than the American general public. I wanted to find out what distinguished *within such a group* those who felt they could do something that might contribute toward the prevention of nuclear war from those who felt they couldn't (French, 1986). I hoped to learn something that might be used to increase the numbers of those who felt they possessed the necessary efficacy. If this number could be increased, the number of individuals who might actually try to act might logically be expected to increase proportionately.

The Stanford students (n = 132; 73 females, 59 males; mean age = 21.0) were separated according to their self-evaluations of being capable (n = 89) or incapable (n = 43) of contributing toward the prevention of nuclear war. Their responses to both knowledge and opinion items on the second edition of the Nuclear War Attitude Survey (NWAS II) were compared. Twice as many students felt "capable" as felt "incapable," and no significant differences in gender were found. No significant differences between the two groups were found in beliefs about the existence of causes justifying nuclear war, the likelihood of nuclear war's occurrence, the limitability of nuclear war, or the value of arms-control efforts. A significant difference (p < .05) was found in scores on the factual knowledge portion of the survey with the "capables" scoring significantly higher than the "incapables." The "capables" also reported thinking about nuclear war more frequently than did the "incapables" (p = .014).

Two other significant differences noted seem at the same time both trivial in their predictability and critical in their implications. It came as no surprise to find a significantly higher percentage of the personally "capables" than of the "incapables" believe nuclear war to be preventable (98% vs. 76%; p < .001). Nor was it surprising to find that a higher proportion of the "capables" (57%) than of the "incapables" (23%) had informed or intended to inform elected officials of their concerns about nuclear war (p < .001). This would seem to represent the "self-fulfilling prophecy" effect. Both the obviousness and the great importance of this is captured in the quip that "those who are convinced they can do something to contribute to the prevention of nuclear war and those that are convinced they are helpless to do so are both correct."

Efficacy and Knowledge

What are we to make of the main findings here—that those who feel capable are distinguished by greater knowledge about our nuclear situation, by greater belief in the preventability of nuclear war, and by greater inclination to take steps to prevent nuclear war? Is this all circularly tautological, or does it contain a meaningful message? M. G. Locatelli and R. R. Holt (1986) studied the differences

between active and inactive "doves," (persons opposed to military actions in set-
tling disputes) using a questionnaire that included an Antinuclear Activism Scale, a
Political Efficacy Scale, and a Powerlessness Scale. Their conclusions point to a
possible meaning of our findings. "Activists," they concluded, "probably scored
lower on powerlessness because they have more information: they know more
answers to the common question 'But what can *I* do about the threat of nuclear
war?' " The greater knowledge of antinuclear activists may give them a perspective from which it's easier to see specific and effective steps that could be taken.
This, in turn, could give them a greater personal sense of efficacy. Perhaps the
most critical feature of the "capables" is one, noted by Locatelli and Holt, that my
survey failed to capture: *they have a perspective on the overall problem which
helps them break it down into manageable tasks.* "[N]onactivists do not have as
sharply differentiated a cognitive means-end structure as activists; between where
they stand feeling helpless and the distant goal of a world safe from war is a vast
but vague territory. For the activist, however, that terrain is filled with concrete,
'do-able' chores. . . . " (Locatelli & Holt, 1986, pp. 158–59). Perhaps even
people who are not usually politically active might feel capable of doing something, if they could just be given a sense of *what* to do that might be effective. This
could account for the widespread success of the nuclear freeze movement in 1983–
84, in which issues were kept simple and the action required was a single vote.

Rogers and Mewborn (1986) conducted studies to find out what worked best to
get people to take steps to protect their own health. Using a combination of films
and written material, they gave different subjects educational presentations on the
dangers of cigarette smoking, unsafe diving, and venereal disease. By varying the
content of the films and written material, the researchers set up different situations
allowing them to compare the effects of the health threat's noxiousness, its probability of occurrence, and the efficacy of the recommended coping responses. They
wanted to see which was the most important factor in increasing people's intentions to comply with recommended threat-averting practices. In all three of the
health-threat areas they looked at, they found the perceived effectiveness of the
action that was being advocated was the most critical factor. How effective the
threat-averting action seemed was more important than how dire or how likely the
threat appeared.

Putting these findings together with the conclusions of Locatelli and Holt, it
would seem that knowing something to do and believing in its effectiveness may be
more important than having a general sense of personal efficacy in determining
whether one acts to prevent non-immediate threats. In other words, to apply this to
the nuclear threat situation, a major distinction between those who believe they can
be effective in averting nuclear holocaust and those who don't may be whether
they know of a *way* to be effective.

Enhancing Efficacy

One approach to enhancing people's sense of their own ability to avert nuclear
holocaust would be to analyze the causes of any feelings of inefficacy. Within a
given group or individual, is the sense of inefficacy attributable to the lack of a
plan? To the lack of group support? To the lack of a skill? To a lack of education?
To a sense of the overall situation being hopeless? To a belief in the unresponsive-
ness of the government? For those who feel themselves helpless through lack of a
plan, imparting a sense of efficacy would involve providing them with such a plan.

For those needing group support, a sense of efficacy might come about through joining one of the hundreds of groups working on these issues from a variety of angles (see below). For those who feel stymied by a lack of skill or knowledge, either the provision of such skill or knowledge, or the convincing of them that such skill or knowledge is unnecessary, would seem a route toward efficacy. (My favorite comment on this latter point was made by former National Security Agency Director Admiral Noel Gayler. He said, speaking to would-be activists paralyzed by self-perceived lack of expertise, "You don't have to know much about the thermodynamics of gasoline engines to get out of the way of a car that's bearing down on you. And that's the situation we're in" [Gayler, 1983, p. 60].) For those believing the government unresponsive, an historical review of such analogous situations as the fight for women's rights or the abolition of slavery could alter attitudes.

But short of such further analysis (and tending to render it unnecessary), there is a more direct approach. One can simply *model* effectiveness. Just as psychologists have found that "learned helplessness" can be learned vicariously by watching others act helplessly in situations, so a belief in efficacy can be inculcated by hearing of or witnessing the effectiveness of others. By witnessing or hearing about other common men and women (and children) who have taken actions toward the prevention of nuclear war, and then seeing these actions have palpable results, people can be given a sense of efficacy no matter what may have stymied them up to that point. They can also get ideas about what to do.

In the early 1980s, when I, like many other physicians, went on a self-created speaking circuit to educate people about the medical consequences of nuclear war, I never hesitated to share with audiences the evidence that my own prior efforts had been effective. I let them know that, aside from my particular medical angle, I was self-educated on our nuclear situation and that they could be too. I shared with them the data I had collected from surveys on the efficacy of the presentations I had made. I let them know the talks had been followed by significant increases in people's belief that they could do something to help prevent nuclear war, as well as by a significant decrease in their willingness to countenance the fighting of a nuclear war.

To serve as a model for them and to teach them about a particular approach, I described and commended to them the process I had used to gain access to congressmen, senatorial aides, major news editors, top scientists, and TV and radio shows—a process I had come to call "leveraging your citizenship." This consisted of finding high-profile physical or political scientists, retired military persons, or other relevant "experts" whose views on nuclear weapons lay along the survival-directed pathway. I would then call them up, asking if they would care to meet with such-and-such a congressman or editor to express their views. If they said yes, as they invariably did (the main constraint being when they might have time), I would then call the representative or editor in question and inquire as to his or her interest in meeting with eminent scientist or admiral or general so-and-so. Again, they would invariably express willingness, but tell me their time constraints. I would then become a time broker until a time could be agreed upon to meet. At that point I would revert to the role of representative of a group of concerned citizens (in my case, Physicians for Social Responsibility), and join in the meeting I had set up.

Through such means, as well as by public speaking, I was able to contribute in a pivotal way to several events. They included (1) two major Sunday editorials in a leading Northern California newspaper (*San Francisco Chronicle*, October 18, 1981, December 18, 1983); (2) the conversion of one congressperson from mild opposition to active support of a nuclear freeze, and of another from strong opposition to leadership of the congressional movement for it; (3) the personal delivery, by the latter congressperson to then-President Reagan, of a petition for an end to the arms race signed by 2,500 local high school students; (4) the founding and/or conversion of three organizations now devoted to the prevention of nuclear war (the Stanford/Mid-Peninsula Chapter of Physicians for Social Responsibility, Beyond War, and Computer Professionals for Social Responsibility); and (5) the people of Palo Alto successfully demanding (against initial 7 to 1 opposition) that their city council take a stand in support of a nuclear freeze. In a ripple effect, the city-council meeting just mentioned happened to get filmed by a local citizen, who made it into a documentary movie (*Peace is a Local Issue*, McFadden, 1987), which in turn won various film awards and was ultimately shown in the houses of Congress.

Others have similar stories of this positive kind of chain reaction, such as the success of a college professor in focusing the concerns of one of his students on the issue of the arms race. The student happened to be the son of a famous American political figure, and in turn convinced his father to become concerned, and finally to speak out and become a national public lecturer on the topic, expressing views divergent from those promulgated while he had been directly active in government.

The number of ways to be effective is limited only by one's imagination. But an essential element in getting started is becoming convinced that one *can* be effective. This conviction, in turn, is acquired through learning about some particular way to be effective and carrying it out. Whether or not people acquire such knowledge is partly a matter of whether or not it is thrust upon them by others, but it is also, quite importantly, a matter of *motivation*. Indeed, to the extent this is true, it could logically be argued that "motivation" should precede "efficacy" in our causal chain. Instead, we have chosen to place it next. We did so for two reasons. The first was our need to place it *somewhere* in the inertia-ridden path from the endorsement of an approach to action. The second was a gut-level sense that in doing anything, one's ability seems a more basic and proximal issue than one's desire.

Becoming Motivated

Let us assume that an individual has acquired a sense of efficacy, through whatever was necessary in the way of favorable socioeconomic circumstances, personal experience, knowledge of an approach, or the example of others. For that person to act, he or she must be motivated.

There appears to be a single, principal force, combined with a number of contributing forces, at work in motivating people to end the nuclear arms race. The major force, which has been referred to as "a chronic personal salience of the nuclear issue" (Fiske, 1987, p. 213), may be experienced as a sense of moral obligation, as a logical cognitive conclusion, or both. It involves belief in a citizen's obligation to prevent nuclear war, with the obligating necessity being perceived alternately as a moral or as a material imperative. What might be referred to as "contributing motivating forces" include such emotionally positive affects as love, hope, affiliation and enjoyment, such negative affects as fear and anger, and such emotionally neutral forces as a strain toward consistency and a tendency to emulate others.

Chronic Personal Salience: The Main Motivating Force

A number of authors speak of this principal force as a sense of "moral obligation." Tyler and McGraw (1983, p. 37) found a "moral responsibility to try to prevent war" more strongly related to prevention behaviors than belief in nuclear war's likelihood, or belief that citizens have the power to prevent nuclear war. Indeed, they felt the strength of this force so great as to explain their finding that "activist behavior is unrelated to judgments about whether past political behavior has been effective." (In contrast to the study of Rogers and Mewborn, which found perhaps preventing nuclear war differs perceived efficacy of approach to be the main determinant in people taking preventive actions in health matters, in having a moral dimension that swamps issues of efficacy?) At the heart of the sense of obligation Tyler and McGraw noted in those acting to prevent nuclear war, was an attribution of current causality to government and future causality to citizens. This attribution pattern is similar to Jesse Jackson's statement "You are not responsible for being down, but you are responsible for getting up" (Brickman et al., 1982). Such an attribution pattern is "the best predictor of prevention behavior," and differs from the pattern of survivalists, who attribute the threat of nuclear war neither to state nor citizen, but to "a complex series of historical forces" (Tyler & McGraw, 1983, p. 37).

Locatelli and Holt allude to resonance with "deeply held values" in explaining activists' impetus towards nuclear war-preventing actions. Mehr and Webster (1985), in surveying anti-nuclearist leaders in Northern California, found "basic value systems" ("religious, ethical, moral, spiritual, or philosophical") to be among the six main factors that had moved their subjects to activism. The Catholic Church in particular, along with various other religions, has taken a strong moral stand against the nuclear arms race and long-term dependence on deterrence. Religiously based motivation has been important for many. Some have experienced it through witnessing or hearing about the individual actions and statements of such figures as the Reverends William Sloan Coffin and Theodore M. Hesburgh, Archbishop Quinn, Bishop Matthiesen, Father Drinan or the brothers Berrigan. Others have experienced it as a general and official position of their church, through such agencies as the pastoral letter on "The Challenge of Peace" drafted by the Catholic bishops' committee headed by Rev. J. Bryan Hehir and adopted by the National Conference of Catholic Bishops on War and Peace.

A number of the physicists involved in the development of nuclear weapons have expressed awareness of a moral dimension to the issue. The (ignored) report of the General Advisory Committee of the Atomic Energy Commission to President Truman recommended that the President not pursue the development of thermonuclear weapons because of their capacity for limitless destruction. In it, Enrico Fermi and I. I. Rabi asserted the hydrogen bomb to be "necessarily an evil thing considered in any light." Physicist Sidney Drell echoes this, asking "What right has man to cause—or even threaten—such a devastating insult to the earth, the ecosphere, the very condition of human existence? If modern civilization is to improve its chances for avoiding nuclear holocaust in the long run, I believe it is absolutely necessary to return the nuclear debate to such fundamental issues" (1983, p. 11).

Action to prevent nuclear war is viewed as moral and embraced by religions because of its altruistic nature: it can be seen as involving individual efforts intended to result in the saving of other people's lives. Perceived as altruism, it is even seen by some as a sign of mental health. Roger Walsh (1984, p. 78) asserts "[c]onsiderable research indicates that psychologically healthy people tend to be particularly concerned for the welfare of others." To the extent this is true, action for prevention could be based on emotional economics—those with their own needs met are the ones in a position to reach out to others—or in psychoanalyst Erik Erikson's terms of reflecting a mature, "generative" stage of ego development, beyond the more narcissistic adolescent phase suitable to guaranteeing one's personal survival into reproductive years. To the extent this is true, regardless of its explanation, the prevention of nuclear war would require the strengthening of the nuclear family or other child-raising unit as a supportive, emotional health-fostering environment. Should a parent ask what single thing he or she could do to guarantee the happiness of his or her child, many counselors would respond "love your spouse." That same prescription could be essential to raising a child who will be concerned enough about others to contribute to the prevention of nuclear war. This seems particularly likely if an emotionally fulfilling home life is combined with setting an example of service.

Fortunately for our chances of survival, however, the prevention of nuclear war is not limited to being a pursuit of the virtuous, or even of those from happy homes. Human beings are capable of, and indeed cannot help, thinking beyond the moment they happen to be in. They also are, necessarily, social creatures. Thus one might think of it as sociobiologically determined, rather than morally inspired, that survival is not just a matter of each individual struggling to save and enhance his or her personal life in an immediate sense. Unless you make it for a few more years beyond today, unless your kids make it, unless your family makes it, unless your co-religionists make it, unless your city, state, or nation makes, it, unless the human race makes it, personal survival is not terribly meaningful.

When I was giving frequent lectures on the medical consequences of nuclear war, people would come up to me and say, in effect, "You're doing such a wonderful thing. God bless you. How altruistic you are! How remarkable that you are taking time off from making money to devote yourself to such a worthy cause!" To me such comments sounded inappropriate. They did not fit my sense of what I was doing. I felt myself to be acting no less selfishly than at any moment of straining for a dollar's pay to feed my stomach, or that of my child or wife. Preventing nuclear war differs from preventing starvation through work by being somewhat less immediate a need; but in any broader perspective, that is a trivial distinction. Would you go up to a man who was turning a hose on his burning house, attempting to put out the flames threatening to consume it, and say "Oh, how noble! Look at you, devoting such energy to putting out that little fire at the corner of your house instead of eating supper over there with the others. How altruistic!" To me this view made no sense, and still doesn't.

I can't help it if others are eating supper and don't seem to notice or care about the flames. I see them, and they still have to be put out. Since I can't do it by myself, the first thing to do is to get a few more people working on it. Giving talks accomplishes that. Spending time thinking about the problem and contributing to this book accomplishes that. It is not time wasted, but neither is it time spent "altruistically." It is simply a *necessary* expenditure of time, just as, until that day when my family's situation is secure enough to guarantee fiscal survival no matter what happens, paying a premium on a life-insurance policy is a necessary expenditure of money. Certainly, other people "live in the house" too. But that's not the principal reason I'm trying to avert its burning up. My child, my wife, and I live in the house. That's my most powerful motivation. Narcissism in most situations stands in opposition to altruism. In the case of the prevention of nuclear war, however, as it necessarily involves forestalling harm to oneself and others alike, these two powerful motivators of human behavior converge into one force.

Regardless of the size of the circle of our concern, how does nuclear war achieve such chronic saliency for myself and others? I have examined this question through my own and others' research, but might have reached the same conclusion via the short-cut of introspective self-examination. Nuclear war achieves salience through a keen awareness of what will happen if we don't act. As *Los Angeles Times* reporter and author Robert Scheer (1984, p. 4) writes, "There are forces working in this society for bigger military budgets and for reliance on the military as opposed to diplomatic efforts. They put tremendous pressure on politicians. Unless those politicians hear other views from their constituents they're not going to do anything." The result of politicians "doing nothing" is an ongoing arms race and an ongoing eventual likelihood of nuclear war. These are the principal flames we see licking the sides of our homes, and their dimensions have been sketched in the previous chapter.

The prospect of actual nuclear war is not the only threat to our "house." Other flames rise up to destroy it in the form of perpetuation and augmentation of unacceptable current costs. Health costs range from lung cancer in radon-exposed Navaho Indians mining uranium, to leaks and intentional ventings at plutonium and tritium plants (with resultant irradiation of workers and neighboring populations). Such plants, as well as high-level nuclear waste storage facilities, stand at risk of major mishap through explosions or earthquakes. At the Savannah River Plant, plutonium has contaminated water supplies in just two decades; the Department of Energy had predicted it would take "millions of years" (Alverez, Blackwelder, & Makhijani, 1988). Psychological health costs doubtless exist as well, and attempts to detail them will be cited below.

Economic costs of both a direct and indirect nature, ultimately threatening our standard of living, are also a major consideration supporting a sense of chronic saliency to the nuclear issue. While only 6 to 7% of the U.S. gross national product goes toward the military (as opposed to 1% in Japan), a significant portion of the defense budget—more than 20%—goes to nuclear research, development, and deployment. Seventy-five percent of all federal research and development funds go into military projects, with work in military areas now involving about one third of America's scientists and engineers (Closson, 1988; Melman, 1988). While it used to be arguable that scientific and technological spinoffs were so enriching as to almost by themselves justify the expenditures involved, the military products being engineered now are so finely turned to the military environment as to be neither in themselves nor in their technology potentially of much use in our daily lives. Instead, the scores of billions of dollars expended annually on nuclear systems seems a one-way economic drain on the civilian population. During the first years of the Reagan administration, while military spending skyrocketed, poverty among U.S. children rose 37%, according to the House Select Committee on Children (Coffin, 1987c). And surely it is not an unrelated fact that a black infant born within 5 miles of the White House is more likely to die in the first year of life than an infant born in Trinidad or Costa Rica (Coffin, 1987c), or that most of the public school buildings in New York City are in drastic need of repair (Melman, 1988).

Awareness of such costs, together with a perception of unacceptable threat to oneself, one's family, or others, combine to produce the principal motivating force behind action to prevent nuclear war: a sense of the task as obligatory. The obligation may be perceived as moral or practical, the saving of one's species or of one's own home. Unremitting efforts at educating people to its threat and costs are thus a critical element in creating motivation to end the nuclear arms race and to help to prevent nuclear war.

It can help *sustain* motivation for people to learn about the various psychological pitfalls tending to undermine it. These include what psychologist Albert Bandura (1988) terms "mechanisms of moral disengagement"—namely, (1) reconstruing detrimental conduct as serving moral purposes; (2) obscuring personal agency in detrimental activities; (3) disregarding or misrepresenting the injurious consequences of one's actions; and (4) blaming and dehumanizing the potential victims. Motivation to end the arms race can be undermined as well by the tendency for individuals to abdicate responsibility when in groups, the tendency to relinquish moral responsibility in the face of "authority" (as in the Milgram experiments), the tendencies toward stereotyped "enemy imaging," "attribution error," and loss of complexity to our thinking when under stress, and finally, the tendency for motivation to evaporate at the first sign of positive movement. (Those who have been so heartened by the INF accord as to lessen their concern over the nuclear weapons issue need to be made aware that more warheads have been constructed during its period of negotiation than the accord retired. On this score, and because it does not involve warhead destruction, for all its accomplishments some cynics have referred to the INF accord as simply a plan to "recycle plutonium," with a move away from land-basing because it "irritated the natives." Others have pointed out how "[t]he INF deal just happens to leave in place the precise Soviet conventional and tactical nuclear forces needed to justify a whole range of Pentagon procurement programs now underway. . . . There isn't a single big-ticket program that is killed outright" [Evans, 1987].).

Education about these human tendencies can help maintain an ongoing sense of moral obligation, freeing it when it gets caught in seductive eddies of contentment or backwaters of disengagement.

Contributing Motivational Forces

In addition to the main motivating force of 'chronic personal salience,' there are a number of contributing psychological forces, each with a positive, negative, or neutral emotional cast. They are in truth intermixed with the sense of "chronic saliency," but will be separately considered here for purposes of clarity.

Negatively charged forces. The powerful emotions of fear and anger can both be strong motivating forces pulling for action to end the threat of nuclear war. Helen Caldicott was masterful at arousing and modeling a potent mix of these feelings in her appeals across America in the early 1980s. The physicians' movement, with its notion of "medical consequences," provided a hard surface upon which to spread out our previously inchoate fears and examine them. And as we saw these consequences spelled out in detail and imagined them occurring to ourselves and to those we love, anger rose up. With it came determination to act. The tight connection of these forces is illustrated by the findings of Fiske, Pratto, and Pavelchak (1983). Antinuclear activists, they discovered, are distinguished by possessing highly concrete imagery of nuclear destruction. They found "[p]eople are most likely to act if they imagine the city they live in being destroyed, or imagine the charred bodies of real people, or imagine their own attempts to survive" (1983, p. 61). And although Sandman and Valenti (1986) have argued that the time for fear appeals is past, the fact is that a new generation of high school students comes along every four years as much in need of education on these matters as the first group, which was coming along at the time of Caldicott's speaking tours.

• *Fear.* It is true, as Sandman and Valenti (1986) point out, that if fear is aroused without presenting a means of reducing the threat, no action will result. Indeed, some people may even become less accessible to information on the topic in the future. Scores of studies on effects of the TV film *The Day After* lead one to the same conclusion Granberg and Faye (1972) reached after showing the film *Hiroshima* to a community about to host a missile base. Granberg and Faye concluded that without specific recommendations as to the proper path for avoiding nuclear war, illustrations of its consequences will produce nothing but heightened anxiety. While this does make the issue more salient, and hence riper for *some* solution, a sincere but ill-informed and misguided salesman of Star Wars (then-President Reagan) could capitalize on that anxiety as readily or more so than an unorganized coalition with an unfocused recommendation and no bully pulpit.

Leventhal, Singer, and Jones (1965) conducted a study to measure the effects of fear and of specificity of recommendations on getting people to take a tetanus shot. While varying the amount of fearfulness of the presentations made no difference in the resultant amount of action, they found a significant ($p < .01$) increase in action on the part of those who were given clear, specific instructions about where to go and how to get the tetanus shot. Although the amount was not critical, it should be noted that they did find *some* quantity of fear essential in producing action. They gave clear instructions without a fear-inducing message to another group of subjects and it resulted in no action to get a shot whatsoever (Feshbach, 1986).

• *Anger.* There is thus a caveat regarding the usefulness of fear as a motivator of action to prevent nuclear war: it must be combined with a clear message regarding the type of action called for. A caveat is also necessary regarding the use of anger as a motivator towards war-preventing action: it must not be stoked up to the point of producing stereotyped images of an enemy. To do so distorts perception of the reality that must be appropriately contended with, just as exaggerated enemy imaging does in fueling the arms race itself.

If such extremism can be avoided, however, anger is undeniably a powerful motivator of human action and should not be ignored in efforts to prevent nuclear war. As Sandman and Valenti (1986, p. 15) stress, "[i]f the world is not all black and white, neither is it all one undifferentiated shade of gray. Honesty and mobilization both require a target for our anger." As a negative emotion, anger is perhaps a particularly strong motivator of forms of action of a negative sort, such as boycott, protest, and civil disobedience.

Practically any aspect of the nuclear arms race is capable of provoking anger—

including the entire situation. The bottom-line prospect of having one's life continually threatened by the Damoclean nuclear sword may be the starting point of anger for some. The notion of pointing nuclear tipped missiles at entire nations may be seen as a level of moral depravity without precedent.

And there is no shortage of more proximal causes for anger in the arms race. Consider the proposal of former Defense Secretary Caspar Weinberger, reported in the *Washington Post*, that "Social Security and Medicare benefits might be cut to finance growth in military outlays." Consider that this is proposed in a nation already spending 27% of its total federal budget on the military (*Washington Spectator*, 1989), a nation where the bill for military research and development each 20 months is greater than the entire amount *ever spent* by the National Institutes of Health (PSR, 1989). Does it make anyone angry to think that our society could spend $68.1 billion to build 132 Stealth bombers (with a principal mission of further preemptive attack after the first wave of a nuclear war), but cannot offer adequate prenatal care to all of its pregnant women, nor immunization against infectious diseases to all its children?

It must be a source of anger for some to think that Northrop Corporation, depending on how one views the MX missile's role, is either risking national security or simply throwing away large sums of taxpayer money, as in its rush to maintain contracts, it puts over-the-counter Radio Shack parts into the guidance systems of the largest of the U.S. nuclear weapons, and then throws away the made-to-specifications fail-safe parts when they are delivered later (ABC-TV, 1988). And surely residents near the Fernald, Ohio, and Hanford, Washington, nuclear weapons material plants have experienced some anger in learning of the Energy Department's intentional secret release of tons of radioactive uranium wastes over the years. By such concealments there, and at Savannah River and Rocky Flats—all part of the U.S. nuclear weapons production complex—"the Department of Energy has broken faith with the people of this country." It has used "deception and secrecy" in a manner that "[has] no place in the United States," where "informed consent is the cornerstone of democracy" (Pastore & Zheutlin, 1988).

Properly exposed to view, the arms race would seem to be able to provide many causes for immediate anger that could motivate action to terminate it.

Mobilization of anger at the incredibly large financial expense of the arms race has unfortunately been muted by several factors, as noted by psychologist Richard Gilbert. These factors have prevented the large and politically influential middle and upper-middle classes from feeling and perceiving the threat to their economic status posed by increasing military spending (Gilbert, 1988). The first is that when "gun" purchasing makes "butter" run short, it is the economically deprived who run out first, having less to start with and less clout to defend it. Cutting social-service programs is experienced as having little direct personal relevance to the middle class. At the same time, the larger dimensions of the social-service cuts tend to distract attention from the middle class "butter" that *is* being lopped off (e.g., cutbacks in federally funded college loan programs—Gilbert, 1988, p. 758). Even more muting in its effect on any angry response to massive "gun" purchases has been the use of deficit spending. While anger at being robbed might serve as a major incentive for social activism, the U.S. government has effectively neutralized it for the time being. It has done so by "adopting the largest line of credit in human history" (Gilbert, 1988, p. 758). In sum, although the potential is there for an economic Three Mile Island, it seems as though it will actually have to occur before sufficient economic salience will accrue to the issue to rouse the majority of Americans to a motivating anger.

Emotionally neutral forces. Certain forces motivating individuals to work to end the arms race are not based on strongly positive nor strongly negative emotions. They are based on aspects of our social behavior less charged than love or hatred. The two motivators in this category I've encountered most often, in the realms of both activism and research, have been the tendency to emulate others (the "band-wagon effect"), and the "strain to consistency" (the tendency of people to seek corroboration for actions they have already taken, and to persist in similar directions once initially moved).

* *Emulation.* Human beings are social creatures with prolonged childhoods, and much of their approach to life is acquired by modeling themselves on others. It is therefore understandable that new behaviors may be seen as "not the thing to do" until other, preferably high-profile and respected, individuals are seen doing them. In addition to reasoned argument, fear appeals, and means-ends structuring, then, potential recruits-to-action need awareness of the commitment of respected others to the sorts of actions hoped for from them. Surgeons need to hear of efforts towards ending the arms race undertaken by Oliver Cope, George Prout Jr., Claude Welch, Augustus White III, Edwin Salzman, William Silen, and others. Psychiatrists should be made aware of the words and actions of Judd Marmor, Roy Menninger, David Hamburg, Eugene Brody, Leon Eisenberg, Robert Lifton, or Jerome Frank. Medical specialists may be motivated by hearing of the anti-arms race attitudes and actions of Lewis Thomas, Robert Berliner, Franz Inglefiner, Mary Avery, Howard Hiatt, Fred Robbins, Alexander Leaf, Herb Abrams, or Paul Beeson. When Robert T. Jones devotes his Cal Tech commencement address to the need to end the arms race, he is attended to as much for his receipt of the Langley award, his Presidential Citations, and other marks of aeronautical-engineering genius, as he is for his logic and persuasive powers. Examples of prominent men and women in active pursuit of our endorsed pathway to survival should not go hidden under bushel baskets. The only caveat here is that one must simultaneously convey to those hearing about these high achievers the message that effective action may equally well be undertaken by everyday individuals.

* *The drive toward consistency.* Once an individual can be induced to partake in an action—even a small one—aimed at ending the nuclear arms race, the "strain to consistency" noted in all of us by psychologist Leon Festinger (1957) and others dictates strongly that that individual will go on to seek arguments in support of such action; further related activities will follow. Thus, as Sandman and Valenti point out, "[t]he growth of commitment is circular . . . with feelings, understandings, and behaviors alternating in complex patterns. Action is as likely as the others—in fact, *more* likely than the others—to begin the process". This is because "behavior itself triggers an effort to regain consistency by finding information and building attitudes to support that behavior" (1986, p. 20). Such a tendency renders us all susceptible to what is known in sales as "the foot-in-the-door technique": the tactic of solicitation which starts with a small request in order to gain eventual compliance with related larger requests.

The strength of this phenomenon was first noted by psychologists Jonathan Freedman and Scott Fraser (1966). They carried out an experiment in which a researcher, posing as a volunteer worker, went door to door in a residential California neighborhood making a preposterous request of homeowners. The homeowners were asked to allow a large, ugly, poorly lettered public-service billboard reading DRIVE CAREFULLY to be installed on their front lawns. While there was only 17% overall compliance, there was a remarkable 76% compliance within a certain sub-group. This group had two weeks earlier been approached by a different "volunteer" with a smaller request so trivial they had almost all complied with it: to accept and display a little 3-inch square sign that read BE A SAFE DRIVER. Their compliance with the trivial request seemed to foster later compliance with the major request. Further research indicated that the small initial request made two weeks before the big one could have related to an entirely different public-service topic and the results would have been almost as impressive. Freedman and Fraser hypothesized that the increased compliance of an individual with the big request was based on a need to act consistently with a newly formed self-image—in this case, as a public service-minded person (Cialdini, 1985). The implications of this mechanism of motivation for steering individuals along the pathway to survival-directed action will be spelled out under "Finding Opportunity" below.

• *Contributing forces of a positive emotional cast.* Emotionally positive experiences of love, hope, and enjoyment can serve as powerful motivators of action to end the arms race. While it may be hard to separate effects of love from those of anger (against threats to those one loves), to distinguish hope from a sense of efficacy, and to differentiate enjoyment in working to end the arms race from that available from other social interactions, it is nevertheless instructive to attempt to look at love, hope, and enjoyment separately and specifically as they relate to efforts at preventing nuclear war.

• *Love.* The willingness of human beings to act on behalf of others in many instances even exceeds our willingness to act on our own behalf, and this is perhaps most strongly in evidence when the others are our children. As Sandman and Valenti (1986, p. 17) put it, in regard to efforts to prevent nuclear war, "[s]omeone to fight *for* is as indispensable to activism as . . . someone to fight against." The ongoing arms race and associated threat of nuclear war constitute a direct threat to our children's lives in the future, and a threat to their physical and psychological growth and well-being now. This has been for many and will continue to be a powerful motivating force.

For myself and countless others, the most outrageous and intolerable feature of the nuclear arms race is the physical jeopardy in which it places our children. In November 1979 in Jonestown, Guyana, the Reverend Jim Jones effected the mass murder-suicide of 700 of his followers and their children. Daniel Ellsberg sees a strong analogy between Jim Jones in Guyana, training his parishioners to react passively as he rehearses them in the gestures of sacrificing their children, and the nuclear governments of this world, exacting calm acceptance of their citizens as they quietly design, build, and prepare for immediate use, thousands of nuclear weapons. He sees the Americans sitting in protest on the railroad tracks at the Rocky Flats plutonium processing plant, and the Europeans marching in protest as nuclear weapons are installed in their countries, as "saying with their presence on the road what the mothers and fathers at Jonestown waited too long to say, what they should have said when the cyanide shipments first arrived or at the first rehearsals for murder and suicide: "No! Not our children! This is craziness; we won't be a part of it" (Ellsberg, 1981, p. xx).

Barbara Wiedner, founder of Grandmothers for Peace, was asked what made her think she could mobilize grandmothers in protest against the nuclear arms race. Her response was that "Grandmothers share our fear that their grandchildren may be the last generation on Earth. That fact has activated us to become peace activists and to encourage others—especially grandmothers—to do the same" (Coffin 1987e, p. 2). Love for her grandchildren certainly served to motivate Wiedner herself, for she has been arrested numerous times in acts of civil disobedience (her first being a 1981 "protest of the presence of 150 nuclear weapons at Mather Air Force Base," 15 miles from her home). Her actions are evidently appreciated in the spirit in which she intends them by her family: her 5-year-old grandson, Edward, saw the Mather action on TV and explained to his friends, "Grandma loves us so much that she went to jail to save us from the bomb" (Coffin 1987e, p. 2).

For some, awareness of possible, current, ongoing damage to children from the nuclear arms race may be a more effective motivator than anticipation of the effects upon them of a future nuclear holocaust. Both physiological damage from inadequate resource allocation and psychological damage from "growing up in the nuclear shadow" seem legitimate areas of concern.

While there is no guarantee that the scores of billions of dollars of U.S. taxpayers' money going annually to feed the nuclear arms race (around $70 billion annually at this point) would be redirected in the event of cutbacks to meet the needs of children, it is hard to think of more pressing uses for it. Decent, affordable housing is essential to stable, happy families, but is in short supply. The National Education Association reports that 2.5 million people are displaced from their homes every year because of "spiraling rents, revitalization projects, and economic development plans. Yet since 1980, federal housing programs have been cut more than 75%. There are more homeless people in the United States today than at any time since the Great Depression—and 700,000 of them are children" (*Washington Spectator*, 1988a, p. 3). Beyond the basic issue of housing, children's education is not what it could or should be in the United States. Senator Claiborne Pell (D-RI) has expressed concern over the "woefully inadequate" school resources in urban areas (ibid, p. 2). And in a less urban territory, it has been noted that one of every three students starting high school in Texas will not finish, with most of the dropouts coming from homes beset by poverty (*Washington Spectator*, 1988a, p. 3).

Of the most immediate concern to those moved by the plight of children may be the fact that somewhere on earth every two seconds a child dies of malnutrition or another equally preventable cause. Instead of spending the approximately $100 per year necessary to forestall this death, the governments of the world spend the equivalent of over $60,000 per dying child on arms (Physicians for Social Responsibility, 1989). Lest one imagine preventable childhood deaths to be strictly a Third World problem, one should be aware than in a comparison of infant deaths among 20 industrialized nations, the United States suffers the most deaths annually, according to the Children's Defense Fund (Coffin, 1988b).

Are there direct, current, harmful effects of the nuclear arms race on children, in addition to the indirect ones attributable to the diversion of resources? A number of experts are convinced there are (see chapter by Judith Van Hoorn & Paula LeVeck in previous companion volume, *Horrendous Death, Health, and Well-Being*). Perhaps the "hardest" evidence bearing on this, the evidence least open to criticism on the basis of biased sampling procedures, has been the massive data collected by Bachman and others in the Monitoring the Future project. In this study, approximately 18,000 high school seniors have been surveyed annually since 1975. Bachman et al. found the proportion of seniors who stated that they "worried often" about the threat of nuclear war rose from 7.6% in 1975 to over 30% in 1982, and had remained at about the same level over subsequent years (Diamond & Bachman, 1986). Psychiatrists William Beardsley and John Mack (1982) assessed the impact of nuclear advances on hundreds of U.S. children across the nation. They found some 50% of the children surveyed were aware of nuclear developments prior to age 12, and over 50% of the children surveyed indicated the shadow of nuclear developments affected their thoughts about marriage and their plans for the future. Beardsley and Mack believe the perception of an unstable future and possible attendant cynicism toward adults could be having a deleterious impact on our children's personality structures, disrupting "impulse management and the building of an 'ego ideal' and enduring values." The development of an ego ideal, that is, a sense of goals and standards worth pursuing, "depends on a stable current environment and a future that is somewhat reliable." In a world perceived as threatened by nuclear war through the folly of adults, "planning seems pointless and ordinary values and ideals appear naive." Instead, Beardsley and Mack assert, impulsivity, a "get it now" value system, drug use, and cults (with an emphasis on afterlife and the extinction of individuality), seem natural developments (Herrington, 1982).

It is inarguably difficult to separate out the impact of anxiety over nuclear war from other factors impinging on today's youth. A host of social, economic, and technological changes have occurred during the same decades as the evolving nuclear arms race. The fact that around 40% of the children in the United States now live in single-parent homes at some point prior to age 18 (Westin, 1988) is doubtless more immediately related to emotional stress in American youth than is the shadow of nuclear war. Nonetheless, it seems likely that when children are exposed to nuclear fears via various media, yet get little or no systematic education or open discussion regarding this immensely important, life-threatening issue at home or at school, it may well contribute to increased anxiety in growing up.

In concluding this brief consideration of the love of children as a motivator of positive actions in issues of life and death, war and peace, I would like to mention two examples of evidence that it works in this regard.

The first is an instance where love of children bore directly on the issue of war versus peace. According to C. R. Rogers, one of the facilitators of President Carter's rapprochement between Begin of Israel and Sadat of Egypt, the incident which turned the Camp David meetings from complete failure into significant success "was a highly personal one." By the thirteenth and last day, Begin had decided he would not sign anything and that the conference was a failure. Photographs had been taken of the three leaders together. Sadat had signed them, and Carter was about to do so as well, with Begin having requested some for his three grandchildren. Carter's secretary, Susan Clough, suggested that he personalize the photographs by addressing them with the children's names when he signed them. Carter did this, and took them to Begin. When he [Begin] saw the names "he became very emotional, and spoke with tears in his eyes about them. An hour later he phoned to accept the new draft of the agreement on Jerusalem" (Thompson, 1985, pp. 99–100).

Rogers commented on how strange it might seem that the outcome of a highly significant international conference "was based on a tearful discussion of grandchildren, rather than the issues of the conference. Yet to us who have experienced intensive groups this seems quite natural. It is when the deepest personal feelings are touched that change takes place in the individual's attitude" (Thompson, 1985, pp. 99–100). Rogers' point, about the power of descent to the personal level, is a valid one. But I would venture to suggest that Rogers, with his focus on the application of techniques of group interactions to diplomacy (and Thompson, who cites him only in this regard) is overlooking the obvious here. There is nothing arbitrary about the nature of the stimulus of Begin's "personal feelings." It was specifically reflection on his grandchildren that lent the necessary perspective and emotional kick to move Begin from a position of nationalistic obstinacy to a broader concern.

The other example of the power of love of children as a motivator in matters of life and death comes from my own experience in dealing with self-destructive patients. As a psychiatrist I am frequently confronted with the need to help depressed individuals find reasons to live that they can be tied to, like life preservers, to get them through the turbulence of their acutely suicidal periods. Time after time, the only thing I can come up with that sparks the slightest will to stay surfaced on their ocean of despair is the thought of how their suicide would affect their children. I lever my self-destructive patients with this unmercifully, detailing what 20 years of psychiatric experience has taught me of the manifold malevolent effects of parental suicide upon offspring. I do this because I know that if by any means they can get through this particularly dangerous period, there is a good chance their thinking will evolve to a point where violent, self-destructive ideas no longer make sense to them. I do this also because I know (better than they, in their distracted thinking and without my experience) what the awful effects of their suicide will actually *be* on their children. I feel an obligation to both them and their children to raise their level of consciousness of these consequences.

The patients I treat are quite seriously disturbed individuals. Their children are sometimes the only human beings for whom they are capable of feeling love. Their own parenting in many cases has left a great deal to be desired, and their capacity for empathy may be limited to identifying with the vulnerability of helpless and innocent children. Later, with their depressions lifted, a number of such patients have told me the only thing that had stood between them and suicide was the thought I had forced upon them of the harm that would befall their children.

Should those who would prevent the world from self-destruction be any less avid in their efforts to remind the militantly nationalistic, the anxious but passive, the short-term profiteers of both faulty and nonfaulty weaponry, that the potential victims of their behavior are all their sons and daughters? Should we be any more hesitant to use this lever of love, this powerful common denominator in a divided world, to get our species through the era of weapons of mass destruction to a point where warfare no longer makes sense?

• *Hope.* Sandman and Valenti (1986) speak of "hope" as a major force in motivating individuals to act to prevent nuclear war. They speak of a "hope cluster," involving elements from both the "Efficacy" and "Motivation" areas of our schema. It is made up of enthusiasm for proposed steps, and belief in one's own ability to help execute them. It is the antithesis of powerlessness, of helplessness. Without it, helplessness and inactivity tend to support each other in a vicious circle. "If you feel powerless to prevent nuclear war, it makes sense to try not to think about it. And if you wish to go about your business without thinking about nuclear war, it serves your needs to decide that you are powerless to prevent it" (Sandman & Valenti, 1986, p. 17). Hope is the breaker of this circle. "[H]opeful people do things, and hopeless people do not" (Sandman & Valenti, 1986, p. 19).

Reasons for hopefulness abound, but people must be constantly reminded of them if they are to effectively break the seductive "powerlessness-inactivity" cycle. Major sources of hope include the increased attention, interest, and respect gleaned by antinuclear issues and forces over the last decade, changes occurring in the Soviet Union, current and potential changes in citizens' attitudes and roles, technological and economic changes, and a number of both recent and remote historical events.

Evidence of increased interest and respect for antinuclear issues and forces include the vast media attention (most books ever written on nuclear weapons and nuclear war have been published since 1979), the increasing interest of philanthropic institutions (Carnegie Corporation, Ford Foundation, George Gund Foundation, Hewlett Foundation, Rockefeller Brothers Fund, etc. [Teltsch, 1984]), and the increased participation of respected members of society in protest against the arms race (college presidents, physicians, bishops and archbishops, etc.). An important result of all this attention has been an increased awareness of the real consequences of nuclear war. Such knowledge, in its stark reality, helps put an end to "conceptual inertia" and to its offspring, "perception theory." Nuclear war—and with it, threats of nuclear war—become no longer viable instruments of national policy, and the arms race becomes more easily recognized as a pointless pursuit. Moreover, as more people recognize this, they see others—for example, adversary nations—recognizing this as well; such knowledge serves to build confidence in moving toward peaceful resolution of conflicts.

Changes in the Soviet Union are operating in several different ways to mitigate the nuclear threat. Firstly, the Soviets have been amazingly forthcoming in the INF treaty, agreeing not only to destroy four of their missiles for every one the West destroyed, but also agreeing to on-site inspections for monitoring the destruction of the nuclear weapons' delivery systems. This represents the reversal of a pattern of governmental secrecy that greatly predates the current Communist regime, and would seem the result of a great deal of effort of Gorbachev's part.

Glasnost. The policy of openness in acknowledging difficulties, has had a side effect of providing considerable reassurance to the Western nations. Both through the drastic step of its adoption in the first place, as well as through the problems its practice has revealed, the West is coming to truly believe that Russia is more interested in attacking its own internal economic difficulties than neighboring (or distant) nations. More heartening of all are such official statements as that of October 4, 1988, by Vadim Medvedev, economist and new chief Soviet ideologist. He declared, to a group of political scientists from Eastern European nations, "Present day reality means that universal values, such as avoiding nuclear war and avoiding ecological catastrophe, must outweigh the idea of struggle between classes." To deal with these problems, his message emphasized, will require peaceful co-existence. What's more, his message went on to say, in regard to economic matters, "a socialist country must learn from . . . the capitalist West" (Bethe, 1989). Facts about the Soviet economic situation and its anti-expansionist requirements are bound to be more reassuring to Americans than attempts to persuade them of Soviet intentions or disposition. At the same time, in its effort to facilitate concentration on its internal problems, the Soviet Union has become more cooperative internationally. It has become more forthcoming and flexible in its give-and-take on arms control matters, more tolerant of emigration, more responsive to demands for release of political prisoners. The dissident physicist Sakharov was not only invited back to Moscow from exile by Gorbachev personally, but allowed to travel to and speak freely in the United States, and was appointed one of the two Soviet representatives to an organization to improve the quality of life for all the countries of the earth (Bethe, 1989). Finally, in *perestroika*, the restructuring required for economic rejuvenation, there has been increased private ownership, an opening up to foreign franchises, a democratization of elections, etc. With each of these changes the Soviet Union has become more like us, less of an alien state, and hence easier to identify with and harder to cast in a stereotyped enemy role.

Technological and economic trends of our time offer hope for international peace as well. The worldwide suffusion of telephones, computers, and the media of radio and television, combined with the potential for satellite-relayed international transmissions, has reduced the world to one "community," in the sense of being a place where a communication is capable of reaching everyone. The growth of the multinational corporation, whose headquarters may be anywhere from Amsterdam to Tokyo but whose divisions are spread across the globe, must also serve as a counterforce to the nationalistic attitudes and nationalistic property bases previously fueling wars. In the long run, the only ultimate guarantee against an outbreak of nuclear war will be a world order with effective institutions for the prevention of all wars. While such a world order remains an unachieved goal, technological and economic trends are serving to bring about a necessary psychological prerequisite of it: a sense of world community among all peoples that transcends national loyalties.

Hope lies as well in the potential for change within individuals and societies. Gallup documented the flexibility of people's "images of the other" in noting the changes in adjectives U.S. citizens used to describe the Communist Chinese over a few years time. Before President Nixon's visit to China, the Chinese were described as "sly, cruel, and treacherous." Afterwards, top adjectives used to describe them were "hard-working" and "practical" (Frank, 1982a). The shift in American attitudes toward Soviet leadership has been no less abrupt in the wake of the changes instituted by Gorbachev. Generational attitudinal changes also augur favorably for an end to the arms race. These include findings within the younger generation of Americans a decreased capacity to countenance nuclear war (Jeffries, 1974; Van Hoorn & French, 1986; Fiske, 1987).

The presence of more and more women in decision-making roles in business and government could be a promising trend—at least to the extent that the female tendency to favor affiliation over competition can be sustained in the face of the more competitive "leadership" traits, in women achieving positions of influence. There has been a slow but steady gain of seats by women in Congress over the recent decades, to the point where women now occupy 5% of the seats in the House of Representatives. In the first half of 1987 there were 15 arms-related matters coming to vote on the floor of the House of Representatives, such as SDI funding, anti-satellite weapons testing, Salt II Treaty interpretation, nuclear testing, and MX missile basing. A comparison of the voting pattern of male and female U.S. Representatives on these issues during this time reveals a "pro-arms control" voting mean of 64% for the women versus 55% for the men. While this 9% difference is not statistically significant, due to the small number of women (22 at that time), it lies in the direction supportive of our hope, and might achieve statistical significance with increasing numbers of female representatives (Report of the Professionals' Coalition for Nuclear Arms Control, 1987).

Finally, historical bases for hope may be found in both the recent and more remote past. As noted above, at least a half a dozen popular movements within the United States over the past 200 years have succeeded in abolishing intolerable policies at the national level, from slavery to women's disenfranchisement. The more recent past yields evidence of hopeful changes brought about by popular concern over the nuclear issue itself, from the congressional resolution on a nuclear freeze, to administrative pressure to achieve the dismantling of a class of nuclear weapons. Meanwhile, increasing regions of the United States (containing 16 million people as of November 1988 [*Nuclear Times*, 1989]) and of the world beyond are declaring themselves, to one degree or another, "nuclear-free zones."

All in all, there are many possible bases for hope that may be cited. Such citation, for a number of individuals, seems essential in getting them motivated to take action to end the nuclear arms race.

Enjoyment. Of all the rewards that working to end the arms race can bring, enjoyment is the most immediate. Roger Fisher, Williston Professor of Law at Harvard Law School and director of the Harvard Negotiation Project, in his pleas to enlist support in the prevention of nuclear war, speaks of "the fun and the joy we can have working together on a challenging task" (Fisher, 1981, p. 236). He sees "exhilaration . . . challenge . . . zest" in "trying to save the world." He describes an opportunity to be "involved, not just intellectually but emotionally . . . a chance to work together with affection, with caring, with feeling." He is contagiously excited about the scope of the task. He points out how "[p]eople have struggled all of their lives to clear 10 acres of ground or simply to maintain themselves and their family," and contrasts this with the awesome historical opportunity offered to us at this point in time to "improve the chance of human survival" (Fisher, 1981, p. 236).

Other authors, in the midst of scientific discourse upon aspects of our nuclear situation, are likewise moved to spontaneous comment on the joys of work in this area and the associations it brings. Acknowledging its share of "petty, narcissistic, even power-hungry people," Locatelli and Holt (1986, p. 159), for example, cite the movement to end the arms race as containing "some of the most committed and altruistic people alive: warm, humorous, and unpretentious, but profound in thought and feeling. It is a privilege to get to know such fine human beings and to work shoulder to shoulder with them." This has, indeed, been the author's experience within the physicians' groups here and abroad.

In addition to the enjoyment of associating with like-minded individuals to work on what W. H. Ferry (1981) refers to as "the supreme challenge of our time," enjoyment can arise from exercising particular endowed or acquired skills. In the "Action" section below, various points of attack on the problem will be discussed. Each one could call upon any of a gamut of human skills, areas of expertise, or knowledge. It matters not whether one is a musician (doing benefit concerts, writing inspirational lyrics, entertaining international conventions, spreading goodwill on foreign tours, etc.) or an accountant (serving as treasurer for a Sane/

FREEZE chapter, estimating realistic costs of SDI, tracking and publishing from non-classified data the actual expenditures on nuclear weapons development projects, etc.). The opportunity is there to engage one's particular talent, knowledge, or interest. The significance of the task will augment whatever usual enjoyment one derives from exercising the skill, talent, or knowledge, to a point where the action may become highly self-motivating.

What Really Happens: Reported Sources of Motivation

The sources of motivation described above were derived from reading, observing, and theorizing. What would one find if one asked people who have been active in these issues what motivated *them*? What would they report? After all, as Mark Twain once said, the best way to ascertain something is to find it out. This method is somewhat less than ideal when it depends on self-reports, but it is more likely to produce accurate and useful information than, say, theorizing.

The only study I am familiar with that attempts to do this was reported in a private publication by Helen Mehr and Marybeth Webster, entitled *Peacemaking Works* (1985). These two psychologists interviewed 204 individuals actively engaged in a variety of efforts to avert a nuclear catastrophe to find out what had moved them to become active. Six categories of "movers" emerged. In order of the frequency of their mention these were:

1. People. Chiefly authoritative speakers—scientists, physicians, converts from roles in developing nuclear weaponry, religious or other leaders—but also family members, friends, and children (discussing their fears).

2. The media. Small group showings of films or videos (e.g., Thiermann & Thiermann's *The Last Epidemic*); books (e.g., Jonathan Schell's *The Fate of the Earth*); commercial movies (e.g., *Fail Safe*); commercial TV (e.g., news, *20/20*, *The Day After*); PBS-TV (e.g., Carl Sagan's *Cosmos*); newspapers; and various other print, radio, music, and theater entities.

3. Group affiliations. Membership in groups where activism is the norm (e.g., peace groups, religious groups, "professional responsibility" groups, or large groups, as in demonstration marches, either directly witnessed or seen via the media).

4. Personal experience. Experiences with war and its victims; cross-cultural experiences.

5. World events. Hiroshima/Nagasaki, "small wars" with the United States and U.S.S.R. taking sides, Vietnam, nuclear accidents, Pentagon Papers, official talk of "winnable" nuclear war, etc.

6. Basic value systems. Having a religious or philosophical value system that promotes assumption of personal responsibility for "changing what's wrong."

It is reassuring to note that, by searching out motivating factors with this self-reporting approach, Mehr and Webster came up with pretty much the same ones we had derived. Our *emulation* category is involved in the power of authoritative speakers, family, and friends to move individuals. *Love of children* is what makes discussion of their fears a motivating force. *Fear* and *anger* are the commonest motivating responses to the various media exposures. *Enjoyment* of association with others in a meaningful task is involved in the motivating power of group affiliations. Finally, *chronic personal salience* derives from basic value systems calling for personal responsibility in matters of mass destruction. (It is no surprise that a self-reporting method of data collection would fail to include our *drive towards consistency* factor, as this is generally an unconscious force. It is nonetheless undoubtedly at work, heightening individuals' attention to relevant media, and moving them to seek out and then persevere in their group affiliations.)

What is different about Mehr and Webster's study is that it indicates the channels through which the forces we have been discussing operate. Moreover, it suggests a ranking for these channels in their order of relative impact (assuming this to correspond with their frequency of mention). "People" first—never underestimate the power of one-on-one, mouth-to-ear resuscitation for breathing the life of an idea into other people. Then media (there is hope for this book!). Then group affiliations, followed by personal experiences and world events. The channels that worked the very best in motivating the people examined in this study seem to have been personal appearances of "heroic" persons and role models, followed by facilitated, small-audience film/video shows.

It must be acknowledged that this ranking is misleading in at least one regard, however. While the individuals surveyed mentioned *world events* less than other motivating factors, the primacy of actual nuclear events as motivators for large masses of people is clear from recent history. Alarm over radioactive fallout, as well as the Cuban missile crisis, both immediately preceded the international protest leading to the Limited Test Ban Treaty of 1963. The prospect of medium-range missiles in Europe is what moved millions of Europeans to march in protest and sign petitions opposing their deployment. Finally, the accident at Three Mile Island, as well as nuclear saber-rattling rhetoric and behavior by the early Reagan administration, served as precursors to the 1982 nuclear freeze movement in the United States. It has only been at times of nuclear stress that large numbers of people have experienced the "personal salience" somehow maintained by the nuclear activists during the intervening periods.

Whether an individual is moved by a world event, a sense of love or anger, or a code of personal values, his or her further movement towards survival-directed action will depend on whether that motivation is stronger or weaker than the competing demands of his or her life. The question is, does the sum of the vectors of the forces pulling for survival-directed action on the nuclear issue outweigh those pulling for work, home, hobbies, study, and social life, at least some of the time?

How Many Need to Be Motivated?

How much motivation is necessary? Enough to activate everyone? Fortunately not. A social psychologist (Lee Ross), consulted on this matter, offered a succinct description of the necessary amount of motivation. It would need to be "enough for the active minority to become active about this issue, and for the inactive majority to become sufficiently outraged for the status quo to be no longer acceptable" (L. Ross, personal communication, July 13, 1984). This is a less daunting task than having to move everyone to the point of significant activity. As has been indicated before, the task viewed this way, in relation to our schema (Figure 1), requires moving the bulk of the people only so far as to choose one of the survival-bound mindsets and endorse its approach. With this accomplished, it is only a minority of the people who need to be moved all the way to frank activity.

Another perspective rendering the task less daunting is that of communications expert Everett Rogers. His research into the diffusion of new ideas throughout populations led him to conclude that once an innovative idea is accepted by a certain minority percentage of the total population, it can't be stopped. "Then, no matter what you do to try to slow further diffusion, the innovation goes ahead and diffuses" (Rogers, 1983). Communications experts, studying such innovations as the introduction of hybrid corn in Iowa, or of a new antibiotic among physicians, have plotted the diffusion process over time on graphs. They use the vertical axis to represent the percent of the population subscribing to the new idea, and the horizontal axis to represent elapsing time. Represented this way, the diffusion process turns out to be an S-shaped curve, with a slow take-off, a rapid upwards acceleration in the midphase, and then a slow trail-off as the most resistant of the ones who are going to convert finally do so. Although it takes some time to get up to the 20% mark, once there, the curve suddenly accelerates upwards. In other words, per the model of Rogers and his colleagues, only about 20% of the population needs to actively accept a new idea. With this achieved, a chain-reaction occurs, spreading the idea through peer networks to a point of major suffusion throughout the population.

Rogers (op. cit.) feels this diffusion model has applicability to ideas about ending the nuclear arms race, and much heart may be taken from the comparatively easier prospect of having to move only 20% rather than 100% of the American citizenry. At the same time, Rogers stresses some important differences between such an "innovation" and hybrid corn—differences rendering its dissemination a somewhat harder assignment. One difficulty in recruiting people to our pathway to survival is that the venture is *preventive* in nature. Something must be done now to avoid something happening in the future that might not happen anyway. This, Rogers says, "requires a great deal of motivation and some special kinds of humans" (op. cit. p. 231). Secondly, ours is not a technological innovation. This means (a) there's nothing as manipulable as a material product to advocate, and (b) the bandwagon won't get the boost provided by America's love of technology. Finally, our "innovation" has strong opposition from various quarters.

Despite these latter sobering considerations, a little knowledge of communications theory seems, in the balance, encouraging. Indeed, the notion of needing to convince only a minority percentage of the whole population has been used by such groups as Beyond War to encourage and sustain motivation in many who might otherwise be daunted.

Finding Opportunity

Let us recapitulate the individual's progress toward survival-directed action at this point in the path (see Figure 1). First, the person's attention is focused through some event on the nuclear threat. The person then ascribes a significant likelihood to the occurrence of a nuclear war (or other nuclear disaster), and decides that more effort toward arms control and some degree of disarmament is in order. The individual judges himself or herself capable of making a difference in regard to this, however slight, and feels strongly enough about the issue to wish to try. What happens next?

The Importance of Opportunity

For a lot of people, what happens next all depends on what opportunities are or are not at hand. A friend of mine, with an ongoing concern about the self-destructiveness of the nuclear arms race, reported that there had been a number of times when his level of alarm had been raised to the point of readiness to take action. This had occurred after seeing *The Day After*, after first becoming aware of Gorbachev's test ban and his offer to continue it if the Americans followed suit, and on several other occasions. Had there been available something quick and easy to do that he had *known* how to do, he said, he'd have done it. But each event had passed by without a clear opportunity for action, and this had resulted in no action ever being taken on his part, despite the existence of some motivation.

In a review of a book on Milgram's obedience experiments, social psychologist Lee Ross (1988) suggested Milgram had overlooked a major explanation for his alarming findings regarding people's compliance in hurting others when under orders from an "authority." Ross felt the lack of any clear method of protest or route of disobedience to be a powerful but ignored explanatory factor. He felt far fewer people might have continued to administer "shocks" to "students" in the experiment if there had simply been, say, a button they could push at any time to end the procedure. Ross shifted emphasis from the traditional explanation of excessive deference to authority, to the notion that the lack of an available means of terminating the situation kept subjects locked into it. To the extent this may be true, having opportunities readily available becomes a very important link in the chain leading to survival-directed action to end the arms race.

Giving People Opportunities

There is a general consensus among those who have studied how to alter people's behavior that the most effective process involves small, easy, manageable steps towards proximal and then intermediate goals, on the way to obtaining the full behavior hoped for. There is also agreement about the need for reinforcement through positive feedback. Such feedback should stress the success of one's initial steps, as well as the attainability of the next proximal goal. It should also make clear the exact nature of the next steps required. Sandman and Valenti describe this process in terms of fostering action to end the arms race. They speak of three requirements necessary to nurture a cycle of increasing engagement. First, one must provide "attractive opportunities for behavioral commitment, 'first steps' such as petitions, buttons, and rallies." Next, one must reinforce those taking the first steps with information—"not just information about nuclear issues but also information about the importance of their contributions." Finally, one must provide adequate opportunities for non-taxing subsequent steps, "so new and tentative activists are not forced to choose between a heavy commitment that they are not yet prepared to make and a relapse into inactivity" (Sandman & Valenti, 1986, p. 21).

For opportunities to be experienced as rewarding, it is important that the objectives they involve are achievable. Moreover, opportunities involving concrete actions and goals are more compelling than ones with more abstract goals and nonspecific means. Collecting children's baby teeth and having them measured for radioactivity (due to strontium 90 from fallout in the milk supply) thus worked well as a generator of motivation for the 1963 atmospheric test ban. It involved a very specific activity and a tangible product, in addition to evoking the motivating force of love for our children and desire to protect them. It is also important that individuals one seeks to motivate receive specific action instructions, as specificity of instructions has been found to facilitate behavioral compliance (Leventhal, 1970).

If the opportunities for actions are public ones, such as signing a petition or sponsoring a statement published in a newspaper, research by Deutsch and Gerard (1955) indicates the commitment involved will be much more lasting. In their experiments, Deutsch and Gerard had students estimate the length of some lines they were shown. They then offered new information suggesting the initial estimates were wrong, and offered an opportunity to change estimates. They found students much more committed to their initial estimates of the lengths if they had written these down, signed their names to them, and handed them into the experimenter, than if they had simply kept the knowledge of their guesses to themselves. (A condition where they essentially wrote their estimates down and then erased them showed an intermediate level of commitment.)

A fine example of an opportunity embodying many of the facilitating features just enumerated is 20/20 Vision. For $20 per year, 20/20 Vision provides its subscribers with typed postcards once a month. These describe an issue relating to the arms race, together with a required action. The action selected represents, in the opinion of expert "peace consultants," the most effective step a citizen in that particular congressional district could take that month in just 20 minutes to stop the arms race. It might involve writing senatorial candidates to question them on their ideas for economic conversion away from excessive military production (Northern California, August 1988), or writing to National Security Advisor General Brent Scowcroft to urge that he advise President Bush not to spend a third of a billion dollars on the MX rail-garrison system (on grounds of local hazard and international destabilization—February 1989). Twenty/20 Vision is the brain-child of an activist art teacher, Lois Barber, and Jeremy Sherman, a man with a background in franchises and marketing. A national office seeks out people across the country to start up new district projects, which it supplies with customized software and promotional materials. The local group then recruits subscribers in its community, and runs its program as it see fit, within certain guidelines. In addition to Congress and the administration, actions recommended may target media heads, chief executive officers of corporations, or others. Twenty/20 Vision prides itself on taking advocacy "out of the realm of plea and into the realm of service" (Triplett, 1988, p. 15).

Twenty/20 Vision may be seen to involve many of the desiderata of opportunities for action that we have been describing. It provides small, easy, manageable steps toward ending the arms race. These steps involve specific instructions, and require little cost in terms of time, money, or effort. They succeed in educating both the subscriber and the actions' targets, providing them with relevant information on timely topics. The 20/20 Vision actions generally require public commitment (e.g., signed letters to legislators). The process involves tangible products—postcards to the subscribers, letters or other communications to the targets—and concrete actions to be taken toward concrete goals. Finally, there is the provision of not just one but successive steps, requiring of necessity an ongoing but unarduous commitment.

Opportunities for action may be additionally enhanced by the presence of high-profile individuals enacting or endorsing them, as has been pointed out above in the section on *emulation*. If a prominent movie actor or physician is arrested in a protest action at a nuclear test site, it not only generates more press, but may cause such action to be reevaluated in a more positive light by some who previously looked at it askance.

Finally, in attempting to provide opportunities for individuals who are motivated (but not to the point of generating their own opportunities), it is important to provide a variety of choices. The opportunities offered should suit the interests of the individual, and should also suit his or her level of comfort, in several senses. It should suit the individual's level of comfort in regard to the amount of commitment called for. Asking too much too soon can produce rapid burnout. An example of an opportunity "integrated into the stream of daily life" in a minimally demanding way is the Working Assets program. Described as "a tool for practical idealists," it offers credit cards, savings, and investment funds free of investment in any areas conflicting with liberal ideals, including involvement with nuclear weapons (Gilbert, 1988). Ideal opportunities for action should also suit the individual's level of comfort in regard to how far they deviate from the status quo in their means and goals. Examples of goals of different distances might be, on the near side, working for a certain candidate's election campaign, versus, on the farther side, demonstrating malfeasance and corruption within the military-industrial complex. In terms of means, closer to the status quo might be voting for a state nuclear freeze referendum, while further along might be trespass on a missile installation for purposes of public protest.

Creating One's Own Opportunities

Helen Caldicott would occasionally become impatient with people who would want her or others to tell them what to do to end the arms race. These people would be inspired by her talks, but then seem helpless to think for themselves of anything that could be done. I expect the impatience of this extremely active woman (and her reluctance to simply respond with directives) was due partly to irritation at what she perceived to be laziness and dependence. But it must also have been due in part to the knowledge that if she came up with suggestions for them, the actions would have less impact, through being less personally meaningful, than if these individuals were to generate their own ideas. People have more ownership, more stock, in ideas they come up with themselves. People's own ideas are more tailored to their interests and resources, both external and internal. Concerned individuals are often in a better position than anyone else to know or find out what local or more distant resources there may be at their particular disposal, and to come up with ideas to use them best suited to their particular level of interest and time constraints.

With this truth in mind, I shall proceed to make a few general comments about creating one's own opportunities, and then offer a brief menu of approaches I have personally enjoyed and found effective. The final section on *Action*, expands this menu far beyond my realm of personal experience. It also includes some recommendations for people who still feel a need for direction from the outside—a need with which I perhaps feel more sympathetic than such a strongly self-directed person as Helen Caldicott.

Using one's loves, interests, skills and expertise. Roger Walsh (1984, p. 87) suggests the two most important questions we can ask ourselves in regard to what we can do are, "What is the most strategic thing I can do?" and "What would I really like to do?" This involves looking for ways to contribute with optimal impact, which often turn out to be identical with "the ways in which the talents and opportunities that are uniquely ours can be put to best use" (ibid.). Whether your job skills, talents, or opportunities lie in fund raising, film-making, music or math, lecturing, researching, preparing food, painting, teaching, setting up businesses, law, accounting, medicine, travel planning, foreign languages, local government, history, chemistry or physics, writing, investing, fast-food franchises, or being a stock holder or consumer or simply a good grandmother, there are people in your position who have already turned that skill to use toward ending the nuclear weapons race. And you can do so too. Artists can make films or posters or illustrate books or pamphlets. They can have their unsold works raffled to raise needed monies. Computer experts and accountants can donate their skills to organizations whose efforts to stop the arms race make particular sense to them, or join together in such groups as Computer Professionals for Social Responsibility to highlight the economic or software problems of the Strategic Defense Initiative. Salespeople can likewise volunteer assistance to groups they deem worthiest, helping improve the effectiveness of solicitations and enlistment. Musicians can, in addition to doing benefit concerts at whatever profit-sharing ratio they require, make soundtracks for films, offer music for organizational events, tour, and establish contact with musicians in other nations. Limits of the possible are set only by the boundaries of each citizen's imagination.

Using what's around. Different geographical locations have inherent in them different opportunities. These include particular aspects of the arms race that can be pointed out and used as focal points for action or discussion, such as probable storage sites for nuclear weapons, probable nuclear weapons targets, processing plants for nuclear materials, weapons assembly plants, etc. Proximity to nuclear testing sites at Las Vegas or to the weapons-related nuclear reactor at Hanford, Washington, brings to mind different educational activities and means of protest than does proximity to legislative officials in Washington, DC, or to missile bases in Cheyenne. Also, different locations provide different sets of human resources. At the national and state capitals there are politicians, at Los Alamos and Livermore there are knowledgeable and involved scientists, in New York City there are corporate executive officers, in Los Angeles there are filmmakers. Some of these people would benefit from dialogue with concerned citizens. Others might respond to petitions, op-ed pieces, or boycotts. Others may already be concerned themselves and searching for the proper avenue to express it. Creative efforts to end the arms race involve creative use of such local resources.

A few personal examples of rewarding self-generated opportunities. My own inclinations and background have steered me toward educational efforts and research. I initially found it easy to approach and gain speaking opportunities at men's service club meetings (Rotarians, Lions, etc., who are always on the lookout for luncheon speakers), after-service meetings at churches, high school and college classes and clubs, educational seminars for business company employees, and various medical rounds and conferences. There were also opportunities I was able to arrange at professional society meetings, from mealtime talks to two-day symposia. There were small home gatherings not unlike Tupperware parties, in which refreshments would be served and I would facilitate the showing of a video or film (Eric and Ian Thiermann's *The Last Epidemic*, and *What About the Rus-*

sians, or Paul Newman's *A Step Away From War*). This latter sort of event turned out to be a very powerful medium, as Mehr and Webster's research indicated. In addition to talking and showing films, I conducted surveys on the different audiences' attitudes before and after the presentations. I published reports of my findings in both popular and scientific journals. This allowed me to arrange radio and television interviews in regard to the research (on shows where I had previously arranged bookings simply to talk as a member of Physicians for Social Responsibility on the medical consequences of nuclear war).

Additionally, I have tried to contribute in different ways to the election of congressional candidates who share the view of the survival-directed pathway expounded in Part I.

But my favorite self-generated opportunities consisted of what I called "leveraging my citizenship." As described above, this was essentially a matter of calling up high-profile individuals who I knew shared my view of the survival-directed pathway and, referring to other high-profile influence-wielding individuals, offer them the invitation "Let's you and he or she talk." If they accepted, I would then call the other high-profile individuals and attempt to complete the brokering of the meeting. By this means I got congressmen and top level physicists together, newspaper editors and Nobel laureates. Editorials were generated, congressional support for the nuclear freeze fostered—all without representing myself as anything but a concerned citizen and member of a group (Physicians for Social Responsibility) dedicated to reducing the threat of nuclear war. A wonderful side benefit of this approach was the opportunity it provided me to meet extraordinary individuals I would never otherwise have had occasion to encounter. I commend the method heartily to all readers of this book. Find out which prominent people with survival-directed ideas live or work near you, which opinion leaders you would like to meet and hear them, and get busy!

Action

In his trenchant analysis of factors inhibiting arms control activism, Richard Gilbert (1988) points out the immobilizing effect of having a maze of objectives. It interferes with people's certainty regarding the correctness and impact of contemplated actions. Since a high degree of certainty is required to justify political action, lack of a unified objective can be quite paralyzing. When arms-control sentiment has been focused on single, specific issues (e.g. atmospheric testing, U.S. missiles in Europe, the freeze), the largest and most effective public demonstrations have occurred (Gilbert, 1988, p. 761). At the same time, the arms race presents a variety of aspects worthy of protest, and a variety of attitudes towards the arms race can reasonably be maintained under the general aegis of opposition to it. Ending the arms race requires action on many fronts. No protest-worthy aspects of the arms race should be neglected, nor should any particular angles of opposition be repudiated.

In the light of these apparently contradictory considerations, our recommendations for individual action involve a two-track approach. We recommend that individuals stand ready to join forces in energetically attacking single local or national issues as they become salient, but that at the same time they also sustain, on a long-term basis, efforts at eradicating the manifold root causes underlying the nuclear arms race.

In reality, division of opinion about ultimate goals is not as major a problem as some believe. Moreover, there is virtual unanimity of opinion among different factions on immediate and intermediate goals. "Absolutist" disarmament groups and "incrementalist" arms-control advocates differ in the amount of weight they feel should be attached to perceptions of military balances (Krepon, 1984). They differ in regard to the number of nuclear weapons nations should disarm down to and the periods of time required for optimal security. But as Michael Krepon of the Carnegie Endowment for International Peace states, "arms controllers are committed to dismantling nuclear weapons, just as those committed to disarmament have respect for the management tools of their operationally minded colleagues" (Krepon, 1984, p. 11). Both camps favor, if not a comprehensive test ban, then a low threshold test-ban treaty, with the threshold so low as to preclude development of new weapons (1–5 kilotons). Both camps view SDI as a high-priced impossible dream. Indeed, they see its pursuit as a nightmare, jacking up the pace of the arms race. Rather than a source of security, if ever it *could* be achieved, disarmists and arms controllers alike see SDI as a destabilizing component of a first-strike capacity. Both camps favor elimination of multiple-warhead weapons, such as the MX— whether viewed as "evil" or "destabilizing." Both camps oppose development of antisatellite weapons. Both camps favor an interpretation of the Anti-Ballistic Missile treaty that means you can't build significant anti-ballistic missile systems. Both camps support an immediate 50% reduction of nuclear forces by the two major nuclear powers, followed by at least one or two more 50% reductions, with the inclusion of other nuclear powers as the numbers get lower. Both groups favor input to Congress and the Administration on arms needs and arms control matters from sources other than weapons labs, weapons manufacturers, and the military. Both are alarmed by the unregulated insularity of the "iron triangle" of military-industrial-congressional interactions with its biggest obstacle of all to ending the arms race: bureaucratic momentum.

We have unanimity up to a point some distance down the road; let us start out together and worry about going separate ways once we reach that point. Indeed, getting that far may generate a new world atmosphere and facilitate further agreement on goals beyond those that can presently be foreseen.

With occasional dramatic single issues of protest, against a background of steady, incremental progress as more people get educated and channels of action are opened up and developed, the course of progress of the movement to end the arms race may come to resemble the upward-tending progress chart of a successful diversified business. Where on the business's chart there might be peaks representing the burgeoning of subsidiaries as one or another makes a major contribution, on the movement's chart there will be peaks representing mass concern generated by galvanizing issues. Where on the business's chart a gradual elevation of the baseline represents the cumulative effect of all the smaller efforts adding up to an increasing market, on the movement's chart it represents the aggregate impact of all the educational efforts, protests, boycotts, editorials, referenda, dialogue, letters, donations, tours, political campaigns, and lobbying efforts, adding up to an eventually unstoppable mandate for drastic if not total disarmament.

For those, then, who on our flow chart (Figure 1) have successfully threaded the inhibiting maze of incomprehension, diverse mindsets, helplessness and rivaling concerns, to arrive finally at a point of readiness to take action, what are the choices?

The menu of meaningful actions one might take is vast, and continues to grow. Our coverage of it is a reflection of our particular exposure, and thus somewhat arbitrary. Numerous worthy endeavors are doubtless omitted, and to these we express our apologies and best wishes. The various actions and organizations we have learned about we shall now present, in the hopes their description may pique the interest of one or another reader, or stimulate thoughts on yet other effective approaches.

As the different actions represent attacks on different points in the process of developing nuclear arms, the schema we shall use to organize their presentation will be the sequential steps in that process. We shall first mention actions designed to reduce the perceived need for developing nuclear weapons. Then we will look at actions affecting the choice of the legislators and administration officials who convert that perceived need into requisitions. Next will come actions bearing on arms-development legislation. Finally, in order, we shall consider actions aimed at stopping weapons development, production, deployment, and transport.

Reducing the "Need" for Nuclear Weapons

If there has been, up to this point, a "need" for nuclear weapons, many of us would see this need as limited to the existence of only enough of these devices to dishearten any nation contemplating global warfare. The political reality we have been operating from, however, has been one in which decision-makers have seen a need for an ongoing nuclear weapons race. This has been based on a fear of specific other nations' intentions, combined with the lack of any recourse other than war, if those other nations should become overly aggressive. Reduction of this "need" might therefore be achieved by either the reduction of tension between nations ("confidence building"), or the development of alternate means of dealing with conflict between nations.

Tension reduction. A variety of creative approaches have been undertaken to reduce tension and build confidence between the United States and Soviet Union. It is unfortunate that most of these, to date, have not originated with the federal government. Mutual government projects, at least prior to the recent thaw in U.S.-Soviet relations, have taken a back seat to military threats and counterthreats. This has been due to the mistaken assumptions that such projects were not the compelling issue, and that they would signal weakness or be premature, false agreements, permitting military maneuvering to run rampant behind them. The reality is that the military maneuvering is secondary to the state of relations. It derives its impetus from tension, its funding from tension, its existence from tension. Lower the tension, put the mutually cooperative understandings first, give *them* priority, and the military maneuverings will fall of their own weight. It should be harder to get Congress to vote funding for multi-billion-dollar space arms race at the expense of education, public transportation, or clean water, if we are working cooperatively on common tasks with our so-called adversary. Such, at least, are the conclusions of Ambassador James E. Goodby, Deputy Chairman of the U.S. delegation to the Strategic Arms Reduction Talks in Geneva, as expressed in various talks at Stanford University in recent years.

• *Joint government projects.* The joint governmental projects that have been arranged (see Chapter 4), from the high-profile Soyuz-Apollo hook-up to the quiet exchange of scientific committees and establishment of a small "crisis center," have been well received by the people of both nations who have heard about them or been a party to them. Groups of private citizens have pushed for more, through lobbying efforts and through the initiation of new legislation at state and national levels. A more complete realization of William Ury's (1985) notion of larger, bilaterally staffed Crisis Centers in both Moscow and Washington still seems a worthy project. So does the notion of a U.S./U.S.S.R. Institute for mutual study and understanding—especially at a time when the chief Soviet ideologist has announced his country's intentions to "learn from the Capitalist West" (Bethe, 1989).

• *Travel.* During the height of the Cold War, many private citizens and private groups arranged one-time or repeated tours of the U.S.S.R. An energetic nurse, Sharon Tennison, from Texas, whipped up a one-woman whirlwind of transcontinental travel, establishing contacts all over the Soviet Union, escorting large groups, taking remarkable photographs, giving video-enhanced lectures, writing up the groups' experiences, and generally inspiring thousands of people. Hundreds of organizations, from Physicians for Social Responsibility to the Institute of Noetic Sciences, regularly arrange tours of the Soviet Union for their membership, generating lectures, articles and/or films each time they do so, spreading a message about Soviets being fellow human beings, about changes towards more freedom and free enterprise in the Soviet Union, and about the Soviets' love of their children and concern for the maintenance of peace. Beyond simple tourism, one method of creating bonds across national boundaries has been the effort on the part of hobbyists, craftsmen, and professionals, from barbers to lawyers to fans of science fiction, to look up their counterparts in other nations in order to discuss and start ongoing dialogue about their mutual interests. A more thoroughgoing means of sharing professional interests is to work or study in the other country.

• *Cultural exchange.* From jazz ensembles to the Bolshoi Ballet to Mickey Mouse to collections of world famous paintings, the United States and Soviet Union have a great deal more to share with each other than threats of destruction, and as the Cold War has drawn to a close, they have begun to do so. Each of the two nations provides wonderfully appreciative audiences for shows from the other—even for shows that may be commonplace in their native country. The risk of international conflict leading to nuclear war among other nations can similarly be reduced by the kind of empathy and mutual understanding that can result from cultural exchanges.

• *Fostering foreign relations at the municipal level.* Chronicled if not inspired by Michael Shuman's Center for Innovative Diplomacy, local U.S. municipalities have been bypassing a recalcitrant, uncreative, undemocratically secretive federal administration to insist on their own voice in foreign-policy matters. Avenues for doing so have included arms race referenda and initiatives, various consciousness-raising publications and activities, including peace studies courses in local schools (e.g., New York City), ordinances requiring the annual publication of reports on the local economic impact of military spending (e.g., Los Angeles, Baltimore), sister-city projects, economic conversion activities (from military to consumer goods), boycotts of city purchasing from corporations heavily involved in the manufacture of nuclear weapons (e.g., Marin County, CA), boycott of the Federal Emergency Management Agency's "crisis relocation planning" (120 cities), participation in global organizations of cities, rejection of home-porting of nuclear warships, declarations of nuclear-free zones (over 900 local governments, including the city of Chicago), "nuclear-free investing" of municipal funds, and trade and cultural exchange initiatives (*Bulletin of Municipal Foreign Policy*, 1987; Shuman, 1987).

• *Education through schools and the media.* A number of organizations have mounted efforts to educate the U.S. citizenry about the Soviet Union, including the Soviet Union itself (e.g., through the magazine *Soviet Life*). Of particular note is the undertaking by Educators for Social Responsibility (ESR) of the Soviet Education Project, which facilitates education about the Soviets within state school systems. Audiovisual media provide a window onto each others' countries for those without the time, means, or inclination to visit in person. Ian Thiermann's documentary film *What About the Russians*, including interviews with ex-CIA director William Colby, Vice Admiral J. M. Lee, ex-Secretary of Defense Robert McNamara, and former Ambassador to the Soviet Union George Kennan, has been shown a number of times in the House of Representatives. Even the popular medium of commercial TV contributes to the thaw in relations, through such entries as *Perfect Strangers*, an ongoing situation comedy featuring a naive but winning young Soviet emigré. Similar educational efforts could foster mutual understanding between peoples of all different cultures throughout the world.

• *Mutual business ventures.* A Soviet law authorizing commercial joint ventures between socialist and capitalist firms came into effect in early 1987. A book entitled *International Joint Ventures* is due to be published by the Center for Foreign Policy Development and two Soviet research institutes in 1991 (Quorum Press, Westport, CT), with alternating Soviet- and Western-authored chapters addressing theoretical questions and stumbling blocks (e.g., communication difficulties, export control, and making the ruble into convertible currency—*Update*, 1989). Ventures that have come to my attention range from the notion of "Peace Fleece" (wool and woolen products from the sheep of both countries—Morton, 1987), to the vastly successful opening of a McDonald's hamburger franchise in Moscow, offering customers 650 seats in which to eat their "Bolshoi Maks," served by restaurant managers trained at the Institute of Hambergerology in Toronto (Wood, 1988, p. 30).

• *Sharing of nuclear weapons information.* One of the most direct confidence-building measures undertaken between the U.S. and the U.S.S.R. is the sharing of information about their nuclear and their military material. This is occurring more and more, starting decades ago with forewarning each other of maneuvers and tests, and progressing now to various sorts of on-site inspections. The Natural Resources Defense Council, a non-profit U.S. organization, added impetus to the movement with its privately arranged measurements of Soviet underground nuclear testing. What's more, they initiated the idea at a time when President Reagan and his colleagues in the Administration were asserting both Soviet cheating on threshold limits, and Soviet intransigence vis-à-vis the notion of on-site inspections.

Developing alternate means of dealing with conflict. The impetus to develop major classes of weaponry declines when a nation no longer feels itself engaged in adversarial relationships internationally. It could also be reduced, despite ongoing international conflict, if confidence existed that such conflict could be resolved by means other than warfare. A number of programs, both national and private, have been set up in the hopes of developing such confidence.

• *The U.S. Peace Institute.* The dream of a series of U.S. citizens, dating from Dr. Benjamin Rush (the "Father of American psychiatry" and a signer of the

Declaration of Independence), the U.S. Peace Institute has finally, if modestly, come to exist. With a two-year operating budget one-fifth the cost of a single F-15 jet fighter, the Institute was finally launched in the late 1980s to study crisis management, the dynamics of conflict, and the science of conflict resolution. As distinct from such institutes as West Point, its intent is to graduate peace*makers*, rather than "peacekeepers."

• *Private conflict management projects*. Several university-based or private projects have been initiated during recent years of the nuclear era to develop "technologies" for conflict management. Common Ground and Project Victory both attempt to engage adversarial parties in "reverse debates," endeavoring to establish points of agreement rather than disagreement in order to work toward acceptable compromises. The Harvard Negotiation Project, consultant to the Camp David Accord meetings, seeks to move away from "positional bargaining" toward what they call "principled negotiation," or "negotiation on the merits." Elements of such negotiation include construing the task as one of mutual problem-solving, concentrating on underlying interests rather than surface positions, generating a variety of possible solutions, and insisting on measurable results (Thompson, 1985, p. 97).

• *World citizenship and the United Nations*. The establishment of transnational institutional forces for keeping peace may one day reduce or remove the felt need for national arms development. While that day has not yet arrived, it may come sooner and we may be more prepared for it as the result of efforts by such groups as the World Federalist Association and the United Nations Association. Their vision of true world law has been moved from the realm of dream to that of necessity by the advent of weapons of mass destruction. These organizations serve to advance the notion of world citizenship—the individual counterpart to world government and the ultimate antidote to the more chauvinistic forms of nationalism. It is through international organizations such as the United Nations that we shall arrive at nonviolent conflict management. A few years back, W. H. Ferry wrote, "If it is argued that these organizations have not proved their effectuality, the answer has to be that they have never been given a proper chance by the major powers" (Ferry, 1981, p. 171). At the time of this writing, there are signs that both the U.S. and the U.S.S.R. are beginning to appreciate the potential of the United Nations for maintaining international stability. Let us do our best to make sure that this trend continues.

Choosing the Decisionmakers

When Harvard Law Professor Roger Fisher (1981) speaks of how "wrong decisions" are made, he states they result from one or more of three potential problems. The first is that there are the wrong decisionmakers in place. The second is that the decision-makers may be operating on wrong information. The third is that the decision-makers may be operating under the wrong constraints. We shall address the education and constraining of decision-makers further below. In avoiding wrong decisions, by most estimates it is a lot more efficient to get the right decision-makers in office in the first place than it is to educate and constrain them once they are there. Methods of accomplishing this include group and individual support for particular candidates, as well as efforts to remove corrupting influences from the general elections process.

• *Electing candidates supportive of disarmament and arms control*. People can affect the outcome of political elections through individual contributions of time, effort, and money to candidates' campaigns. A sufficiently enthusiastic individual might even choose to join the campaign staff of a candidate, integrating his or her own network of resources and contacts directly into those of the candidate's office.

People can increase their influence to affect the outcome of a number of elections by joining together in groups. There are several national political action committees (PACs) devoted to the election and support of Representatives and Senators who are committed to the survival-directed pathway endorsed in Chapter 4. Council for a Livable World was founded by Leo Szilard, a scientist who felt a particular responsibility for preventing nuclear war because of his earlier participation in the Manhattan Project to develop the first atomic weapons. The council pools the contributions of its members (almost $1.5M in 1988), and channels what it deems to be appropriate amounts of them to the campaign chests of candidates for the Senate who share the Council's views on arms control. To qualify for support, these candidates, in addition to having propitious views, must be in tight contests and up against candidates with clearly *un*propitious views. The Council, the largest of the "peace PACs," calls itself "the electoral arm of the peace movement." It focuses on the Senate because of its being the smaller legislative body, where contributions can be concentrated to make the most difference.

PeacePAC, headed by the activist Catholic priest-turned-representative, Father Robert Drinan, functions in a similar manner to support candidates for the House of Representatives. Though a larger body than the Senate, PeacePAC argues that "the House is the lever by which we move Washington" (Drinan, 1988). Peace-PAC asserts that House members are more responsive to public pressure than senators because they must run for re-election every two years and because they have smaller constituencies. Congressional Agenda 90's is a Congressional PAC with a somewhat wider social agenda, of which arms control and disarmament are key elements.

• *Cleaning up the election process.* Opposing all PACs, including such survival-minded ones as Council for a Livable World, is the organization Common Cause. In the near term it is at cross purposes with "peace PACs," but in the long term its goals are similar. Common Cause is attempting, through campaign finance reform initiatives and the arousal of public concern, to decrease the influence of wealthy corporations on the election of leaders. If this means eliminating all PACs, including ones like Council for a Livable World, it might still, in the balance, be a step in the right direction. This is because the PACs with the most to spend are those with major corporation sponsorship. With 32 of the top 50 corporations in the U.S. making and/or exporting weapons or weapons parts, their stake in the status quo is great. Legislators free to receive large "lecture honoraria" and other forms of contributions from such companies are then able to build massive campaign war chests. These permit them to scare off or beat off any opponents who dare come against them, so that turnover in Congress is becoming rare. It is said that, as of the 1988 elections, tenure in the legislature had become more durable than that in the old Soviet Politburo.

To the extent this is true—a very great extent, it would seem—our legislators are rendered less accountable to their constituents and more accountable to their "sponsoring" corporations. The money almost always goes to those already in power, with such campaign contributions often being quite transparent gifts. In

1986, for example, GE PAC gave money to 34 House candidates who faced *no opponent whatsoever*, and to another 34 who had won by at least three-to-one margins in the last four elections (Philip Stern, author of *The Best Congress Money Can Buy*, cited in *The Washington Spectator*, 1988c, p. 2). It has reached the point where former Senator Barry Goldwater (R-AZ) says, "It is not 'we the people' but political action committees and moneyed interests who are setting the nation's political agenda and are influencing the position of candidates on the important issues of the day" (*Washington Spectator*, 1988c, p. 4).

A number of actions have been suggested to clean up this situation. Perhaps all donations to a candidate for Congress should come from within the candidate's own voting area. Limits could be placed on the amount of money that could be collected or spent by candidates for federal office. Paid political advertising could be banned. In its place, TV and radio stations could be required to give equal time to opposing candidates to discuss real issues (*Washington Spectator*, 1988c). In the meantime, free copies of PAC contribution printouts on every candidate for elected office may be obtained from the Secretary of State in each relevant state, as well as from the Federal Election Commission in Washington, DC. To get the full picture, one can look up in the book *Congress and Defense 1988* both the military-related voting record and the top military contractor campaign contributors of every member of Congress. It includes listings of defense spending by congressional districts and 200 top defense-related PACs (published by Cardiff Publishing, Englewood, CO). Perusal of this book or the state or federal printouts might give the electorate a better profile of what to expect from a candidate's continued tenure than the candidate's campaign promises.

The Making of Legislation

Once the legislators and members of the Administration are in place, short of impeachment (or offering them more attractive jobs—the option used in Leo Szilard's novel, *The Voice of the Dolphin*), the only ways to deal with those opposed to the survival-directed path are to try to educate them or to try to put constraints upon them. As stated above, this is a more difficult task than choosing the right representatives in the first place. With varying degrees of success, it can nevertheless be done.

Before discussing actual methods of educating and constraining legislators, let us consider for a moment what some examples of survival-directed legislation could be that we might wish to educate or constrain legislators to support.

• *Some survival-directed legislation.* Legislation that could serve to move us along the survival-directed path might include such measures as the following: (1) establishment of a mutually verifiable, bilateral (with the Soviets), and later multilateral freeze on the testing, production, and deployment of nuclear weapons; (2) more narrowly, a bilateral (later multilateral) comprehensive (or very low threshold) test ban; (3) further elimination of nuclear weapons from tactical arsenals now in place; (4) halting of all phases of SDI save for whatever research might be prudent to forestall any unforeseen breakout in this direction by another power; (5) a bilateral 50% reduction by the United States and U.S.S.R. of their strategic nuclear forces, to be followed by further reductions involving other nuclear nations as our arsenals begin to approach their size. The Soviets have already indicated readiness to meet us at least halfway on these measures. In the one accord we have reached lately, the Intermediate Nuclear Forces treaty, the Soviets, in fact, agreed to scuttle four of their missiles for every one of ours—meeting us a good deal more than halfway.

Additionally, there are related matters requiring some sort of legislation that are less directly focused on arms control or disarmament. Examples of these include opposition to expensive, provocative, and ineffective efforts at civil defense, and the establishment of a more independent and objective method of providing scientific and technical advice to the President and subcommittees of Congress.

Of all these measures, the one to focus upon and achieve first—other than completing the START negotiations, which could lead to 30% reductions in nuclear forces—should be the comprehensive test ban treaty (CTBT). One good reason for this is that the Soviets have already put themselves on record as supporting it by carrying one out unilaterally for 18 months, starting on Hiroshima day, August 6, 1985. They said at that time that should the United States join them, they would extend it indefinitely. They have said since, that they would resume it whenever we chose to join them in doing so. Thus there would be no question of their willingness to comply, if we adopted such a policy. Arguments in favor of a CTBT are these: (1) it would provide a very effective brake on the arms race, as tests are essential for weapons development; (2) it is a measure that does not require trust, being readily verifiable by current seismologic techniques, especially given the Soviets' now proven willingness to permit monitoring within their national boundaries; (3) it is necessary if we in the United States and Soviet Union are to uphold our end of the Non-Proliferation Treaty, wherein scores of other nations agreed not to develop nuclear weapons provided that the superpowers demonstrated such constraint; (4) extended to other nations, a ban on testing would help prevent the spread of nuclear weaponry worldwide; (5) it would reduce U.S.-Soviet tensions, improving the chances for meaningful arms reductions beyond the bare beginning with INF; (6) it would prevent further work on nuclear-based directed energy weapons for SDI, alleviating fears aroused by the Star Wars program that we are seeking a first strike potential; (7) its enforcement would be free of complex technological problems, unlike agreements calling for quantitative measurements of weapon sizes or numbers.

A comprehensive test ban treaty has been endorsed as a high priority action to end the arms race by at least 50 major national and international organizations, including SANE/FREEZE, Physicians for Social Responsibility, Women's International League for Peace and Freedom, the American Friends Service Committee, the National Committee for Radiation Victims, Psychologists for Social Responsibility, the Sierra Club, the Union of Concerned Scientists, the Center for Defense Information, and the Natural Resources Defense Council. On June 17, 1987, the U.S. Conference of Mayors (a national organization representing mayors from cities with populations of 30,000 or more) passed a resolution calling on the President to "immediately announce a U.S. suspension of nuclear testing, and to resume negotiations with the Soviets leading to a Comprehensive Test Ban as a first step towards reversing the arms race and reducing the risk of nuclear war" (Lown, 1987). As part of the FREEZE package in the early 1980s, initiatives were passed in support of it in 22 out of 23 states where it was on the ballot. With powerful arguments in favor of it, and clear popular support, it is time for a substantive bill on the matter to be passed in both houses of Congress and be signed into law by the president. A move is already afoot in the United Nations to expand by amendment the existing Limited Test Ban Treaty, making it into a

Comprehensive Test Ban Treaty. Thirty-nine nations sufficed to call an Amendment Conference, which will take place in January 1991. Support in the U.S. Congress for such a move, pressuring ourselves (the United States) not to veto it in the UN Security Council, could put us on the shortest road to a CTBT.

• *Educating and constraining legislators.* A number of organizations have been set up to educate or constrain legislators regarding the nuclear arms race, or have taken this task upon themselves in addition to ongoing priorities. Any mention of them by name here must be understood to be a partial listing only. In addition to the groups mentioned above as being supportive of a CTB, there are ones as old and established as the Arms Control Association, a research organization called upon by the government to fine-tune SALT II in the 1970s, or as new and grass-roots as Nuclear Dialogue, the brainchild of Rachel Findley in Princeton, NJ. The latter already has dozens of chapters throughout the U.S. directly linking concerned citizens with people who determine nuclear weapons policy at the highest levels, for purposes of probing, nonadversarial discussion (Findley, 1988).

Groups like Common Cause, the Union of Concerned Scientists, the Natural Resources Defense Council, and the League of Women Voters took up the issue of nuclear arms and arms control as a new or newly revitalized priority in the early 1980s. Such groups are devoted both to the education of the public, in the form of their membership as well as others exposed to their messages, and the education and lobbying of politicians in Washington. In a representative democracy, this dual approach is more unified than it seems, as the people and their representatives are two tines of the same fork. Lobbying congresspeople is working on decision-making by the people at its focal point, while educating the public stimulates them to "lobby" their representatives. Some groups, like the Center for Defense Information, have a significant focus on providing information to the decision-makers directly, while other groups, like Mobilization for Survival, strive to shape a concerned and informed coalition of "the people."

Similarly, there is a tendency for the fine line between the "educating" and "constraining" of elected officials to dissolve on scrutiny. If a politician is hearing from numbers of his constituents that they favor certain arms-control measures for certain reasons, is he or she being educated or constrained? The politician knows those citizens will be watching his or her vote on related issues, and that these citizens' own votes for a representative will be influenced thereby. Thus when Nuclear Dialogue informs citizens about the decision-making process and about the decision-makers they are setting them up to meet, and "enhances their communication skills," they are preparing people to constrain as well as educate. Services like the Council for a Livable World's Arms Control Hotline ([202] 543–0006), with its two-minute recorded educational messages followed by "this week's Action Request," or 20/20 Vision's monthly education/action postcards, represent direct hook-ups of public education with appeals to constrain legislators by letting them know exactly how one might wish them to act in specific instances.

Stopping Weapons Development

Once the government has set out on a non-survival-directed pathway, having legislated a weapons system that seems clearly destabilizing, immoral, or both, various efforts may be launched to stop the development of such weapons. The Comprehensive Test Ban and the Freeze, already discussed, represent legislation that would effectively halt nuclear weapons development already under way. Another channel, legitimate and in place, through which weapons development might be curtailed, would be the exercise of adequate oversight by the University of California over the weapons labs at Berkeley and Los Alamos. By insuring that false or misleading statements about weapons test results do not get transmitted to decision-makers, the University could curtail funding of unwarranted projects and block lab interference with the arms-control process.

Other legal though less orthodox approaches to blocking weapons development exist. They tend to involve independent, private actions of a creative sort. Two examples of action at this level have come to our attention. The first is the boycotting of work on SDI projects by a number of top U.S. scientists (see Gollon, 1986; Kogut & Weissman, 1986; Gurman, 1988). The second was the "separate peace" move by the Natural Resources Defense Council (NRDC) to monitor, on a private basis, Soviet nuclear testing. As noted above, they did this at a time when Washington, without ever pursuing the issue to actually test it, was frequently alluding to Moscow's recalcitrance to on-site monitoring. While the move by NRDC was inspired, it was not out of keeping with their basic mandate as a group concerned about the future of the earth. The boycotting of work on Star Wars by U.S. scientists, on the other hand, required a great deal of courage and sacrifice, as well as imagination. In abandoning weapons research, many of the scientists have lost financial security, prestige, and professional advancement. Should they attempt to speak out and stay in, as Colonel Robert Bowman tried briefly to do as a General Dynamics executive, the going gets pretty rough. "The company," he said to writer Lew Gurman, "warned me to shut up or get out. I had even less freedom of speech in industry than I'd had in the military" (Gurman, 1988, p. 6).

What do actor Robert Blake, actress Teri Garr, disc jockey Casey Kasem and former nuclear strategist Daniel Ellsberg all have in common? They were all arrested at the U.S. nuclear testing ground 65 miles northwest of Las Vegas, together with 1,100 other protesters, on March 12, 1988. They had climbed the barbed wire fence surrounding the 1,350 square mile site and begun walking across the desert when they were arrested by 300 officers from the Nevada Highway Patrol, the Nye County Sheriff's Office, and the Department of Energy security force (*San Jose Mercury News*, 1988). One method of stopping nuclear weapons development is nonviolent civil disobedience. To pursue it requires a willingness to place moral dictates above such civil laws as those of trespass, and a readiness to accept consequences that may include prosecution and loss of liberty and/or income. For activists like Jessie Cocks, however, who split with the Freeze campaign to lead the American Peace Test (APT) test site protest group, these costs are outweighed by advantages. She sees people who engage in on site protests "go through a life-changing experience. They become completely empowered and go home with a sense of hope and passion that many have not felt since we first started the Freeze" (Ferguson, 1988). Such forms of nonviolent civil resistance are aimed at creating social change by "dramatically demonstrating through personal risk the 'moral crisis' caused by the arms race" (Ferguson, 1988).

Stopping Weapons Production

The Freeze movement, and the SANE/Freeze group organizing it, are hopeful of passing legislation that will curtail the production of nuclear weapons, as well as their testing and deployment. In addition to such congressional legislative actions, there can be other actions designed to stop nuclear weapons production. Two that have already proven capable of at least occasional success are direct protest, similar to that involved in the protesting of weapons testing, and local legislation of "nuclear-free zones."

Protest activities. With the dual aim of public education and corporate consciousness-raising, civil disobedience has been used to expose and obstruct the role of corporations in the nuclear arms race. Two organizations that have been doing this are the Honeywell Project in Minneapolis, Minnesota, and the First Strike Prevention Project in Santa Clara and Santa Cruz counties, California. The former group opposes Honeywell Corporation's production of guidance system components for the cruise, MX, and Pershing II missiles. It has been involved in a number of major civil disobedience actions and dozens of smaller ones, altogether involving thousands of arrests and the closure of Honeywell's headquarters for at least one full day (Friedman, 1988). The First Strike Prevention Project, together with the National Mobilization for Survival, the California Alliance to Stop First Strike, and others, focuses on protest of Trident II D-5 missile production by the Lockheed Corporation, in Sunnyvale, California. Their choice of this weapon system is based on the observation that missiles with the accuracy and payload of the Trident II D-5 appear to be uniquely suited for first strike, rather than defensive or retaliatory use.

The protesters at Lockheed and elsewhere, when brought to court following their arrests for trespassing, argue that their actions were not only morally justified, but actually legal. They base their defense on three points: (1) the constitutional stipulation that all treaties made under the authority of the United States are part of the supreme law of the land; (2) the fact that the United States has entered into treaties which prohibit, as war crimes, the use of weapons which cause unnecessary and indiscriminate injuries or death to non-combatant civilians; and (3) the privilege to take reasonable action, provided by common, statutory, and international law, to resist a public offense, based on a reasonable belief that the public offense is occurring or about to occur (Jones, 1988). Where such defenses have even been allowed to be entered into evidence at trials, they have been, to date, set aside in decisions based on narrow interpretations of traffic or trespassing laws.

Nuclear-Free Zones. While the federal government has legislated funds for the manufacture of a variety of nuclear weapons systems, it has not legislated where they must be built. The power to do this, at least in a negative sense, has instead been exercised by a number of local communities. The total number of nuclear free zones (NFZs) in the United States is now 172, representing over 17 million people (C. Johnson, personal communication, October 26, 1990). The ordinances establishing these zones ban the presence of nuclear weapons within them, and a number of them, including Oakland's, ban as well the community government's purchasing from, investing in, or contracting with companies involved in nuclear weapons production (*Nuclear Times*, 1989). These U.S. NFZs are part of an international movement including a score or more foreign nations with declared NFZ policies. Some of these, such as Iceland and New Zealand, have insisted on making these policies stick, despite pressure from the U.S. Navy to permit docking of nuclear-weapons-carrying ships. Others, such as Japan, Spain, Denmark, and the Philippines permit the presence of U.S. naval nuclear-armed ships, but either do so with considerable internal embarrassment or with plans to desist from doing so in the future (Ross, 1989). The ultimate objective of the establishment of individual nuclear-free zones, as Olaf Palme stated at a Special Session of the United Nations in 1980, is that "of achieving a world entirely free of nuclear weapons" (Coates, 1981, p. 205).

Michael H. Shuman (1987), founder and director of the Center for Innovative Diplomacy, strongly promotes the notion of municipal foreign policies. He speaks of the need and right of cities to be heard on issues of international relations and military expenditures, and of the injustice that results from the absence of municipal voices on such matters. He cites historical support for both the legality and the power of such actions. He points to the effect 800 local governments passing nuclear-freeze resolutions had on turning a refractory President Reagan around on arms control. He asserts, it seems accurately, that the action of over 120 cities in rejecting the Federal Emergency Management Agency's "crisis relocation planning" helped cancel the federal government's nuclear war civil defense program. And as an example of the power of municipalities to affect U.S. foreign policy, he points to the role played by over 65 cities and 19 states in ending the Reagan policy of "constructive engagement" with South Africa through divesting billions of dollars in assets out of firms doing business with that nation. Cities have a stake in the nuclear issue, he asserts, both because they are the principal potential victims of a nuclear war, and because they are principal victims of the shunting of some $300 billion or more annually to the military (with approximately 22% going directly into nuclear forces). In the absence of sufficient input from individual citizens and local levels of government, the Reagan and Bush administrations avoided putting on the negotiating table a freeze proposal indicated by polls to be endorsed by between 70 and 80% of the American people. Cities have planning and zoning authority in regard to such matters as affect the health, safety, welfare, morals, and aesthetics of local life, and their right to register support for a freeze or to establish nuclear free zone ordinances under such authority has not been challenged by the federal government.

In testimony before the budget committee of the U.S. Congress on February 14, 1987, Larry Agran, the mayor of Irvine, California, spoke of an "undeclared war on America's cities." He pointed out that in "spending nearly $300 billion per year for military purposes—roughly one-third of our national treasure—we have neglected the serious technical and social problems of urban and suburban life" (Shuman, 1987, pp. 18–19). Chicago, Illinois, and Oakland, California, are two of the largest U.S. cities to have declared themselves nuclear-free zones. Los Angeles is the largest city to have passed an ordinance requiring its staff to prepare and publish an annual report on the economic impacts of military spending. Los Angeles mayor, Tom Bradley, asserted in his 1985 keynote address to the congress of the National League of Cities, that cities have not only a right but an obligation to be part of the national debate on nuclear weapons. Is it just a coincidence that the men who were mayors of these three large American cities at the time they legislated their concerns about the negative effects of the nuclear arms race all happened to be black? Was it not relevant that they were members of a group of Americans particularly hard hit by the lopsided favoring of military expenditures over social welfare, health, child-care, and education programs?

Decreasing the Incentive and/or Ability to Manufacture Nuclear Weapons

Resolutions and votes. Nuclear free zoning directly inhibits the ability of manufacturers, in districts where the NFZ is being enforced, to produce nuclear weapons. NFZs result from voting by citizens who believe themselves to have a personal stake in the issue. In addition to local citizens, at least two other bodies of people who might feel they have a stake in the issue can, through voting, potentially inhibit companies from the production of nuclear weapons. These groups are the companies' employees and the companies' stockholders.

The workers of Lucas Aerospace and Vickers companies in England have earned a worldwide reputation for their proposals and campaigns to achieve socially useful production. Their efforts have been based on "the simple but revolutionary idea that in a society where there are substantial unfilled needs it makes no sense to put people, who could be making products to fill those needs, on the dole or into arms manufacturing" (Kaldor, 1981, p. 186). The workers' unions achieved conversion from military production to the production of consumer goods with the help of unions in supplier industries, on the one hand, and consumer organizations, on the other. The Lucas Aerospace workers, in getting their management to undertake the manufacture of socially useful products, are inserting their own criteria, as both producers and consumers, into the choice of items their company makes.

A surge of socially responsible activity involving voting has taken place on the shareholder front over the past few years as well. This has occurred in regard to South African involvement, with Sara Lee Corporation, for example, withdrawing from South Africa in the face of a shareholder resolution that they should do so. As chair John Bryan said, "You can debate the moral question of whether it's better to stay or go, but the shareholder is the one who owns us. If he says 'Get out,' and it can be done without penalizing the company, that's what you do" (Marlin, Lydenberg, & Strub, 1987). There is no reason why shareholders of AT&T or GE might not, at some future date, develop sufficient inclination and clout to effectively insist, in like manner, that their companies get out of the manufacturing of components for nuclear weapons systems—perhaps starting, conservatively, with the most destabilizing ones. (A GE Stockholders Alliance Against Nuclear Power and Nuclear Weapons has existed for several years and has representatives in nearly every state, but its resolutions and dialogue with corporate management have yet to bear significant fruit [Tritch, 1986]).

Conversion. Many of the disarmament efforts described in previous sections have been aimed at the role of armaments as objects of use. As analyst Kaldor points out, to reverse effectively the armament process, we also need to undermine the weapons' role as objects of production (Kaldor, 1981). To do this, conversion should actively *precede* disarmament, rather than being a begrudgingly undertaken post-disarmament-treaty obligation. Conversion can remove an aggravating cause of war. The more successfully it is pursued by corporate America, the less economic incentive there is to continue the arms race and the militarization of thinking and priorities that accompany it. As far as the Soviets are concerned, the timing is promising. Their State Planning Commission, which had long taken the position that conversion planning would be carried on only after the achievement of full political détente with the United States, has changed its view in recent years. As of March, 1987, representatives of the State Planning Commission assured American economist Seymour Melman that it had become the policy of their government and Mikhail Gorbachev to support planning for conversion from a military to a civilian economy, and they pledged cooperation in a joint U.S.-Soviet symposium on the topic.

Several U.S. nonprofit organizations are devoted to promoting conversion through reestablished channels. These channels include education (of both the public and relevant high level decision-makers—e.g., 20/20 Vision, Nuclear Dialogue) and the putting together of and lobbying for legislation (e.g. Nuclear Free Zones groups). Arguing that America's real national security comes from jobs and prosperity, not missiles and warheads, JOBS WITH PEACE registers voters, sponsors referenda, conducts town meetings, and testifies at government hearings in its efforts to "reduce military spending and reinvest in America." By freezing the arms race and reducing Pentagon waste, they assert, some $55 billion could be made available for more reasonable priorities annually. In their mailings, they bring the issue down to the immediate level of the individual. "This year [1989], the average household in the United States will pay $5,767 in federal taxes. [Of this], $3,103 will go for military spending; $115 will go for housing; $126 will go for education," they write, citing the Office of Management and Budget (Jobs With Peace Campaign, 1989). With similar alarm at over 50% of the federal budget going to the military, the Ad Hoc Committee for a Better Budget of the Women's International League for Peace and Freedom in Santa Clara County, California, set out to educate its membership and local elected congressional representatives on how the budget process can and should be influenced to reflect more peace-oriented priorities. Also in California is the Center for Economic Conversion, with a major focus on the companies—heavily invested in military contracting—located in the "Silicon Valley" area south of San Francisco. In Washington, DC, one may now find a non-governmental organization called the National Commission for Economic Conversion and Disarmament. Its purpose is to educate the public on why transfer of military resources to civilian uses through conversion and disarmament planning is necessary for reversing the arms race and restoring the nation's economic health.

Boycott. Two somewhat less established and direct, but nonetheless legitimate and effective, means of creating an incentive toward conversion are the economic tactics of the boycott and investment conversion. Both tactics are readily available to every citizen; the means of effecting them lie squarely in the hands of any consumer. Both approaches, actually, represent forms of boycott, with the first a boycott of purchasable products and the second a boycott of purchasable stock. In the last decade, INFACT created an effective boycott of the Nestle company, outraged at the sickness and death of thousands of African children due to Nestle's socially irresponsible practices. In the present decade, INFACT has taken on the General Electric corporation. It has done so out of anger at its lobbying for, promoting, and generally profiteering from the production of nuclear weapons. They call upon GE to "cease production, marketing, and promotion of nuclear weapons; stop interfering with government decision-making on military matters; and draw up conversion plans" (Tritch, 1986). The boycott claims some success to date, with hospitals shunning half-million-dollar GE CATscanners, major universities pulling GE products off shelves at campus stores, "GE free" apartment complexes going up, over 3.5 million Americans boycotting GE goods as of November 1990, and more than 15% of the American public now aware that the boycott is underway. Goals for next year include 5% of the U.S. population involved in the boycott and 33.3% aware of it, with 100 community-based GE Boycott Action Committees building nationwide. The group believes it has cost GE $18 million in lost medical sales and more than $100 million in lost general sales to date (K. Zamarin, personal communication, October 26, 1990).

Amy Domini, an investment counselor and co-author of the book *Ethical Investing*, sees the goal of the INFACT boycott as not so much a matter of affecting sales, as one of altering GE's corporate image. Inherent in the boycott she sees "a threat that business as usual ought to consider the welfare of humankind, that business as usual is about more than money. There is a fear about how far *this sort of thing* is going to go" (Tritch, 1986). That it goes, in fact, beyond INFACT, is indicated by the existence of other boycotts. Nuclear Free America, a Baltimore-based organization, is boycotting AT&T for its major role in running the Sandia nuclear weapons lab, as well as its role in developing, producing, and selling a number of critical nuclear weapons parts. As part of a broader campaign against the top 50 nuclear weapons contractors, Nuclear Free America, in a campaign whose flyer reads "Reach Out and Touch a Nuclear Weapons Contractor," urges citizens to switch their long distance phone service from AT&T, signaling the move on a post card labeled "AT&T, The *wrong* choice" (*The New Abolitionist*, 1987).

Socially responsible investing. The boycotting of nuclear weapons-producing firms in terms of investment can, of course, be done via the selection of individual investments managed by private citizens. It needn't be, however. One can take advantage of professional management and diversification by investing in a growing number of socially responsible mutual funds. Pax World lays claim to being the "first social responsibility fund to stress investment in non-war-related industries" (Pax World Fund, 1988). The Fund is a "no-load, open end, diversified mutual fund" that "endeavors to make a contribution to world peace through investing in companies producing life-supportive goods and services." The Fund is set up to meet economic as well as social criteria, and points out in its prospectus that it has not only paid dividends each year since its inception in the early 1970s, but has also made capital gains payments from time to time. The San Francisco-based Working Assets mutual fund, founded in 1983, has assets approaching $100 million. It shuns companies holding military contracts, generating nuclear power, supporting repressive regimes, or following bad labor policies. Two other similar mutual funds are Calvert and New Alternatives (Marlin, Lydenberg, & Strub, 1987). As with the boycotting of consumable products, investment boycotting so far has undoubtedly done more in the way of raising consciousness and affecting corporate images than it has in the way of undermining corporate funding. A notion of its potential, however, can be glimpsed from the tens of billions of dollars mandated for divestment from companies with holdings in South Africa once mammoth pension funds (e.g., New York State; college and university teachers nationally) got into the anti-apartheid act.

The talk-show host Phil Donahue, an educated commentator on the national scene, recently stated that in the United States, "we have an economy built on war and Christmas." Instead of accepting this, he went on to imply, we need to adopt the perspective of William Winpisinger, the respected union leader of the International Association of Machinists and Aerospace Workers (many of whose members work in defense plants). He applauds Mr. Winpisinger for his courage in asserting that "we have got to begin to convert our economy from one that is vulnerable to being described as militaristic and move it toward the production of products that create an aftermarket. A tank has no aftermarket. It sits in a field and it eventually rusts . . . " (*Beyond War*, 1989, p. 8). Whether through legislation, nuclear-free zoning ordinances, boycotts of products or stock, or protest, efforts must be continued and increased to stanch the flow of corporation profits which the Center for Defense Information, among many others, contends are driving the arms race (Tritch, 1986).

Protesting Nuclear Weapons Deployment and Transport

At the end of the chain of events involved in the development of nuclear weapons are the nuclear weapons themselves. They sit in silos in the middle of the country. They are loaded in and out of nuclear submarines in seaports. They are stored and loaded on and off aircraft at airforce bases. They are transported from plants to deployment sites by truck.

Possible legal, non-military channels for removing these weapons from their routes of transport and sites of deployment have been discussed already. They include the legislation of a freeze, the making and ratifying of arms-control treaties, and (potentially) the establishment of nuclear-free zones.

What remains to be discussed are interference with and attempts to disable weapons, weapons bases, or weapons transport, that do not come under the aegis of established approaches. Out of respect for the arguments of the persons of conscience who carry them out, these approaches shall not be referred to here as "illegal." We shall, however, refer to these as acts of civil disobedience—despite some of their authors' objections to this phrase as well, and their preference of the term "divine obedience" (Friedman, 1988, p. 37). The actions we are referring to clearly involve disobedience of various posted signs and rules, a fact that we feel can be acknowledged without a necessary finding of illegality. They are essentially symbolic acts, intended to arouse the conscience of the nation, and do not tend to represent significant degrees of sabotage.

At the beginning of 1988 it was reported that there had been over 15,000 arrests in the United States and Canada for antinuclear civil disobedience since the heyday of the Freeze movement in 1983 (Friedman, 1988). Despite this, publicity has been minimal. What's more, judges, for the most part, have refused to permit discussion of perpetrators' motives in their courtrooms. This has resulted, as the attorney of Plowshares protestor Katya Komisaruk put it, in the trials amounting to an opportunity for the defendant to "be present while the government presented its case to 12 people." In her case, and many others, defendant and lawyers were forbidden by a gag rule to speak about ethics or morality, U.S. policy, the Geneva Convention, protection of our children, the Nuremberg Principles, or international law. In short, all evidence and testimony of intent to help prevent nuclear war was excluded from the trial. Sentences have been extremely heavy in many cases. Komisaruk walked through an unguarded gate at Vandenberg Air Force Base on June 2, 1987, and damaged a computer linked to a missile guidance system. After waiting two hours to be arrested she left, leaving a bouquet of flowers for the absent security guards and the words "Nuremberg" and "international law" spray-painted on the walls. She turned herself in the following day at a press conference in San Francisco. Found guilty at her "trial," she was sentenced to five years in federal prison and "restitution" of a half-million dollars. Other Plowshares defendants have had stiffer sentences, Father Carl Kabat receiving 18 years, and Helen Woodson, a mother of 11 children, serving a sentence of 12 years (Goldberger, 1988).

With prison terms more punitive than the average rapist or kidnapper might expect, how is it the press has been so silent on these cases? Is it, as Steven Ladd of the Education Film and Video Project in Berkeley, California, suggests (Friedman, 1988, p. 27), just that "it's become so commonplace"? I don't think so. I think it reflects several serious problems with the use of civil disobedience in the effort to end the arms race—problems that go back to the "distance" we spoke of having to overcome to get people to comprehend the threat in the first place.

When a video clip can be seen of a bloodied black person being pushed off a bus by white men after defiantly sitting in the "wrong" section, there can be instant and widespread sympathy with the plight of the "disobedient" individual. Such sympathy is evoked by several factors: (a) the clear unacceptability of the rule defied; (b) the immediacy of the rule's effect on the individual who defied it; (c) the obvious, physical nature of the suffering inflicted on the individual who defied the rule; (d) the lack of recourse one imagines the individual to have to any other method of redressing the wrongful rule. Not one of these factors exists in any immediate, filmable form in regard to acts of antinuclear civil disobedience. Instead: (a) the laws being defied are laws protecting public and private property, "which are not inherently offensive statutes," as law professor Charles DiSalva points out (Friedman, 1988, p. 28); (b) the connection between the nuclear arms race and injury to the trespassing individual is by no means clear and direct— indeed, the connection between his or her symbolic pouring of blood on the missile or hammering on its concrete cover and the ending of the arms race is a bit of a stretch; (c) the suffering of demonstrators put away in prisons is neither visible nor photographically compelling even if it could be filmed; (d) there exist numerous other approaches (see above) by which to attempt to end the arms race accessible to the generally middle-class individuals undertaking the acts of civil disobedience. For all these reasons, then, antinuclear civil disobedience lacks prime-time punch, and *that*, I would assert, rather than its being commonplace, is the reason for its neglect by the media.

The issue simply lacks immediacy. For starters, as has been mentioned before, we are not even genetically hard-wired to react to the sight of a bomb with fear—if we should ever be able to see one. As for what present harm the arms race does, the harm is not *directly* connected to the race. You can't walk over to an SAC commander, or a GE chief executive officer, with a hungry, sick, uneducated child in your arms, say "You did this," and expect to have it make any sense to anyone. Concern over the weapons as objects of use faces an equally great comprehension gap. A present-time desperate act, engaged in against an imagined future harm, appears as unseemly as does a desperate act in any particular location, engaged in against a chain of events occurring remotely from the locus and from one another. American Peace Test (APT), in its search for some purchase hold of immediacy on the body of the slippery, vague beast of nuclear militarism, goes straight to the warhead testing site. But even the scene there lacks poignancy. The tests are underground. Instead of a pitiful boatful of brave souls X-rayed *in situ* by an atmospheric blast over the cruel waves of the Pacific, we have a group of people trespassing over a fence and walking across some ground miles from some spot where the ground will shake and cave in a bit. Where's the picture for page one?

Nukewatch, a national organization based in Madison, Wisconsin, strives for immediacy through their H-Bomb Truck Watch and their Missile Silo Campaign programs. In the former, they follow and draw attention to the unmarked Department of Energy convoys transporting nuclear weapons. They stage demonstrations along the routes. In their Missile Silo Campaign, they distribute maps to familiarize the public with the location in their midst of the 1,000 Minutemen ICBMs, buried across seven Midwestern and Great Plains states (Humanitas, 1987). As with APT, this seems a worthy attempt. But with the sight of trucks as unfrightening as it is, it shows the lengths to which one must go to achieve any immediacy at all in the matter.

I raise these problems in the hopes they can somehow be overcome, and nonviolent demonstrations be made to work more effectively than they have to date. I do believe antinuclear demonstrations have had some positive effects, as intended, serving to rouse the consciences of a number of U.S. citizens. Depending on the exact nature of the demonstration, such effects can outweigh the negative ones of disaffecting a certain number of people with the unseemliness or temporal "illegality" of the acts. Though I would hope it would not be necessary to go to the lengths some of them did, the Suffragettes proved at the start of this century that an issue lacking in immediate physical imagery can nonetheless be demonstrated against with adequate effect.

CONCLUSION: WHAT THE READER CAN DO

In the previous chapter, we examined the national options in the nuclear era. In this one, we have traced the path that individuals must follow to get from "business as usual" to the point of action to end a nuclear arms race that threatens our children's lives, while eroding their happiness, prosperity, and true security. We have defined, albeit with a certain acknowledged arbitrariness of sequencing, a pathway with specific branching points leading towards action to end the arms race. In doing so, we hope to have created a model useful both for planning effective interventions and for conducting further research. Studies might be undertaken, for example, to determine the relative importance of the different branching points in our schema in different segments of the population. It is also hoped that readers may find our model, or at least particular aspects of it, applicable to the movement of individuals from "business as usual" to action against other horrendous death-producing behaviors. Such movement will be necessary for humankind to survive for very long, as disaster from ecological devastation lies, in the evolutionary scheme of things, only a moment or two behind the prospect of devastation from weapons of mass destruction.

I indicated above that I would list some recommendations for any persons unsure of what they would like to do. It is fitting in a time that has seen a rebirth of behavioral psychology that we should conclude our section on the psychology of survival-directed action with suggestions for specific survival-directed behaviors— actions that could be carried out by the reader, or others the reader might wish to inspire.

Self-Education

Before taking action involving others, it is a good idea to inform yourself on various matters relevant to ending the arms race. This can be accomplished through listening to informed others, reading informed sources, and joining groups whose aims include education of their membership.

Listening. You can attend public and university lectures on topics from weapons accidents to grass-roots organizing. The Houses of Congress may be heard and witnessed on television (C-Span Cable TV) in debate on matters ranging from defense appropriations to confirmation of Secretaries of Defense. You can rent or purchase audio tapes, video tapes, or films (e.g. via the Educational Film & Video Project, 5332 College Ave., Suite 101, Oakland, CA 94618 [tel. (415) 655–9050]). Or you can call the Council for a Livable World Arms Control Hotline and listen to its biweekly updated information and suggested action message [(202) 543–0006].

Reading. Important books abound on different aspects of ending the arms race. My own list of just a few would have to include Freeman Dyson's *Weapons and Hope* (Harper & Row, 1985), Jerome Frank's *Sanity and Survival in the Nuclear Age* (Random House, 1982), Ralph K. White's (Ed.) *Psychology and the Prevention of Nuclear War* (University Press, 1986), Ruth Adams' and Susan Cullen's (Eds.) *The Final Epidemic* (University of Chicago Press, 1981), Jonathan Schell's *Fate of the Earth* (Knopf, 1982), E. P. Thompson and Dan Smith's (Eds.) *Protest and Survive* (Monthly Review Press, 1981), Steve Kull's *Minds at War* (Basic Books, 1988), and Robert Jay Lifton's and Richard Falk's *Indefensible Weapons* (Basic Books, 1982). Additionally, Roger Walsh's *Staying Alive* (Shambhala, 1984) provides a stimulating blend of the spiritual and psychological aspects of the challenge, while a book like Robert Cialdini's *Influence: Science and Practice* (Scott, Foresman & Co., 1985) offers a highly readable smorgasbord of social-psychology findings with direct application to the "selling of peace." Absolutely essential subscriptions for anyone wishing to keep up with the academic, Washington, and grass roots developments in the arms control/disarmament race are *The Bulletin of the Atomic Scientists* (don't be put off by its title, it is intended to be read by the public and is quite reader-friendly) and *Nuclear Times. Common Cause Magazine, The Washington Spectator*, and *the Nation* run pertinent articles at frequent intervals. For those with only one minute for reading and nineteen minutes for action on this topic each month, a subscription to 20/20 Vision's monthly postcard is the answer.

Joining. For those with sufficient interest and lots of time, a truly significant means of educating yourself and others might be by joining the staff of a candidate for Congress whose position on arms control you'd like to see reflected in national policy. Education may also be had by joining whatever public gallery of auditors may be welcome at relevant governmental meetings, or at international security and arms-control centers or other university-based or private organizations bent on studying the arms race from a scholarly or professional perspective.

A number of groups have already been mentioned above that have far-flung chapters (probably one near you) and focus on particular aspects of the arms race or on particular approaches towards ending it. These include Jobs With Peace, SANE/Freeze, INFACT, United Nations Association, Beyond War, Nuclear Dialogue, American Peace Test, Common Cause, and others. If one or another of the aspects represented seems particularly germane to your understanding of the problem, by all means look into joining that group.

In the American tradition of forming societies around every issue imaginable, a variety of specialized groups have sprung up, focused on the contribution that specific roles, trades, or professions might be able to make to ending the arms race. Joining one of these can prove an extremely enjoyable and effective means of magnifying your influence. As with all similar American societies, these may be joined in expectation of making valuable social and professional contacts, as well as utilizing your particular training to promote the survival-directed pathway. A listing of some of these may provide you with an idea of one particularly appropriate for you to locate and join: Lawyers Alliance for Nuclear Arms Control (LANAC, 43 Charles St., Boston, MA [(617) 227-0118]—"attorneys are the experts at negotiation . . . "); Architects/Designers/Planners for Social Responsibility (ADPSR, 225 Lafayette St., New York, NY 10012 [(212) 334-8104]—"build homes—not bombs"); Business Executives for National Security (BENS, 601 Pennsylvania Ave. NW, Washington, DC 20009 [(202) 737-1090]—"Defense is a business . . . it could be better managed . . . "); Educators for Social Responsibility (ESR, Dept. NT, 23 Garden St., Cambridge, MA 02138 [(617) 492-1746]—education about nuclear war, the arms race, the Soviet Union, conflict and its management . . .); Women's Action for Nuclear Disarmament (WAND, 691 Massachusetts Ave., Arlington, MA 02174 [(617) 643-4880]—"Mother's Day for Peace . . . "); Physicians for Social Responsibility (PSR, 1601 Connecticut Ave. NW, Washington, DC 20009 [(202) 939-5750]—the medical consequences, the social costs . . .); Psychologists for Social Responsibility (PsySR, 1841 Columbia Rd. NW, Washington, DC 20009 [(202) 745-7084]—the arms race as human behavior . . .]; Librarians for Nuclear Arms Control (LNAC, P.O. Box 1496, Santa Monica, CA 90406—establishing a national peace information network . . .); the International Society for the Study of Nuclear Texts and Contexts (ISSNTC, c/o Paul Brians, Dept. of English, Washington State University, Pullman, WA 99164-5020—confronting the nuclear threat through the study and teaching of modern languages and literature . . .); Foundation for the Arts of Peace (1918 Bonita Ave., Third Floor, Berkeley, CA 94704 [(415) 486-0264]—Communications and marketing for global peace and security . . .); Computer Professionals for Social Responsibility (CPSR, P.O. Box 717, Palo Alto, CA 94301 [(415) 322-3778]—reliability and risk in critical systems; the unfeasibility of Star Wars software; privacy and civil liberties . . .); the Union of Concerned Scientists (UCS, 26 Church St., Cambridge, MA 02238 [(617) 547-5552]—the dangers of nuclear power and nuclear weapons); the Federation of American Scientists (FAS, 307 Massachusetts Ave. NE, Washington, DC 20002 [(202) 546-3300]—research, education, and lobbying on aspects of the arms race); Grandmothers for Peace (909 12th St., Ste. 118, Sacramento, CA 95814 [(916) 444-5080]—activists, putting love on the line . . .); Economists Against the Arms Race (—30 W 95th St., New York, NY 10025—Founded by Ken Arrow and Lawrence Klein, it has six Nobel Laureates in Economics on its Board of Directors). If your own niche isn't there, chances are a group exists and I haven't happened to hear of it. If it doesn't, why not start one? There is hardly a human enterprise imaginable that couldn't be creatively related by some means or other to ending the nuclear arms race.

Action

Having read and listened, subscribed and joined, you are ready for action. We shall end our description of a pathway to action with a few basic suggestions for types of activities you might want to consider, in addition to others mentioned earlier in this section.

Arrange meetings. The research of Mehr and Webster (1985) indicates that one of the most powerful activities for creating more active individuals is the arranging of group meetings with audio-visual presentations and/or speakers. This may be done by renting public halls and printing up your own flyers, but it may be done a good deal more easily by lining up such events within ready-made contexts. Examples of these include after-service religious forums, school classes, company employee seminars, club luncheons or other club get-togethers (with the clubs being of a social, political, recreational, activist, or other nature), and hospital or other institutional rounds or seminars. Such gatherings, indeed, are often eager for suggested topics, films, and/or speakers. Simplest of all may be to invite people over to your own home to watch a film or meet a speaker. Friends invited to private homes for such meetings may be particularly affected.

Write. Never hesitate to write to elected representatives. It helps greatly to indicate you live in their district and vote in every election, as well as to indicate your affiliation with a group of like-minded individuals (who also vote). It is said that elected officials receiving letters count each as representing hundreds of other people with the same opinion who didn't get around to writing. You may wish to be brief and quick, in which case send a telegram. Sending letters to the editor of a newspaper, or writing freelance editorials (especially when made topical to a certain newsworthy event or holiday or time of year) can be a very effective way of getting material widely read. Other worthy targets for writing include the programming managers of radio and TV shows (to seek more programming educating people to the need to end the arms race), chief executive officers of nuclear weapons-related contracting corporations (indicating unhappiness, urging conversion), and people who devise school curricula (urging education on the medical, social, economic, and psychological aspects of the arms race, as well as human conflict behavior and its management).

Talk. Telephone the offices of your local representatives or other decision-makers. If you can't speak with the principal individuals, talk with their assistants in the relevant area. Call in to radio or TV talk shows. Attend governmental hearings or the local meetings of elected representatives and speak up. Give talks to groups yourself: become the speaker at the meetings you arrange. Join Nuclear Dialogue (106 Fitz Randolph Road, Princeton, NJ 08540, [609] 924-1015], or work through the speakers' bureau of the concerned organization you have joined, and become versed on particular issues to discuss with particular decision-makers or other audiences.

Demonstrate. If you feel it is indicated and you are inclined to do so, demonstrate. Demonstrate against whatever point in the arms race feels most salient to you, or against a part of it that is nearest at hand. If you are considering the pros and cons of participating in a large demonstration, recall how effective they can be. When, by some estimates, over a million people demonstrated in New York City on June 12, 1982, it sent a signal to Washington that forced a shift away from a policy of nuclear saber-rattling and confrontational rhetoric towards the Soviet

Union. When hundreds of thousands marched on the Pentagon in a "moratorium" during the late '60s, both Nixon's and Haldeman's memoirs indicate the action was critical in changing Nixon's decision to deliver a nuclear ultimatum to Hanoi.

Donate. If you approve of the efforts of a particular organization, if it seems to you to have a particularly advantageous leverage point from which to upset the nuclear status quo, support it. Donating to a "peace PAC" like Council for a Livable World while simultaneously supporting Common Cause in its efforts to end PACs is not necessarily a contradiction. It's like betting on specific numbers at roulette while covering the double zero that wins when all bets are off; it makes sense, at least at this point in time. Groups involved in lobbying, research, or education, as well as the many organizations involved in all three of these activities, need our financial support to carry out work that can be extremely influential. And if you sympathize with civil disobedience, but for a variety of possible reasons may not feel like engaging in it yourself, give it your financial support. Contribute to Plowshares Defense Fund (36 E. 12th St., New York, NY 10003) in support of the Plowshares defendants on trial for direct assaults upon nuclear weapons in a symbolic carrying out of the Biblical injunction of Isaiah to beat "swords into plowshares." Become a "Friend of the Rainbow Warrior" (P.O. Box 96099, Washington, DC 20090–6099), in support of the nonviolent navy that Greenpeace launches against the nuclear threat, among others. If you have a desire to help financially but no strong preferences as to how you wish to do so, your smartest investment in the future might well be a professionally managed charitable "mutual fund." Ploughshares Fund, based at Fort Mason in San Francisco [telephone: (415) 775-2244], is a fine example of such a publicly supported charitable foundation. Established by Sally Lilienthal in 1981, it funds a multitude of projects, selected through careful research, which are likely to promote arms reduction and nuclear disarmament.

Volunteer. If you don't feel like joining an organization to end the arms race on a "full-time member" basis, consider volunteering time or energy in spare moments when you have it. As with water conservation, every drop counts. One should never refrain from an action, no matter how small, thinking it inconsequential. Perhaps you could volunteer to make a poster for an event, to play music at a benefit concert. Or perhaps your skills lie in clerical, accounting, sales, advertising, communications, marketing, or fundraising. Any such skills are more than welcome on either a short- or long-term basis by the various sorts of organizations discussed above.

Travel. Given the right circumstances, travel can be an effective means of (a) spreading good will and dispelling mistrust; (b) learning of the "humanity" of people in adversarial nations, as well as the strengths and problems of their countries; (c) developing specific ties of individual friendship and/or professional association; (d) developing a sense of world citizenship; (e) acquiring knowledge and "credentials" with which to become an educator of others upon these subjects. Post-travel education may be a matter of slide shows or articles. The travel itself may be either as an individual or with an organized group, either as a tourist or with a professional or avocational interest in mind. The motivation is often irrelevant to the value it can provide. "Living and studying in other peoples' countries," Senator J. William Fulbright once stated, "helps get over the human tendency to go to war every little bit" (Fulbright, 1987).

REFERENCES

ABC-TV (1988, December 1). The business of defense: Flaws in the shield. An ABC *Close Up* news special anchored by Tom Jarriel.

Alvarez, R., Blackwelder, B., & Makhijani, A. (1988). Letter to shareholders of Westinghouse from the Environmental Policy Institute. Reprinted in *Greenpeace*, 13(6), 13.

American Psychological Association. (1990). The Seville statement on violence. *American Psychologist*, 45(10), 1167–1168.

Bandura, A. (in press). Social cognitive theory of moral thought and action. In W. M. Kurtines & J. L. Gewirtz (Eds.), *Moral behavior and development: Advances in theory, research, and applications* (Vol. I). Hillsdale, NJ: Erlbaum.

Bandura, A., Underwood, B., & Fromson, M. E. (1975). Disinhibition of aggression through diffusion of responsibility and dehumanization of victims. *Journal of Research in Personality, 9*, 253–269.

Beardsley, W., & Mack, J. (1982). The impact of nuclear advances on children and adolescents. In Rogers, R., Beardslee, W., Carson, D., Frank, J., Mack, J., & Mufson, M. (Eds.), *The psychosocial aspects of nuclear developments* Task Force Report No. 20, pp. 64–93. Washington, DC: American Psychiatric Association.

Beck, K., & Frankel, A. (1981). A conceptualization of threat communications and protective health behavior. *Social Psychology Quarterly, 44*, 204–217.

Bethe, H. (1989, February 1). The future of arms control. A talk given at the Center for International Security and Arms Control, Stanford University.

Beyond War (1989, February). TV's spacebridge veterans speak out. On *Beyond War, 46*. Palo Alto, CA: Author.

Blight, J. G. (1987). Toward a policy-relevant psychology of avoiding nuclear war. *American Psychologist, 42*(1), 12–29.

Blum, D. (1988). Weird science: Livermore's X-ray laser flap. *Bulletin of the Atomic Scientists, 44*(6), 7–13.

Brickman, P., Rabinowitz, V. C., Karuza, J., Coates, D., Cohn, E., & Kidder, L. (1982). Models of helping and coping. *American Psychologist, 37*, 368–384.

Bulletin of Municipal Foreign Policy (Spring, 1987). (A quarterly publication of the Local Elected Officials Project of the Center for Innovative Diplomacy, Irvine, CA.)

Center for Foreign Policy Development (1988). Public Summit '88 results. *Update, 3*(1) 2–3. Providence, RI: Brown University.

Chaiken, S., & Eagly, A. (1976). Communication modality as a determinant of message persuasiveness and message comprehensibility. *Journal of Personality and Social Psychology, 34*, 605ff.

Chivian, E., Mack, J. E., Walotzky, J., Lazaroff, C., Doctor, R., & Goldenring, J. M. (1985). Soviet children and the threat of nuclear war: A preliminary study. *American Journal of Orthopsychiatry, 55*(4), 484–502.

Cialdini, R. (1985). *Influence: Science and practice*. Glenview, IL: Scott, Foresman.

Closson, M. (1988, October). Jobs, defense, and the U.S. economy. On *Beyond War, 43, 8*. Palo Alto, CA: Beyond War.

Coates, K. (1981). European nuclear disarmament. In E. P. Thompson & D. Smith (Eds.), *Protest and survive* (pp. 189–213). New York: Monthly Review Press.

Coffin, T. (1987). The quest for peace. *The Washington Spectator, 13*(22), 2.

Coffin, T. (1987a). The American mood: Protest and concern. *The Washington Spectator, 13*(13), 2.

Coffin, T. (1987b). A changing political scene. *The Washington Spectator, 13*(15), 1.

Coffin, T. (1987c). The American scene: The plight of children. *The Washington Spectator, 13*(19), 1.

Coffin, T. (1888a). The children of our cities. *The Washington Spectator, 14*(22), 3.

Coffin, T. (1988b). The high cost of health. *The Washington Spectator, 14*(8), 1.

Coffin, T. (1988c). For sale: The American political system. *The Washington Spectator, 14*(18), 4.

Coffin, T. (1988d). A look at the news media. *The Washington Spectator, 14*(4), 1.

Coffin, T. (1989). Home front problems for the new president. *The Washington Spectator, 15*(1), 1–4.

Cohn, C. (1987). Slick 'ems, glick 'ems, Christmas trees, and cookie cutters: Nuclear language and how we learned to pat the bomb. *Bulletin of the Atomic Scientists, 43*(5), pp. 17–24.

Deutsch, M., & Gerard, H. B. (1955). A study of normative and informational social influences upon individual judgment. *Journal of Abnormal and Social Psychology, 51*, 629–636.

Diamond, G., & Bachman, J. (1986). High-school seniors and the nuclear threat, 1975–1984: Political and mental health implications of concern and despair. In M. Schwebel (Ed.), *Mental Health Implications of Life in the Nuclear Age* (pp 210–241). Armonk, NY: M. E. Sharpe.

d'Heurle, A. (1987). The role of psychology in the development of the theories and strategies of peace. *Current research on peace and violence,* 10(223), 31–77.

Drell, S. D. (1983). *Facing the threat of nuclear weapons.* Seattle: University of Washington Press.

Drinan, R. P. (1988, January). Letter in solicitation of contributions to PeacePAC. Washington, DC: PeacePAC.

Dyson, F. (1985). *Weapons and hope.* New York: Harper & Row.

Eisenhower, D. (1960). *Public papers of the Presidents: Dwight D. Eisenhower, 1959.* Superintendent of Public Documents (Ed.). Washington, DC: U.S. Government Printing Office.

Ellsberg, D. (1981). Introduction: Call to mutiny. In E. P. Thompson & D. Smith (Eds.), *Protest and survive* (pp. i–xxviii). New York: Monthly Review Press.

Erikson, E. (1983, October). A developmental crisis of mankind? In *Prescription for prevention— Nuclear war: Our greatest health hazard* (pp. 112–120). Proceedings of the symposium at Stanford University sponsored by The Stanford University School of Medicine.

Evans, D. (1987, September 20). What both sides could gain in arms deal. A *Chicago Tribune* article reprinted in *the San Francisco Examiner,* p. A-20.

Ferguson, B. (1988). Different agendas, styles shape SANE/Freeze. *Bulletin of the Atomic Scientists,* 44(3), 26–30.

Ferry, W. H. (1981). By what right? In E. P. Thompson & D. Smith (Eds.), *Protest and Survive* (pp. 166–172). New York: Monthly Review Press.

Feshbach, S. (1986). Introduction and highlights of the literature, re Section XII: Changing war-related attitudes. In R. K. White (Ed.), *Psychology and the prevention of nuclear war* (pp. 513–516). New York: New York University Press.

Feshbach, S., Kandel, E., & Haist, F. (1985). Attitudes toward nuclear armament policies: An example of social research in behalf of social advocacy. In S. Oskamp (Ed.), *Applied social psychology annual* (vol. 6, pp. 107–126). Beverly Hills, CA: Sage.

Festinger, L. (1957). *A theory of cognitive dissonance.* Stanford, CA: Stanford University Press.

Findley, R. (1988, Spring). Nuclear dialogue: News from the Nuclear Dialogue project. Princeton, NJ: Nuclear Dialogue Project.

Fisher, R. (1981). Preventing nuclear war. In R. Adams & S. Cullen (Eds.), *The final epidemic: Physicians and scientists on nuclear war* (pp. 223–236). Chicago: University of Chicago Press.

Fiske, S. (1987). People's reactions to nuclear war. *American Psychologist,* 42(3), 207–217.

Fiske, S., Pratto, F., & Pavelchak, M. (1983). Citizens' images of nuclear war: Contents and consequences. *Journal of Social Issues,* 39(1), 41–65.

Flay, B., & Cook, T. (1981). Evaluation of mass media prevention campaigns. In R. E. Rice & W. J. Paisley (Eds.), *Public communication campaigns* (pp. 239–264). Beverly Hills, CA: Sage.

Frank, J. (1982a, May). Talk given at the symposium on psychological aspects of nuclear war, 1982 annual meeting of the American Psychiatric Association, Toronto.

Frank, J. (1982b). *Sanity and survival in the nuclear age.* New York: Random House.

Frank, J. (1987). The drive for power and the nuclear arms race. *The American Psychologist,* 42, 337–344.

Fransden, K. (1963). Effects of threat appeals and media of transmission. *Speech Monographs,* 30, 101ff.

Freedman, J. L., & Fraser, S. (1966). Compliance without pressure: The foot-in-the-door technique. *Journal of Personality and Social Psychology,* 4, 195–203.

French, P. (1983). Ignorance and the capacity to countenance nuclear war. Unpublished manuscript.

French, P. (1984). The physician as nuclear-war educator. *New England Journal of Medicine, 310*(21), 1397–1398.

French, P. (1986, March 1). Determinants of antinuclear activism. Talk given at seminar on Responses to the Nuclear Arms Race (H. Mehr, Chairperson), California Psychological Association annual meeting, San Francisco.

French, P., & Van Hoorn, J. (1986). Half a nation saw nuclear war and nobody blinked? A reassessment of the impact of *The Day After* in terms of a theoretical chain of causality. *International Journal of Mental Health,* 15(1–3), 276–297.

Friedman, M. (1988). Acts of conscience. *Nuclear Times,* 6(3), 22–37.

Fryszman, A. (1984, October/November). "Rapture" master Ronnie. *Nuclear Times,* 3(1), 10.

Fuguta, G. (Interviewee-1981, Jan. 29). *CBS News* with Walter Cronkite.

Fulbright, J. W. (1987). Changing minds. *The Washington Spectator,* 13(19), 1.

Gallup, G. (1956). Atomic warfare. Survey No. 566-K. *The Gallup poll.* Princeton, NJ: Author.

Gallup, G. (1986a). Federal budget deficit. Survey No. 261-G. *The Gallup Poll.* Princeton, NJ: Author.

Gallup, G. (1986b). Survey on national defense. Survey No. 262-G. *The Gallup Poll.* Princeton, NJ: Author.

Gallup, G. (1987). War and peace. Survey No. 269-G. *The Gallup Poll.* Princeton, NJ: Author.

Gayler, N. (1983, October). Nuclear weapons vs. security: A strategic analysis. In *Prescription for prevention—Nuclear war: Our greatest health hazard* (p. 60). Proceedings of the symposium at Stanford University and sponsored by The Stanford University School of Medicine. Stanford, CA.

Gilbert, R. K. (1988). The dynamics of inaction: Psychological factors inhibiting arms control activism. *The American Psychologist, 43*(10), 755–764.

Goldberger, P. (1988). Plowshares defense fund. A mailing from the Disarm Education Fund, 36 E. 12th St., New York, NY 10003.

Goldenring, J. M. & Doctor, R. (1986). Teenage worry about nuclear war. *International Journal of Mental Health, 15*(1–3), 72–92.

Gollon, P. J. (1986). SDI funds costly for scientists. *Bulletin of the Atomic Scientists, 42*(1), 24–27.

Granberg, D., & Faye, N. (1972). Sensitizing people by making the abstract concrete: Study of the effect of Hiroshima-Nagasaki. *American Journal of Orthopsychiatry, 42*, 811.

Greenwald, D., & Zeitlin, S. (1987). *No reason to talk about it: Families confront the nuclear taboo.* New York: W. W. Norton.

Gregory, W., Cialdini, R., & Carpenter, K. (1982). Self-relevant scenarios as mediators of likelihood estimates and compliance: Does imagining make it so? *Journal of Personality and Social Psychology, 43*, 89–99.

Ground Zero (1982). *Nuclear war: What's in it for you?* New York: Pocket Books.

Gurman, L. (1988). Walking away from Star Wars. *Bulletin of the Atomic Scientists, 44*(3), 6–8.

Hamilton, S., Chavez, E., & Keilin, W. (1986). Thoughts of Armageddon: The relationship between attitudes toward the nuclear threat and cognitive/emotional responses. *International Journal of Mental Health, 15*(1–3), 189–207.

Herken, G. (1987). The earthly origins of Star Wars. *Bulletin of the Atomic Scientists, 43*(8), 20–28.

Herrington, B. (1982). APA report warns of impact of nuclear world. *Psychiatric News, 17*(4), p. 1–29.

Humanitas International. (1987). Nukewatch. *Humanitas newsletter, 2*, 7. Menlo Park, CA: Author.

Janis, I., & Feshbach, S. (1953). Effects of fear-arousing communication. *Journal of Abnormal and Social Psychology, 48*, 78–92.

Jeffries, V. (1974). Political generations and the acceptance or rejection of nuclear warfare. *Journal of Social Issues, 30*, 119–136.

Jobs With Peace Campaign (1989, February 2). A national budget for jobs with peace. Flyer sent with letter from J. Nelson, Executive Director, Jobs With Peace. Boston, MA.

Jones, S. (1988, January). Arrested Lockheed protesters cite defense of necessity. *Peace Times*, pp. 1–3. San Jose, CA: San Jose Peace Center/Fellowship of Reconciliation.

Kaldor, M. (1981). Disarmament: The armament process in reverse. In E. P. Thompson & D. Smith (Eds.), *Protest and survive* (pp. 173–188). New York: Monthly Review Press.

Kaplan, D. E. (1981). Where the bombs are. *New West, 6*,(4), 76–.

Klineberg, O. (1984). Public opinion and nuclear war. *American Psychologist, 39*(11), 1245–1253.

Kogut, J., & Weissman, M. (1986). Taking the pledge against Star Wars. *Bulletin of the Atomic Scientists, 42*(1), 27–30.

Kotz, N. (1988, July/August). The mysterious case of the B-1 bomber. *Common Cause Magazine, 14*(4), 36–38.

Krepon, M. (1984). *Strategic stalemate: Nuclear weapons and arms control in American politics.* New York: St. Martin's.

Kull, S. (1985). Nuclear nonsense. *Foreign Policy, 58*, 28–52.

Kull, S. (1988). *Minds at war: Nuclear reality and the inner conflicts of defense policymakers.* New York: Basic.

Latane, B., & Darley, J. (1968). Group inhibition of bystander interventions in emergencies. *Journal of Personality and Social Psychology, 10*, 215–221.

Leventhal, H. (1970). Findings and theory in the study of fear communications. In L. Berkowitz (Ed.), *Advances in experimental social psychology* (Vol. 5, pp. 114–86). New York: Academic Press.

Leventhal, H., Singer, R., & Jones, S. (1965). Effects of fear and specificity of recommendations upon attitudes and behavior. *Journal of Personality and Social Psychology 2*, 20–29.

Lifton, R. (1987, May 12). Nuclear normality: Dubious assumptions. In P. French (Chair), *Psychoso-*

cial research on adaptation to the nuclear age. Symposium conducted at the annual meeting of the American Psychiatric Association, Chicago.

Lifton, R., & Falk, R. (1982). *Indefensible weapons: The political and psychological case against nuclearism.* New York: Basic Books.

Locatelli, M., & Holt, R. (1986). Antinuclear activism, psychic numbing, and mental health. In M. Schwebel (Ed.), *Mental health implications of life in the nuclear age* (pp. 143–161). Armonk, NY: M. E. Sharpe.

Mack, J. (1981). Psychosocial trauma. In R. Adams and S. Cullen (Eds.), *The final epidemic* (pp. 21–34). Chicago: University of Chicago Press.

Manoff, R. K. (1983, October). The role of the media in war and peace. In *Prescription for prevention—Nuclear war: Our greatest health hazard* (pp. 203–212). Proceedings of the symposium at Stanford University sponsored by The Stanford University School of Medicine, Stanford, CA.

Markey, E. J. (1985). The politics of arms control. *The American Psychologist, 40*(5), 557–560.

Marlin, A. T., Lydenberg, S., & Strub, S. (1987). Give your dollars a political spin. *The Nation, 246*(3), 75.

McFadden, J. (1987). *Peace is a local issue* [Film]. Project of Mid-Peninsula Peace Center. Palo Alto, CA: Peace Video.

McTigue, B. (1986, May 9). KRON-TV Exclusive: Do Soviets cheat on nuclear tests? Pentagon scientists say top Reagan official rejects their evidence. Evening news special. Interviews by R. Post. San Francisco, CA: KRON-TV.

Mehr, H., & Webster, M. (1985). Peacemaking works. Reprints of brochure available from Helen Mehr, Ph.D., 1240 Scott Blvd., Santa Clara, CA 95050 (408) 248-2509.

Melman, S. (1988). *The demilitarized society.* Montreal: Harvest House.

Milgram, S. (1974). *Obedience to authority.* New York: Harper & Row.

Morton, S. (1987). That sheep may safely graze: On a Maine island, a peace initiative. *Harvard Magazine, 89*(6), 34–40.

Nash, H. T. (1981). The bureaucratization of homicide. In E. P. Thompson & D. Smith (Eds.), *Protest and survive* (pp. 149–160). New York: Monthly Review Press.

Nelson, L. L., & Slem, C. M. (1984, August). Attitudes about arms control and effects of *The day after.* Paper presented at the meeting of the American Psychological Association, Toronto.

The New Abolitionist (1987). AT&T challenges boycott. *The New Abolitionist, 5*(2), 1. Baltimore, MD: Nuclear Free America.

Nuclear Times (1989). Dispatches: NFZ victories. *7*(3), 6.

Pastore, J., & Zheutlin, P. (1988, October 30). "Consent" on weapons can't be based on lies. *Los Angeles Times,* Part 5, p. 5.

Pax World Fund (1988, April). Pax World Fund Inc.: Questions and answers about Pax World Fund. Portsmouth, NH: Pax World Fund.

Physicians for Social Responsibility. (1989). Militarism's social costs. *Nuclear Times 7*(3), 28–29.

Rogers, E. (1983, October). How new ideas are adopted. In *Prescription for prevention—Nuclear war: Our greatest health hazard* (pp. 225–231). Proceedings of the symposium at Stanford University, sponsored by The Stanford University School of Medicine, Stanford, CA.

Rogers, R., & Mewborn, C. R. (1986). Fear appeals and attitude change: Effects of a threat's noxiousness, probability of occurrence, and the efficacy of coping responses. In R. K. White (Ed.), *Psychology and the prevention of nuclear war* (pp. 517–526). New York: New York University Press.

Rosen, J. (1987, January/February). Public knowledge/Private ignorance. In *Deadline* (pp. 1–4) a publication of the Center for War, Peace, and the News Media, contained in *Nuclear Times.*

Ross, L. D. (1988). Situationist Perspectives on the Obedience Experiments. *Contemporary Psychology, 33*(2), 101–104.

Ross, M. (1989). 'Nuclear allergy' spreads. *Nuclear Times, 7*(3), 7.

Sandman, P., & Valenti, J. (1986). Fear, psychic numbing, and empowerment: Scared stiff or scared into action. Original manuscript published in condensed form as an article in the *Bulletin of the Atomic Scientists, 42*(1), 12–16.

San Jose Mercury News. (1988, March 13). Nuclear foes arrested at Nevada test site. *San Jose Mercury News,* p. 17A.

Seligman, M. E. (1975). *Helplessness: On depression, development, and death.* San Francisco: Freeman.

Scheer, R. (1984, Summer). Reporting should reach beyond "big bang." *Media and Values, 28.* Los Angeles: Media Action Research Center.

Schofield, J. W., & Pavelchak, M. A. (1984). Fallout from *The Day After.* Content relevant effects. Paper presented at the meeting of the American Psychological Association, Toronto, Canada.

Schofield, J. W., & Pavelchak, M. A. (1985). *The Day After:* The impact of a media event. *American Psychologist, 40,* 542-548.

Shuman, M. H. (1987). *Building municipal foreign policies: An action handbook for citizens and local elected officials.* Irvine, CA: Center for Innovative Diplomacy's Local Elected Officials Project.

Solantaus, T. (1986). Young people and the threat of nuclear war in Finland. In B. Gould, S. Moon, & J. Van Hoorn (Eds.), *Growing up scared? The psychological effect of the nuclear threat on children* (pp.77-84). Berkeley, CA: Open Books.

Teltsch, K. (1984, March 27). Foundations' new interest in studying war and peace. Reprinted from *The New York Times,* in the *San Francisco Chronicle,* p. 9.

Thiermann, E., & Thiermann, I. (1981). *The last epidemic.* [Film]. Available from the Educational Film & Video Project, 5332 College Ave., Ste. 101, Oakland, CA 94618 (415 655-9050).

Thompson, J. (1985). *Psychological aspects of nuclear war.* New York: John Wiley & Sons.

Triplett, W. (1988). Instant activists: 20/20 Vision helps people do their part in just 20 minutes a month. *Nuclear Times, 6*(5), 14-15.

Tritch, T. (1986, September/October). INFACT targets GE. *Nuclear Times, 4,* 14-15.

Tversky, A., & Kahneman, D. (1973). Availability: A heuristic for judging frequency and probability. *Cognitive Psychology, 5,* 207-232.

Tyler, T., & McGraw, K. (1983). The threat of nuclear war: Risk interpretation and behavioral response. *Journal of Social Issues, 39*(1), 25-40.

United Press International (1987, September 24). Well-off say they need lots of dough. *San Francisco Chronicle,* p. A8.

Update (1989) *3,* 2. A publication of the Center for Foreign Policy Development, affiliate of The Institute for International Studies, Brown University. Providence, RI.

Ury, W. L. (1985). *Beyond the Hotline: How crisis control can prevent nuclear war.* Boston: Houghton Mifflin Co.

Van Hoorn, J., & French, P. (1986). Facing the nuclear threat: Comparisons of adolescents and adults. In B. Gould, S. Moon, & J. Van Hoorn (Eds.), *Growing up scared? The psychological effect of the nuclear threat on children* (pp. 57-75). Berkeley, CA: Open Books.

Van Hoorn, J., LeVeck, P., & French, P. (1989). Transitions in the nuclear age: Late adolescence to early adulthood. *Journal of Adolescence, 12,* 41-53.

Walsh, R. (1984). *Staying alive.* Boulder, CO: New Science Library/Shambhala.

Washington Spectator, The (1987a). The American mood: Protest and concern. *13*(13), 2.

Washington Spectator, The (1987b). A changing political scene. *13*(15), 1.

Washington Spectator, The (1987c). *13*(19), 1.

Washington Spectator, The (1987d). *13*(22), 1.

Washington Spectator, The (1987e). The Quest for Peace. *13*(22), 2.

Washington Spectator, The (1988a). *14*(22), 3.

Washington Spectator, The (1988b). The high cost of health. *13*(8), 1.

Washington Spectator, The (1988c). For sale: The American political system. *14*(18).

Washington Spectator, The (1988d). A look at the news media. *14*(4), 1.

Washington Spectator, The (1989). Home front problems for the new president. *15*(1), 1-4.

Weiler, L. D. (1983). No first use: A history. *Bulletin of the Atomic Scientists, 39*(2), 28.

Westin, A. (1988). *America's kids: Why they flunk.* ABC TV 60-minute documentary film in the series *Burning Questions.* Anchored by Barbara Walters.

Wood, C., & Wilson-Smith, A. (1988, May 16). A 'Bolshoi mak' attack. *Maclean's, 101*(21), 30.

6

Educational Approaches for Helping the Young Cope With the Prospect of Nuclear Annihilation

---

Art Newman
University of Florida, Gainesville

This chapter suggests various educational measures which might be adopted to enable the young—adolescents and children alike—to relate effectively to the nuclear weapons peril. The first section address the 11–18 age range; the second relates to those of more tender ages. Predominantly cognitive and predominantly affective approaches are described. Some of the orientations are traditional and can be rather easily incorporated into the schooling (and other institutional) context(s). Others are rather unorthodox and imply an imaginative—if modest— restructuring of the usual learning fare dished up to the young. The underlying thesis is that we have a moral obligation to the young to engage them in a process of evolving out of the pre-nuclear world view to which they have become accustomed into a nuclear-age mentality.

INTRODUCTION

In turning to the educational implications of the nuclear peril, we are going to use the term *education* in a wide, generic sense, a sense that embraces any social institution that has the capacity of facilitating heightened consciousness about the problem. Moreover, we'll be concerned with informal learning experiences, such as casual home conversations, as well as formal, systematic approaches adopted by agencies such as the public schools.

Another important point which must be stressed at the outset is that the concept of nuclear age education suggested in this essay relates to both the predominantly cognitive and predominantly affective learning domains. A predominantly cognitive approach, distinguished by efforts to inform youngsters about nuclear armaments and facilitate their ability to analyze nuclear weapons matters, while crucially necessary, is not sufficient. This informational-analytic emphasis must be related integrally to such emotion-laden considerations as the moral justification for the possession and possible use of nuclear weapons.

The formal/informal, cognitive/affective approach to education for nuclear sensitivity should include as its recipients both those youngsters who are already knowledgeable and/or concerned about nuclear warfare as well as those who— through indifference, ignorance, denial, or whatever—are not. Those who are already reasonably knowledgeable and concerned have a "leg up" on their more complacent peers. Regarding this more sophisticated group, all who educate— parents, teachers, the clergy, television producers, and others—have an obligation to capitalize on the heightened interests and the raised consciousness of these worried youths. Regarding those who are neither knowledgeable nor concerned, all societies have a moral obligation to engender a cognitive sophistication and deep level of concern in this population.

LEARNING EXPERIENCES
FOR THE PUBESCENT-ADOLESCENT POPULATION
(AGES 11 TO 18)

Assuming that rationality presupposes awareness, at the very least, teaching agents ought to provide our nuclear-imperiled youth with the opportunity to know about the nature of that which menaces them. This type of learning experience might be approached either through a given academic discipline or it might be treated in a multidisciplinary manner. Regarding the former, among the more obvious choices are the biological and physical sciences (Whitney, 1983) because of the nature of their conceptual structures. For example, young people can be introduced to the nature of fission and fusion processes, or they might learn about the biological impact of radiation. Virtually all the academic disciplines can be adapted for nuclear education purposes (Ringler, 1984). For a more multidisciplinary approach, several texts and curriculum guides are available (*Choices*, 1985; Grover, 1983).

Another important learning component for teens and preteens is the inclusion of lessons on the media and how they present news; the aim is to encourage a sophisticated awareness of media manipulation. Accounts of nuclear-related matters may well be of questionable validity, so a critical eye is needed. In two penetrating essays, "The Media: Playing the Government's Game" and "Soviets Seen Through Red-Tinted Glasses," journalism professor William Dorman alerts us to the distortion that characterizes a good deal of purportedly accurate journalism (Dorman, 1985).

Closely related to facilitating the development of the ability to distinguish between specious and reliable news items is the ability to appreciate the insidious nature of Nukespeak. Quite often, weapons included in (or being developed for—the most notorious being "Star Wars") the American nuclear arsenal are labeled with high-sounding, moralistic names. Caldicott observes that "the President [Reagan] renamed the MX 'Peacekeeper.' (To call a missile that carries 10 hydrogen bombs, each about 27 times bigger than the Hiroshima bomb, the Peacekeeper is a cynical travesty)" (Caldicott, 1984, p. 187). Other scholars have forcefully addressed the blatantly propagandistic nature of nuclear nomenclature. In an excellent essay, "Nukespeak: Language Culture and Propaganda," the linguist Paul Chilton reveals the ideologically loaded nomenclature our leaders attach to nuclear arms.

> . . . this variety of English is not neutral and purely descriptive, but ideologically loaded in favor of the nuclear culture and . . . this matters, insofar as it possibly affects how people think about the subject and probably determines to a large extent the sort of ideas they exchange about it. (Chilton, 1986, p. 128)

Distorted images of the nuclear period may also be propagated by American and world history texts. In a 1984 study of such texts, Dan Fleming found that most reflected an alarming omission of material on nuclear armaments (Fleming, 1984). Responsible adults—parents, school-board members, teachers—have an obligation to make sure public school learning materials are adequate to the task of educating for nuclear literacy.

As suggested above, even a young person acquainted with technical, political, and military insights about nuclear arms can be said to be only semi-literate regarding a sophisticated appreciation of the nature and implications of these lethal weapons. Informational and analytic skills per se do not equip the young citizen to behave wisely and sensitively in situations involving nuclear arms. Not only must the intellect be appreciably engaged, the emotions and especially, the imagination must come into play as well.

To facilitate young people's ability to feel deeply the awesome power of nuclear weapons and the awful suffering which would attend their use, a carefully selected use of audiovisual material is highly recommended. Visual images of horrendous death captured by audiovisual productions can add flesh and blood, as it were, to the rather dry conceptual bones provided by a predominantly informational-analytic approach. As Zuber observes:

> Films have a unique ability to transmit images and ideas in a way that provides a satisfying, common group experience, one which can successfully promote analysis and discussion of the nuclear threat. There is no other medium that can communicate as graphically the destructive capabilities of our nuclear arsenals. (Zuber, 1983, p. 521)

In a 1984 study of high school students and college freshmen, one researcher concluded: "Our findings suggest that today's students have been influenced primarily by what they have seen on film or television—such as *The Day After* or the popular film *War Games*—rather than by what they have read" (Zweigenhaft, 1985, p. 27).

Listening to audiotapes can also have a powerful impact on young people; the present writer has very effectively used a recording of a Helen Caldicott address in his university classes.

The reading and discussion of good science fiction accounts that treat the problem can be a frequently overlooked means of helping young people appreciate holistically the implications of the use of nuclear arms. An excellent anthology appropriate for the 11- to 18-year age level is *Countdown to Midnight* (Franklin, 1984). Classics such as *A Canticle for Leibowitz* are also powerful pedagogical tools for older adolescents.

The frequently quoted observation of Einstein that the splitting of the atom has changed everything but our way of thinking reminds us of the critical need for adopting unorthodox angles of vision for comprehending the nuclear age. For the mindful, the potentially catastrophic consequences implied by the use of nuclear weapons are reason enough to realize that some traditional modes of political-military conceptualization are morally untenable. Prenuclear notions such as absolute national sovereignty, accompanied by Von Clauswitz's insistence that war is a logical extension of national policy, have become dysfunctional. Prenuclear saber rattling is a monumentally weak metaphor for the threatened use of nuclear-armed guided missiles.

The arts in general are superbly equipped to help facilitate the development of engaging in varying modes of perception. The point is cogently made by Lawrence Frank who, shortly after the conclusion of World War II, made the following observation:

> If we are to have any order and meaning in our personal lives and in our society, if we are to conserve our enduring human values and our persistent aspirations toward human dignity, we must renew our traditional culture, providing equivalent formulations for all these obsolete, archaic assumptions and developing new patterns and roles through which we can live more sanely and fully and can more nearly approach our enduring goals and values. (Frank, 1946, p. 139)

Frank's position is reinforced by Mihaly Csikszentmihalyi in an essay which appeared in *The Arts, Cognition and Basic Skills*:

> From an evolutionary viewpoint, the value of aesthetic cognition is that it provides models for human experiences with which reason alone cannot cope. Artists see their task as using all their sensory and cognitive skills to tackle global existential problems. In so doing, they inevitably enter realms of reality that are still uncharted, that have not yet been colonized by the rules of reason. Therefore artistic cognition can provide the novel concepts and the unthought-of rules constituting that variation without which knowledge could not evolve. (Csikszentmihalyi, 1978, p. 118)

An excellent example of an aesthetic approach to nuclear age education is a high school curriculum guide prepared by David Schwartz et al. to stimulate a global disposition for students enrolled at the Hillcrest (New York City) High School's School of International Studies (Schwartz, Marcus, & Fine, 1980). This manual is rich with examples of how students' appreciation and creation of virtually all art forms can promote the varying paradigms for which Einstein pled.

Not only can artistic involvement help our youth value conceptual structures that contrast with prenuclear-age paradigms, it can also be a powerful vehicle for fostering a deep appreciation of human universality. All artistic media, whether fine, folk, or popular, abound with expressions of an irreducible, invaluable human condition (King, 1971). Poetry, in particular, lends itself to facilitating the teen or preteen's identification with all people (Newman, 1983). John Donne's "No man is an island entire of itself . . . " is emblematic of a treasure-trove of materials which can be drawn upon by those who are committed to stimulating a nuclear-age consciousness (Gardner, 1952).

An emotional commitment to help prevent horrendous nuclear death is one whose role models—heroes and heroines—represent a nonviolent approach to resolving conflict; identification with the John Waynes of this world is intrinsically a prenuclear-age process. At every turn we—teachers, parents, advertisers, TV producers, whoever—should present our youth with the opportunity of appreciating great-souled and noble people. Perhaps having a picture of "Mahatma" Gandhi in every school classroom and every home would be a good place to start.

The learning approach thus far presented, although necessary, is not sufficient if one of the major objectives of the process is helping young people become committed to engaging in constructive social behavior. Somehow a way must be found to involve them in "hands on" activities that confront directly the nuclear peril. Joanna Macy's *Despair and Personal Power in the Nuclear Age* (Macy, 1983) contains a host of compelling suggestions for involving people in learning experiences which relate to their own deeply experienced thoughts and feelings. While the book is not targeted specifically for youths, the many techniques of group interaction advanced by Macy recommend themselves.

LEARNING EXPERIENCES FOR YOUNGER CHILDREN (TODDLERHOOD TO 10 YEARS)

In turning to a discussion of the provision of nuclear age learning experiences for younger children, we are obliged to respond to a cluster of frequently voiced objections. There are, for example, many well-intentioned adults who protest that the nuclear war issue should not be discussed with young children because it may frighten them unnecessarily (Weber, 1983; Adelson & Finn, 1985). With all due respect, their position relies on an observation that is significantly inaccurate and therefore irrelevant. The sad fact is that a very sizable proportion of our very young are already scared (Gittelson, 1982; Mackey, 1983; Reifel, 1984, Yudkin, 1984). Although most can't articulate clearly their nuclear-related fears, many are apparently affected adversely by nagging images of an amorphous evil force capable of annihilating them and their loved ones.

Another objection sometimes invoked is that young children can't understand the nuances of the nuclear armaments issue. In this, the critics are partially correct: of course it's true that those aged 3 to 10 years can't understand much regarding international military and political matters. Nor can we reasonably expect them to comprehend the technical nature of nuclear weapons. However, although children may not understand all the issues, their awareness of the nuclear peril can be raised. Like all societies, we're constantly providing our youngsters with developmentally appropriate materials which help them cope with harmful and dangerous things in their environment. Smokey Bear signs, anti-litter cartoons, and comic-strip characters inveighing against tobacco use come readily to mind. The "kids-aren't-sufficiently-sophisticated" argument is largely fatuous.

If age and developmental differences are allowed for, the moral argument for helping young children cope with the nuclear threat is not different from that which was presented above for the 11- to 18-year-old population. To reiterate, it is simply wrong—and undemocratic—to avoid familiarizing all youngsters with those conditions that threaten to extinguish their future.

What, then, can reasonably be done to provide nuclear-age learning experiences for this admittedly not-too-sophisticated, frequently frightened population? As a response, we can do no better than refer to a very cogent, engaging set of recommendations suggested by Judith A. Myers-Walls and Kathleen M. Fry-Miller (1984). We should, these writers suggest, help children deal with their fears by listening to them in a warm, receptive, and understanding way, so that they can freely express their nuclear-related (and other) concerns. We should help children realize that the nuclear armaments problems *is* something that can be controlled. This latter objective can be greatly enhanced by communicating to them that many adults are actually engaged in efforts to diminish the possibility of international or accidental nuclear conflict. The best examples of such efforts are, of course, significant other adults who might serve as reassuring role models.

Joanna Macy, in her *Despair and Personal Power in the Nuclear Age* (1983), has some advice for adults committed to helping children deal with the nuclear menace. After posing the question, "What can we do to break the silence and meet children on the level of their own deep responses?" Macy makes the following recommendations:

1. *Know your [significant other's] own feelings . . . about what is happening to our world.*
2. *Invite children to share their feelings about the world.*
3. *Give your complete attention [to children's behavior].*
4. *Let yourself listen . . . accept the challenge not to interrupt them.*
5. *Help children define their feelings. . . . Help them gain control over vague feelings by putting them into words.*
6. *Let them know they are not alone in these fears.*
7. *Acknowledge what you don't know.*
8. *Don't feel you must relieve your children of their painful feelings . . . anguish over the nuclear peril is a component of our experience in this time and cannot be taken or washed away.*
9. *Let children make choices.*
10. *Watch your children, take joy in life. . . . We . . . can convey our own sense of the sacredness and health of the web of life.*
11. *Show them you care enough about your world and about them to engage in actions to avert disaster.*
12. *Support children in taking action in their own right. There is a great deal to do to work for peace and justice. (Macy, 1983, pp. 52–54)*

Conflict resolution research is a gold mine of promising leads for helping children—both younger and older—develop dispositions consonant with preventing a nuclear holocaust.[1,2] In his classic *The International Dimension of Education*, Leonard Kenworthy states the case forcefully:

> *Long before children come to school they have begun to grapple with conflict and with cooperation. They will not use these terms, but they will have experienced their meaning in many ways. In the classroom and in school at large, they should be learning ways of resolving conflicts and the attitudes and skills involved in fostering cooperation. But they should go further. They should learn about these twin themes as they relate to the families, the communities, and the countries they study.*
>
> *As a special part of the curriculum they should also learn about some of the regional and international organizations which have been created to promote international understanding and cooperation. (Kenworthy, 1970, p. 55)*

Intercom, a publication of the Center for Global Perspectives, frequently contains imaginative examples of conflict resolution lessons that might be adopted by nuclear-age educators (Otero and Levy, 1975; "Move, Feet," 1976). Some young children's stories, such as Dr. Seuss's *The Sneetches*, are tailor-made to help children identify with characters embroiled in conflict.

A crucially important dimension of any effort to help children develop attitudes compatible with the prevention of nuclear annihilation is steering them away from

[1]The remarks regarding the utility of a conflict resolution approach apply with equal force to the 11- to 18-year-old age group discussed above.

[2]The major source of scholarly inquiry in this area is *The Journal of Conflict Resolution*, published continuously since 1957. The publication "is an interdisciplinary journal of social scientific theory and research on human conflict" that emphasizes international conflict. Currently, it is published at Yale University.

toys that reinforce a war mentality. If this is impossible, parents can capitalize on children's interest in such toys to help them appreciate the moral questions inherent in the taking, however "pretend," of human life. A publication has observed that "Sales of war toys have risen 500% since 1982 to a record of $1.2 billion projected for 1985. They are the leading category of toys sold, making up five out of six of the best-selling toys in the United States" (*Sharing Space*, 1985, p. 3). A 1986 article reported:

> A child will be able to pit a robot he is controlling against one responding to TV signals. The robots, six to eight inches tall, will move, make sounds, and fire infrared beams at each other on command; a direct hit will temporarily disable the enemy robot. ("*Toy Soldiers Go High-Tech: Five Wizards Build a Remote-Control Robot Army*" 1986, p. 54)

An Associated Press dispatch that appeared shortly before the height of the 1986 Christmas buying season announced: "The year's biggest toy fad," according to *Fortune* magazine, is Lazer Tag, a $40 kit that includes a light-emitting pistol, a belt and holster, and a sensor that automatically records each 'hit' " ("Products of Year Include Album and Dental Rinse," 1986). We can, of course, argue until eternity about the causal relationship between playing with war toys and warlike attitudes. However, common sense would suggest that a significant relationship exists between war-playing behavior and a disposition to accept easily a prenuclear national "defense" policy.

Closely related to war toy hysteria, and highly illustrative of a patently unwholesome approach to resolving conflict, is the video game craze. As Helen Caldicott reminds us:

> Many of these computer games are nuclear war games that are, in effect, conditioning our offspring from a very early age to the prospect of nuclear war. I can think of no more insidious and invidious influence that could be distorting these lovely, innocent, and open minds than genocidal games. (Caldicott, 1984, p. 143)

Caldicott's remarks apply, of course, to all children (including those disguised as adults) who get their thrills out of extinguishing the "enemy." Youngsters seduced and mesmerized by the electronic gadgetry represented by so many video games might, unless enlightened by responsible adults, grow up to endorse computerized atomic weaponry without question.

Another admittedly controversial approach to helping children develop an awareness of the nuclear scourge is deliberately to inculcate antinuclear-war ideas in their consciousness. Fables, parables, aphorisms, lullabies, nursery rhymes, and reading primers are among the vehicles which might be used for this purpose. Such an orientation is certainly not unAmerican; the McGuffy readers are ample testimony to the popular acceptance of this type of moral instruction (Ornstein & Levine, 1985). Nor need it be at all undemocratic. The philosopher Sidney Hook reminds us that in all societies, democratic or otherwise, the young necessarily experience a socialization process whereby they are conditioned to accept a constellation of cherished social mores. Referring to this mode of learning as "nonrational indoctrination," Hook reconciles it with democratic theory by proposing that, so long as the indoctrinated young, as they mature, are permitted and encouraged to examine reflectively the inculcated content, there is nothing undemocratic about the process (Hook, 1963, pp. 169–170). In myriad insidious ways—much parental conditioning, some religious education, Nukespeak content conveyed by the media, war toys, many video games, some patriotic ceremonies, and others— we are already conditioning our young to adopt a nationalistic-militaristic mentality, in other words, a disposition that easily allows an obscene acceptance of horrendous death. Why not provide equal time for instilling attitudes of peace?

The public schools are particularly well-adapted to facilitate children's ability to experience and express the joy of peace. Art classes, discursive and/or non-discursive, are ideally suited for this purpose. An inspiring example is reflected by *A Chance to Live: Children's Poems for Peace in a Nuclear Age*, an anthology written in 1982 by children enrolled at the Berkeley (California) Arts Magnet School (Peterson & Kelley, 1983). Those concerned with helping our children cope with nuclear insanity could do no better than to peruse this little book. Another example of how artistic expression might relate to nuclear-age education is *Children as Teachers of Peace*. This booklet contains both writing and drawings depicting themes of peace (Jampolsky, 1982). Other sources for materials that embrace children's expressions of peace and related themes are various publications of the United States Committee for UNICEF.

CONCLUSION

This chapter has suggested that in a planet bristling with nuclear weapons, the adult inhabitants should feel a compelling moral obligation to teach the young how to cope adequately with nuclear-related fears and anxieties. More importantly, this moral debt must include liberally funded opportunities supportive of the prevention of death by nuclear war. The educational measures advanced, while necessary, are clearly not sufficient. Regardless of how audacious, imaginative, and far-reaching our efforts to help the young, similar programs must be put in place to raise the consciousness of their elders. Nor is this sufficient, for unless these older folks include the world's political leaders our own endangered species well might become extinct. Are Messrs. Bush, Gorbachev, and their colleagues up to the task of rescuing us from nuclear bondage? If not, perhaps their more enlightened progency may. Perhaps.

REFERENCES

Adelson, J., & Finn, C. (1985). Terrorizing children. *Commentary, 79,* 29–36.
Caldicott, H. (1984). *Missile envy.* New York: Bantam Books.
Children's creative response to conflict program newsletter. (1985). *Sharing Space, 8*(3), 3.
Chilton, P. (1986). Nukespeak: Nuclear language, culture, and propaganda. In D. Gregory (Ed.), *The nuclear predicament.* New York: St. Martin's.
Choices: A unit on conflict and nuclear war. (1985). Washington, DC: Union of Concerned Scientists, Massachusetts Teacher's Association and National Education Association.
Csikszentmihalyi, M. (1978). Phylogenetic and ontogenetic functions of artistic cognition. In S. Madeja (Ed.), *The arts, cognition, and basic skills.* St. Louis, MO: Cemeral. Reprinted by permission.
Donne, J. (1624/1952). Devotions upon emergent occasions. In H. Gardner (Ed.), *The Divine Psalms.* Oxford: Clarendon Press.
Dorman, W. (1985). Soviets seen through red-tinted glasses. *Bulletin of the Atomic Scientists, 41*(2), 18–22.

Dorman, W. (1985). The media: Playing the government's game. *Bulletin of the Atomic Scientists*, *41*(7), 118–124.

Fleming, D. (1984). Nuclear war: What place in secondary education? *The High School Journal*, *67*, 72–76.

Frank, L. (1946). The arts in reconstruction. *The Journal of Aesthetics and Art Criticism*, *IV*, 135–140. Reprinted by permission.

Franklin, H. B. (Ed.). (1984). *Countdown to midnight*. New York: Dow Books.

Gittelson, N. (1982, May). The fear that haunts our children. *McCall's*, *77*, 144–150.

Grover, T. (1983). *The nuclear arms race*. A curriculum packet prepared for the Calgary (Alberta) social studies curriculum team, Calgary Public Schools.

Hook, S. (1963). *Education for modern man*. New York: Knopf.

Jampolsky, G. G. (Ed.) (1982). *Children as teachers of peace*. Berkeley, CA: Celestial Arts.

Kenworthy, L. S. (1970). *The international dimension of education*. Washington, DC: Association for Supervision and Curriculum Development. Reprinted with permission of the Association for Supervision and Curriculum Development. Copyright 1970 by the Association for Supervision and Curriculum Development. All rights reserved.

King, E. (1971). *The world: Context for teaching in the elementary school*. Dubuque, IA: Wm. C. Brown.

Mackey, J. A. (1983, May). Living with the bomb: Young people's images of war and peace. *Curriculum Review*, 126–129.

Macy, J. (1983). *Despair and personal power in the nuclear age*. Philadelphia: New Society Publishers. Reprinted by permission.

Move, feet, move! (1976). *Intercom*, *84/85* 46–47.

Myers-Walls, J. A., & Frey-Miller, K. M. (1984). Nuclear war: Helping children overcome fears. *Young Children*, *38*, 27–32.

Newman, A. (1983). Poetic license for appreciation of human universality. *The Social Studies*, *74*, 188–192.

Ornstein, A. C., & Levine, D. U. (1985). *An introduction to the foundations of education*. Boston: Houghton Mifflin.

Otero, G. G., & Levy, M. J. (1975). Activity cards on conflict. *Intercom*, *79*, 3–7.

Peterson, G., & Kelley, J. (Eds.). (1983). *A chance to live: Children's poems for peace in a nuclear age*. Berkeley, CA: Mindbody Press.

Products of year include album and dental rinse. (1986, Nov. 20) *The Gainesville (FL) Sun*.

Reifel, S. (1984). Children living with the nuclear threat. *Young Children*, *39*(5), 74–80.

Ringler, D. (Ed.). (1984, December). Nuclear war: A teaching guide. *Bulletin of the Atomic Scientists*, *10*, 1s–32s.

Schwartz, D., Marcus, J., & Fine, H. (1980). *School of International Studies Curriculum Guide*. New York: New York City Board of Education.

Toy soldiers go high-tech: Five wizards build a remote-control robot army. (1986, May 5). *Newsweek*, 54, 57.

Weber, N. (1983, November). Stop scaring our kids. *Redbook*, 226.

Whitney, L. J. (1983). Scientific truthfulness in the nuclear age. *Curriculum Review*, *22*(2), 177–180.

Yudkin, M. (1984, April). When kids think the unthinkable. *Psychology Today*, 18–25.

Zuber, R. (1983). The role of film in nuclear education. *Social Education*, *47*, 521–522.

Zweigenhaft, R. (1985). Students surveyed about nuclear war. *Bulletin of the Atomic Scientists*, *41*, 26–27.

APPENDIX: RESOURCES

Background Reading

Teachers and Senior Students

Canada and the Nuclear Arms Race. Edited by Ernie Regehr and Simon Rosenblum, introduction by Margaret Laurence. (Toronto: Lorimer, 1983). A much-

I am indebted to the Alberta Teachers' Association, Edmonton, Alberta, Canada, for permission to reproduce this material.

needed look at Canada's role in the nuclear dilemma. This collection of 15 essays provides a great deal of basic information.

The Fate of the Earth. By Jonathan Schell. (New York: Knopf, 1982). Originally written as a series of three essays for the *New Yorker*, this is an eloquent analysis of the devastating consequences of a major nuclear attack.

Nuclear Peace. (Toronto: Canadian Broadcasting Corporation, Box 500, Station A, M5W 1E6). This transcript of a series originally broadcast in the fall of 1982 covers the breadth of nuclear issues in interviews and includes comments from Hiroshima survivors, military strategies, and peace activists. Excellent bibliography.

World Military and Social Expenditures. By Ruth Leger Sivard (Leesburg, VA: World Priorities Inc., Box 1003, Leesburg, VA, 22075, published annually). Documents world expenditures for arms and money spent for social needs. This highly regarded and reputable gathering of statistics contains many charts and tables.

Hiroshima. By John Hersey (New York: Bantam, 1968). An early classic about the effects of the atomic bomb attack on Hiroshima in 1945.

On the Beach. By Nevil Shute (New York: Ballantine Books, 1957). The setting for this story is a fictional post-nuclear-war Australia. Centers on a group of inhabitants awaiting the drift of a cloud of radiation from the Northern Hemisphere. Helpful for teaching about the effects of nuclear war in grades 8 to 12.

The Bomb. By Sidney Lens (New York: Lodestar Books, 1982). One of the most easily understandable books about the history of the atomic bomb and U.S. weapons policy for junior and senior high school students. When selecting this book, teachers should be aware of Lens' strong disarmament stance.

Ground Zero. Nuclear War: What's in It for You? (New York: Pocket Books, 1982). It contains basic information on the development of nuclear weapons, current weapons, and the effects of their use.

Indefensible Weapons: The Political and Psychological Case Against Nuclearism. By Robert Jay Lifton and Richard Falk (Toronto: CBC Publications, 1982). This book served as a comparison to a series of broadcasts by Lifton and Falk on CBC Ideas Network in 1982. Lifton, a psychiatrist, explores the psychological effects of nuclearism. Falk, a political scientist, discusses the way that nuclearism undermines national security and destroys political legitimacy. It is an excellent resource for teachers.

This is the Way the World Will End. This is the Way You Will End Unless . . . . By Harold Freeman (Edmonton: Hurtig Publishers, 1983). Written in an effort to open citizens' eyes to the real threat of nuclear war, this book gives a great deal of factual information, as well as possible scenarios of attack sites.

War: Four Christian Views. Edited by R. G. Clouse (Downers Grove: Intervarsity Press, 1981). This well-balanced source presents a spectrum of Christian views, from pacifism to crusading.

Children

Once Upon a Mountain. By Don Bolognese (New York: Lippincott, 1964). A mountain shepherd prepares for war when he mistakenly thinks people in the village opposite are laughing at him. Grades K to 3.

Tiger Eyes. By Judy Blume (Scarsdale, NY: Bradbury Press, 1981). A young girl's values undergo a change through a series of crises beginning with her father's death. Grades 7 to 9.

Walk a Mile and Get Nowhere. By Ivan Southall (Scarsdale, NY: Bradbury Press, 1979). Set in Australia on a national holiday, this book deals with personal and national insecurity and response. Grades 7 to 9.

Henry Three. By Joseph Krumgold (New York: Atheneum, 1967). A story about a panic as the threat of a nuclear attack seizes a suburban community and how two boys keep their heads. Grades 4 to 6.

Curriculum Guides and Teaching Units

Alberta Education Social Studies Teaching Unit Project—Grade 12. "Should we encourage the development of world government?" A unit designed to teach about nuclear awareness, it contains activities that attempt to ascertain the potential for nuclear war, develop research procedures, understand conflict and war, and inform students on ways to work for peace.

Choices: A Unit on Conflict and Nuclear War. (Available from the National Education Association, 1201 16th St. N.W., Washington, DC 20036). A junior high school curriculum consisting of ten lessons "designed to help students understand the power of nuclear weapons, the consequences of their use, and most importantly, the options available to resolve conflicts among nations by means other than nuclear war."

Crossroads: Quality of Life in a Nuclear World. Prepared by the Education Task Force of Jobs with Peace, 1982. Three 10-day high school curricula for social studies, science, and English. Available from Jobs with Peace, 2940 16th Street, San Francisco, CA 94130; telephone (415) 558–8615.

A Day of Dialogue: Planning and Curriculum Resource Guide Dealing with Issues of Nuclear War in the Classroom. (Educators for Social Responsibility, 23 Garden St., Cambridge, MA 02138, 1982). Deals with the role teachers and parents can play in supporting issues related to war and peace. Provides sections from the psychological effects of the arms race on children to a wide variety of classroom activities, along with sample letters to parents, faculty, and staff. Lists places to look for support (professional, political, community groups) and many other resources.

Dialogue: A Teaching Guide to Nuclear Issues K-12. (Educators for Social Responsibility, 23 Garden St., Cambridge MA 02138, 1983). This is an expanded version of the 1982 *Day of Dialogue.* It consists of a 250-page manual containing suggestions on how to introduce nuclear education into schools, guidelines for appropriate ways to talk to young people about nuclear issues and presenting difficult points of view, curriculum ideas, an adult study guide for self education and teacher background, and an annotated bibliography of resources.

The Friendly Classroom for a Small Planet. By Priscilla Prutzman et al. (Children's Creative Responses to Conflict, Box 271, Nyack, NY 10960, 1978). Methods of building caring for others and self-worth. Evaluations and good bibliography included. Grades K to 6.

Educating for Peace and Justice: A Manual for Teachers. (The Institute for Peace and Justice, 414 Lindell Blvd., St. Louis, MO 63108, four vols). I. National

Dimensions; II. Global Dimensions; III. Religious Dimensions; IV. Teacher Background Readings. Curriculum units contain teaching strategies for elementary, secondary, and college levels, action possibilities, student readings, case studies, and bibliographies.

A Manual on Nonviolence and Children. By Stephanie Judson. (Friends Peace Committee, 1515 Cherry St., Philadelphia, PA 19102). Provides detailed theory and activities for teaching peacemaking skills, concepts, and values to young children. Accounts from teachers who have used the approach are a useful feature.

Militarization, Security, and Peace Education: A Guide for Concerned Citizens. By Betty Reardon. (United Ministries in Education, Valley Forge, PA 19481). A new resource study action curriculum intended to help people study about and work on ways in which peace and justice concerns can be included in the ongoing activity in the classroom. Also available is the supplementary packet, a super bargain of useful material.

The Nuclear Arms Race: Technology, History, Politics, Social Issues. A curriculum packet prepared for the Calgary Social Studies Curriculum Team, Calgary Public Schools. By Trudy Govier (Available from Project Ploughshares, 2932 13 Avenue N.W., Calgary, Alberta T2N 1M2). A much-needed Canadian look at the nuclear arms race prepared for both teachers and students with Social Studies 30 in mind. Takes the form of a series of questions and answers and uses a variety of sources.

Let Peace Begin With Me. By Mary Lou Knownacki. (Pax Christi, 3000 N. Mango Ave., Chicago, IL 60634, 1984, teacher's guide and student material). Excellent lesson unit for elementary grades. The theme is simple—"why war should be eliminated" and "how to become a peacemaker." The few references to religion can be omitted; the message will remain.

Peace Studies in the United Kingdom. (Specific information on Peace Studies in the United Kingdom can be obtained from Dr. David Hicks, St. Martin's College, Bowerham, Lancaster, England LAI 3JD). Peace education has taken a firm hold in the United Kingdom and many prominent educators have now found it to be a necessity in schools. The emphasis for peace education has been directed toward the understanding of conflict and violence and exploring ways of resolving them. Dealing with the reasons for violence leads to the questions of unjust and oppressive societies and of contemporary world tensions and how these might be eased. The United Kingdom has found resources thin on these subjects, with the result that many colleges and universities have now set up sites to centralize all the new resources.

Perspectives: A Teaching Guide to Concepts of Peace K-12. (Educators for Social Responsibility, 23 Garden St., Cambridge, MA 02138, 1982). This guide will help teachers discuss with students their personal experiences, social and international peace, and the means and structures by which peace can be promoted and preserved.

A Repertoire of Peacemaking Skills. By Susan Carpenter. (Kent State University, Kent, OH 44242, 1977). Basic for curriculum development in peace education. The listing of skills is an excellent starting place for developing course objectives. Suggestions for teaching peacemaking skills.

Restoring American Power in a Dangerous Decade. By Richard Barnet. (New

York: Simon and Schuster, 1981). An outstanding discussion of the philosophy and use of nuclear weapons as part of U.S. foreign policy. Addresses the meaning of real security in a nuclear age. Concise, can be effective in high school teaching.

Growing up in a Nuclear World: A Resource Guide for Elementary School Teachers. By Paulette Meier and Beth McPherson. (Nuclear Information and Resource Service, 1346 Connecticut Ave. NW, 4th Floor, Washington, DC 20036, 1983). This guide is divided into background materials for teachers and approaches to teaching about nuclear issues, classroom material such as curriculum guides and teaching units, books for children to read on their own, and audiovisual resources.

ESR Bibliography of Nuclear Education Resources. Edited by Susan Alexander. (Educators for Social Responsibility, 639 Massachusetts Ave., Cambridge, MA 02139, 1983). Covers the whole spectrum of educational materials from young children to adults. Sometimes prices are noted, and usually the grade level and address, and all titles are annotated. Topics covered include the Soviet threat, the arms race, peace education, ethics, the social and economic impact of military spending and conflict resolution.

Organizations

The Arms Control Association, 11 Dupont Circle N.W., Washington, DC 20036. A nonpartisan organization founded in 1971 by a group of individuals with extensive experience and expertise in the field of arms control and national security policy. *Arms Control Today* is a monthly publication of opinion, analysis, and factual information.

Center for Defense Information, 303 Capital Gallery West, 600 Maryland Avenue S.W., Washington, DC 20024. An organization financed solely by voluntary contributions. The organization supports a strong defense but opposes excessive expenditures for weapons and policies that increase the danger of nuclear war. *The Defense Monitor* (10 issues per year) is mailed without charge to all donors of $25 or more.

Edmonton Learner Centre, 10765 98 Street, Edmonton, Alberta T5H 2P2. A variety of materials dealing with nuclear issues is available.

Children's Creative Responses to Conflict (CCRC), Box 271, Nyack, NY 10960. Exercises to increase cooperation, communication, affirmation, and conflict resolution are the core of the CCRC program. Produces a newsletter, *Sharing Space*. They have a book, *The Friendly Classroom for a Small Planet*, which is a handbook on techniques they have found successful.

Citizens Against Nuclear War (CAN), 1201 16th Street, N.W., Washington, DC 20036. A coalition of unions that includes national women's groups and civil rights groups, as well as religious, environmental, and business groups.

The Committee for National Security, 2000 P Street N.W., Suite 515, Washington, DC 20036. A nonprofit, non-partisan organization formed in 1980. Since its founding, the committee has sought, through its activities and educational programs, to promote a broader understanding of national security issues. Produces publications and educational material.

Common Cause, 2030 N Street N.W., Washington, DC 20035. A nonprofit, non-partisan citizens' lobbying organization that works to improve the way federal and state governments operate. *Common Cause Magazine* is published six times a year. A special publication called *You Can Prevent Nuclear War* is in its second printing.

Educators for Social Responsibility (ESR), 639 Massachusetts Avenue, Cambridge, MA 02139. ESR was established in 1981 to educate teachers at all grade levels, parents, and school administrators about issues related to dangers of nuclear war and the arms race. Publishes an annotated bibliography of books and materials, handbooks for teachers, and a regular newsletter.

Federation of American Scientists (FAS), 307 Massachusetts Avenue N.E., Washington, DC 20002. FAS is an organization of more than 6,000 scientists concerned with the use of science in society, especially regarding nuclear weapons. Produces a newsletter and resource material for educators.

Global Education Associates, 552 Park Avenue, East Orange, NJ 07017. An educational organization that facilitates the efforts of concerned people of diverse cultures, talents, and experience in contributing to a more humane and just world. Publishes a newsletter and a *Global Education Resource Guide* on all their issues, including war/peace.

National Clearinghouse, Nuclear Weapons Freeze Campaign, 4144 Lindell Boulevard, Suite 404, St. Louis, MO 63108. The Nuclear Freeze Campaign is one of the major reasons for the new interest in prevention of nuclear war. Produces a newsletter of interest to high school students.

Nuclear Information and Resource Service (NIRS), 1346 Connecticut Avenue N.W., Fourth Floor, Washington, DC 20036. An excellent resource service for teachers.

Peace Child Foundation, P.O. Box 33168, Washington, DC 20033. *Peace Child* is a musical fantasy about children who bring peace to the world. The Peace Child Foundation has two immediate goals: first, to legitimize peace education as a curriculum subject in schools; and second, to find ways to give children an effective voice in the direction of world affairs.

Peace Research Institute-Dundas, 25 Dundana Avenue, Dundas, Ontario L9H 4B5, Canada. Publishes *Peace Research Abstracts Journal* which contains abstracts from over 600 journals published throughout the world.

Physicians for Social Responsibility (PSR), P.O. Box 144, Watertown, MA 02172. Materials aimed at adults. PSR publishes books, pamphlets, and audiovisual materials concerned with health effects of nuclear war. Dr. Helen Caldicott is this group's most effective spokesperson.

Public Education Resource Centre (PERC), 1111 6th Avenue, 2nd Floor, New Westminster, B.C., Canada. One of the primary objectives of PERC is to develop materials on the issue of nuclear weapons and disarmament suitable for use in schools.

The Riverside Church Disarmament Program, 490 Riverside Drive, New York, NY 10027. Excellent resource list entitled "Peace Teaching and Children" with classroom activities and cooperative games. Focuses on the teaching of peaceful conflict resolution.

Citizens' Organization for a Sane World (SANE), 711 G Street S.E., Washington, DC 20003. SANE is a good source of a large variety of educational materials on nuclear disarmament and peace. A free resource list available.

Stanford Program on International and Cross-Cultural Cultural Education (SPICE), Lou Henry Hoover Building, Room 200, Stanford University, Stanford, CA 94305. The International Security and Arms Control Project (ISAAC) is SPICE's newest curriculum program. An annotated bibliography of materials for all grade levels is available from the SPICE director, Dr. David L. Grossman.

Student/Teacher Organization to Prevent Nuclear War (STOP), Box 232, Northfield, MA 01360. STOP is an educational organization of high school students and teachers committed to reducing the threat of nuclear war. Publishes a newsletter which offers cartoons, high school activities and news of what other students are doing.

These resources were compiled by the editor with suggestions from Ida Wyllie, librarian with the Calgary Board of Education, and Professor Terry Carson and graduate students David Calvert and Errol Miller of the University of Alberta.

7

The Consortium on Peace Research, Education, and Development (COPRED), Peace Education, and the Prevention of War

Maire A. Dugan
Consortium on Peace Research, Education, and Development
George Mason University, Fairfax, Virginia

This chapter serves as an introduction to the importance of peace education in the development of a strategy of war prevention. It utilizes a perspective from the Consortium on Peace Research, Education, and Development (COPRED), the oldest and largest peace education organization in North America. The article indicates not only that peace education itself is important, but that it is important to maintain an ongoing connection among research, action, and education on and about peace.

INTRODUCTION

The importance of war as a public health concern arises from several sources. The most obvious and most discussed has to do with the species-destruction capability of nuclear weapons. Such concerns have been the motive force behind the Nuclear Freeze campaign, the emergence of SANE/Freeze as a large national group, and the development of Physicians for Social Responsibility (and its sister groups such as Educators for Social Responsibility) and the writings of its founder, Helen Caldicott.

Even were the specter of nuclear annihilation completely removed, however, preventing war is probably the most important single thing one can do to promote physical health and well-being. Here the other reasons come into play: the large numbers of people killed, injured, or displaced as a result of conventional wars; the increased frequency of war; the devastation of the natural and human-made environment on which we depend; and the psychological damage and pain wreaked on survivors.

To focus on the first two mentioned, wars have taken 86 million lives thus far in the 20th century. This is up from 6 million in the 18th century and about 10 million in the 19th. To put this in a broader context, the world population has increased by a factor of approximately three-and-a-half since the 18th century while deaths resulting from war have increased by a factor of thirteen-and-a-half. Aside from the horror of the loss of life itself, then, one must be concerned with war's rapidly growing capacity for human destructiveness. Since the 18th century, war deaths have increased at a rate four times that of population growth (Eckhardt, 1987).

There are many models for responding constructively to the need to prevent war; and most people, regardless of their ideology, nationality, or religious background, consider preventing war a noble goal. Some would respond through political means, whether their strategy is deterrence at one extreme or unilateral disarmament at the other. Some would stress religious strategies, whether they involve a focus on inner transformation or on liberation theologies. Some emphasize increasing understanding and transmitting knowledge of the nature of peace, the conditions which make it more likely, and the processes through which individuals and groups bring these conditions into being. Many of this last group identify themselves as peace educators.

Peace studies as a formal, institutionalized field of endeavor is a relatively new one—basically a post-World War II phenomenon. One of the primary organizations that has provided leadership in the development of peace studies is the Consortium on Peace Research, Education, and Development (COPRED).

THE ESTABLISHMENT OF THE CONSORTIUM ON PEACE RESEARCH, EDUCATION, AND DEVELOPMENT

On May 8, 1970, some 35 people representing approximately 30 professional associations and peace research institutes gathered together in Boulder, Colorado, to give birth to a new organization—the Consortium on Peace Research, Education, and Development (COPRED). They had gathered there at the invitation of Gilbert White, Kenneth Hammond, and Kenneth Boulding of the Institute of Behavioral Science at the University of Colorado at Boulder. The invitation suggested the need for a new organization which would promote interdisciplinary research on peace, influence policy making, and encourage international cooperation among peace scholars.

On May 10, they named an organizing committee composed of Chad Alger (then representing Northwestern University's Research Program in International Relations and now at Ohio State's Mershon Center), Kenneth Boulding (University of Colorado), Israel Charny (then representing the American Orthopsychiatric Association, now director of Human Rights Internet in Jerusalem), Bob Hefner (Center for Research on Conflict Resolution, University of Michigan, the first peace research institute in the United States, now defunct), and Hanna Newcombe (Canadian Peace Research Institute, now of the Peace Research Institute-Dundas). Elise Boulding agreed to act as Executive Secretary to the organizing committee and newly formed organization; Oscar Schachter of UNITAR and Col. Kent Parrot of ACDA agreed to act as consultants.

Purposes

The founders defined the new organization as a transnational body (originally intended to include South as well as North America) with seven functions: (a) facilitating communications and exchanging information; (b) strengthening existing peace research groups and supporting formation of new ones; (c) strengthening support for peace research and training in the Americas; (d) strengthening flows of information and collaborative research; (e) facilitating development of graduate programs of research and training in conflict and peace; (f) fostering constructive relationships with national governments; and (g) compiling and publishing periodically an inventory of peace research findings having potential policy and action implications.

By the time COPRED was actually incorporated a year later, the almost exclusive emphasis on research had already been broadened to include education, particularly on the collegiate level; within another year or two, the peace action dimension was an equally strong orientation of the organization.

Thus COPRED emerged as a response to a need for an ongoing communications forum for people involved in peace research, education, and action. While the organization has grown significantly since its beginnings (current membership includes approximately 150 institutes, programs, and organizations as well as over 600 individuals), it has maintained this purpose as its basic foundation. The current constitution of the organization states that "The purposes of the Consortium shall be to foster research, education, and training in the area of peace, social justice, and other global concerns, [and] to facilitate such activities of its members as are related thereto . . . " COPRED's goals are also discussed in a recent membership brochure, which states that "COPRED's purpose is to advance peace studies at all levels. It encourages interchange and support among peace educators, researchers, professionals, and practitioners."

Activities

From its origins, COPRED has attempted not only to provide a network for the broadest possible constellation of peace groups and individuals, but also to provide or identify resources and materials that will enhance their efforts.

One of the first projects in which COPRED engaged was one identified in the list of functions identified by the organizing committee—to periodically compile and publish an inventory of peace research findings having potential policy and action implications. Several researchers, coordinated by Elise Boulding, set out to provide a subject-coded listing of all English-language publications in the field of peace and conflict studies. The most current manifestation of this effort, *Bibliography on World Conflict and Peace: Second Edition* (Boulding, Passmore, & Gassler, 1979) was published by Westview Press in cooperation with COPRED and the Section on World Conflicts of the American Sociological Association. It includes over 1,000 entries published from 1945–1978 organized in 26 major categories, as well as relevant bibliographies, abstracts, collections, annuals, series, and periodicals.

Of other activities, some of the most important resource development projects undertaken in the 1970s were the work of COPRED's primary and secondary education group, the Peace Education Network. PEN produced a 20-minute slide show called *Creating the Future* (Carpenter & Solo, 1977) which provides an introduction to peace education particularly useful to primary and secondary teachers. PEN also joined PEN member Susan L. Carpenter in producing a skills development tool, *A Repertoire of Peacemaking Skills* (Carpenter, 1977) still widely used today.

Another publication that COPRED has provided is *A Directory of Peace Studies Programs* (Cianto, 1990). The current edition, produced in 1990, lists 220 programs, primarily in the United States and Canada, with short descriptions of their course content and orientation. The immediately previous edition, published in 1986 (Segedin), listed over 100 such programs. Help in this expansion was provided by Daniel Thomas of the Five Colleges Program in Peace and World Security Studies located at Hampshire College. Thomas compiled a list of 255 programs internationally as part of the fifth edition of *Peace and World Order Studies: A Curriculum Guide* (Klare & Thomas, 1989).

The expansion of the field can be seen in many ways. For example, the field is now large enough to support not only a full-time COPRED office, but also a new organization, the Peace Studies Association, which has emerged to cater to some of the specific needs of college peace studies programs not provided by the more broad-based COPRED. COPRED's own membership increased by more than a third since July 1987.

As the field has grown and more research institutes and educational programs have developed, there has been less of a need for COPRED itself to generate resources; it has therefore placed increased emphasis on publicizing resources and making them available. Two main avenues are used for this. The first is a bimonthly newsletter, the *COPRED Peace Chronicle,* which provides annotated lists of new publications and other resources, a calendar of upcoming events, a bulletin board of news notes in the field, and program and network news, as well as substantive feature articles. The second is a literature list, which identifies over 30 materials that may be ordered directly from COPRED.

COPRED is also currently working on projects to develop careers for peace studies and conflict resolution graduates and to develop curriculum materials and models for infusing peace studies into traditional curricula.

Assumptions

COPRED is based on the proposition that peace studies has both similarities and differences from other intellectual fields of endeavor. It is similar in that it is dedicated to rigorous and intellectual analysis, that it assumes that knowledge can be accumulated, transmitted, and learned, and that it has a definable subject matter that distinguishes it from other fields. It is different in that it is inherently interdisciplinary and avowedly value oriented. One may then define peace studies as

> *an academic field which identifies and analyzes violent and nonviolent behaviors as well as structural mechanisms attending social conflict with a view toward understanding those processes which lead to a more desirable human condition (Carey & Dugan, 1982).*

Its similarities to other academic pursuits create the need for forums through which professional peace studies educators and researchers can meet, share knowledge, and continually define and refine the field. Its dissimilarities demand that at least one of these forums be open to people who are not "peace studies professionals" but are involved in the search for peace in other ways. In order for peace studies education and research to have a broader audience than the academic community (absolutely necessary if the field is going to have an impact in the real world that lies beyond the ivory tower and thus have the opportunity to realize its values of bringing about a more desirable, peaceful, and just human condition), it is important to stay regularly informed by and informing of the people who use this knowledge, for example, peace activists and conflict resolution practitioners.

COPRED attempts to provide the forum for the cross-fertilization so necessary in turning ideas into realities and keeping action informed by thought. At the 1987 annual conference in Milwaukee, Chadwick Alger of the Mershon Center at Ohio State University gave a good example of how this works. He indicated that when he first became involved in COPRED, he was a rather traditional international-relations scholar. But he found that when he tried to use traditional perspectives in talking to activists at COPRED, his paradigms were not very helpful in describing or explaining their experiences. He hypothesized that the reason for this is that most traditional international relations models deal only with state actors. Some more progressive IR models included international governmental and nongovernmental actors as well, but even here the actors in the paradigm were too distant from local activists to be particularly useful in identifying how the "ordinary citizen" might have an impact on world events in areas of his or her concern, nor did the paradigms themselves have any room for such things as local peace movements. Yet Alger was convinced that local peace movements and other local actors did have an impact on the global order and that if traditional international relations theory was unable to perceive or explain this impact, let alone suggest how to undertake effective action of this kind, then IR theory was not adequate.

He set about turning the theory on its head and coming up with a very new model, one which assumes that not only states but also local communities have international relations. Citizens, equipped with an understanding of the international relations of their own communities, can begin to understand how to affect world affairs through their own localities. The pyramidic structure of affecting world events through impact on national leaders is not the only strategy which can be successfully followed.

His model set the groundwork for a number of applied research projects, beginning with his own "Columbus [Ohio] in the World." It provides a theoretical framework for understanding how citizen diplomacy campaigns, sister-city connections, and second track diplomacy should be undertaken, and how and why they can work (Alger, 1977, 1978–79, 1984–85, and 1988). But the theory would not have come into being without the opportunity COPRED provided for Alger to interact with activists and practitioners.

It is somewhat early to assess, and we currently lack any systematic analysis of the long-term impact of, intellectual developments such as Alger's new model or educational developments such as the expansion of the field of peace studies in North America from one program in 1948 to almost 200 in 1988. Nonetheless, I cannot but hope that peace research, education, and action, informed by each other, will make a significant contribution to the quest for peace. When humankind has diverted concerted mental energy to a specific problem, the results have often been monumental. Witness the way in which the Manhattan Project changed the world. If we can commit ourselves to diverting a portion of our energies to inventing technologies of peace rather than weaponry of war, we will invent technologies no more imaginable to the average human mind now than mushroom clouds were to our great-grandparents.

CONCLUSION

The nature of war as a public health concern has become more and more obvious. As weapons technology has developed, medical science can no longer deal with the devastation it causes. The only reasonable course is prevention. This is true not only in the case of the battlefield itself, where triage would assign a higher and higher percentage of victims to doom, but beyond the battlefield or even the course of a particular war itself. Survivors of the atomic blasts at Hiroshima and Nagasaki still contract terminal diseases as a result of the radiation exposure they suffered almost a half-century ago; so too do the Vietnam War veterans (both here and in Vietnam) who were exposed to the defoliant Agent Orange.

Fortunately, the notion of prevention is not as conceptually undoable in the case of war as it is in the area of natural disasters over which we have no control; as the UNESCO charter states, it is in the human mind that wars begin and therefore in the human mind that peace must begin—thus the primacy of the strategy of peace education.

Appropriately enough, the most public manifestation of the recognition of war as a public health concern on the part of the health care profession is an organization alluded to in the first paragraph of this article, Physicians for Social Responsibility. The notion of social responsibility in this context is a very important one and rests squarely on the concept of citizenship and the duties thereof.

Not long ago in our history, children and college students took courses in a subject called civics. Civics curricula were born of a rich tradition that called for full participation by all citizens in a democracy and a concomitant realization that such participation required an understanding of the political system. More recently, these courses have been superseded by a more positivistic approach in the form of disciplines such as social studies, political science, and sociology. This approach largely ignores the role of citizen as participant, focusing instead on the role of objective observer and analyst. Peace studies returns the original notion of civics—of learning about our social and political system in order to participate in and have an impact upon it—but in a broader sense, one which recognizes that we are citizens not only of our nation, but of our world. This is the perspective that Elise Boulding states so ably in her recent book on educating for peace called, appropriately enough, *Building a Global Civic Culture: Education for an Interdependent World* (Boulding, 1988).

Although peace studies programs have often been hampered by a perception of their ideological nature, this is not a valid criticism as peace studies begins to come of age. To the contrary, peace studies must be avowedly inclusive in that it is hard to identify anything that should be less limited by boundaries of any sort—be they disciplinary, ideological, or methodological—than the search for peace.

H. G. Wells has said that "human history becomes more and more a race between education and catastrophe." From this point of view, peace education represents the true hope of humankind in continuing our history.

REFERENCES

Alger, C. F. (1977). 'Foreign' policies of U.S. publics. *International Studies Quarterly, 21, 2.*

Alger, C. F. (1978-79). Role of people in the future global order. *Alternatives, 4, 233-62.*

Alger, C. F. (1984-85). Bridging the micro and the macro in international relations research. *Alternatives, 10, 319-44.*

Alger, C. F. (1988). Perceiving, analyzing, and coping with the local-global nexus. *The Local-Global Nexus, International Social Science Journal, 117, 321-40.*

Boulding, E. (1988). *Building a global civic culture: Education for an interdependent world*. New York: Teachers College Press.

Boulding, E., Passmore, J. R., & Gassler, R. S. (Compilers) (1979). *Bibliography on world conflict and peace* (2nd ed.). Boulder, CO: Westview Press. Available through COPRED, George Mason University, Fairfax, VA 22030.

Carey, D. P., & Dugan, M. A. (1982). Towards a definition of peace studies. In *Proceedings* of the International Peace Research Association Conference held in Orillia, Ontario, Canada.

Carpenter, S. L., with the assistance of COPRED-PEN and the Institute for World Order. (1977). *Repertoire of Peacemaking Skills*. Boulder, CO: Author. Available through COPRED.

Carpenter, S. L., & Solo, P., in collaboration with COPRED-PEN. (1977). *Creating the Future*. Boulder, CO: COPRED. Available through COPRED.

Cianto, D. (Compiler) (1990). *A directory of peace studies programs*. Fairfax, VA: COPRED.

Eckhardt, W. (1987). Civilian deaths in wartime. *COPRED Peace Chronicle, 12*(5), 8–9.

Klare, M., & Thomas, D. C. (in press). *Peace and world order studies: A curriculum guide* (5th ed.). Boulder, CO: Westview Press. *Peace and world order studies: A curriculum guide* is a series of edited works which include listings and outlines of college peace studies, course syllabi, and program descriptions, the first four of which were published by the World Policy Institute (formerly the Institute for World Order) in 1972, 1978, 1981, and 1984.

Segedin, P. (Compiler), & Fink, C. F., & Mohraz, J. E. (Eds.), with assistance from Groppe, E. (1986). *A directory of peace studies programs*. Urbana, IL: COPRED. Available through COPRED.

8

Religious Insights Into a Response

John F. Tuohey
The Catholic University of America, Washington, DC

In spite of the many differences that exist between the religions of the world, there is at least one place of agreement: the need for a religious response to the threat of horrendous death in the world. Rooted in religion's respect for humanity and the earth can be found an urgent concern that humanity begin to hold itself accountable for the reality of death that it has imposed and threatens to impose on itself. This concern is often expressed in what might be called "Religious Commandments," which essentially link the obligations to protect and preserve life. Through these common "commandments," religion calls on humanity to inform its conscience with a deep respect for life, to pray and to do penance. In so doing, humanity is offered a way to stop the incidence of horrendous death and to promote life and well-being.

INTRODUCTION

One commandment shared by nearly all religions is a fundamental commitment to life and well-being. In the words of the Dalai Lama,

> *Every major religion of the world—Buddhism, Christianity, Confucianism, Hinduism, Islam, Jainism, Judaism, Sikhism, Taoism, Zoroastrainism—has similar ideals of love, the same goal of benefiting humanity through spiritual practice, and the same effect of making their followers into better human beings.* (the Dalai Lama, 1984, p. 13)

Further, as will be developed below, there is a common religious conviction that *life-threatening* issues, such as abortion, capital punishment, modern warfare, and euthanasia, and *life-diminishing* issues, such as prostitution, pornography, poverty, and discrimination are essentially linked to one another. All are issues of human dignity (Bernardin, 1988a).

These two insights, that all religions share a common commitment to life and well-being, and that no one life issue is essentially isolated from another, will serve as the foundation for this chapter. Rather than developing each religion or issue separately, this chapter will seek to identify some common religious insights into an understanding of and a response to the threat horrendous death poses to the protection and promotion of life and well-being. This will be done within a fourfold framework: first, the linkage of life-threatening and life-diminishing issues; second, the Protection of Life: "No Killing"; third, the Promotion of Life: "Thou Shalt Not Steal"; and fourth, Toward a Religious Response.

While it may be true that all religions share a common commitment to human well-being, it is not true that all share a common structure or method. In view of this, the reflections offered here will focus on representative statements from different religious perspectives, rather than on official teachings as such. This will, it is hoped, avoid the suggestion that any one tradition has a superior insight. The chapter will be developed with the understanding that,

> *All authentic religions are valid, lawful, legitimate ways of salvation, as social, institutional communities of men who, within their own existential situations, respond in their own way positively to God's salvific revelation as it is manifested to them. (De Graeve, 1979, p. 317)*

THE LINKAGE OF LIFE-THREATENING AND LIFE-DIMINISHING ISSUES

In his work with the Pro-Life Activities Committee of the National Conference of Catholic Bishops, Joseph Cardinal Bernardin has attempted to demonstrate a linkage between *life-threatening* issues, such as abortion and the death penalty, and *life-diminishing* issues, such as inadequate nutrition, health care, and housing. While acknowledging that each issue is distinct, he nevertheless finds a linkage rooted in the nature of the human person. The human person is, Bernardin (1988a) suggests, both sacred and social: because the person is sacred, life must be protected; because each person is social, an environment which fosters personal life must be promoted. Life must be both protected and promoted. In praxis, this linkage means that,

> *as individuals and groups pursue one issue, whether it is opposing abortions or capital punishment, the way we oppose one threat should be related to support for a systematic vision. . . . And it is very necessary . . . that individuals and groups who seek to witness to life at one point of the spectrum of life not be seen as insensitive to or even opposed to other moral claims on the overall spectrum of life. (Bernardin, 1984, p. 15)*

The linkage of which Bernardin speaks is found within the Christian tradition as a whole. Reformation leaders Martin Luther (d. 1546) and John Calvin (d. 1564) both spoke of an underlying principle beneath the life-protecting prohibitions of the Decalogue[1] (Exodus 20, 1–21) that prescribed positive life-promoting actions. Calvin wrote that the commandment *Thou Shalt Not Kill*, which seeks to protect life, was also to be understood to mean that, "if we find anything of use to us in serving our neighbor's lives, faithfully to employ it; if anything harmful, to ward it off" (*Institutes*, II, viii, 37).

This is not unlike the Buddhist understanding of the Five Grave Precepts.[2] Zen Buddhist ethical writer Robert Aitken (1984) suggests that, though negatively framed, these precepts are to be interpreted both negatively and positively. The First Grave Precept, *No Killing*, intends that people should be protected from harm, and that life in general should be promoted. The Second Grave Precept, *No Stealing*, can be understood in a similar way: to not steal means both to protect and promote another's well-being.

---

[1]The Decalogue, or Ten Commandments, are often referred to as the foundations of Jewish and Christian ethical thought.

[2]The basic ethical precepts in Buddhism are contained in the Five Grave Precepts: No Killing; No Stealing; No Unchastity; No Lying; and No Intoxicating Beverages.

Bernardin, as noted, roots his linkage of life-threatening and life-diminishing issues in an anthropological understanding of the person as both sacred and social. This linkage can also be rooted biblically within the Judeo-Christian notion of *berit*, covenant. Covenant denotes a general obligation between two or more parties. Left as such, it might be thought to be similar to a contemporary understanding of contract. This is not the case. Whereas a contract is limited to a statement of an agreed-upon exchange of goods or services, a covenant bespeaks an internalized personal commitment. Roman Catholic scholar William E. May (1986) points out in his discussion of marriage as a covenant that covenanting involves each party taking on a new identity. More precisely, when people enter into a contract, they agree to meet certain expectations which are extrinsic to each person. In a covenant, each person chooses the other to be the one with whom he or she will take on a new identity. In the Pentateuch, for example, the God of creation becomes the personal *your God* and those who were once *no people* become *a people* (Deuteronomy 7:7–15). In marriage, a woman chooses a man not so much to be her husband as to be the one with whom she becomes a spouse.

In a covenant, one's own fidelity is not dependent upon the other's. Instead, it is rooted in fidelity to the *who* one has become. In the Judeo-Christian covenant tradition, people have become each other's *keeper* (Genesis 4:1–16). This relationship is not unlike the mutuality found in the Buddhist notion of self-realization.

Buddhists regard self-realization as a central aspect of religious development (Aitken, 1984). However, there is also the recognition that, if one is to be faithful to the pursuit of one's own self-realization, he or she must also seek to promote the other's self-realization. It is in this that the Five Grave Precepts find their essential meaning. They assist in the individual's pursuit of self-realization by offering guidance for the promotion of the other's self-realization. As Aitken points out, "The fundamental fact is that I cannot survive unless you do. My self-realization is your self-realization" (Aitken, 1984, p. 19).

For the Hindu Gandhi (d. 1948), this commitment of one person to another is rooted in *Satyagraha*, the clinging to truth (Fisher, 1962). A *satyagrahi* is a person who clings to the truth that everyone is always a brother or sister. This remains true regardless of how that brother or sister behaves. One's enemy, he said, is never a person. The only enemy anyone has is the evil which a person might commit (Kumarappa, 1951).

Protestant theologian Paul Ramsey (1970) wrote that an essential element of *berit* is *hesed*, steadfast love. Covenant necessarily entails a steadfast, unqualified love of the other. Ramsey also suggested that this is an age when *hesed* often becomes *perhaps*. One's fidelity to a covenant relationship can become conditional. An Anglican study group warns of this tendency in stating that

> *the value of human life does not depend only on its capacity to give. Love . . . is the equal and unalterable regard for the value of the other human being independent of their particular characteristics. It extends especially to the helpless and hopeless. . . . In the giver it demands unlimited caring, in the recipient absolute trust. (As quoted in McCormick, 1988, p. 107)*

When acceptance becomes conditioned by the appropriateness of the other's race, behavior, sexual orientation, gender, social status, or state of health, a type of death results. Qualified fidelity in a covenant leads to a horrendous death embodied in racism, revenge, heterosexism, sexism, classism, healthism, and other forms of discrimination.

The shift from *hesed* to *perhaps* in covenant is illustrated in decisions concerning human reproduction. Jean Bethke Elshtain (1984) suggests that advanced technology has made it possible to detect and abort any fetus that will fail to meet parental expectations, such as appropriate gender or mental or physical wholeness at birth. What is at stake, she writes, is the human capacity for risk-taking, spontaneity, and unconditional welcoming.

The issue Elshtain raises has explicit implications for some instances of death associated not only with abortion, but also with euthanasia, suicide, the death penalty, and war as well. The human capacity for risk-taking, spontaneity, and welcoming can only be lived out in a community bound together in unconditional mutual concern for one another. Only a community that regards the other as the self (Leviticus 19:18), regardless of who, what, how, or why the other is (John 13:34–35), can risk welcoming and protecting, or keeping and promoting anyone in its midst.

Finally, this linkage is not just one of protecting and promoting the life of individuals. It always is a question of protecting and promoting all life. In speaking of the creation of Adam, one Talmudic text reads,

> *Therefore only a single human being was created in the world, to teach that if any person has caused a single soul of Israel to perish, Scripture regards him as if he had caused an entire world to perish; and if any human being saves a single soul of Israel, Scripture regards him as if he had saved an entire world. (Veatch, 1981, p. 30)*

It is not possible to protect and promote some life through some acts. In every act or omission, either all life is protected, or all life is threatened; either all life is promoted, or all life is diminished.

The Protection of Life: "No Killing"

In *The Heritage Dictionary* (Morris, 1973, p. 720), killing is defined as (a) the act of putting to death, slaying; and (b) the depriving of life. The second definition reflects more closely the religious understanding. Killing is the result of the deprivation of any of those conditions necessary for another's life and well-being. The World Council of Churches teaches that racism, which is present

> *whenever persons, even before they are born, because of their race, are assigned to a group severely limited in their freedom of movement, their choice of work, their places of residences, and so on. . . . (Jersild & Johnson, 1983, p. 131)*

is killing.[3] In Buddhism it is taught that, in a person's need to protect him or herself, another's point of view is sometimes killed (Aitken, 1984). Ideologuism is killing. Killing has other manifestations as well:

> *. . . oppression of the poor, deprivation of basic human rights, economic exploitations, sexual exploitation and pornography, neglect or abuse of the aged and the helpless, and innu-*

---

[3]See also, Pontifical Justice and Peace Commission (1989) "The Church and Racism: Toward a More Fraternal Society," *Origins, 18,* 614–626.

merable other acts of inhumanity. (National Conference of Catholic Bishops, [NCCB], 1982, no. 285)

Careers or activities that harm others, such as trading in arms or poisons, drinking and driving, fraud, and polluting are also forms of killing (Rahula, 1959; Carmody & Carmody, 1988).

Any act or attitude that deprives another of those conditions necessary for well-being may be properly defined as killing. For the sake of clarity, this section will discuss religious views on physical killing. The following section will discuss the broader understanding of killing within the context of stealing.

Historically, numerous attempts have been made to justify some forms of physical killing. In Christianity, the ideal of turning the other cheek (Luke 6:28) seems to have been modified by at least the fifth century, when Augustine allowed that there could be such a thing as a *just war*, made necessary by human sin (*City of God*, 19, 7). Pope Urban II threw all caution to the wind in 1095 and called on Christians to embark on an armed Crusade to recapture the Holy Land from the Turkish infidels (Pelikan, 1985). By the 12th century, Thomas Aquinas (d. 1274), while recognizing that Jesus taught his disciples not to resist evil with evil (Matthew 5:29), wrote that it was, nevertheless "sometimes necessary for the common good for a man to act otherwise" (*Summa Theologica* II, II 40). On that premise, he formulated his Just War Theory.

The Protestant Reformation of the 16th and 17th centuries did little to challenge these attitudes. Although it is true that the crusade ideal was generally rejected, the fighting itself was not uniformly condemned. Instead, different reasons were given to justify it. Luther, for example, argued that the fighting could be justified by appeal to the just war principle of legitimate authority. He reasoned that as long as Charles V was legitimately protecting his subjects, the fighting was justified (Pelikan, 1985).

The only Christian challenge to this attitude came from people like Erasmus (d. 1566), John Amos Comenius (d. 1670), the Anabaptists, and the Religious Society of Friends, known as Quakers. These Christians rejected fighting and killing as a violation of the teachings of Christ. Prominent 17th century Quaker theologian Robert Barclay expressed this rejection in his *Apology*:

> *Whoever can reconcile this, "Resist not evil," with "Resist violence by force," again, "Give also thy other cheek," with "Strike again"; . . . or "Pray for those that persecute you, and those that calumniate you," with "Persecute them by fines, imprisonments, and death itself," whoever, I say, can find a means to reconcile these things may be supposed also to have found a way to reconcile God with the Devil. (As quoted in Marsh, 1984, p. 2)*

At the center of this rejection is the notion of Christian discipleship. Religious groups like the Quakers insisted that in order to be a disciple, one had to come to know the life of Jesus as the only way to live. In imitation of this life, disciples were to love each neighbor as self, and return good for evil received.

This attitude toward violence should not to be understood as passive tolerance in the face of injustice. The Quakers have a long tradition of working to overcome injustice and oppression. This reform, however, is always pursued through non-violence.

> *We have thought of the widespread exploitation of economically underdeveloped peoples,*
> *and of those industrial and other workers who are also exploited and heavily burdened. . . .*
> *Subjection, poverty, injustice, and war are closely allied. This situation demands sweeping*
> *political and economic changes; and we are convinced that the hope of freedom does not lie in*
> *violence, which is at its root immoral, but in such changes as may be brought about by fellow-*
> *ship and mutual service. (Marsh, 1984, p. 8)*

Gandhi also believed that to be truly nonviolent one had to be both resolute in renouncing violence and actively engaged in social reform (Carmody & Carmody, 1988). This combination, Gandhi wrote, is only possible through an absolute refusal to hate another human being:

> *I see neither bravery nor sacrifice in destroying life or property . . . I would rather*
> *leave . . . my homestead . . . for the enemy to use . . . There is . . . bravery in so leaving my*
> *homestead and crops, if I do so not out of fear, but because I refuse to regard anyone as my*
> *enemy. (As quoted in Fisher, 1961, p. 332)*

This perspective on nonviolence is not held universally within Hinduism, just as it is not within Christianity. The *Bhagavad Gita* tells the story of Arjuna, a member of the warrior caste, who is repulsed by his obligation to do battle and risk killing. Arjuna is told by Krishna that he ought to fulfill his duties to his caste rather than to seek *ahimsa*, noninjury.[4] Gandhi, as well as other Hindu teachers, sought to reform this attitude.

Efforts to reform Christian attitudes have gone on as well. During the Vatican Council II (1963–1965) debate of "The Pastoral Constitution of the Church in the Modern World" (*Gaudium et Spes*, 1965), the question of whether or not a just government could legitimately order its citizens to fight was addressed. In the original draft of this document an appeal was made to the principle of the *presumption of justice* (Zahn, 1986), the long-held Christian principle that governments are presumed to be just and to legislate justly. If included, the text would be understood to give a benefit of the doubt to government military policies, and continued ecclesial rejection to conscientious objection.[5] As a result of the debate, appeal to the principle was dropped. Instead, the Council document offers praise to those who renounce the use of violence in the vindication of their rights, and expresses explicit ecclesial approval of such nonviolent acts as draft resistance and deferred military service (*Gaudium et Spes*, 1965, no. 78). The Pastoral Letter *On Human Life in Our Day* speaks of the value to society of those who refuse to engage in acts of violence:

> *If war is ever to be outlawed . . . it will be because the citizens of this and other nations*
> *have rejected the tenets of exaggerated nationalism and insisted on principles of nonviolent*
> *political and civic action in both the domestic and international spheres. (NCCB, 1968, p. 148)*

---

[4]Zaehner, R. C. (Ed.). (1969). *The Bhagavad-Gita: With a Commentary Based on the Original Sources* (pp. 48–53). London: Oxford University Press. The doctrine of *ahimsa* is especially important in Jainism.

[5]In a 1956 Christmas radio address, Pius XII (d. 1958) said, "A Catholic citizen may not make appeal to his own conscience as grounds for refusing to give his service to the state, and to fulfill duties affirmed by law."

Within Christianity today, opinions regarding the appropriateness of fighting and the risk of killing remain similar to those formulated by the World Council of Churches in its first Assembly of the Commission of the Church on International Affairs in 1948:

> 1. *There are those who hold that, even though entering a war may be a Christian's duty in particular circumstances, modern warfare, with its mass destruction, can never be an act of justice.*
>
> 2. *In the absence of impartial supranational institutions, there are those who hold that military action is the ultimate sanction of the rule of law, and that citizens must be directly taught that it is their duty to defend the law by force if necessary.*
>
> 3. *Others, again, refuse military service of all kinds, convinced that an absolute witness against war and for peace is for them the will of God, and they desire that the Church should speak to the same effect. (Peace and Disarmament, 1982, pp. 15–16)*

The difficulty in living a life of nonviolence may lie in its conviction of the absolute goodness of others. Gandhi believed that a wrongdoer will ultimately grow weary of wrongdoing in the absence of violent resistance (Kumarappa, 1951). Although most people are not that trusting, Gandhi was convinced:

> *Even if Hitler was so minded, he could not devastate 700,000 nonviolent villages. He would himself become nonviolent in the process. (As quoted in Fisher, 1962, p. 327)*

As mentioned earlier, each precept or commandment is not merely a statement of prohibition. It is also a call to positive action. The Grave Precept, *No Killing*, is also the command, *Promote Life*. Religion teaches that this is done through a search for genuine peace.

Just as killing is not restricted to war, so too is peace not restricted to the absence of war. United States military language often refers to peace as *permanent prehostility*. Within the religious traditions, peace does not consist of an absence. For the Buddhist, peace is neither a vacuum of sense perception, nor a harmony created by authority. Rather, peace is the calm of the one who has forgotten the self in doing the work of the world (Aitken, 1984), where the persecution of the innocent is vehemently denounced and compassion is the driving force of all actions (Rahula, 1959). For the Quaker, peace is "love conquering fear . . . a lovely concern for all men, for friend and for rival" (Marsh, 1984, p. 14). For the Hebrew prophets, peace is the centerpiece of justice (Jeremiah 8:11; Ezekiel 13:16).

The Hebrew word of peace is *salom* or *shalom*. *Shalom* is best understood as an order or harmony placed by God in creation (Genesis 1:1–31). Roman Catholic Scripture scholar John Gillman (1989) speaks of *shalom* as the realm where the chaos of sickness, war, social strife, and infidelity to covenant is not allowed to enter. Peace is the presence of divine harmony.

In the Jewish mystical tradition *Kabbalah*, it was understood that one of the purposes of the commandments was to strengthen the presence of a divine harmony in the universe (*Encyclopaedia Judaica*, 1971). Through the performance of the commandments, a person helped to bring harmony (*shalom*) to the disunited (*chaotic*) world.

The religious insight concerning peace and the practice of nonkilling is that it is not attained merely by doing away with violence. Peace is established by promoting life through the observance of such commands of the Law as assisting the widow and the orphan (no. 256, Exodus 22:21); respecting another's possessions (no. 265, Exodus 20:17); using weights and measures honestly (no. 271, Leviticus 19:35); and giving only true testimony (no. 285, Exodus 20:16).

The Promotion of Life: Thou Shalt Not Steal

To take what belongs to another is stealing. To keep for oneself what is needed by another is also stealing. Gandhi expresses it this way:

> *In India we have got three million people who have to be satisfied with one meal a day. You and I have no right to anything . . . until these three millions are clothed and fed better. (As quoted in Aitken, 1984, p. 31)*

The remedy to this form of theft and the horrendous death which it causes is the practice of nonstealing; that is, the reduction of personal wants.

In the Christian tradition, the practice of nonstealing is reflected in the understanding of the common nature of all property. In the first modern social encyclical, *Rerum Novarum*, (1891) Leo XIII (d. 1903) taught that attention must always be paid to the universal purpose for which all things were created. The practice of nonstealing entails an attitude of regarding all personal possessions as not merely one's own, but as common property. By this it is meant that what is owned by one should accrue to the benefit of all (*Gaudium et Spes*, 1965, no. 69). In a way similar to Gandhi's insistence that no one has a right to any possession until the needs of the poor and hungry have been addressed, Vatican Council II asserts that if a person is in extreme necessity, that person has the right to take what is needed from the riches of others (*Gaudium et Spes*, 1965, no. 69). These riches, it should be noted, are not just one's extras. To those who insist on coming to the relief of the poor only out of their superfluous wealth, John XXIII (d. 1963) responded that the obligation of all people, and indeed the urgent obligation of the Christian, is to reckon what is superfluous by the measure of the needs of others.

By promoting life through the practice of nonstealing, horrendous death can be prevented. Aitken's (1984) view of the two ways of achieving peace and well-being in the world illustrate this. One way to peace is to satisfy everyone's desire. The other has to do with each person being content with the good. Due to physical limitations, the former is impossible. That leaves only the second alternative, contentment with the good, as the way to peace. This does not mean doing away with all competition, acquisition, and possession. These only become a problem when charity is missing. Charity needs to be at the root of all human acquisition. As is taught in Hinduism, "neither profit nor pleasure should rule over peace, self-possession, purity of intention, and compassionate help for others" (Carmody & Carmody, 1988, p. 123). When this is the case, people acquire things for the benefit of all, and not just for the self.

The notion of nonstealing may challenge common notions of justice. Justice, it might be argued, upholds a person's right to private property. It would, in this scenario, be unjust to demand that one's own property be understood in any sense as being common. The question of natural rights in this discussion of horrendous death from a religious perspective will be addressed in more detail below. For now, one point will be made.

The religious notion of justice does not connote the minimal requirements for fairness, as does a secular understanding. As such, it is not rooted in, nor does it necessarily demand, a system of natural rights. In Christianity, for example, justice is rooted in the biblical ideal of charity. Charity, as the apostle Paul teaches, does not seek its own interests (1 Corinthians 13:5). This can be taken to mean that the demands of justice are not so much directed toward upholding one's own rights, as they are directed toward the active pursuit of the interests of the other. Justice itself demands that the economic community, for example, not make decisions concerning labor, wages, and the distribution of goods merely on otherwise legitimate economic considerations. Decisions should be based on the criteria of the interests of others, particularly those most vulnerable. A "trickle-down" approach to prosperity, within this perspective, is not just if it fails to actively seek the other's interests. As such, it is a form of stealing, and ultimately, killing.

This option for the poor is expressed by some within contemporary Hinduism as a form of worship. Swami Vivekananda, as one example, taught that the poor ought to be regarded as the presence of the divine in the world. Work such as educating the illiterate, feeding the hungry, visiting the imprisoned, and caring for the ill should be seen, Vivekananda taught, as expressions of love for God (Carmody & Carmody, 1988).[6]

Another point that is made in religious thought concerns the treatment of those who steal by breaking into a house, exploiting the poor, or by standing idle in the face of injustice.[7] These people may not, in turn, be made victims of another theft. That is, the criminal should not have the opportunity of life and well-being stolen as a punishment for having stolen. Buddha opposed harsh punishments for crime because poverty, which itself results from breaches of the precept of nonstealing, is the root and cause of crime (Rahula, 1959). The thief in crime is also a victim of crime. If punishment becomes vengeful, it too will destroy rather than promote life. When justice seeks the others' interests, the appropriate response to a breach of nonstealing will be to provide opportunity.

Religious opposition to the death penalty is rooted here. Killing someone for committing a crime is not in the criminal's best interest, so justice will not be served. As Buddha taught, "Hatred is never appeased by hatred in this world; it is appeased by love" (Rahula, 1959 p. 125).[8] Gandhi also speaks against harsh punishment for those who commit crimes and perpetrate violence:

Instead of bearing ill-will towards a . . . criminal and trying to get him punished . . . try to . . . understand the cause that has led him into crime and try to remedy it . . . [T]each him a vocation and provide him with the means to make an honest living and thereby transform his life. (As quoted in Kumarappa, 1951, p. 350)

[6]See also Proverbs 19:71; Matthew 25:31–46.

[7]According to Gandhi, the difference between being rich and being a thief is often only one of degree. The one who obtains money by exploitation or other questionable means is as guilty of robbery as the one who picks a pocket or breaks into a house (Kumarappa, 1959, p. 351).

[8]There is, admittedly, a great public debate as to whether or not the death penalty serves the interest of the state in preventing crime. Even if the interests of the state are served by the death penalty, it is difficult to see how it could serve the interests of the criminal.

The Commandment, *Thou Shalt Not Steal*, applies to all sisters and brothers. The practice of nonstealing and the promotion of life refuses to admit any form of stealing (killing), even as a remedy for social ills.

Toward a Religious Response

The religious insights noted here affirm the relationship that binds all people together. Each person is the other's keeper and brother or sister; everyone depends on the other's self-realization for his or her own. Each tradition also lays a firm injunction against committing acts of horrendous death, of which this chapter discusses only a few. Most importantly, perhaps, is the consensus that religious precepts and commandments are not merely negative injunctions intended to protect life. They are also positive admonitions intended to promote life. That is what Buddhists refer to as *right livelihood*.[9] To protect life by not killing necessarily entails a corresponding call to promote life by nourishing it. The protection and promotion of life are intricately linked.

Insights are for the purpose of facilitating action, and this chapter will not be complete until some call to action is articulated. This final section will make use of the four areas of concern mentioned in the pastoral letter *The Challenge of Peace* (1983), as a framework for this reflection: education programs and the formation of conscience; reverence for life; prayer; and penance.

Education Programs and Formation of Conscience

The picture formed by the instances of horrendous death in the world can be overwhelming. In the face of such a reality, how is it possible to begin to protect and promote life and well-being? Learning the facts is one way. In Buddhism, awareness lies at the root of *right action*.[10] Gandhi writes that awareness begins with the self:

> We are not always aware of our real needs, and most of us improperly multiply our wants and thus unconsciously make thieves of ourselves. If we devote some thought to the subject, we shall find that we can get rid of quite a number of wants. (As quoted in Aitken, 1984, p. 30)

In becoming more aware of self, people are freed to become more aware of others. Education and conscience formation means becoming aware that the U.S. nuclear arsenal has targeted 60 military sites within the city limits of Moscow; that 35 million Americans have no health insurance; that one in four children under the age of 6 is poor; that two out of three poor adults are women; that approximately 33% of all teenage women and men who commit suicide do so in part because of society's lack of acceptance of their homosexuality. Beyond the local scene, there is a need for an awareness of the plight of the 800 million people throughout the world who live in absolute poverty. Awareness is the key to an appropriate response to the many threats of horrendous death.

---

[9]In Buddhism, *right livelihood* means that one should abstain from making one's living through a profession that brings harm to self, others, or the environment. This would include such careers as trading in arms and lethal weapons, using poisons or pollutants, killing animals, cheating, and so forth (Carmody & Carmody, 1988).

[10]In Buddhism, *right action* is one of the eight paths to the attainment of the Fourth Noble Truth of detachment. See footnote 12.

Once aware, it is possible to learn how to act. Kathleen and James McGinnis (1986) suggest that good places to learn the value of common ownership and the practice of nonstealing are public facilities, such as libraries and pools. They offer other suggestions as well, intended to help raise an awareness of the issues of materialism, individualism, racism, sexism, militarism, and family violence. Awareness of the death entailed in these attitudes can lead to greater efforts toward well-being.

Financial institutions committed to aiding the poor can be chosen by those who seek to avoid engaging in multinational theft and killing. Many corporations regularly contribute to funds aimed at human development. Choosing career positions in, or doing business with, institutions which respect the dignity of human labor and the common need for a healthy and safe environment help to respond to the insight that life is to be protected and promoted.

Money-markets can be of use in contributing to the ending of the incidence of horrendous death. Some credit cards, for example, donate a percentage of each transaction to organizations such as Oxfam to feed the hungry and Amnesty International to free those unjustly detained. As important as what such purchasing practices accomplish is the attitude they help to foster. When one is aware that a percentage of everything spent is used to promote the cause of justice and the prevention of horrendous death, awareness of the impact one person can have on the community as a whole is strengthened. The reality of human covenantedness is enhanced, and all move toward the achievement of self-realization by constantly keeping, and not turning a back on, their own (Isaiah 58:1–9). While some may object that life is too short to be worried about the life-and-death implications of the purchase of a shirt, it can be pointed out that life is too long for any of it to be an experience of horrendous death.

True Peace Calls for "Reverence for Life"

When violence or death, in any form, becomes an accepted part of everyday life, respect for all life is diminished. When dimensions of life become separated into categories based on the *quality* of that life, life as such loses its dignity. Even so, the Christian tradition has often made appeal to various philosophical principles to justify violence against some life. Many of these principles are rooted in the notion of *natural rights*.

It is often pointed out that society has the *right* to put a criminal to death and to defend itself against an aggressor, that a woman has a *right* over her body, that individuals have a *right* to free speech, and so forth. These statements have merit, and it is not the intent here to diminish in any way the importance of natural, personal rights in society. Nevertheless, it is appropriate to question the proper authority these principles possess in light of the imperative placed before the religious person, *No Killing*.[11]

---

[11]In Buddhism, the Grave Precept, No Killing, and the ideal of *ahimsa* in Hinduism has generally led to a negative evaluation of war, the death penalty, and abortion. With respect to abortion, however, there are some exceptions. Aitken (1984) suggests that in Zen Buddhism, abortion may sometimes be seen as a lesser of two evils. In the Hindu tradition, the Upanishads could speak of a person being united to divinity and therefore beyond the reach of crimes such as murder or abortion (Carmody & Carmody, 1988). Although admitting of exceptions, there is a subtle yet important distinction to be made. In these exceptions there remains a negative evaluation of the act itself. Unlike the common Western view, there is no affirmation of the appropriateness of the act by appeal to a natural, personal right.

Roman Catholic theologian Fans Jozef van Beek argues that "Dedication to compassionate service in imitation of Christ, not appeal to natural law or natural rights, is the primary source of Christian life-ethics" (van Beek, 1988, p. 133). An examination of the example of compassionate service as it was lived out by Jesus would seem to indicate, as the Quakers point out, that the follower of Christ is called to reject violence as a means to correct an injustice, and to foster an attitude of willingness to give one's life for others, including one's enemies (Fendall, 1988). Religious insight asks the question whether society's appeals to natural rights is in service to a fundamental respect for life, or to a justification for a qualification of that respect. As the justification of any form of horrendous death becomes easier, respect for life and well-being becomes more difficult.

One point that Bernardin (1988b) makes in his formulation of a consistent ethic of life is the insistence that any group's efforts to protect or promote one dimension of life must respect the efforts of other groups. In the case of abortion, for example, it can be argued that it is counter-productive to bomb abortion clinics, or to insist that the availability of abortion is a necessary part of any program to help people to break out of poverty. One of the inconsistencies that can mitigate a reverence for life is the tendency to view a particular life issue with such a degree of urgency that violence becomes a permissible way to deal with it. This does not work toward an atmosphere in which all life is protected, promoted, and reverenced.

Prayer

Religion offers people a way of reflecting upon or gaining insight into reality. Protestant theologian James M. Gustafson (1984) speaks of the Scriptures as a medium through which reality is revealed. That is, it is a place where the reality of the divine, self, and others is discovered. It follows from this, Gustafson writes, that when people know God, the self, and the other, it is possible to know how to live rightly.

Prayer is another place where reality is revealed. Again, with a knowledge of reality comes the knowledge of how to protect and promote life. The Buddhist tradition, with its emphasis on self-realization, echoes this. Part of self-realization is the coming to an awareness of who one is in order to learn compassion for one's self (Aitken, 1984). Having done this, it is then possible to be compassionate with others.

Prayer can also be a way of discovering one's commitment to life. Take, for example, the words in the Christian text of *The Lord's Prayer*, "Grant us peace in our day." Referring to these words, the National Council of Catholic Bishops (NCCB) reminds the person using them that peace is requested *today*, and not at some future time (NCCB, 1983). Prayer is not simply a request for something to be done or given. Rather, it expresses a commitment on the part of the person at prayer to work for the realization, with divine assistance, of what is requested. It does no good to pray for something one is not committed to making possible. In reflecting on the practice or content of prayer, it is possible for each person to discern how committed he or she is to eliminating horrendous death from this world.

Penance

In a quotation cited above, Gandhi suggested that if people thought about it long enough, they would discover that they unconsciously make thieves of themselves by multiplying wants. The practice of nonstealing is a way to gradually reduce those wants. In some traditions, this learning to do with less is known as penance:

> You and I, who ought to know better, must adjust our wants, and even undergo voluntary starvation in order that they [the poor] may be nursed, fed and clothed. (As quoted in Aitken, 1984, p. 31)

Buddhism, too, entails this kind of penance. All life is suffering, Buddha taught, because of our desires[12] (Rahula, 1959; Carmody & Carmody, 1988). Letting go of desires and learning to live with less, doing penance, is the Buddhist way to well-being.

At the end of World War II, an ecumenical Commission of Theologians issued a statement saying that the first word of the churches in that postwar situation needed to be a call to active penance. They defined penance as an exercise in humility:

> . . . the humility of clear-headed, honest men who see how grievously they have squandered resources inherited from a long, laborious past and jeopardized what should have been a more enlightened future. (Lunger, 1988, p. 307)

Penance is also needed today. As expressed in these examples, this cannot be a penance expressed in accusations against oneself or others. A penance of this type would only encourage other forms of horrendous death. Rather, what is needed is life-giving penance: a penance that helps people learn the distinction between real needs and those things they have convinced themselves they need; a penance which reflects on the goods of humanity that have been squandered and need to be promoted, as well as the goods that have been endangered and need to be protected.

CONCLUSION

There are many issues concerning horrendous death and well-being, many more than have been discussed here. The purpose of this chapter, however, was not to address each issue, but to offer insights for personal reflection on the life-and-death issues of today. Religious insights offer a place to start this reflection by describing the relationships each person shares with others, the meaning of horrendous death, and the link between the protection and promotion of life. These insights also offer a source of hope that humanity can begin to recognize the reverence due to life and well-being and the threat posed to it by horrendous death. There is hope that one day, there will be no more death on all of God's holy mountain (Is 26:6–8).

REFERENCES

Aitken, R. (1984). *The mind of clover: Essays in Zen Buddhist ethics.* San Francisco: North Point Press.

[12]The Four Noble Truths of Buddhism are: all life is suffering; all suffering is caused by desire; the remedy to suffering is detachment; the way to detachment is through the eightfold path of right view, right thought, right speech, right action, right livelihood, right effort, right mindfulness, and right concentration (Rahula, 1959; Carmody & Carmody, 1988).

Bernardin, J. (1988a). A consistent ethic of life: An American-Catholic dialogue. In T. Fuechtmann (Ed.), *Consistent ethic of life* (pp. 1–11). Chicago: Sheed & Ward.

Bernardin, J. (1988b). A consistent ethic of life: Continuing the dialogue. In T. Fuechtmann (Ed.), *Consistent ethic of life* (pp. 12–19). Chicago: Sheed & Ward.

Carmody, D. L., & Carmody, J. T. (1988). *How to live well: Ethics in the world religions.* Belmont, CA: Wadsworth.

The 613 commandments (1971). *Encyclopaedia Judaica: Vol 5* (pp. 760–783). Jerusalem: Keter Publishing.

The reason for commandments. (1971). *Encyclopaedia Judaica: Vol 5* (pp. 783–791). Jerusalem: Keter Publishing.

Cooney, R., & Michalowski, H. (Eds.). (1987). *The power of the people.* Philadelphia: New Society Publishers.

The Dalai Lama. (1984). *A human approach to world peace.* London: Wisdom Publications.

De Graeve, F., S.J. (1979). From O.T.S.O.G. to T.A.S.C.A.S.: Eleven theses toward a Christian theology of interreligious encounter. *Louvain Studies, 7,* 315–325.

Elshtain, J. B. (1984). Reflections on abortion, values, and the family. In S. Callahan & D. Callahan (Eds.), *Abortion: Understanding differences* (pp. 47–72). New York: The Hasting Center Series in Ethics/Plenum Press.

Fendall, L. (1988). Theology and the bloodless revolution. *Quaker Religious Thought, 23,* 1–22.

Fisher, L. (Ed.). (1962). *The essential Gandhi, his life, work and ideas: An anthology.* New York: Random House.

Gaudium et spes (1966). In W. M. Abbott, S.J. (Ed.). *The documents of Vatican II* (pp. 199–308). New York: Guild Press.

Gillman, J. L. (1989). Biblical understanding of peace. In B. L. Marthaler (Ed.), *The New Catholic Encyclopedia: Vol. 18* (pp. 365–366). Palatine, IL: Jack Hearty & Associates.

Gustafson, J. M. (1984). The changing use of the Bible in Christian ethics. In C. E. Curran & R. A. McCormick (Eds.), *Readings in moral theology No. 4: The use of Scripture in moral theology* (pp. 133–150). New York: Paulist Press.

Jersild, P. T., & Johnson, D. A. (Eds.). (1983). *Moral issues and Christian response* (3rd. ed.). New York: Holt, Rinehart, & Winston, citing the Commission on Faith and Order and the Programme to Combat Racism of the World Council of Churches. (1975). *Racism on theology, theology against racism.* Geneva, Switzerland.

Kumarappa, B. (Ed.). (1951). *M. K. Gandhi: Collected writings on nonviolent resistance (Satyagraha).* New York: Schocken Books.

Lunger, H. L. (Ed.). (1988). *Facing war/Waging peace: Findings of the American Church Study Conferences, 1940–1960.* New York: Friendship Press. Excerpts used with permission.

Marsh, M. (Ed.). (1984). *Quakers on peace.* Washington, DC: Friends Meeting of Washington.

May, W. E. (1986). Marriage and human dignity. In J. A. Dwyer, S.S.J. (Ed.), *Questions of special urgency: "The Church in the modern world" two decades after Vatican II* (pp. 19–36). Washington, DC: Georgetown University Press.

McCormick, R. A., S.J. (1988). The consistent ethic of life: Is there an historical soft underbelly? In T. Fuechtmann (Ed.), *Consistent ethic of life* (pp. 96–122). Chicago: Sheed & Ward. Citing *On dying well* (Church Information Office, Church House, Dean's Yard, SWIP 3NZ, 1975) 1–67 at 22.

McGinnis, K., & McGinnis, J. (1986). The social mission of the Christian family. In J. A. Dwyer, S.S.J. (Ed.), *Questions of special urgency: "The Church in the modern world" two decades after Vatican II* (pp. 37–52). Washington, DC: Georgetown University Press.

Morris, W. (Ed.). (1983). *The heritage illustrated dictionary of the English language: International edition* New York: American Heritage Publishing.

National Conference of Catholic Bishops. (1968). *On human life in our day.* Washington, DC: United States Catholic Conference.

National Conference of Catholic Bishops. (1983). *The challenge of peace: God's promise and our response.* Washington, DC: United States Catholic Conference.

Peace and disarmament: Documents of the World Council of Churches and the Roman Catholic Church. (1982). Geneva, Switzerland: Commission of the Churches on International Affairs of the World Council of Churches.

Pelikan, J. (1985). *Jesus through the centuries: His place in the history of culture.* New Haven: Yale University Press.

Pontifical Justice and Peace Commission. (1989). The church and racism: Toward a more fraternal society. *Origins, 18,* 614–626.

Rahula, W. (1959). *What the Buddha taught.* New York: Grove Press.
Ramsey, P. (1970). *The patient as person: Explorations in medical ethics.* New Haven: Yale University Press.
Valentine, L. (1988). Power in pacifism. *Quaker Religious Thought, 23,* 23–35.
van Beek, F. J., S.J. (1988). Response: Weakness in the consistent ethics of life? Some systematic-theological observations. In T. G. Fuechtmann (Ed.), *Consistent ethic of life* (pp. 123–139). Chicago: Sheed & Ward.
Veatch, R. M. (1981). *A theory of medical ethics.* New York: Basic Books.
Zaehner, R. C. (Ed.). (1969). *The Bhagavad-Gita: With a commentary based on the original sources.* London: Oxford University Press.
Zahn, G. C. (1986). The church's "new attitude toward war." In J. A. Dwyer, S.S.J. (Ed.), *Questions of special urgency: "The church in the modern world" two decades after Vatican II* (pp. 203–220). Washington, DC: Georgetown University Press.

APPENDIX: RESOURCES

American Friends Service Committee
1501 Cherry St.
Philadelphia, PA 19102

Amnesty International
322 Eighth Ave., 10th floor
New York, NY 10001

Catholic Peace Fellowship
339 Lafayette St.
New York, NY 10012

Catholic Worker
36 East First St.
New York, NY 10003

Center on Law and Pacifism
P.O. Box 308
Cokedale, CO 81032

Central Committee for Conscientious Objectors
2208 South St.
Philadelphia, PA 19146

Church of the Brethren World Ministries
1451 Dundee Ave.
Elgin, IL 60120

Clergy and Laity Concerned
198 Broadway
New York, NY 10038

Episcopal Peace Fellowship
Hearst Hall
Wisconsin Ave. at Woodley Rd. NW
Washington, DC 20016

Greenpeace
1611 Connecticut Ave. NW
Washington, DC 20069

Interfaith Center on Corporate Responsibility
475 Riverside Drive, Room 566
New York, NY 10115

International Fellowship of Reconciliation
Hof van Sonoy 15–17
N-1811 LD Alkmaar
Netherlands

Jewish Peace Fellowship
P.O. Box 271
Nyack, NY 10960

Martin Luther King, Jr. Center for Social Change
449 Auburn Ave. NE
Atlanta, GA 30312

Mennonite Central Committee
21 South 12th St.
Akron, PA 60614

National Council of Churches of Christ
475 Riverside Drive
New York, NY 10015

National Inter-Religious Service Board of Conscientious Objectors
800 18th St. NW, Suite 600
Washington, DC 20006

Pax Christi
348 E. Tenth St.
Erie, PA 16503

Religious Task Force
85 South Oxford St.
Brooklyn, NY 11217

Sojourners
P.O. Box 29272
Washington, DC 20017

Southern Christian Leadership Conference
334 Auburn Ave. NE
Atlanta, GA 30303

Source: Cooney & Michalowski, 1987, pp. 262–263.

9

Leader Control: Peace Through Participation

Michael H. Shuman
Institute for Policy Studies, Washington, DC

INTRODUCTION

In 1945 two atomic bombs fell on Hiroshima and Nagasaki and killed 200,000 Japanese civilians (The Committee for the Compilation of Materials on Damage Caused by the Atomic Bombs in Hiroshima and Nagasaki, 1985). Since then the United States and the Soviet Union have stockpiled more than 50,000 nuclear weapons—enough firepower to fuel a Hiroshima-sized blast every second for nearly twelve days. Even if a small percentage of these weapons were ever used in combat, hundreds of millions of people, perhaps even billions, would die. Nuclear War I would instantly become the worst tragedy ever to befall humanity—the most extreme example of horrendous-type death imaginable.

For more than 40 years, few horrendous-type death threats have hung over civilization more ominously than nuclear war. And yet few threats have resisted solution as persistently. Advances in medicine have wiped out many diseases and prolonged human life. Technologies for predicting hurricanes, tornados, floods, volcanic eruptions, and earthquakes can now prevent the catastrophic losses that once accompanied these natural disasters. Even in social development we have made considerable progress in stigmatizing and reducing the incidence of slavery, child labor, torture, and capital punishment. But when it comes to prevention of horrendous-type death from war—particularly a nuclear war that could wipe out most of civilization in a matter of hours—we have made remarkably little progress.

Optimists argue that nuclear weapons have reduced the intensity and frequency of conventional warfare and that arms control will gradually eliminate whatever risks of nuclear war remain. The first part of their argument is dubious. Roughly 10 million combatants and 12 million civilians have died during the 20th Century's first 44 years with nuclear weapons (Sivard, 1987). In 1983 some 40 major and minor armed conflicts were raging around the planet, involving nearly one-third of the world's nations (Center for Defense Information, 1983). Perhaps nuclear weapons have prevented some conventional wars that otherwise might have occurred—we can never know—but the cost has been a serious risk of nuclear war. According to the *Canadian Army Journal*, of the 1,587 arms races between 600 B.C. and 1960, all but ten ended in war (Lens, 1983). Thomas Powers has written in the *Atlantic* that "many Russians cite Chekhov's famous principle of dramaturgy: If there is a gun on the wall in the first act, it will fire in the third" (Powers, 1984).

The second part of the optimists' argument, that arms control will gradually reduce the risks of nuclear war, is equally questionable. The actual results of arms control have been disappointing. True, both superpowers have agreed to put their weapons tests underground and limit the yield on these tests, to forego extensive anti-ballistic missile systems, to keep nuclear weapons out of outer space and off the ocean floor, to set ceilings on their offensive launchers, and to limit the spread of nuclear weapons to other nations (Barton & Weiler, 1976). But never have these agreements amounted to anything more than minor constraints. Despite the end of the Cold War, both the Soviet Union and the United States have continued to modernize their arsenals, building ever faster, ever more accurate, and ever deadlier nuclear weapons, with no end in sight.

In the years ahead, arms control could play a more constructive role. In 1987, President Ronald Reagan and Soviet General Secretary Mikhail Gorbachev signed an agreement scrapping about 1,500 intermediate-ranged missiles in Europe—the first agreement ever actually to dismantle nuclear weapons. Other more ambitious treaties are certainly possible. A complete ban on the testing of nuclear warheads and missiles would halt much of the qualitative arms race, in which each superpower has sought to obtain a technological edge over the other. And a cutoff on the production of fissionable uranium and plutonium, coupled with deep cuts in strategic arsenals, would cap and reverse the quantitative arms race.

Yet even if arms control were to make unprecedented headway in maximizing lifegenic factors on the planet, it would only reduce the risks of nuclear war, but not eliminate them. As Jonathan Schell has written, "[A]rms control can theoretically eliminate redundancy, but it must never touch the essential capacity for 'assuring' the annihilation of the other side. In other words, it can get rid of the overkill but not the kill . . . " (Schell, 1984, p. 71). So long as nuclear weapons exist, nuclear war will remain possible through any number of conduits: a political dispute like the Cuban missile crisis that leads to reckless nuclear brinksmanship; an escalating conventional war that tempts one side to fire nuclear weapons in desperation; computer errors leading to accidental launch; mutiny by a nuclear submarine crew; or sheer madness by any nuclear nation's leadership.

Despite its dismal track record and limited long-term promise, arms control has remained the central pursuit of the American peace movement. Sometimes the peace movement has sought narrow treaties such as the test ban in the late 1950s or the Strategic Arms Limitation Talk (SALT) treaties in the early 1970s. Sometimes it has sought to halt specific weapons systems such as the B-1 bomber or MX missile. Sometimes it has sought a broader agreement such as nuclear freeze.

Remarkably, however, the totality of the peace movement's promotion of lifegenic factors has directed almost all of its efforts at restructuring or eliminating weapons hardware—precisely the area of policy over which Americans have the least political influence. While Americans can often take initiatives—as individuals, corporations, organizations, or local governments—that have profound effects on a wide variety of domestic and foreign policies, weapons policy lies almost exclusively in the hands of national leadership, primarily the president's. For example, we can encourage the president to enter arms control talks but we can do very little to shape his negotiating positions. Our founding fathers deliberately centralized national power over weapons, and yet it's precisely that centralization that makes grass roots influence so difficult, for at least two reasons.

First, national decision-makers with responsibility for foreign and military policy are generally inaccessible to the American public. Despite the fact that Americans pride themselves on their democracy, U.S. foreign policy is largely set by the president and the National Security Council, a small group of appointed officials. Congress plays a primarily negative role, denying budget authorizations or outlawing certain international transactions. The positive vision of foreign policy is usually articulated by the president. Popular democratic controls over foreign policy are expressed in votes for national leaders, but since these votes are based on domestic as well as foreign policy positions and are expressed at most biennially, the input of the public into foreign policy is irregular and attenuated. The judicial branch could play a role, but generally has dismissed foreign-policy lawsuits as raising "political questions" that it is incompetent to answer, no matter how glaring the violations of actual law. The only other popular control left is the press, which sometimes plays an independent role, but is often reluctant to challenge official policies for fear of alienating official sources.

The result is a runaway foreign-policy establishment, geared toward continuous military mobilization and giving only minimal attention to public opinion or the long-term national interest in preventing nuclear war. Opinion polls indicate that most Americans are generally satisfied with presidential conduct in foreign affairs, but profoundly disenchanted on a growing number of specific security issues. Although between 70% and 80% of the American public in the early 1980s favored a nuclear weapons freeze, the Reagan administration consistently refused to put a freeze proposal on the negotiating table (Yankelovich & Doble, 1984). Despite opposition by two-thirds of the American public to a military overthrow of the Nicaraguan government, the Reagan administration continued pressuring Congress to support the contra rebels (Roberts, 1985).

Compounding the inaccessibility of national decision-makers is a second obstacle for citizen influence over arms policy, office secrecy. Much of U.S. nuclear policy, including weapons characteristics and strategic doctrines governing the weapons' use, is classified. The U.S. Navy, for example, refuses "to confirm or deny" the presence of nuclear weapons on its ships. Because Soviet intelligence no doubt knows a great deal about the status of the ships it tracks, this policy results in the American people knowing less about U.S. weapons policy than the Soviet military does (van Ness, 1988).

Taken together, the centralization of weapons policies, the inaccessibility of leaders overseeing them, and the cult of secrecy protecting them from public scrutiny all undermine effective public pressure for arms control. Is it really surprising, then, that the peace movement has had so few successes in reversing the risks of horrendous-type death from nuclear war? The peace movement has concentrated its efforts on changing precisely those national policies most insulated from popular opinion. A strategy more capable of eliminating the threat of nuclear war is one that would empower Americans to play a more direct, participatory role in promoting peace, both as individuals and through their cities.

DEMOCRACY: A NEW PEACE STRATEGY

Arms control focuses on weapons, not conflict. Yet weapons do not pull their own triggers, leaders do. And unless we figure out a strategy for preventing leaders from pulling nuclear triggers, all arms control will be for naught. An alternative strategy for preventing nuclear war is to focus not on arms control but leader control—political structures that can restrain leaders from launching wars.

History suggests that one reliable means to control the bellicose inclinations of national leaders is participatory democracy. Several empirical studies of conflicts between nations over the past two centuries have revealed that, while democracies and nondemocracies have been equally likely to get involved in wars with nondemocracies, wars *between* democracies have been exceedingly rare (Singer & Small, 1976; Wallersteen, 1973; Rummel, 1980). One strains to find two relatively well-developed democracies in modern times which have even come close to war with one another. Apparently nations in which a small number of leaders can launch a war without popular support have a greater propensity to fight wars than others.

Intuitively, most Americans suspect that democracy fosters peace. They were relieved when recent democratic revolutions ousted the military dictators of Argentina, Brazil, the Philippines, and South Korea. And they have been even more enthusiastic about Gorbachev's *glasnost* campaign in the Soviet Union and the struggles for democracy by students in China. These intuitions are not groundless, for there are at least four important connections between democracy and peace.

First, a nation going to war needs to imbue the public with images of a brutal enemy. Since war necessarily involves heinous acts of killing and maiming—especially, in modern warfare, of civilians—soldiers are less willing to commit such acts and the public less willing to support them if the enemy is not seen as deserving such treatment. Where participatory forces operate, the citizens of a country can speak and meet freely with citizens of potential adversary nations. Traveling members of a democracy often discover that the causes of their anxiety are not nearly as nefarious as government and private-interest propaganda maintains. This suggests why democracies rarely fight one another. "Perhaps," writes Yale political scientist Bruce Russet, "our elites cannot persuade us to fight other peoples who we imagine, like us, are self-determining, autonomous people—people who in some substantial way control their own political fate" (Russett, 1982, pp. 189–90).

Second, people participating in their government also can form with the supposed enemy valuable relationships, whose beneficiaries then pressure leaders to maintain the peace. Even when official relations become strained, businesspeople want to protect their trade contracts, scientists and academicians want to pursue their research across national borders, and cultural colleagues (writers, artists, and musicians) want to continue communicating with and seeing each other. For example, after President Carter imposed an embargo on grain sales to the Soviet Union in 1979, the many Midwestern farmers and their suppliers who had benefited from earlier grain sales to Soviets became vocal advocates of restoring economic relations. By 1983, according to William Bundy, then editor of *Foreign Affairs*, President Reagan "responded to heavy domestic political pressures from the U.S. farm belt" when he scrapped the embargo and signed a new 5-year contract that prohibited interruptions for political reasons (Bundy, 1983, p. 503). The web of relationships made possible by U.S. pluralism has also helped to reduce American hostility toward the Chinese. Widely regarded in the late 1960s as a "yellow menace"—the menace against which the United States considered building a "light" ABM system in 1969—China has since become an American ally because of what Arthur W. Hummel, Jr., the U.S. Ambassador to China in the early 1980s, has called "an amazing web" of relationships: "The multiplicity of relationships which we have—perhaps the majority of them having nothing to do with the U.S. government—is a genuine stabilizing force and a force which through the decades will produce much better understanding" ("Multiplicity of Relationships with Chinese," 1985, p. 6). Even after Chinese troops killed thousands of pro-democracy protesters near Tiananmen Square in June 1989, these relationships allowed Americans to express their anger through dialogue, protest, and divestment, rather than through a renewed nuclear arms race.

A third way democracy promotes peace is by permitting citizens to take peacemaking initiatives which constructively supplement and improve governmental relations. Formal negotiating demands that leaders protect national interests and make worst-case assumptions about an adversary's intentions, but informal negotiating, according to Joseph V. Montville, a Foreign Service officer in the State Department, and William D. Davidson, a psychiatrist specializing in foreign affairs, is "always open-minded, often altruistic, and . . . strategically optimistic, based on the best-case analysis. Its underlying assumption is that actual or potential conflict can be resolved or eased by appealing to common human capabilities to respond to goodwill and reasonableness" (Montville & Davidson, 1981–1982, p. 155). Thus during the late 1950s the democratic nature of the United States enabled *Saturday Review* editor Norman Cousins to launch the annual Dartmouth Conferences, high-level, off-the-record Soviet-American discussions that played an important role in helping the superpowers reach formal agreements banning above-ground nuclear tests, installing the original "hot line," allowing direct commercial air service between the United States and the Soviet Union, and expanding trade (Warner & Shuman, 1987).

A fourth explanation of how democracy promotes peace is that war is often more fatal or costly to ordinary people than it is to the leaders who promote and plan it. Even when the public gives preliminary consent to such adventures, the consent rarely lasts long, and in a democracy, the withdrawal of popular consent will ultimately stop the international adventure. As the Vietnam War demonstrated, public support for military involvement abroad crumbles as young friends and neighbors return dead or injured, as news reports graphically depict atrocities on the front lines, and as international opinion leaders condemn the supposedly just cause. In a participatory culture, negative news easily spreads to the public and the public can then more readily pressure their leaders to avoid or halt the war. Thus political pressures against the Vietnam War were able to build more rapidly than the analogous domestic pressures in the Soviet Union against that country's misadventures in Afghanistan.

Together, these explanations suggest how public participation can restrain leaders' foreign interventions by rendering them accountable to real facts about "the enemy," the benefits of peacetime relationships, the possibilities for better relationships, and the human costs of warfare. Public participation can act as a check against abuse, overzealousness, and rash exercises of power by individuals and small groups in government. A new challenge for the peace movement, therefore, is to promote leader control in hot spots throughout the world.

Promoting Leader Control Abroad

The United States now spends almost $300 billion per year to deflect military threats from adversaries abroad, but virtually nothing on creating political structures within its adversaries that might restrain their ability to launch wars. Policymakers typically assume that adversaries are politically unchangeable. As recently as 5 years ago, for example, neoconservative Irving Kristol wrote about the Soviet Union: "'Liberalization' remains a fantasy. . . . [t]he party still rules supreme, its Leninist orthodoxy intact; the Soviet people remain sullen, intimidated and coerced into passivity" (Kristol, 1985, p. 26).

But before describing what our leader control policies toward other countries might look like, it is worth stressing what leader control should not be: a cover for U.S. military intervention. The imposition of participatory democracy through violent or provocative means should be unequivocally rejected for several reasons. First, a democracy imposed from the outside rarely remains democratic. In the name of democracy, the United States overthrew the leaders of Guatemala (1954), Iran (1954), and Chile (1970–1973), only to put in their place repressive dictators that brutalized their people for decades, giving both the United States and democracy a bad name (Kwitney, 1984). Second, every time the United States uses violence internationally to forward its goals, no matter how worthy the goals, it gives legitimacy to other nations' acts of violence. This is why the United Nations overwhelmingly condemned the U.S. invasion of Grenada, widely regarded here as a successful effort to impose democracy through violence. As Robert C. Johansen of Notre Dame University has written, "[T]he many countries that condemned the U.S. invasion, including most of America's allies, did so not out of baseless hostility but in deference to the Charter principle prohibiting the aggressive use of force and out of concern that the U.S. action would establish a dangerous precedent for conflict resolution" (Johansen, 1986, p. 609).

As Americans promote leader control abroad, they should seek to empower individuals abroad to reform their own systems according to *their own* values and visions—to exercise more fully for themselves the democracy which Americans exercise, or at least seek to exercise, at home. And Americans should be willing to accept the results of participatory processes even when they seem disappointing by American standards. In the past, such tolerance would have led Americans in 1984 to accept the election of the Sandinistas in Nicaragua instead of funding a covert war that ultimately cost the Nicaraquan people 26,000 lives and many billions of dollars of property damage. In the future, Americans should be prepared to accept that an increasingly empowered Soviet or Chinese people may want greater freedoms of speech and assembly, but still may prefer large-scale government management of their economies.

To suggest what leader control policies might look like, let's briefly look at one of the hardest and most important examples—the Soviet Union. Aaron Wildavsky, a professor of political science at the University of California at Berkeley, has urged that Americans seek to pluralize the Soviet Union: "[T]he larger the number of independent centers of power with the USSR, the more the Soviets will be constrained to secure domestic consent for their foreign policy" (Wildavsky, 1983, p. 128). What could the United States do to help democratize the Soviet system in a nonviolent and nonprovocative way?

The few American efforts that have been undertaken to reform the Soviet Union in the past decades have been mainly provocative and counterproductive. For years, many U.S. policymakers like Richard Pipes have argued that a vigorous arms race would stimulate political change in the Soviet Union by placing intolerable economic burdens on the Soviet people and thus sparking open revolt. Greater economic burdens have indeed fallen upon the Soviet people, but the result, comparable to the consequences of the United States bombing North Vietnam or the

Nazi blitz of London, has been exactly opposite—greater resentment toward the United States. Congress tried a different provocative tactic when it passed the Jackson-Vanik Amendment to the Trade Act of 1974, withholding most-favored-nation status until the Soviet Union loosened emigration policies. Again the provocation backfired, motivating the Soviet Union to cut off emigration and blocking off many channels of constructive communication (Cullen, 1986–1987). The United States has long been beaming Radio Liberty and Voice of America into the Soviet Union both to spread higher-quality information and to foment dissent, yet because these transmissions have been so clearly designed as propaganda highly antagonistic to the Soviet government they did little to spawn revolt (Nichols, 1984). Surveys suggest that fewer than one in ten Soviets even tuned into Radio Liberty once or more a month and that most of those listening were tuning into entertainment programs.

An alternative security agenda that aims to reform the Soviet Union must be grounded in two tactics that are wholly nonprovocative: persuasion and cooperation. Obviously these cannot effect radical changes overnight, but, like the competing tactics of the arms builders or arms controllers, these tactics are part of a long-term process. Unlike arms building or arms control, however, persuasion and cooperation have already begun working, and there are real prospects of significant success in the future.

Even before *glasnost*, Soviet leaders were not completely insulated from their people. Politburo members always have needed some popular support both to ensure that their economic and social policies were carried out smoothly and to fend off rivals who might otherwise capitalize on popular discontent. Past shifts in Soviet public opinion clearly have had an impact on policy. Gorbachev's decision to withdraw from Afghanistan, for example, was at least partially a reflection of growing Soviet public frustration with the dead and wounded there. Even hardline U.S. arms builders believe that the Soviet people have considerable political power: Why would they support spending most of the U.S. Information Agency's $820 million annual budget on Radio Liberty, Radio Free Europe, and Voice of America if the listeners were powerless (Hughes, 1988)? And why were the Soviets reportedly spending $1 billion per year to jam these broadcasts (until jamming ceased in late 1988) (Schmemann, 1988)?

In the face of recent political reforms in the Soviet Union, old arguments about the powerlessness of the Soviet people have become untenable. In mid-1988, the Central Committee voted to limit the term of most party and government officials to 10 years, to expand the power of popularly elected legislatures, and to assure competitive candidates and secret ballots for each seat. The debates leading up to the March 1989 election for the Congress of People's Deputies proved to be the most open and unrestrained in the nation's history, and the election itself wound up bringing dozens of new reformers like Andrei Sakharov into Soviet politics, returning popular radicals like Moscow's Boris Yeltsin to power, and putting numerous conservative party bosses out to pasture. From this Congress emerged a new Supreme Soviet, which, if Foreign Minister Eduard Shevardnadze has his way, will soon be empowered to debate the nation's foreign and military commitments—the Soviet equivalent of the War Powers Act (Isaacson, 1989).

As we use the tools of persuasion and cooperation to assist this process of democratization, we should avoid the temptation of focusing solely on dissidents, refuseniks, or political prisoners. American initiatives in the past few years have suggested that some of the most promising reformers are progressive yet loyal members of Soviet society—people such as the poet Yevgeni Yevtushenko, who has become an advocate of greater literary freedom, and Alexei Yablokov, an environmentalist who is a member of the Supreme Soviet and chairman of Greenpeace-USSR. Diverse reformers can be found—and helped—at all levels of Soviet society. Lost in the debate over "linking" various Soviet-American transactions to reformed Soviet human-rights behavior is the fact that many of these transactions themselves exert a democratizing influence. Every one of the more than 100,000 Americans who visit the Soviet Union each year meets Soviet citizens formally and informally and has some kind of impact. Whether or not these Americans realize it, they are walking, talking banned books, expressing facts and attitudes at odds with the prevailing party line. Because Soviet citizens are more likely to trust American friends than faceless Radio Liberty announcers, one wonders if the hundreds of millions annually spent on these radio broadcasts might have been better invested in citizen exchange programs.

Improved citizen exchanges with the Soviet Union can enhance all of the mechanisms for nonprovocative leader control. In the early 1980s, the goodwill of American visitors often stood in sharp contrast to the Nazi-like depictions of Americans in *Pravda* and reduced the ability of Soviet leaders to characterize Americans as barbaric monsters worth going to war against. As more Soviets have been swept into relationships with Americans—whether economic, scientific, cultural, or personal—they have put pressure on Communist party leaders, in their own small ways, for improved ties with the United States. According to the *Christian Science Monitor*, some exchange experts believe "that 30 years of travel to the United States by the Soviet political, cultural, and scientific elite have fueled demand for Gorbachev's reforms" (Feldman, 1988, p. 5). When Americans meet high-level Soviets, new possibilities for political cooperation are uncovered. Such encounters in the mid-1980s seemed to play a prominent role in encouraging the Soviets to halt nuclear testing unilaterally for 18 months, to release prominent dissidents, and to allow on-site inspection of their nuclear test site by the Natural Resources Defense Council, a U.S. environmental group. American "citizen diplomats" also may have nudged the government toward rejecting nuclear warfighting strategies (Levin, 1986). For example, Dr. Bernard Lown, cofounder of the International Physicians for the Prevention of Nuclear War, managed to convince Soviet officials in 1982 to broadcast during prime time a frank, uncut discussion among Soviet and American doctors about the medical consequences of nuclear war and the uselessness of the Soviet government's civil defense program (Warner & Shuman, 1987). Today, citizen diplomats are reaching the highest levels of the Politburo. According to *New York Times* correspondent Philip Taubman, "Mr. Gorbachev's education about the United States has been rounded by his frequent meetings with delegations of visiting Americans" (Taubman, 1988).

Greater Soviet-American trade is another promising area for Americans eager to exert nonprovocative leader control. Samuel Pisar, an international lawyer specializing in East-West trade, has written: "The new Soviet leaders know that the choice before them is fateful: either to face up to the challenges of an advanced economy, with the free movement of ideas, people, and goods that this presupposes, or to isolate themselves in an armed fortress condemned to obsolescence" (Pisar, 1985, p. 6). The old guard may still try to keep foreign "ideas, people, and goods" away from the general Soviet populace, but the hundreds of thousands of foreigners who enter the country for business relations will inevitably develop ties with millions of Soviet citizens. As Soviets encounter more American products, they begin to see the virtues of other economic systems, and more comfortably support both internal economic reforms and greater trade with the West. Franz Schurmann, a professor of sociology and history at the University of California at Berkeley, suggests that the Soviets have located the first McDonald's near Red Square to expose their people to the efficiency of American fast food (Schurmann, 1987). A concerted effort by the United States to open up trade with the Soviet Union can help diversify and decentralize the Soviet economy, all of which will help the Soviet people exert greater control over their leaders. After PepsiCo recently purchased 17 submarines, a cruiser, a frigate, and a destroyer for scrap metal from the Soviets, Donald Kendall, the company's president, chided National Security Advisor Brent Scowcroft, "We're disarming the Soviet Union faster than you are" (Lewis, 1989, p. A35).

New Jersey Senator Bill Bradley, among others, has taken a more jaundiced view toward expanding Soviet-American trade and has argued against our providing cheap credit to Soviet Union because "reform means making tough choices—butter not weapons, efficiency not useless output, consumption not forced saving. . . . Cheap credits play into the hands of perestroika's opponents by deferring the day of reckoning" (Bradley, 1989, p. A19). Bradley's argument, however, misses the mark in two ways. Gorbachev has already begun making tough choices—and making the right choices. At this point, harder economic times for the Soviet Union could precipitate a political crisis and end the Gorbachev reform era. Moreover, if credits help accelerate the flow of Western goods, people, and ideas into the Soviet Union, the United States will be assisting the very movements of *glasnost* and democratization that already are promoting greater leader control there.

In the early 1980s, a high-level advisor to President Reagan prepared a memo recommending U.S. initiatives in Eastern Europe and the Soviet Union "aimed at subtly strengthening free market forces, private ownership of land, worker ownership and self-management of industry, decentralized economic (and ultimately political) decision-making . . . and ultimate integration of the [East Bloc economies] into the relatively free market economies of the OECD" (personal communication). The memo urged technical assistance for helping East Bloc countries privatize national industries, give workers more control of their factories, develop profit-sharing plans, establish small family-sized farms, set up urban and rural credit unions, and establish genuine cooperatives for farmers, consumers, producers, and renters. The attraction of these policies was that they would have been simultaneously nonthreatening to the recipient governments, consistent with current directions of East Bloc reform, and capable of being undertaken by U.S. churches, civic organizations, and local governments. But the Reagan administration was so consumed with arms building that it never translated these proposals into policy.

Another promising leverage point for Americans is computerization. As the *Economist* recently argued, information technologies "have shown themselves time and again to be destructive of centralized control, in private companies or dictators' states. A Russia stuffed with Xerox machines, personal computers, and electronic telephone switches humming with too many conversations to be monitored is more the West's kind of Russia" ("Cuddly Russia?," 1987). In the early 1980s a number of Americans helped interest top Soviet officials in personal computers and international computer networks, and by late 1988 the Soviet Union agreed to allow Americans to mail computers, diskettes, and videotape recorders to Soviet friends. IDG Communications began a joint venture in April 1988 to print and distribute a Russian edition of *PC World* magazine to 50,000 paid Soviet subscribers. The result of this dispersion of personal computers, laser printers, and desktop publishing has been the rapid proliferation of *samizdat* (unofficial press) on controversial issues of foreign policy, economic reform, and human rights; Sergei Grigoryants' magazine *Glasnost* is a prime example. Underground publications also have been assisted by the emergence of public photocopy shops established by Western companies. In the years ahead, as computers multiply and get smaller, as diskettes move in and out of the country the way audiotapes and videotapes do now, and as computer networks begin connecting to satellites instead of telephones, a whole generation of young Soviet "hackers" will gain access to information at home and abroad that their parents never dreamed possible. A strong case can be made for the United States to subsidize, wherever possible, exports of shortwave radios, video recorders, telephones and telephone directories, and even television shows—every conceivable technology that erodes the government's monopoly on information and empowers individuals to hold Soviet leaders accountable to their own rhetoric for peace.

Outside the Soviet Union, the United States already has begun employing some of these leader control tactics. Between 1985 and 1988, for example, the U.S. Congress and the National Endowment for Democracy (NED) provided more than $5 million in cash assistance to Solidarity and other underground groups to bring into Poland printing presses, ink, publications, radio equipment, microfiches and microfiche readers, and videocassettes and videocassette players (Pear, 1988). In Chile, NED gave $1 million to help fund parties opposing General Pinochet and to assist voters in getting free photographs for their registration cards prior to the October 1988 election (Christian, 1988). In Peru and Argentina, the United States has successfully discouraged coups by letting would-be military-junta leaders clearly know that U.S. economic and political support would be cut off if their democratically elected leaders were toppled (Cohen, 1989). And in countries as diverse as Chile, Haiti, Pakistan, Panama, and the Philippines, private groups like the National Democratic Institute for International Affairs (an affiliate of the Democratic Party) and the Center for Democracy have helped monitor elections for fraud or irregularities (Pear, 1989).

There are enormous opportunities for leader-control policies in the years ahead. In Eastern Europe, Americans have expanding opportunities for making loans, providing IMF debt relief, entering joint ventures, and funding exchanges. In Central America the United States could supply advanced communications technologies to oppressed minorities, whether strafe-bombed villagers in El Salvador or harassed Miskito Indians in Nicaragua. In South Africa, Americans might form stronger personal relationships with white Afrikaaners to sway them toward compromise, while equipping the black majority with technical, financial, and educational assistance that could reduce their vulnerability to apartheid's leaders in Pretoria. Renewed American economic contacts with Havana could expose the Cuban people to the virtues of the market economies that surround them. Throughout the Third World, Americans can help developing political cultures adopt constitutions that protect free speech, promote the separation of church and state, check and balance power, and ensure fair judicial review. And now that the Ayatollah Khomeini is gone, relationships with true Iranian moderates might be developed, not for illegal arms transfers, but for joint projects in agriculture, medicine, science, and law.

None of this will be easy, but these projects are certainly more promising routes to change than tinkering with levels of weapons hardware.

Leader Control at Home

If a U.S. policy on behalf of the control of leaders abroad is to survive criticisms of "cultural imperialism," Americans must be willing to apply the same policy in their own homeland. Just as democracies have more mechanisms, and more effective mechanisms, for constraining foreign policy adventures than nondemocracies, higher levels of participation within democracies can increase restraints on *their* adventures. Consequently an important goal for Americans promoting leader control is to strengthen democracy at home.

One way Americans can help democratize U.S. foreign policy is through more people-to-people exchanges. These leave the U.S. government less able to perpetuate the "evil empire" rhetoric that fueled both the Cold War and the arms race. Critics of Soviet–American exchange programs, such as Milan Svec, a senior associate at the Carnegie Endowment for International Peace, claim that "American perceptions about the U.S.S.R. are basically correct" (Svec, 1986, p. 8). Nothing could be further from the truth. A recent *New York Times* survey showed that 44% of Americans did not know that the Soviet Union fought against Nazi Germany in World War II (Shipler, 1985). The information gap is so wide that Americans who do no more than travel to the Soviet Union, take some notes, snap some photographs, speak with some Soviets on the streets, and tell what they have learned to their friends are serving a valuable function for peace by helping to deny U.S. leaders the power to misrepresent the Soviet people or exaggerate the Soviet threat.

Over the years, convinced that federal officials have superior knowledge and that secrecy is a necessary evil to combat adversaries abroad, Americans have become accustomed to unchecked executive power. Whatever the validity of these rationales in the past, recent history has rendered them obsolete.

International affairs have become too complicated for anyone to claim exclusive expertise. Billions of significant transactions now take place between the United States and other nations every day in such areas as international communication, tourism, trade, investment, cultural exchange, and political cooperation ("Risky Movements in the Money Markets," 1987). Increasingly, foreign policy has come to mean setting broad guidelines for the ways in which goods, capital, people, and ideas may cross borders while leaving the details to organizations, multinational corporations, and individuals. If the U.S. government attempted to control all of these transactions, it would scare off international trade and stifle the domestic economy, as the East Bloc discovered in its self-destructive pursuit of autarky.

The need for governmental secrecy also seems less important in an era of expanding mass communications. With agile reporters, broad networks of people interconnected through telephone, radio, and computer networks, and with high resolution satellites coming increasingly under private control, very little information can long remain under national lock-and-key—even information about relatively closed societies like the Soviet Union. Some Americans visiting the Soviet

Union with technical expertise have been able to tell Soviet experts facts they didn't know about *their own* country's military capabilities, which enabled the Soviets to do their jobs better, increasing both Soviet and American national security. Against this background, secrecy is increasingly used by decision-makers not to foil adversaries abroad, but to thwart critics at home.

The closed nature of the U.S. foreign-policymaking apparatus does not seem to have served national security interests well. In a climate of more open dissemination and evaluation of information some of the most serious foreign-policy blunders in modern history could have been avoided. If the public had known the strength of the Viet Cong, which the Pentagon consistently underestimated to present a more sanguine evaluation of the U.S. war effort, the Vietnam conflict might have been cut short by several years (Dworkin, 1987). President Carter's secret effort to bring the Shah of Iran into the United States for medical treatment triggered the takeover of the American Embassy in Tehran, helping to bring down Carter's own presidency. The Iran-Contra scandal involved largely unchecked executive authority in trading arms for hostages and funneling profits through Swiss banks to the *contras* in Nicaragua to wage their covert war against the government there. Most fundamentally, secrecy has enabled the Pentagon to persistently exaggerate Soviet military strength, hornswoggling the American people into excessive military spending. In all of these cases the public was excluded not out of a principled concern for the public interest, but because successive administrations concluded that their policies could not have withstood correctly and fully informed public scrutiny. To view these events simply as misjudgments within each administration is to miss the larger point. Scandals and bad judgment are inevitable without vigorous public scrutiny, and the more they are covered up, the worse they become and the longer incompetent government officials continue to compound their concealed mistakes.

We now must control our own propensities for conflict by increasing public participation in the foreign-policymaking apparatus. Abolishing the military operations unit of the National Security Council, as the Reagan administration did following the "Iranamok" scandal, was a useful step. Three areas of further improvement should be considered.

First, congressional oversight of the President's foreign policy powers, particularly with regard to military operations, needs to be enhanced. The founding fathers placed war powers in the hands of the Congress to prevent precisely the kinds of indiscreet military adventures and entanglements which successive presidents have launched since World War II. Alexander Hamilton, a stalwart advocate of a strong executive, said, "The history of human conduct does not warrant . . . [committing] interests of so delicate and momentous a kind as those which concern [a nation's] intercourse with the rest of the world, to the sole disposal of . . . a president of the United States" (Lewis, 1988, p. A14). The War Powers Act needs to be revised so that it not only demands Presidential consultation with Congress before using force, but also prohibits the President from using force unless a true national emergency exists. Laws that govern covert intelligence operations should be moved beyond weak, after-the-fact reporting provisions to stringent limitations on presidential discretion (Halperin, 1987). Narrow and explicit criteria should be written into these laws to encourage judicial review and allow citizen litigation to require compliance.

The most serious yet least discussed presidential usurpation of war powers relates to the command and control structure overseeing nuclear weapons. That the

President can unilaterally launch a nuclear first strike, committing the United States to a war certainly killing more Americans than all previous wars combined, underscores how seriously the war-powers provision of the Constitution has been eroded. Worse still, to the extent that U.S. ICBMs have been placed in a launch-on-warning status, *all* human decision-makers have been excluded from the critical question of when and under what circumstances the fateful decision to authorize a nuclear retaliation should be made. Jeremy Stone, executive director of the Federation of American Scientists, has suggested that a nuclear planning committee of Congress be established to work closely with the President's national security advisors and to exercise veto power over the first use of nuclear weapons (Stone, 1984). Yale political scientist Robert Dahl proposes that nuclear decision-making be overseen by a council of enlightened citizens exerting guidance and control (Dahl, 1985). Congress should begin to explore these and related proposals.

Democratic control of American leaders could be further strengthened by greater public openness about our strategic doctrines, weapons deployments, and intelligence activities abroad. This might be accomplished by narrowing the national security exceptions to the Freedom of Information Act (FOIA). Openness could also be enhanced by engaging as well as informing the general public. For example, the National Environmental Policy Act requires environmental impact statements and public review for every major federal action, a process which has often led to less expensive and more environmentally sound decisions. An analogous process requiring national-security impact statements with public review for every major action in foreign or military policy, could lead to new possibilities of preventing bloodshed and reducing money costs. Simply getting the government to consider more diverse information could break the all-too-established pattern of U.S. meddling in other countries' affairs—often on behalf of the wrong side.

Third, a growing number of Americans are practicing some type of diplomacy, as the once-prohibitive costs of international transportation and communication continue to plummet (Shuman, 1987). As already noted, tens of thousands of private American citizens are working with Soviets on joint cultural, scientific, and economic projects and are communicating regularly through telex messages, faxes, slow-scan video machines, satellite "space bridges," and computer networks. As citizens find ever more powerful ways to participate in foreign affairs, national politicians should welcome and support them. Most of these citizen initiatives are based on constitutionally protected freedoms of speech, assembly, and travel. Citizen diplomacy should be viewed as an inevitable and desirable step in the maturation of democracy.

ACTING LOCALLY: A NEW WAVE IN GLOBAL ORGANIZING

The Need for Institutionalization

Besides addressing the roots of conflict rather than the symptoms, leader control has a critically important advantage over arms control—it fosters policies in which every American can participate. No longer must the peace movement relegate itself to petitioning the least accessible decisionmakers to make improbable changes in our weapons policies. Instead, Americans can promote democracy directly. They can establish contacts with the Soviets and other adversaries and reduce the probability of war by breaking dangerous stereotypes, lobbying bellicose elites, establishing valuable relationships, and informing people of the costs of war. These contacts also have the salutary effect of persuading our own leaders to move away from violent confrontation and toward peaceful cooperation. At the same time, Americans can pressure Congress to democratize our own foreign policy structures—a task more concrete and meaningful than begging the President to conclude desired arms control treaties.

Yet no matter how much citizens and nongovernmental organizations (NGOs) try to promote leader control, they will be impeded by two profound barriers. Unlike nation-states, which have the vast resources available from taxation, most citizen diplomats and NGOs operate on financial shoestrings. Citizen diplomats and NGOs also lack the "color of authority" of national diplomats and therefore are much less likely than national officials to get meetings with, let alone influence, officials abroad. The challenge for Americans trying to promote nonprovocative leader control is how to get more resources and clout outside the traditional national conduits of power. One of the most promising answers, they have found, lies in their own backyards.

In recent years, millions of Americans eager to influence international affairs have turned to their nearly half-million local elected officials, who, unlike inaccessible national officials, are rarely more than a telephone call or public meeting away. They have discovered that, unlike NGOs, local governments can confer on their foreign affairs activism both money and legitimacy. As financially pinched as America's cities are, were they persuaded to allocate one percent of their budgets to promote world peace, they could expand the entire U.S. peace movement by more than ten-fold (Forum Institute, 1985). As for legitimacy, mayors may lack the same clout as national ambassadors, but they often receive red-carpet treatment, far better than most citizens or NGOs. That Mayor Feinstein and seven other mayors convinced the Soviet Union in early 1986 to allow 36 people to emigrate after so many analogous private initiatives failed can be attributed, in part, to the legitimacy of their offices (Rosenheim, 1985).

Were the peace movement to institutionalize itself in local governments throughout the country, it could escape the inaccessibility and secrecy of national leaders and still have access to substantial resources and legitimacy. A brief analogy is illustrative.

In the late 1960s and early 1970s, as the American public grew restive over the risks of nuclear energy, a large protest movement emerged to shut down nuclear power plants (Patterson, 1976; Faulkner, 1977; Berger, 1976). Dismissing these concerns as largely irrational, the federal government responded by pumping tens of billions of additional dollars into further expansion of U.S. reactors (Lovins & Lovins, 1980). Within a few years, however, nuclear power expansion came grinding to a halt. Despite intense promotion by the U.S. government, concerned Americans essentially vetoed the nuclear option. While protest undoubtedly played a role, the public really succeeded by implementing an alternative policy that rendered nuclear power irrelevant—energy efficiency. Between 1979 and 1986, the United States obtained more than seven times as much new energy from improved efficiency as from *all* net expansions of its energy supply (Lovins & Lovins, 1989). Throughout the country, regional and local energy conservation programs covered for federal neglect. States such as California and Oregon established special energy commissions and revamped their public utility commissions. Many communities prepared detailed blueprints for a nonnuclear energy future, including: Geneva County, Alabama; Humboldt County, California; Carbondale, Illinois; Franklin County, Massachusetts; Fulton, Missouri; Salem, Oregon; Philadelphia, Pennsylvania; and Madison, Wisconsin (Lovins & Lovins, 1982).

Today, the so-called peace movement is roughly where the antinuclear-power movement was two decades ago—impoverished and on the fringes of power. Whether the peace movement ultimately succeeds will depend on how well it learns the lesson of the antinuclear-power movement and begins cloning itself within the institutions of state and local government. Once this happens, the peace movement will become, as the environmental movement did, a multibillion-dollar-a-year enterprise providing hundreds of thousands of jobs—an enterprise that no national politician could reverse by fiat.

Fortunately, there are encouraging early signs of institutionalization. More than 1,000 local governments have begun to enter international affairs, and their numbers are growing daily.

Sprouting Municipal Foreign Policies

Local governments have been surprisingly receptive to citizen requests for their involvement in foreign policies. In the early 1980s, for example, grass-roots pressure for the nuclear freeze motivated nearly 700 local officials to join two organizations committed to reversing the arms race: Local Elected Officials of America (LEO-USA) and Local Elected Officials for Social Responsibility (LEO/SR).

During the December 1985 convention of the National League of Cities, Mayor Tom Bradley of Los Angeles discerned sufficient interest in municipal foreign policies to make them the centerpiece of his keynote address: "I submit to you that cities have the right—indeed, even the obligation—to be a part of the great national debate in these weighty issues. From foreign trade policies to opposing South African apartheid, from immigration policies to the proliferation of nuclear weapons, the right of cities to be heard on these crucial issues derives from two fundamental principles. First, local government is closest to the people. In fact, one of the few ways citizens can register their dissent is through locally elected representatives. . . . [Second,] many of our national policies are felt first—and in the end most profoundly—in America's cities. . . . " (Dunn, 1985, p. A8).

Following the words of Mayor Bradley, over a thousand American municipalities have entered international affairs, with increasing impact on foreign policy:

• More than 800 local governments (Nuclear Weapons Freeze Campaign, 1984) passed a nuclear freeze resolution and helped pressure Ronald Reagan—the only modern U.S. president to enter office on a platform condemning arms control—to launch the START negotiations in Geneva (Talbott, 1983).

• By refusing to cooperate with the Federal Emergency Managements Agency's "crisis relocation planning," more than 120 cities helped put its civil defense program to pasture ("Civil Defense Plan on Relocation Out," 1985).

• By divesting more than $20 billion in assets away from firms doing business in South Africa, more than 70 cities, 13 counties, and 19 states helped persuade the government to replace "constructive engagement" with serious economic sanctions (Richard Knight, American Committee on Africa, personal communication, 20 October 1986).

Contrary to critics' assertions, these municipalities have launched foreign policies not to "meddle" in other people's affairs, but to protect their own local interests being directly affected by international affairs, especially the arms race. "Cities of the world unite," Kenneth Boulding once wrote, "you have nothing to lose but your slums, your poverty, and your military expendability" (Boulding, 1968, p. 1,123). It is no accident that cities like Verdun, Berlin, Guernica, Dresden, and Coventry, all of which were destroyed in battles, also have some of the most active foreign policies (Shuman, 1985). Cities throughout the world have come to realize that, inasmuch as it is their people and their buildings being held hostage for national security, it is also their civic responsibility to ensure that war, especially nuclear war, never happens.

For American cities, a compelling reminder of their connection to global problems is the economic impact of the $300 billion now being drained each year from domestic programs into military spending ($1 trillion worldwide). In autumn 1986, Congress axed $3.5 billion from General Revenue Sharing while approving $3.5 billion to support Star Wars research. Cities are beginning to understand that high levels of military spending are associated with high unemployment, poor economic growth, high inflation, and regressive wealth redistribution (Mosley, 1985). Even the minority of communities that benefit in the short term from military contracting—cities like Los Angeles, San Jose, and Boston that have traditionally lobbied for more military contracts—have passed Jobs With Peace Resolutions, articulating their concern that long-term dependence on military spending may ultimately leave them economic ghost towns (Jobs With Peace, 1985).

With these kinds of arguments, cities are playing an increasingly active role in promoting progressive foreign policies. Here are some examples (Shuman, 1987):

- *Education:* New York and Milwaukee high schools now teach peace studies courses (LEO/SR, 1985). San Francisco, Cambridge, and Boulder have produced and disseminated pamphlets describing the effects of nuclear war and arguing for a nuclear freeze ("Cambridge Hires Nation's First 'Peace Director'," 1984). The California Department of Education has appropriated money for every local school district to assess and develop curricula for teaching grade school and high school courses about the implications of "nuclear age problems."
- *Research:* Undaunted by the glacial progress of the National Peace Academy, some states like California and Iowa have established their own peace programs. Los Angeles, Pittsburgh, and Baltimore have passed ordinances requiring their staffs to prepare and publish annual reports on the economic impacts of military spending.
- *Lobbying:* The city of Cambridge has a full time "Peace Commissioner" whose responsibilities include lobbying local, state, national, and international bodies on behalf of peace. In Hiroshima and Nagasaki, where one percent of their municipal budgets is spent on peace activities, the mayors have spent 40 years lobbying leaders worldwide to reverse the nuclear arms race.
- *Nonbinding resolutions:* Many municipalities have sought to educate constituents, other citizens, and national politicians through nonbinding resolutions. Using these measures, San Francisco and Seattle have protested U.S. policy in Cen-

tral America; Los Angeles has registered its concern on Soviet human rights policies; and Berkeley has condemned the U.S. invasion of Grenada, supported the fatal hunger strike of Irish Republican Army leader Bobby Sands, and urged a halt to U.S. support for aerial bombing in El Salvador.

• *Policing:* Using their police powers, New York State and New Jersey, in cooperation with the cities of New York and Newark, protested the Soviet shooting down of a Korean Air Lines (KAL) 747 jet by denying Soviet representatives at the United Nations access to local airports. More than a dozen state liquor commissions responded to the KAL incident by banning sales of Soviet vodka. Twenty-eight cities (and the state of Wisconsin), declaring themselves sanctuaries, have instructed their police forces not to cooperate with the U.S. Immigration and Naturalization Service's efforts to round up and deport Salvadoran and Guatemalan refugees.

• *Selective zoning:* Through their zoning powers, the cities of Chicago and Cambridge have launched projects to assist military contractors in alternative use planning. Three thousand five hundred communities internationally (and more than 165 in the United States) have tried zoning out nuclear-weapons manufacturing, deployment, and transportation entirely. While these measures are often more educational than restrictive, they are rarely just symbolic. Nuclear free zones in the United Kingdom, for example, have educated their communities with special newspapers, leaflets, videos, booklets, speaking tours, conferences, workplace seminars, exhibitions, research studies, road signs, billboards, plaques, advertisements, postcards, banners, badges, peace parks, town shows, bunker parties, exhibitions, curriculum guides, adult-education courses, libraries, sister cities, and peace shops.

• *Selective contracting and investing:* With U.S. states and cities spending $500 billion annually and overseeing $300 billion in investments, they are increasingly recognizing their power in selectively contracting and investing. Newark prohibits any person who has entertained in South Africa or Namibia from performing in any facility owned, leased, or regulated by the city. Hoboken, New Jersey and Takoma Park, Maryland are among nearly a dozen jurisdictions that have prohibited any municipal contracts with firms producing nuclear weapons.

• *Transboundary relationships:* For decades, American states and communities adjacent to Canada or Mexico have entered into agreements with these nations (and sometimes their local subdivisions) on such issues as road and bridge oversight, water management, motor vehicle registration, civil defense, fire prevention, and border patrolling. One estimate is that American states and Canadian provinces have signed over 600 protocols.

• *Sister cities:* To demystify the Soviet Union, a growing number of American cities are entering sister city relationships with Soviet cities. The superpowers had only five sister city relationships in the 1970s (four of which were moribund after the Soviet military entry into Afghanistan). But within the next 5 years, four of these sisters sprang back to life, many new sister relationships were formed, and the Ground Zero Pairing Project got 55 U.S. cities to establish less formal ties with Soviet cities. Today, there are nearly 50 Soviet-American sister-city projects at some stage of formation.

• *Trading:* More than 180 U.S. cities are now actively promoting economic city-to-city ties abroad, and, again, a growing number of these are with "adversary" nations like the Soviet Union and China. In 1984, for example, San Francisco Mayor Dianne Feinstein signed a trade pact with the Chinese city of Shanghai. In Western Europe, more than 1,000 cities have created Peace Corps-like economic development programs with their "twins" in the Third World.

• *Political alliances:* Many city-to-city agreements are tantamount to political treaties. To challenge U.S. policy in Central America, 87 U.S. cities established formal ties with cities in Nicaragua. The City of Burlington, Vermont arranged for a ship to carry 560 tons of supplies to its sister city, Puerto Cabezas, including 30 tons of medical supplies the city collected from local hospitals.

• *Municipal state departments:* In an effort to carry out their foreign policies with the greatest possible coherence and effectiveness, a few cities have established permanent governmental bodies—bodies that could be viewed as miniature state departments. Seattle, for example, has an Office of International Affairs to coordinate its $250,000 annual programs involving trade, tourism, and sister cities. Between 1981 and 1982, Washington, DC, Cambridge, and Boulder established peace commissions with modest budgets and staffs. By 1986, Cambridge was using its commission to create a sister city relationship with Yerevan in the Soviet Union, a sanctuary for Central American refugees, a peace library, a peace curriculum, a conversion committee, and a "work camp for world peace" involving inner-city youths.

As is evident from these examples, some municipal activism has focused on arms control. But there is no reason why cities cannot be persuaded to promote leader control policies in the future. Indeed, the seeds of these policies may already be planted. The nearly 50 American cities paired with Soviet cities could try helping their counterparts to democratize by setting up exchange programs, exporting computer technology, or helping them to set up small-scale businesses. American cities interested in promoting leader control at home could direct their lobbyists to Washington, D.C., to fight for a stronger War Powers Act or a ban on covert actions. The possibilities are as broad as a local jurisdiction's imagination.

Future Directions

In the years ahead, American local governments will undoubtedly try strengthening their municipal foreign policies by connecting and working with ideologically friendly local governments abroad. A glimpse of this process was provided by the August 1985 "First World Conference of Mayors for Peace through Inter-City Solidarity." Sponsored by the mayors of Hiroshima and Nagasaki, the conference brought together more 200 local officials from 100 cities in 23 countries to discuss how their cities could help prevent nuclear war (Shuman, 1985). While much of the conference was consumed in formal ceremonies commemorating the 40th anniversary of the first nuclear bombings, it was an unprecedented opportunity for local officials to begin exploring ways they could cooperate. Despite radical differences in ideology, the officials openly criticized the limited accomplishments of their national leaders and passed three resolutions unanimously condemning the arms race and advocating several concrete arms control measures. One resolution, negotiated primarily by American and Soviet mayors, endorsed a comprehensive test ban, which General Secretary Gorbachev had just entered unilaterally, but in terms that, eschewing Soviet rhetoric, legitimized President Reagan's counter-offer for open inspection of both side's test sites (Shuman, 1985).

The First World Conference of Mayors for Peace suggested a whole new arena for international politics. Most officials attending expressed a strong desire to meet again and to begin developing a coordinated global lobby for reversal of the nuclear arms race. A second conference took place in 1989 and a third is under discussion. Similar dialogues have emerged in the International Union of Local Authorities and the United Towns Organisation.

Over the next decade or two, there may well be enough cities participating in foreign affairs to establish one or more "global unions" of local officials— permanent, ongoing organizations in which local representatives could devise common global agendas and lobby national leaders through pooled resources. Predicting the exact complexion of these organizations is of course premature, but three of their probable features are worth noting. First, with city-sized units of representation, many minorities silenced in today's nation-state politics would be given a real voice in international affairs. Second, the sheer number of participants would ensure that critical issues embarrassing to nations that often get buried in nation-state organizations—issues like torture or United Nations reform, for example—would finally get an airing. Third, as the inner politics of the Hiroshima conference demonstrated, a global union of municipalities might foster new alliances on such bases as size, industry, bioregion, religion, and language—natural alliances that nation-state politics now obscure. While a Camp David summit among the national leaders of Israel, Egypt, Syria, Jordan, and Lebanon now seems implausible, it would be less difficult to gather from each of these countries one or two of its most forward-looking mayors. If global dialogues emerge where a growing number of municipalities find themselves agreeing with one another on some issues but disagreeing on others, they might serve as an important moderating force in preventing conflicts between their national governments.

How far these unions could go without provoking a backlash from their national governments is hard to say. In theory, national governments have sovereign control over their local governments and could easily silence them. In practice, however, official repression will face profound limits (Shuman, 1986–1987). Democracies will be especially reluctant to commit ideological suicide by quashing citizens' rights of speech, travel, and association.

The argument can be made that an international politics in which thousands of independent local officials from democracies interact with thousands of controlled local officials from nondemocracies would simply strengthen the hand of nondemocracies. Yet just the opposite is probably true. The diversity of city-to-city contacts will probably spawn a diversity of new agreements for economic, scientific, and cultural exchange—agreements that inevitably expose the nondemocracies to new products, ideas, and people. As more Japanese, Western Europeans, and Americans meet and work with Soviets, pressures mount on the Soviets to enter the global economy (Hough, 1985–1986). In promoting the freer movement of ideas, people, and goods, a union of local officials might emerge as a powerful force for global democratization and leader control.

CONCLUSION

Clearly we as Americans have many more options for eliminating the risks of horrendous-type death from nuclear war than arms control. By seeking to control leaders rather than weapons, we can address the causes of war and not just the symptoms. Moreover, by promoting direct citizen participation in foreign policy, whether through individual initiatives or municipal foreign policies, we can exert powerful checks on national leaders and promote the most important lifegenic factors of our time.

In the 1970s, international relations scholars began recognizing the growing power of nonstate actors, especially those possessing enormous economic power—multinational corporations (Keohane & Nye, 1977). Now we must begin recognizing those actors possessing enormous political power—municipal governments. For citizens throughout the world terrified by escalating global problems and frustrated with the responses of the national governments, municipal foreign policies are beginning to offer a concrete, realistic alternative to apathy and despair. These citizens are beginning to see how they can mobilize local governments, at home and abroad, to influence and change the behavior of national governments, including their own. Municipal foreign policies offer a realistic conduit for citizens to put permanent restraints on leaders throughout the world, making it ever more difficult for them to launch wars with impunity.

Political power is always a double-edged sword, and it is possible that municipal foreign policies could produce 100 Colonel Khaddafis. Certainly local leaders are no less prone to error, terror, or madness than are national leaders. What municipal foreign policies ultimately offer, however, is a better system of political accountability—the essence of leader control. They provide unprecedented opportunities for the world's people to launch constructive foreign policies and desperately needed safety valves to halt disastrous policies. Whether 5 billion people can better mold international relations than fewer than 200 national leaders is a matter of political judgment, but it's precisely that judgment that underlies America's longstanding faith in democracy. As Thomas Jefferson once wrote. "The good sense of the people will always be found to be the best army" (Koch & Peden, 1944, p. 411).

REFERENCES

Barton, J. H., & Weiler, L. D. (Eds.). (1976). *International arms control: Issues and agreements.* Stanford, CA: Stanford University Press.

Berger, J. J. (1976). *Nuclear power: The unviable option.* Palo Alto, CA: Ramparts Press.

Boulding, K. E. (1968). The city as an element in the international system. *Daedalus,* 1123.

Bradley, B. (1989, January 3). Perestroika, without western subsidies. *New York Times,* p. A19.

Bundy, W. (1983). A portentous year. *Foreign Affairs, 62*(3), 485–520.

Center for Defense Information (1983). A world at war—1983. *The Defense Monitor, 7*(1), 1.

Christian, S. (1988, June 15). Group is channeling U.S. fund to parties opposing Pinochet. *New York Times,* p. 1.

Civil defense plan on relocation out (1985, March 4). *New York Times,* p. 7.

Committee for the Compilation of Materials on Damage Caused by the Atomic Bombs in Hiroshima and Nagasaki (1985). *Impacts of the A-Bomb.* Tokyo: Iwanami Shoten.

Cuddly Russia? (1987, February 14). *The Economist,* pp. 13–14.

Cullen, R. B. (1986–87). Soviet Jewry. *Foreign Affairs, 65,* 252–266.

Dahl, R. (1985). *Controlling nuclear weapons: Democracy versus guardianship.* Syracuse, NY: Syracuse University Press.

Dunn, A. (1985, December 11). Cities must speak out. *Seattle Post-Intelligencer,* p. A8.

Dworkin, R. (1987, February 26). The press on trial. *New York Review of Books,* pp. 27–37.

Faulkner, P. (1977). *The silent bomb: A guide to the nuclear energy controversy.* New York: Vintage Books.

Feldmann, L. (1988, February 25). From hand to hand flows . . . trust or manipulation. *Christian Science Monitor,* p. 5.

Forum Institute (1985). *Search for security: A study of philanthropy in international security and the prevention of nuclear war.* Washington, DC: Forum Institute.

Halperin, M. (1987, March 21). The case against covert action. *The Nation,* p. 363.

Hough, J. F. (1985-86). Beyond the summit. *World Policy Journal, 3*(1), 1-28.

Hughes, J. (1988, August 8). Don't weaken USIA: War of words continues. *Wall Street Journal,* p. 14.

Isaacson, W. (1989, April 10). A long, mighty struggle. *Time,* p. 58.

Jobs with Peace. (1985). *Proposal for funding.* Boston, MA: Author.

Johansen, R. C. (1986). The Reagan administration and the U.N. *World Policy Journal, 3*(4), 607.

Keohane, R., & Nye, J. (1977). *Power and interdependence: World politics in transition.* Boston: Little, Brown.

Koch, A., & Peden, W. (1944). *The life and selected writings of Thomas Jefferson.* New York: Modern Library.

Kristol, I. (1985, December 17). Coping with an 'evil empire.' *Wall Street Journal,* p. 26.

Kwitney, J. (1984). *Endless enemies.* New York: Penguin.

Lens, S. (1983, December 25). Deterrence hardly deters. *New York Times.*

Levin, A. (1986, November 13). U.S., Soviet scientists progress in nuclear test monitoring effort. *Christian Science Monitor,* p. 5.

Lewis, A. (1988, March 23). Reagan's obsession with Nicaragua. *San Francisco Chronicle,* p. A14.

Lewis, F. (1989, May 10). Soviets buy American. *New York Times,* p. A35.

Lovins, A. B., & Lovins, L. H. (1980). *Energy/war: Breaking the nuclear link.* San Francisco: Friends of the Earth.

Lovins, A. B., & Lovins, L. H. (1989). *Drill rigs and battleships are the answer! (But what was the question?).* Snowmass, Colorado: RMI.

Lovins, A. B., & Lovins, L. H. (1982). *Brittle power: Energy strategy for national security.* Andover, MA: Brick House.

Montville, J. V., & Davidson, W. D. (1981-82). Foreign policy according to Freud. *Foreign Policy, 45,* 145-157.

Mosley, H. (1985). *The arms race: Social and economic consequences.* Lexington, MA: Lexington Books.

Multiplicity of relationships with Chinese (1985, October). *Surviving Together,* p. 6.

Nichols, J. S. (1984). Wasting the propaganda dollar. *Foreign Policy, 56,* 129-140.

Nuclear Weapons Freeze Campaign (1984, December). *The Freeze Focus, 4*(10), 2.

Patterson, W. C. (1976). *Nuclear Power.* Middlesex, Great Britain: Penguin.

Pear, R. (1988, July 10). U.S. helping Polish underground with money and communications. *New York Times,* p. 1.

Pear, R. (1989, May 7). Poll watching becomes a growth industry. *New York Times,* Sec. 4, p. 2.

Pisar, S. (1985, December 26). A red or green light for East-West trade: Gorbachev's pragmatic generation. *The Wall Street Journal,* p. 6.

Powers, T. (1984, January). What is it about? *The Atlantic Monthly,* p. 48.

Risky movements in money matters (1987, March 2). *U.S. News and World Report,* p. 44.

Roberts, S. V. (1985, June 9). Of two minds. *New York Times,* p. 1E.

Rosenheim, D. (1985, December 30). Feinstein's coup on emigres. *San Francisco Chronicle,* p. 1.

Rummel, R. J. (1980). *Understanding conflict and war: Volume 4.* Beverly Hills, CA: Sage.

Russett, B. (1982). Causes of peace. In Stephenson, C. M. (Ed.), *Alternative methods for international security* (pp. 189-190). Lanham, MD: University Press of America.

Schell, J. (1984, January 2). The abolition—Part I. *The New Yorker,* p. 71.

Schmemann, S. (1988, December 1). The Soviets stop years of jamming Radio Liberty. *New York Times,* pp. A1-A2.

Schurmann, F. (1987, December 3). Fast food outlets symbolize capitalist spirit at Communist shrines. *East-West News,* p. 7.

Shipler, D. (1985, November 10). The view from America. *New York Times Magazine,* p. 40.

Shuman, M. H. (1985). The world's mayors meet in Hiroshima. *The CID Report, 2*(4).

Shuman, M. H. (1986-87). Dateline main street: Local foreign policies. *Foreign Policy, 65,* 154-74.

Shuman, M. H. (1987). *Building Municipal Foreign Policies.* Irvine, CA: Center for Innovative Diplomacy.

Singer, J. D., & Small, M. (1976). The war-proneness of democratic regimes, 1815-1970. *Jerusalem Journal of International Relations, 14,* 50-69.

Sivard, R. L. (1987). *World military and social expenditures—1987.* Washington, DC: World Priorities.

Stone, J. J. (1984). Presidential first use is unlawful. *Foreign Policy, 56,* 94–112.
Svec, M. (1986, December 26). That airwaves exchange. *Wall Street Journal,* p. 8.
Talbott, S. (1983). Buildup and breakdown. *Foreign Affairs—Chronology 1983, 62*(3), 605.
Taubman, P. (1988, May 29). Gorbachev has come a long way, too. *New York Times,* Sec. 4, p. 1.
van Ness, P. (1988, March 12). Concealed weapon. *The Nation,* p. 329.
Wallersteen, P. (1973). *Structure and war.* Stockholm: Raben and Sjogren.
Warner, G., & Shuman, M. (1987). *Citizen diplomats: Pathfinders in Soviet-American relations.* New
    York: Continuum.
Wildavsky, A. (1983). *Beyond containment: Alternative American policies toward the Soviet Union.*
    San Francisco: Institute for Contemporary Studies.
Yankelovich, D., & Doble, J. (1984). The public mood: Nuclear weapons and the U.S.S.R. *Foreign
    Affairs, 63,* p. 46.

APPENDIX: ADDITIONAL READING

Books/Handbooks

Michael Shuman. "Dateline Main Street: Local Foreign Policies," *Foreign Policy,* Volume 65, Winter 1986/87, pp. 154–174.

Michael Shuman. **Building Municipal Foreign Policies.** August 1987. (Available from the Center for Innovative Diplomacy at 17931 Sky Park Circle, Suite F, Irvine, CA 92714).

Michael Shuman and Jayne Williams. **Having International Affairs Your Way: A Five-Step Briefing Manual for Citizen Diplomats.** January 1986. (Available from the Center for Innovative Diplomacy).

Gale Warner and Michael Shuman. **Citizen Diplomats: Pathfinders in Soviet-American Relations** (New York: Continuum, 1987) Paperback edition by Seven Locks Press, 1991.

Periodicals

The Bulletin of Municipal Foreign Policy. (Available from the Center for Innovative Diplomacy, 17931 Sky Park Circle, Suite F, Irvine, CA 92714).

Surviving Together: A Journal on Soviet-American Relations. (Available from the Institute for Soviet-American Relations, 1608 New Hampshire Ave. NW, Washington, DC 20009).

10

Bridge Building from the Grass Roots: Organization and Management of Citizen Diplomacy Programs

Earl A. Molander
Portland State University and Ground Zero Pairing Project
Portland, Oregon

Citizen diplomacy—outreach programs whose purpose is to link the people of the United States and the Soviet Union at the grass-roots level—is one aspect of the horrendous-type death/ fear of death/denial/action model.

This chapter describes the goals, operation, and successes and failures of citizen diplomacy as it has been practiced in the United States over the past 30 years, with particular emphasis on the period since 1982.

The primary analysis of this contemporary period derives from the author's own experience as founder and executive director of the Ground Zero Pairing Project, a leading citizen diplomacy organization.

INTRODUCTION

Whether spurred by divine inspiration, frustration, or careful analysis and calculation, the mid-1980s saw the proliferation of a variety of people-to-people programs whose purpose has been to link the people of the United States and the Soviet Union at the grass-roots level. Known as citizen diplomacy, citizen summitry, or grass-roots diplomacy, the number of organizations with a national scope actively involved in these activities was well over 100 by the end of 1987, after which time the number plateaued.

Citizen diplomacy is one aspect of the horrendous-type death/fear of death/ denial/action model outlined earlier in this book. Spurred by the threat of nuclear war and deteriorating U.S.-Soviet relations that increase the prospects of such a war, individuals across the United States have worked their way through their fears and denial. Often the outcome of this process is action, like citizen diplomacy, in which they seek to take their own fate into their own hands, no matter how small their efforts might appear in the larger equation of U.S.-Soviet relations.

This chapter will describe the goals, operation, and successes and failures of citizen diplomacy (the term I will use hereafter) as it has been practiced in the United States over the past 30 years, with particular emphasis on the period since 1982. The main substance of the coverage in this contemporary period derives from my own experience as founder and executive director of the Ground Zero Pairing Project, a leading citizen diplomacy organization.

Since 1983, the Ground Zero Pairing Project has emerged as the largest supplier of educational materials on the Soviet Union and U.S.-Soviet relations to schools and community groups in the United States. It is also a major participant in the citizen diplomacy movement through its "Global Leader" program to establish informal linkages between U.S. and Soviet cities.

Except where there is significant overlap, I will narrow the focus of this chapter to only those organizations and programs which are truly grass roots in character and that have as their intended market ordinary citizens, not specialized experts in a profession or discipline. I also will leave aside an extensive discussion of cultural exchange programs. The focus here will be on genuine people-to-people programs at the grass roots of American political and civic life.

Although my hope is to inspire others to join the citizen diplomacy effort of which the Ground Zero Pairing Project and I are a part, my tone will be more pragmatic than ecstatic, my purpose more to inform than inspire. I establish these parameters because there is an ample inventory of inspiration and plenty of inspired people ready to give of their time and even their entire lives to this critical area of citizen involvement and peacemaking. But there is a near total absence of an honest assessment of the mechanics of the process and the requirements to succeed over the long haul. What the last four years have taught us at the Pairing Project is that the critical ingredient lacking in the entire grass-roots diplomacy movement, and in the United States peace movement generally, is "staying power." This lack of staying power is a product of the lack of education and understanding about the nature of the Soviet Union and U.S.-Soviet relations, and about the lengthy and mine-filled road of citizen diplomacy.

THE ORGANIZATIONS INVOLVED: GOALS, STRATEGY, AND STRUCTURE

The character of the individuals and organizations that have been "called" to organize and actively participate in citizen diplomacy varies widely, from the traditional people-to-people exchange programs which began in the 1950s to the "New Age" or "Aquarian" individuals and organizations of the 1980s. Some organizations are established institutions for which citizen diplomacy with the Soviet Union is only a small program within a broader one of educational and other activities. Others are small, informal groups or even single individuals, often masquerading as established organizations but in fact lacking a solid financial foundation and membership base.

Figure 1 summarizes the overall strategy of the citizen diplomacy movement. Essentially, it represents an effort on the part of citizen diplomacy organizations to persuade U.S. peace activists and organizations to add citizen diplomacy to their agendas, and to mobilize U.S. citizens toward citizen diplomacy both directly and through these peace groups. Citizen diplomacy has two targets: policymakers in the U.S. and policymakers in the Soviet Union. By mobilizing grass-roots sentiment in the U.S., the movement hopes to influence Sovietologists and national security experts in the U.S. to recommend policy changes that would reduce U.S.-Soviet tensions. Simultaneously, the efforts of the movement are directed toward Soviet citizens, Soviet Americanologists, and exchange organizations in order to educate them about American perspectives, build bridges between the two countries, and persuade them to implement policy changes that would reduce U.S.-Soviet tensions and the threat of horrendous death for Soviet and other people.

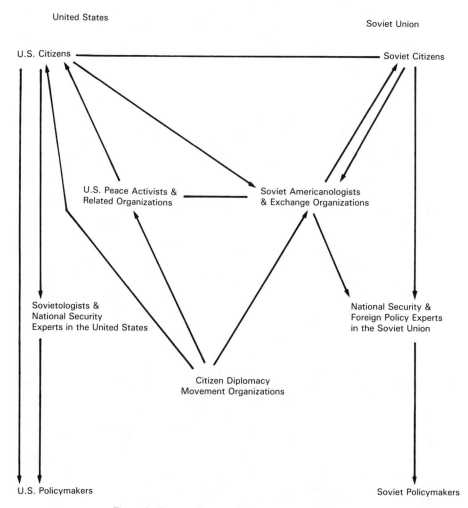

Figure 1 Target audiences of the citizen diplomacy movement.

Appendix A gives a more detailed outline of the operational goals and strategy inherent in Figure 1.

The activities of the individual citizen diplomacy organizations and programs that make up the movement represent a mix of two related objectives:

1. Education: to educate the people of the United States to the nature of "real people" in the Soviet Union as well as the social, economic, and cultural realities that lie beneath the awesome Soviet political and military system—which is its most visible feature in the West. To a lesser extent, the reverse goal—educating the Soviets about the United States, is also present.

2. Outreach: to establish a network—a set of relationships or "linkages"—on which to construct a system of long-term communication wherein the citizens of

the two countries, on a one-to-one basis, learn to better understand and even like each other. These interpersonal sentiments, then, percolate through the respective political systems to make each government less hostile to the other, more inclined to communication and cooperation, and less inclined to provocation or use of nuclear weapons.

Peace organizations allocate their scarce resources to a broad range of efforts. Some focus their efforts on education, including the development of educational materials and quasi-formal educational programs in which citizen diplomacy becomes a component or concluding activity. Programs such as those conducted by schools and universities are of this character. Direct contact with Soviet citizens is thus a part of a well-designed educational process.

Other organizations focus on the travel aspects of citizen diplomacy, with actual face-to-face encounters, a minor part of the grass-roots diplomacy experience. These groups do some amount of "orientation" for participants, but the educational dimensions of this orientation are usually quite limited.

That idealized citizen diplomacy experience—a well-developed educational program followed by extensive direct contacts between U.S. and Soviet citizens at the grass-roots level, stripped of the encumbrances of formal diplomacy and governmental oversight—is an altogether rare experience in the annals of citizen diplomacy. In those instances where it has occurred it has been a case of serendipitous circumstances, rather than a carefully planned and replicable part of a particular organization's citizen diplomacy program.

With all of the enthusiasm for citizen diplomacy in this country, and with more than 150,000 Americans and 30,000 Soviets travelling to each other's countries each year, why has citizen diplomacy to date been so weak? There are a variety of possible explanations, not the least of which is that the citizen diplomacy movement is only 8 years old. Yet these 8 years have seen a number of problems develop which have plagued primary efforts as far back as their origins in the post-Stalin thaw in the late 1950s.

The adage that "those who do not learn from history are condemned to repeat it" is particularly appropriate for individuals contemplating active participation in the citizen diplomacy effort, because reliving the experiences of the last 30 years and especially the early 1980s means a predominant experience of frustration, hostility, alienation, and failure, and a limited experience of success.

In the balance of this chapter, I will trace those experiences, highlighting those features from which we can learn better how to approach citizen diplomacy and maximize the enthusiasm for this enterprise among the American public so it may achieve the most satisfaction from its efforts. Citizen diplomacy, if properly practiced, can achieve its full potential in reducing the ignorance and hostility between the United States and Soviet Union and ultimately, the risk of horrendous death in nuclear war.

PEOPLE-TO-PEOPLE EXPERIENCES PRIOR
TO THE 1980s

The grass-roots, people-to-people experiences of American and Soviet citizens in the last 30 years can be divided neatly into four periods: (a) the post-Stalin thaw and the cold war, 1958–1973; (b) détente, 1973–1979; (c) the new cold war, 1979–1983; (d) the contemporary era, 1983–present.

Post-Stalin Thaw and the Cold War: 1958–1973

The first U.S.-Soviet exchange agreement was signed in 1958. Known as the "Cultural Agreement," it included exchanges in a variety of areas, including science and technology, agriculture, radio and television, youth, athletics, medicine and public health, culture, and tourism. The fact that the Soviets insisted on a formal exchange agreement when exchanges had been ongoing with other countries for decades pointed to four aspects of U.S.-Soviet exchanges that would surface continuously over the next 30 years:

1. In a highly centralized and bureaucratic system like the Soviet Union, Soviet officials are accustomed to having agreements of any kind written down in copious detail.
2. Formalized agreements carry legitimacy within the Soviet Union, enabling those responsible for their execution to proceed without fear of charges that they are overstepping the boundaries of their responsibilities, and especially that they are being excessively friendly to the capitalist West.
3. Formalized agreements can be budgeted for.
4. Formalized agreements with the United States that emphasize strict reciprocity—a nearly precise symmetry in exchanges—carry the implication of Soviet equality or parity with the United States in the area of exchange, as well as generally.

Over the next 30 years, further exchange agreements were signed, with nearly all traceable to this first exchange agreement. The Soviet insistence upon a formal agreement carried an implicit requirement that the U.S. signatory of such an agreement have an official or quasi-official status, and that the agreement have boundaries. Later, and especially in the 1980s, the informal "Let a Thousand Flowers Bloom" approach of many peace groups, who courted Soviet authorities for grass-roots diplomacy, would find this requirement a major roadblock in their efforts.

Because governmental activities in the principal areas of exchange are largely in the private sector in the United States and in the public sector in the Soviet Union, this very first agreement also clarified what was to become a major problem in all forms of exchange activities between the two countries. Because the various forms of grass-roots citizen exchange that would eventually take place represented the most private, and thus least organized and legitimized area of exchange, this public/private asymmetry would prove even more of a problem in this sector than in others. For example, although it was rarely a routine matter, it was possible for private universities and athletic associations to arrange exchanges with their Soviet counterparts. They possessed the organizing skills, the funds to sustain the project to completion, and the capacity to promote the activity to their member individuals and organizations. In many instances, they had already participated in similar exchange activities with their counterparts in other countries in the past, often informally.

By contrast, grass-roots citizen groups, usually lacking the experience and resources of these other organizations, had a difficult time in arranging people-to-people contacts both in the United States and in dealing with the Soviets. Citizen groups, by nature accustomed to informal relationships within and outside of their organizations, were unable to formalize their efforts enough to deal with the needs and requirements of potential Soviet counterpart organizations, for example, Komsomol (the Communist Party organization for Soviets aged 16–29), the Soviet Peace Committee, or the Soviet Women's Organization, all of which were logical contact points for people-to-people exchanges. Nor did they have the quasi-official status or legitimacy which were accorded other private U.S. organizations, such as universities and professional associations. As a result, the overwhelming people-to-people experience from 1958 to 1973 was a by-product of the formal exchanges which took place in science and technology, academia, athletics, and other professional areas, rather than specifically grass-roots outreach efforts.

This early period also highlighted a third problem which would hamper all future grass-roots exchanges: the Soviet desire—eventually mirrored in the United States—for strict control over all visitors to the Soviet Union. Part of this control was achieved through the requirement that U.S. visitors to the Soviet Union stay only at Soviet-authorized locations, which usually meant Intourist hotels or in the case of longer stays, foreign compounds within the major cities of the Soviet Union. No U.S. citizens were permitted to stay in private homes of Soviet citizens. Further control was implicit in the rigidly specified and supervised movements for American visitors once inside the Soviet Union. This tight control created an atmosphere of sterility, if not artificiality, in many early U.S.-Soviet exchanges.

Deténte: 1973–1979

In 1973, in conjunction with the signing of the SALT I (Strategic Arms Limitations Talks) Agreement, President Nixon and Party Secretary Brezhnev signed a new cultural exchange agreement. The agreement was more ambitious than those of the past, indicating the greater importance the two sides assigned to cultural relations as part of their overall foreign relations and of the peacemaking process whose centerpiece was the new arms control agreement. As a result, exchanges increased, and some Soviets were even permitted to visit the United States as individuals and in small groups rather than as part of a tightly bound delegation.

A key feature of the new cultural exchange agreement was the establishment of five U.S.-Soviet "sister cities," to be organized through the quasi-official Sister Cities International organization in the United States, and the Association for Relations between Soviet and Foreign Cities in the Soviet Union. These city-to-city pairings were to be the framework for an array of exchanges in education, culture, and economic areas, and for citizen delegations.

The five Sister City pairings—Seattle/Tashkent, Jacksonville/Murmansk, Baltimore/Odessa, Houston/Baku, and Oakland/Nakhodka—were inaugurated with the exchange of delegations of up to a dozen people in the following 2 years. However, only the Seattle/Tashkent relationship ever blossomed. The other four pairings fell victim to developments in the United States, not the Soviet Union. In Baltimore, the Ukrainian community objected almost immediately and was able to frustrate the effort at the start. In Oakland, the exchange never penetrated City Hall, but was limited almost exclusively to the exchange of members of the respective port commissions. In Houston, once it became apparent that the opportunities for sale of oil drilling equipment in Baku were limited, local business support for the effort (the primary driving force behind it) faded. And finally, in Jacksonville, as well as in the other cities, the Soviet invasion of Afghanistan created such antipathy toward the Soviet Union that the mayor was unwilling to risk his political capital by pushing the program. Only in Seattle, where large delegation exchanges have been continuous over the past 10 years, has there been a genuine people-to-people experience for the participants, and there it has been largely structured around tourist visits by Seattle citizens to Tashkent and the rest of the Soviet Union.

The New Cold War: 1979–1982

By late 1979, the Soviet arms buildup of the 1970s and the Soviet invasion of Afghanistan had quashed not only grass-roots exchanges through Sister Cities International, but also other exchange efforts. Those exchange agreements covering space, science, and other areas which were due for renewal in the 1979–1981 period were not renewed, and the two countries settled into the "new cold war." In 1980, for example, only 13,000 visas were issued for U.S. citizens to visit the Soviet Union, down from 44,000 the previous year and 65,000 in 1976.

The first two years of the Reagan administration saw further polarization of U.S.-Soviet relations and virtual stagnation of all forms of exchange. However, deteriorating U.S.-Soviet relations and the arms buildup in the U.S. by 1982 had catalyzed a renewed peace movement in the United States. While focusing primarily on the threat in an ever-expanding nuclear arms race and an accompanying appeal to "freeze" nuclear weapons at existing levels, that movement eventually turned to a closer examination of the U.S.-Soviet relationship.

ANSWERING THE "WHAT ABOUT THE RUSSIANS?" QUESTION: BRIDGE BUILDING FROM 1983 TO THE PRESENT

The key factor in the renewed interest in learning about the Soviet Union was the revival of the antinuclear-war movement in 1981 and the well-worn "What About the Russians?" question which greeted it in so many circles. The phrase carried a variety of meanings:

1. The literal meaning—"tell me more about the Soviet Union and Russian people."

2. The well-considered observation that no progress in controlling nuclear arms could be seriously pursued without the participation of the Soviet Union. The problem was how to get the two sides together and working on genuine arms control.

3. The assertion that any well-informed person knows the true nature of the Communists who run the Soviet Union and their hostility to any concept of arms control unfavorable to them and beneficial to the United States. Here, the questioner already knew all he or she needed to know about the Russians.

Awareness that there was a sizable audience for answers to the first two of these questions sparked an effort aimed at education about the Soviet Union and the U.S.-Soviet relationship. In the newer, more activist organizations involved in this effort (I would include the Ground Zero Pairing Project in this category), it became apparent that among the American public this interest in learning gave way to a more action-oriented desire to reach out to the Soviet people for the purpose of understanding the shared threat. Thus by the summer of 1983, some half-dozen U.S. organizations were engaged in both education and outreach programs focused on the Soviet Union. By 1986, that number had grown to almost 200. These groups joined a small cadre of organizations whose primary activity had involved study tours of the Soviet Union for, in the case of the Citizen Exchange Council, up to 20 years.

Current Status

Currently, there are about 50 U.S. organizations sending delegations to the Soviet Union, delegations whose primary goal and activities would fall within the "grass-roots diplomacy" category. Of these, a half-dozen organizations account for over 90% of the 1,000 or so travellers in this category. (The Citizen Exchange Council alone accounts for about one-fourth of the total.) Thus, of the 120,000 Americans who visited the Soviet Union in 1987 (up from 45,000 in 1985), less than 1%, representing a minuscule .0004% of the total U.S. population, were consciously "citizen diplomats."

In 1985, 42 U.S. organizations involved in educational and exchange activities hosted 491 Soviet citizens in the United States. These numbers did not change appreciably in 1986 and 1987. However, less than half of these organizations receive Soviet visitors on a regular basis, and one organization, the National Council of American/Soviet Friendship, regularly accounts for over 25% of the total number of Soviet visitors. These guest Soviets represented less than 7% of the 7,000 Soviet visitors to the United States in 1985, or .0002% of the Soviet population. These numbers demonstrate that the magnitude of the organizational effort far exceeds the actual numbers of citizens in each country who encounter each other with the conscious purpose of improving U.S.-Soviet relations through citizen diplomacy.

THE GROUND ZERO PAIRING
PROJECT EXPERIENCE

The Ground Zero Pairing Project is an organizational spinoff from Ground Zero, the nonpartisan educational organization which conducted a nationwide educational campaign on nuclear weapons and nuclear war in April 1982. Local organizers in the more than 1,000 communities and universities which participated in the program reported a high frequency of "What About the Russians?" questions in their educational efforts: the organizers in turn sought advice and materials on how to respond to the question. As a result, in the summer of 1982, Ground Zero started the Ground Zero Pairing Project in order to focus its educational efforts exclusively on the Soviet Union and U.S.-Soviet relations and to include exploration of the possibility of linking of U.S. and Soviet cities for educational exchanges. (The "Ground Zero Pairing Project" name implies the pairing of communities which have equal probability of being "ground zeros"—the point of detonation of a nuclear weapon.)

We undertook the pairing of U.S.-Soviet cities after Sister Cities International announced that they had no further intention of pursuing this activity because of the mid-1980s breakdown of the exchange activities among four of the five proposed U.S.-Soviet Sister Cities.

The Ground Zero Pairing Project began active promotion of its educational materials in the spring of 1983. The program proposed using special study of a "Soviet community just like your own" as a means of the focusing educational efforts at the community level.

The pilot study made clear that Americans, while showing some interest in conducting educational programs for local citizens, were far more interested in more aggressive outreach to a Soviet city. Armed with this information, we targeted the autumn of 1983 for a nationwide promotion of the Pairing Project focused on the Thanksgiving weekend effort; we called the outreach, "Make the First Strike a Knock on the Door."

In order to prepare, in the late spring we made an effort to solicit the assistance of the USSR-USA Society in Moscow in this outreach effort, directing our request through the Cultural Affairs Section of the Soviet Embassy in Washington, DC. They passed our program proposal on to Moscow, but we received no response. Nor did the Washington embassy.

By the summer of 1983 we decided to make a frontal grass-roots-based citizen diplomacy assault on the Soviet Union. We set as a goal convincing community groups in 1,052 U.S. communities (the number of ICBMs in the U.S. nuclear arsenal at the time) to mail portraits of their communities to 1,052 comparable Soviet communities. We recognized the risks in this strategy, since we had been advised that the Soviets took a dim view of unilateral action and programs outside centralized Moscow control. Yet without this frontal assault, we felt that the attention of the Soviets would never be drawn to the importance of people-to-people exchanges within a paired community framework. Nor would the Soviets recognize the strong sentiment in the American public for such contacts and accompanying exchanges.

KAL 007: Horrendous Death and the Impact on Citizen Diplomacy

In August 1983 we put some 20,000 promotional pieces into the mail, only to have them drop through mail slots around the country in the 2 weeks following the Soviet shooting down of Korean Air Lines flight 007, with the loss of almost 500 lives, including many Americans. Initially, the sentiment for outreach to the Soviet people was buried in the angry reaction of the American public against this act. When this anger passed, however, many people came away from this face-to-face encounter with the horrendous death of innocent people—a microcosm of the effects of conventional or nuclear war—with a sense of just how deeply strained U.S.-Soviet relations were, and how threatening this condition was to international stability and security.

From this nadir of U.S.-Soviet relations emerged a strong desire on the part of many Americans to minimize the strain between the superpowers. Those Americans who held this sentiment and had received our promotional materials became the organizing core of our First Strike program. While we did not reach our goal of 1,052 communities mailing community portraits to Soviet communities on Thanksgiving weekend 1983, groups in over 800 communities eventually did participate. This was approximately one-third of the number of communities (over 2,400) from which we received individual inquiries about the program. In about a third of the participating communities, the main organizing thrust came from schools, a third from local peace groups, and the remaining from a mix of other local groups and individuals. (Although only about one-fourth of participating local groups who initially sought the support of mayors or city-council members were successful, from October 15 onward well over half gained some form of official support.)

The Pairing Project provided, free of charge, an extensive package of educational materials and curricula to all local groups. Although participating local groups with close ties to schools used the materials extensively, outside of the schools only about half the community groups made any significant effort to conduct education about the Soviet Union and U.S.-Soviet relations as part of their First Strike effort. This reinforced our previous experience, which suggested that Americans wanted to act on their concerns, not wait to learn more. Knowing that U.S.-Soviet relations were at their lowest point since the cold war was enough.

The First Strike program achieved considerable local publicity in the communities which participated. In addition, there was considerable national publicity, including a feature news story in the *New York Times*.

This extensive local and national publicity brought hundreds of additional inquiries from around the country about the outreach program. We supplied these individuals and groups with educational and organizational materials. Over the next 2 years, an additional 200 communities participated in the program, again, about half the number from which we received individual inquiries.

Low Response and Weak Follow-Up

The first U.S. community to receive a Soviet response was Eureka, Montana, a small city near Glacier National Park in northwestern Montana. The town received a package of letters, local postcards, photos, and children's artwork from Rebrikha, a Soviet city of similar size in central Siberia. This first response led CBS Evening News to do a feature story on the Pairing Project and the Eureka-Rebrikha connection. Over the next 2 years, some 65 U.S. cities would receive responses from Soviet cities, representing about an 8% response rate.

The packages sent by the Soviet cities were generally mirror images of what had been sent over and were similar to that received by Eureka, Montana. Some represented very ambitious undertakings, especially in the area of children's art. Two cities, Eau Claire, Wisconsin, and Portland, Oregon, received a substantial collection of children's art of high quality which then became travelling exhibits in their states. In the case of Portland, the exhibit has hung in the City Hall, the state capitol rotunda, and in numerous schools, churches, and libraries.

Despite its best efforts, the Pairing Project was unable to sustain its citizen diplomacy program. The low response rate deterred new participants, and even in those communities that did receive a response, follow-up outreach efforts were limited. At the end of 1987, it was estimated that only 10 of the original 65 communities that had received packages from Soviet cities had maintained an active local program and contacts with their Soviet communities.

The Decline of the Ground Zero Pairing Project

The Pairing Project also faced severe problems in dealing with Soviet exchange organizations, brought on partly by the reticent Soviet response to the aggressiveness of the Pairing Project program. Another deterrent to success was the systematic effort by a major U.S.-based pro-Soviet organization to portray the Pairing Project as a front for U.S. intelligence agencies. Despite numerous trips to Moscow by Pairing Project personnel and local groups, we were unable to persuade Soviet authorities of the nonpartisan, nonconspiratorial, and nongovernmental goals of the organization. As a result, association with the Pairing Project became a handicap for local communities soliciting the assistance of Moscow-based Soviet exchange organizations—the Soviet Friendship Society and its key elements, the USSR-USA Society and the Association for Relations between Soviet and Foreign Cities.

There is an important lesson here for those whose entrepreneurial spirit would lead them to organize their own citizen diplomacy groups and programs. Enthusiasm, risk-taking, and innovation—characteristics long rewarded in the United States—can be genuine liabilities when dealing with the Soviet Union. Citizen diplomacy *is* diplomacy, and entrepreneurship is not a characteristic of that profession.

The Pairing Project's hope to be the leading, if not the umbrella, organization for city-to-city citizen diplomacy efforts was further damaged by the emergence of competitors for this role. Most prominent was Sister Cities International, the quasi-official U.S. organization that handles all other pairings of U.S. and Soviet cities. In addition, there was a handful of other organizations who sought to exploit the opening left by the Pairing Project's difficulties. These problems are summarized in Appendix B.

Problems with other peacemaking organizations were an unexpected part of the Pairing Project environment. Whereas we had expected our greatest political threat to come from conservative, pro-military organizations, they were a minor problem. Organizations on the far left and liberal groups who sought to displace us at the head of the movement proved to have a far more negative impact on our operations. The head of one far-left organization wrote a review of our Soviet primer entitled, "With friends like this, who needs enemies?" We would echo that sentiment.

CONCLUSION

Current Status of the Project and Some Lessons for Would-Be Social Movement Entrepreneurs

Since 1987, Sister Cities has been in virtual control of all U.S.-Soviet city-to-city linkages. Dozens more cities had been added to the original five pairings established in the mid-1970s: half of them had originally come into being as part of the Ground Zero Pairing Project. However, pairings were restricted to cities with population over 100,000, leaving all other cities to fend for themselves with no assistance from any other organization. Those other organizations which had sought to displace the Pairing Project as the lead organization in city-to-city citizen diplomacy were left with a "cheerleading" role, promoting the concept while lobbying for the expansion to smaller cities. Pairing smaller cities was an idea which the Soviets resisted because of the limited capital resources for travel available to Soviet cities and their citizens.

Certainly the Pairing Project could take considerable credit for and satisfaction in its leading role in promoting citizen diplomacy and its pioneering city-to-city program. Still, it found that this entrepreneurial role left it on the sidelines when the city-to-city program began to achieve legitimacy and be supported by more established groups in the United States and the Soviet Union. In the process, the Pairing Project's overriding hope—that of using city-to-city pairings as a framework for education about the fundamental divisions between the two countries, the risks of horrendous death, the various arms control efforts to minimize the risk of its occurrence, and the general concern for greater mutual understanding—has taken a back seat to superficial exchanges typical of casual tourist encounters anywhere in the world. Whether current citizen diplomacy efforts can be linked to more fundamental concerns in the future remains a speculative matter on which opinions within the citizen diplomacy community vary widely.

On a personal level, as an entrepreneur in this area, I have mixed feelings. I felt I had done just about all that I could to deal with the personal anxiety which the threat of horrendous death in nuclear war had created. Like most individuals in the position of starting a movement, I felt gratified at having provided a mechanism for others like me to do what they could at a personal and community level, not only to deal with their anxiety but to make a positive contribution to a solution.

I remain somewhat pessimistic about the potential of those organizations which have succeeded us to have any fundamental impact on the root problem in U.S.-Soviet tensions. They seem almost universally unwilling to address the fundamental issues that have divided the United States and Soviet Union over the past 17 years, and still divide us in many ways today. However, I do not rule out the possibility that they, too, will be succeeded by more politically attuned organizations and leaders who will cut to the core of the issues which divide the United States and the Soviet Union while pursuing citizen diplomacy tied to community, professional, and avocational interests.

The key to the future of citizen diplomacy remains in the Soviet Union, however, not in the United States. Until the Soviet Union demonstrates a willingness to accept some of the problems in opening up its organizations, communities, and homes to American citizen diplomats, citizen diplomacy will always fall far short of its full potential. Secretary Gorbachev's *glasnost* has started down this path, but there is still a long distance to go.

In February 1988 a group of over 100 Soviet citizens arrived in the United States to participate in a commemoration of the 30th anniversary of the first cultural exchange agreement. For the first time, Soviet citizens were being permitted to stay in the homes of American citizens without the usual tight controls imposed on Soviet travellers to the United States. This is perhaps the most dramatic development yet in the annals of citizen diplomacy. Not only should it open up more doors in the Soviet Union to American citizen diplomats, but it opens up the opportunity for Americans and Soviets to act in new and inspired ways to deal with their fears as they confront the possibility of horrendous death from nuclear war.

APPENDIX A: OPERATIONAL GOALS AND STRATEGIES OF THE CITIZEN DIPLOMACY MOVEMENT WITH RESPECT TO VARIOUS TARGET AUDIENCES

U.S. Peace Activism

Primary Goal

To channel the energy, frustration, concern, and knowledge base of the antinuclear-war movement toward citizen diplomacy by presenting the possibility that an "end run" around the U.S. and Soviet governments was not only possible but also desirable.

Secondary Goals

1. To provide an alternative to arms-control based activities, (e.g., the Freeze campaign).
2. To provide a more relaxing and pleasant activity in which activists could keep a hand in a less strenuous activity while recuperating for a return to the political trenches.
3. To demonstrate that the antinuclear-war movement has staying power and can survive various policy defeats at the hands of any administration.
4. To educate antinuclear activists on the Soviet Union so as to answer the "What About the Russians?" challenge.
5. To educate antinuclear activists about Soviet perspectives (e.g., on verification and Star Wars) vis-à-vis U.S.-Soviet relations so as to better devise strategies for promoting arms control.
6. To provide a holding action for the antinuclear-war movement until such time as a hostile administration and policymakers have either altered their policy or are out of office.

Strategies

1. To actively promote educational materials and programs on the Soviet Union and U.S.-Soviet relations to antinuclear-war organizations and activists, emphasizing the tie-in with the antinuclear-war movement and its goal.
2. To offer citizen diplomacy programs and activities to the antinuclear-war movement to highlight the desirability and ease of bridge-building to the Soviet Union—the essence and symbolism of the Ground Zero Pairing Project's inaugural "Make the First Strike a Knock on the Door" program.

U.S. Citizens

Primary Goal

To convert enough U.S. citizens, organizations, and communities to the idea of citizen diplomacy that it would form a self-augmenting social movement for bridge-building between the people of the United States and Soviet Union.

Secondary Goals

1. To develop a better understanding in the United States of the Soviet Union and its people.
2. To develop a better public understanding of Soviet perspectives on U.S.-Soviet relations.
3. To "de-demonize" the Soviet Union.
4. To put a human face on the "Russians."
5. To persuade the U.S. public that its views on the Soviet Union and U.S.-Soviet relations are important to politicians and experts.
6. To persuade U.S. citizens to articulate actively their views to elected officials.
7. To persuade U.S. citizens to continue attentiveness and self-education on the Soviet Union and U.S.-Soviet relations.

Strategies

1. To promote citizen involvement in bridge-building activities.
2. To offer educational programs and materials on the Soviet Union and U.S.-Soviet relations.
3. To present opportunities for travel to the Soviet Union and meetings with Soviet citizens.
4. To emphasize nonpartisanship so as to garner a broad base of public support, including local elected officials and traditionally nonpartisan organizations.
5. To use names emphasizing world community (e.g., "Fellowship of Reconciliation") and the common threat (e.g., "Ground Zero Pairing Project").
6. To present a positive image of the future in which the United States and Soviet Union live together on the same planet, if not harmoniously then at least without the threat of nuclear war.

Sovietologists and National Security Experts in the U.S.

Primary Goal

To neutralize those experts with a traditionally distrustful posture toward the Soviet Union and stimulate those with a more moderate view toward the Soviet Union to speak out more vigorously.

Strategy

To catalyze and then draw significant attention to a broad-based social movement for better U.S.-Soviet relations.

U.S. Policymakers

Primary Goal

To persuade U.S. policymakers up to and including the president to reexamine existing policy vis-à-vis the Soviet Union, especially as it relates to national security and nuclear war.

Secondary Goals

1. To persuade policymakers that the U.S. public no longer supports the traditional approaches to the Soviet Union and U.S.-Soviet relations.
2. To provide a buffer against entrenched paranoia about Soviet intentions among some U.S. policymakers.
3. To persuade U.S. policymakers that mutually verifiable nuclear arms control and reduction with the Soviet Union are both possible and desirable.
4. To persuade U.S. policymakers that the U.S. public does not support launching nuclear weapons.

Strategies

1. To create a groundswell of public support for cooperation rather than confrontation in U.S.-Soviet relations.
2. To create an educated public that is sufficiently informed about the Soviet Union and U.S.-Soviet relations to not accept overly-simplistic characterizations of Soviet goals and problems in the relationship.
3. To create an interest group among peace activists advocating improved relations with the Soviet Union.

Soviet Americanologists and Exchange Organizations

Organizations in this category would include Soviet Embassy and Consulate personnel; Soviet Friendship Society; USA Institute; Soviet Academy of Sciences; Soviet Peace Committee; other Soviet committees charged with international relations (e.g., Soviet Womens Committee); Soviet cultural institutions; Soviet writers, artists, and intellectuals; Soviet media (e.g., *Pravda, Izvestia,* and electronic media such as *Gostelradio;* Intourist.

Primary Goal

To encourage Soviet institutions to expand their exchange activities and offer special assistance to U.S. citizens wishing to establish contacts with their Soviet counterparts.

Secondary Goals

1. To provide a U.S. grass-roots perspective on the Soviet Union and U.S.-Soviet relations
2. To encourage representatives of these institutions to lobby Soviet policy-

makers for a more cooperative rather than confrontational approach to U.S.-Soviet relations.

3. To convert professional staff in these organizations into active lobbyists for citizen diplomacy within the Soviet system.

4. To demonstrate U.S. grass-roots interests in improved U.S.-Soviet relations and exchanges.

Strategies

1. To encourage representatives of U.S. organizations to visit Moscow.
2. To demonstrate workable citizen diplomacy programs.
3. To demonstrate the media potential of city-to-city diplomacy.
4. To emphasize the complementarity between citizen diplomacy and the official goals of the respective Soviet organizations.
5. To assure Soviet officials that citizen diplomacy programs are not a front for espionage or any other threat to the Soviet system and thus are no threat to them professionally or to their organizations.

Soviet Citizens

Primary Goal

To persuade Soviet citizens to open themselves to the overtures of U.S. citizens who are trying to bridge the gap between the two countries.

Secondary Goals

1. To extend a hand of friendship to the Soviet people.
2. To educate Soviet citizens about the U.S. and U.S. perspectives on U.S.-Soviet relations.
3. To encourage Soviet citizens to articulate their views to Soviet policymakers.
4. To persuade Soviet citizens, communities, and organizations to lobby Soviet exchange officials and local Party officials for expanded contact with U.S. counterparts.

Strategies

1. To proffer city-to-city pairings and other forms of ongoing exchanges.
2. To arrange delegation visits from U.S. citizens.
3. To initiate letters and other forms of communication from U.S. communities and citizens.

Soviet Policymakers

Primary Goal

To persuade Soviet policymakers that citizen diplomacy is in the national interest of the Soviet Union.

Secondary Goals

1. To persuade Soviet policymakers of the U.S. public's earnest support for peace and nonconfrontational relations with the Soviet Union.
2. To discourage Soviets from any decision to launch nuclear weapons against the United States.
3. To persuade Soviet policymakers to adopt a cooperative, not confrontational, approach to relations with the U.S.
4. To persuade Soviet policymakers to share in the effort for controlling and reducing levels of nuclear arms.

Strategies

1. To stimulate a more positive posture toward the Soviet Union on the part of the U.S. government through the Citizen Diplomacy movement in the U.S.
2. To galvanize U.S. citizen diplomats who will persuade the Soviet public of the U.S. interest in cooperative relations and world peace.
3. To structure positive citizen diplomacy experiences for the Soviet public, who will hopefully then press for a more cooperative posture by its government toward the U.S.

APPENDIX B: IMPEDIMENTS TO DEVELOPMENT OF A WORKING RELATIONSHIP BETWEEN THE SOVIET FRIENDSHIP SOCIETY AND THE GROUND ZERO PAIRING PROJECT

Characteristics of Earl Molander, GZPP Founder and Executive Director, and the Ground Zero Pairing Project

1. The perception that GZPP was a one-man show.
2. The fact that the director had not participated in peace-related activities prior to 1982.
3. The director's position as a professor of business administration at Portland State University, an unlikely place to find a successful grass-roots organizer in the peace movement.
4. Soviet suspicion that the director might be connected to U.S. intelligence agencies through his brother Roger, whose career included employment in the Defense Department and on the National Security Council staff.
5. The director's authorship of *What about the Russians—and Nuclear War?*, a book seen as misrepresenting the Soviet Union, thereby preventing more informed and enlightened views of the Soviet Union from reaching the American people.
6. The director's persistence, including multiple trips to Moscow and to the Soviet embassy in Washington, DC.
7. The support for the Pairing Project from a member of the Rockefeller Family.
8. The perception that the director could not be manipulated or controlled.
9. The declared nonpartisan approach of the Pairing Project.

Characteristics of the GZPP "First Strike" Program

1. Soviet distaste for the aggressiveness of the "First Strike" name.
2. The dramatic success of the "First Strike" program—800 cities participating—which suggested that the organization had considerably more funding and other forms of support than it claimed.
3. The basement office of the Pairing Project in the director's home.
4. The minimal ($30,000) annual budget for the program.
5. The fact that the program was undertaken unilaterally without the formal support of Soviet exchange agencies.
6. The extensive national media coverage the "First Strike" program received.
7. The fact that some of the community portraits were targeted on Soviet cities that were sensitive for national security reasons.

Characteristics of the Soviet Friendship Society Bureaucracy

1. The Soviet desire to channel the majority of grass-roots contacts through the National Council of American-Soviet Friendship, an organization the Soviets knew well and trusted, thereby to expand its size and legitimacy.
2. The Soviets' declared inability to respond to our initiatives until they received a signal or directive from higher authority, presumably the Foreign Ministry, to change existing policy and procedures.
3. The shortage of staff and funding for Soviet exchange organizations. The USSR-USA Society has only two professional employees, and the Association for Relations between Soviet and Foreign Cities only three or four. As a result, the magnitude of the Pairing Project initiative overwhelmed them.
4. Desire to avoid political risk among Friendship Society bureaucrats, especially once questions had been raised about the origins and goals of the Pairing Project.
5. Resurfacing of long-standing distrust of U.S. initiatives in U.S.-Soviet relations.
6. The Soviet desire to deal only with official or quasi-official organizations in the U.S., such as Sister Cities International, or organizations they knew, such as the National Council of American-Soviet Friendship and the Citizens Exchange Council.
7. The Soviet desire to avoid agreements or activities where details were not clear and thoroughly worked out.
8. The limited hard currency resources of Soviet cities, making travel for Soviet delegations to the U.S. difficult.
9. Soviet insistence on pairings built on delegation exchanges, in contrast to the Pairing Project's desire to build pairings primarily by letter.

11

From Theory to Practice: The Adult Health and Development Program and Theories of Children's Love and Peace Behaviors

Daniel Leviton
University of Maryland, College Park

Action toward eliminating horrendous-type deaths while increasing lifegenic factors is an individual matter. This chapter describes two examples of action *developed by the author that he deems appropriate for other like-minded university professors. The first is an intergenerational health and well-being program in which play, physical activity, and health education are used as both a means to bring people together in common effort and to eliminate stereotypes and labels.*

The second is a more formal academic course in which the goal is to teach the art and science of love and peace behaviors to actual and potential parents and teachers. The rationale is that no formal or informal education is required for parenthood, allowing any one, no matter how ill-qualified, to become a parent. Therefore education helpful to rearing children so that they get on well with one another has health and survival value.

INTRODUCTION

In the Introduction to this book, we established that anyone who wants to live long and well—and to secure that safety for family and friends—needs to act to improve the quality of global health by eliminating horrendous-type deaths while increasing lifegenic factors. As other chapters have indicated, such action needs to be perceived as effective, and it needs to be suited to the individual or group. In this chapter the purpose is to describe two academic courses I have developed. They are appropriate to my role as a professional health educator and they satisfy my desire to transform the theory of horrendous-death prevention into action. Both courses resulted from the study of thanatology in general and the threat of horrendous death in particular.

THE ADULT HEALTH AND DEVELOPMENT PROGRAM

The Adult Health and Development Program (AHDP) began in 1972. Its development was motivated by two factors: first, the desire to extend to the general population the theory and methods of the Children's Health & Developmental clinic begun some 35 years ago by the late Professor Warren R. Johnson at the University of Maryland. After working in that clinic for 7 years, it became obvious to me that other populations, such as university students and the elderly, could benefit from modifications of Johnson's approach.

A second motivation derived from my involvement in the field of thanatology. That is, if the elimination of horrendous-type death is the highest global priority, then anything that allows us to see one another as friendly human beings would serve us well. If this is true, there is a need to study and apply the art and science of getting on well with other people. The AHDP provides such a model.

Goals

The goals of the AHDP are:

1. to affect positively the health, sense of well-being, physical fitness, and health knowledge status of the older adult;
2. to allow students and other staffers to learn about aging, old age, history, and different cultures in our particular environment; and
3. to have the AHDP serve as a catalyst for integrating various ages, ethnic groups, and members of the University of Maryland and the community (including the private sector) to work toward the common purpose of the first two goals.

Nature of the AHDP

Members and Staffers

In the spring of the 1989 semester, there were approximately 70 older adults ("members") and 85 university students and others ("staffers"). Among the latter were two high school students and three over-50 adults who volunteered their services. The average age of the members was approximately 68 years; ages ranged from 48 to 94 years. Ten members were residents in a Veterans Administration (VA) nursing home; 15 were Hispanic elderly from the community (matched with Spanish-speaking staffers), and the remainder were non-Hispanic members from the community. In 1990, 15 persons with developmental disabilities were welcomed into the program. About 33% of the members had been in the AHDP for eight semesters and one had been in the program for 13 years.

It terms of health status, about 33% of members were classified as being at a high level of health and physical fitness, while others suffered from a variety of symptomatic conditions including sensory deficits, obesity, arthritis, Parkinson's disease, Alzheimer's disease, and depression. Others were recovering from bypass surgery, experiencing psychological and emotional distress due to death of a spouse or the "empty nest" syndrome, and so forth. Most of the VA members were wheelchair-bound due to single- or multiple-limb amputation.

About 70 of the staffers were enrolled in the AHDP for academic credit; 15 were volunteers. The average length of stay for senior staffers in the AHDP is 10 semesters (one has served for 19 semesters). Many staffers become motivated to devote their professional and/or advocacy life to gerontology or geriatrics. Student-staffers come from such diverse academic fields as human development, psychology, health education, therapeutic recreation, physical education, physics, law enforcement, business administration, journalism, and public relations.

The average age of staffers was about 24 years. Two in 1989 were over age 60 years and two were 16 years old (specially selected high school students).

The integration of a heterogeneous staff and members is intentional, as it contributes to the notion that young and old can learn much from and be helpful to one another. Also, working toward a common purpose in a supportive environment is the basis for developing peaceful relations between individuals, groups, and I believe, nation states.

Keys

The four keys to the AHDP are:

1. The unique use of exercise, play, sport, recreational activities, and fun as a means to improving physical fitness, body image, self-concept, perceived health and well-being, perceived control over one's own health, and the development of friendship between staffers and members.

2. The special bond that develops between paired staffers and members as they engage in exercise, other activities, and learning. Because of the nonthreatening and supportive environment within the AHDP, the staffer serves as a coach and friend to the member. In turn, the member may be helpful to the staffer in resolving some of his or her problems. Also, the member may serve as a teacher of history (our members have *experienced* historical events such as World War I and II, and the Great Depression, which are only concepts to younger staffers). Finally, staffers have the opportunity to learn about different cultures and languages.

3. The systematic education and training of staffers.

4. The practice of honoring the wishes and expressed needs of the member rather than telling him or her what is "best."

Schedule

The AHDP meets for nine Saturdays each semester from 8:00 a.m. to 1:00 p.m. The first half hour is concerned with Group Leaders' Training. Group leaders are experienced staffers who have shown leadership and teaching abilities. They meet on Saturdays and during the week to plan the events for the day and subsequent weeks, monitor the progress of both staffers and members, deal with problems, and think of ways to improve the program.

Training

Staff training is the *sine qua non* of the AHDP's success. It runs from 8:30 to 9:30 a.m. and, at the end of the morning from noon to 1:00 p.m. Topics include: AHDP theory and philosophy; the AHDP coaching model; psychosocial stress theory; empathy exercises; safety; physical fitness, health and aging; organic brain syndrome; working with the wheelchair-bound individual; motivation of the AHDP member and staffer; preparing for the end of the semester's program; disengagement; intimacy and sexuality; and drug interactions and side effects. As the senior staffers gain in experience they increasingly conduct training. Training involves both the dissemination of knowledge and processing. Concerning the latter, it is important for staffers (and members) to express their feelings, anxieties, fears, and frustrations. After 17 years we are able to assuage concerns and show

that a member is making progress often without the novice staffer being aware of
it.

Staffers are trained to follow our *ACAEM* paradigm:

• Assessment: Staffers make an assessment of the member's physical and medical fitness as well as their psychosocial health status.

• Creativity: A plan consisting of physical activity, health education, and
friendship is designed to meet needs identified under the assessment. The plan is
always designed in collaboration with the member. (We also train to prevent coercion and patronizing behavior).

• Action: The member-staffer couple engages in the activities mutually agreed
upon.

• Evaluation: The staffer evaluates results. Did the member enjoy the activity?
Was there any progress or potential for progress? If the activities were not well
received, how might they be modified?

• Modification: The results of evaluation are then incorporated into the plan of
action, and the process begins anew.

A Typical Day

At 9:30 a.m. the members arrive and are met by their staffers. From 9:30 to
11:00 is the activity hour: the member and staffer engage in activities including
walking, bowling, swimming, jogging, square-dancing, aerobics, yoga, singing,
t'ai chi, games, sports, resistance exercise, and so forth. Because *fun*, in itself, is
therapeutic and worthwhile, the ambience is one of smiles, laughter, joy, and
affection. This happens because of the nonthreatening and spontaneous nature of
play and noncoercive learning. A 70-year-old member from El Salvador or Puerto
Rico may walk down the corridor with his or her bilingual staffer for a workout on
the stationary bicycle or the Universal Gym, or may join in the popular square-
dancing, exercise, t'ai chi or yoga sessions. The staffer might be a medical student, a law-enforcement major, or language major receiving some informal lessons
in conversational Spanish while learning of the members' life and home in Latin
America.

Health Education

Because *preventive intervention* is an important aspect of the AHDP, a health-
education hour is conducted from 11:00 to noon. During this time topics such as
coping with stress, physical fitness, prevention of osteoporosis, grief and bereavement, the intelligent use of medications, medical problems, and others of interest
are discussed by experts in each respective field.

Every semester the topic of global health and well-being is discussed in an
intergenerational format. Since most of the members are grandparents, they have a
special interest in insuring that their children and grandchildren live long and well.
Again, the emphasis is on action. Many members already belong to the Gray
Panthers and other groups devoted to the improvement of global health as defined
in the Introduction to this volume. Others want concrete suggestions of what do to.

Several members and a few staffers are refugees from oppressive regimes, war, or terrorism in Latin America, the Middle East, or Asia. One of our staffers was a "boat person." During her escape from Vietnam with 80 persons crowded on a small boat, the boat was overtaken by pirates. Her sister was raped and killed before her eyes. She was spared because she was deathly ill and hid unnoticed.

With older individuals one doesn't always have to resort to mental imagery of a beloved child or grandchild being napalmed to death. Many have lived through World War I with its gas and trenches; the Great Depression with its breadlines and unemployment; or World War II with the Holocaust, perhaps the most infamous of all crimes against society. I find older adults to be the most receptive of audiences. They ask, "What can I do?" and then do it!

We also have other intergenerational discussions. "What was it like growing up when you were a child?" is a favorite question of the staffers. We learn a great deal from all of the participants, but especially from those members who have suffered persecution or prejudice.

When student-staffers and members are given an opportunity to evaluate the AHDP and asked what aspect of the health education discussions are most enjoyable, they always list the intergenerational discussions first.

Special Events

Often a special event such as Hispanic Day or the AHDP version of the Olympics will be held. In the enjoyable and friendly ambience, members and staff eat together, either in a party or dining situation. During Hispanic Day, fried chicken is purchased from a local restaurant to supplement the home-cooked Mexican, Spanish, or Cuban food brought in by members and staff. Special events, meals, aquatic activities, and "new games" (Fluegelman, 1976) are excellent means for integrating our heterogeneous group, because everyone can participate regardless of impairment or age.

Follow-up

At the end of the day staffers escort members to their vehicles while recapitulating the day's events, progress made, and plans for the next week. Staffers contact "their" members during the week by telephone or in-person visits.

Of course, planning goes on during the week and during those times when the AHDP is not in session. The time and energy staffers devote to the program are quite amazing.

Vignettes

Learning About Dignity

A graduate student-staffer and I once visited a dignified Black woman in her 70s who was respected, along with her husband, by everyone in the AHDP. Her husband had died and we wanted to share our grief with Mrs. H. We talked of Mr. H. and how much he had meant to us and the hundreds with whom he had come in contact in the AHDP. He had been a physics major as a young man in college. When the Great Depression came, he was unable, as a Black physicist to find a job. So he became a vaudeville pianist and a barber.

His wife, Mrs. H., then told us what it was like for her growing up in the South. There were tales of "Jim Crow" and the Ku Klux Klan. There was the story of the White woman who took a liking to Mrs. H., then a feisty, obviously intelligent, young girl of 15, and told her, "I will teach you what I know as a beautician . . . I think you have a talent." So Mrs. H. was trained, and eventually came to work in her patron's shop, which was, of course, segregated. That kind lady lost some customers but she stood by Mrs. H. There were tears in Mrs. H.'s eyes as she told her story. My graduate student and I learned a lot. Later, I asked Mrs. H. if she would tell our entire AHDP group her story. She did. Students, staffers, members, and other learned of the indignity of racism. It was obvious that those listening suffered vicariously the humiliation Mrs. H. had suffered so many years ago. On the one hand, we were ashamed as members of the human race. On the other, we were heartened by the strength and resiliency shown by Mrs. H. If she could overcome, so could we.

Live and Let Live

One gentleman who came to the AHDP for years was a habitual smoker. We allowed this habit, and simply requested that he be considerate of the sensitivity of others to tobacco smoke. Why did we act this way? This man was a veteran of World War II, a paraplegic living in a VA Medical Care Facility. Smoking was one of his pleasures. He knew it was bad for his health—but it relaxed him. He had done "cures" before but he loved his cigarettes. Should we have added stress to his life by harping on his smoking? This man, old enough to be my father, had made a conscious decision to smoke. We learn *not* to be health dogmatists in the AHDP. We learn to respect that most profound of all behavioral concepts—individuality and human variation. Live and let live is our motto. On the other hand, many of our staff and members dislike tobacco smoke. Also, the University of Maryland has a policy forbidding smoking in classrooms and other closed areas. We find that smokers are quite willing to hold their pleasure until they are in a proper environment. Many of our members give up smoking while in the program. Whether the effect is long-lasting is unknown.

The Deaths of Staffers

The death of the young is always an abomination, intolerable to the senses. It is one thing to die in old age, but it is another to die in youth. Several of our staffers have died or been killed. One, a Vietnam veteran who served as an advocate for the VA group, had a host of pathological conditions that he attributed to the effects of Agent Orange. When he appealed his case to the government they denied that his ill health was their responsibility. He died before the age of 40. All of the members were shocked and numbed by the announcement of Bob's death. Having medical problems is one thing, dying is another. Many were angry at the U.S. Government for avoiding its responsibility for Bob's illness. Others were saddened that he hadn't had the chance to marry and raise a family. He had wanted children in the worst way. Many members and staffers went to his funeral. We gathered afterwards and talked a long time about Bob. Nearly every semester someone remembers an anecdote about him: his good nature, his ideas and leadership, his genuine affection for people, and his ability to barbecue the most succulent ribs around.

Meaning to Life

Mr. R. was a White, middle-class, retired man who came to the program after being forcibly retired. His children were grown, and had their own careers and families thousands of miles away. Mr. R.'s relations with his wife were anything but ideal. By his own admission, during our training he had been suicidal. The reasons given by Mr. R. for his remaining involved with the AHDP for more than 10 years was that it provided him with something to live for—a meaning to his life. Certainly the bond he developed with his staffers over the years was primary. He knew he was being helpful to them by giving solid advice on a host of problems. He did not come to the program for exercise or physical activity, but for the social and educational benefits. He enjoyed the give-and-take of the health-education hours, especially the intergenerational dialogue.

The VA patients who come to the AHDP are living examples of the cost of war. Many are amputees or have other war-related injuries. Ruth Frank, a nurse who sacrifices her Saturdays to bring the vets to the AHDP, said,

> We have people who don't want to be discharged because they'll miss their Saturday at the Program. Many of them have no one left. These young people add a lot of spark and enthusiasm to their lives. The Veterans just blossom. They've been out, met somebody new, and have a new friend who cares about them. They now have a reason for living ("One-on-one for fitness, friendship," 1989, p. 3).

Touching

Affectionate touching seems to be necessary to the healthy development of infant and young animals and humans (Harlow, Gluck, & Suomi, 1972; Harlow, 1974; Montague, 1986). I think it is developmental necessity for all ages. Too often the older adult is bereft of such contact due to lack of a mate, children, or friends. While many enjoy hugging a child, and everyone else enjoys hugging a sexually attractive, youthful individual, the older adult is often perceived as physically displeasing. By and large, in the United States, beauty and youth are often equated while old age, with its decrepitude, decay, and dependency, reminds one of the approaching, inevitable process of old age and dying.

Western society generally does not sanction many situations allowing the exchange of affectionate touching between the older adult and others. Same-sex expressions of affectionate touching are approved most often in greetings and goodbyes, and during and after athletic contests (take as an example the predictable pat on the fanny by a coach when an athlete leaves a contest). Most adults over age 50 are no longer members of organized athletic teams. Thus the older adult is bereft of affectionate touching because of the lack of appropriate social situations or any people with whom to exchange such contact.

Playful activity may offer opportunities for nonthreatening, fun physical contact. Square dancing, trampolining, and swimming all involve skin contact.

When one member, years ago, came to the program, she would not communicate verbally. (Never mind the psychiatric label: We tend to ignore them and focus, instead, on the problem.) One day her staffer enticed her to get on the trampoline. The staffer suggested that the member simply bend her knees and sway. A novice on a trampoline immediately feels off balance, so the member threw her hands out for support and the member grasped the hands of her staffer. The member visibly relaxed. Then the two gently swayed in unison while holding hands. Soon the two were jumping together to a height of about one foot. Never having done anything like this before, the member was smiling and excited. When she eventually dismounted she calmly said to the staffer, "Can we get a drink of water?" It was the first time she had spoken in years. I think the combination of trust and skin contact, that is, affection, prompted the great change in communication. The effect of this exchange on both the member and staffer was the growth of affection and admiration between them.

The ambience of the program reinforces the expression of affection whether one is in a wheelchair or not, attractive or less so. Staffers and members get into the relaxed, fun mood of the program. As a side note, in our training staffers are told to do what is natural for them. If they do not feel comfortable with such affectionate gestures early in the program they wait until they do. Similarly, with our members, we ask them if they prefer being called by their first name or last. If holding hands or hugs are disliked by the member, the staffer refrains. Yet affectionate touching is generally perceived by both members and staffers as pleasurable and desirable.

Fund-Raising Activities

The AHDP is self-supporting, raising funds by charging a fee for services ($50 per semester). However, no one is ever turned away for lack of funds. We also developed Camp Rediscovery, a health and well-being camp for the adult age 50 and older. A percentage of profits from the camp is returned to the AHDP.

Research and Evaluation

Each semester the AHDP is evaluated by staffers and members. In one study, over 80% of the members rated themselves as high or very high in health, sense of well-being, physical fitness, social relations, and health knowledge *as a result of participating in the program*. More than 85% of the members very much looked forward to the program the following semester, and most strongly agreed or agreed that the program contributed to their sense of happiness (94%) and well-being (84%) (Leviton & Santa Maria, 1979).

Fretz (1979) examined the effect of the AHDP and its sister program, the Children's Health and Developmental Clinic (CHDC) on the personal development of staffers; Fretz also compared their characteristics with those of staffers who dropped out of training and a control group (matched by sex and age). Results indicated that there were few differences between the two groups of staffers who remained in their respective programs. Both groups of staffers' modal responses indicated that they were more (a) tolerant with people in general, (b) relaxed with people, and (c) accepting of other peoples' problems.

When compared to a control group, those participating in the AHDP showed significantly greater increases in inner-directedness, spontaneity, and self-acceptance. Those participating in the CHDC showed no significantly greater change than control groups. These characteristics are similar to those associated with what Abraham Maslow called *self-actualization* (Maslow, 1968).

Both formative and summative research has been conducted by graduate students with the recommendation that although the AHDP fits no theory of voluntary organizations, it works well (Cook, 1986; Dixon, 1989). Staffers are motivated beyond what is usually found in essentially volunteer organizations. They support one another, insuring that the AHDP accomplishes its mission, and the staffers are very protective of the AHDP.

Dixon (1989) compared AHDP staffers enrolled for credit to students enrolled in other health-education classes. No pretest differences between groups existed on variables of age, gender, religion, term in school, volunteerism history, self-health ratings, ethnicity, marital status, and family income, or by initial tests of health attitudes, health behaviors, or perceived value of kindness. Process evaluations confirmed that the AHDP group experienced successful, caregiving health experiences, and that these experiences were not reproduced for control groups. Statistical analysis of changes in health behaviors and attitudes showed slight, but not significantly higher, gains for AHDP staffers than for control groups over a 9-week period. Using anecdotal data, treatment group students were more likely to express altruistic and social motivations for enrolling in the AHDP and to attribute classroom success to altruistic and social factors. Dixon's conclusion, similar to Cook's, was "that the AHDP works but the mechanism for its success remains unknown." Dixon concluded, "I don't know what it is about the class that is special. There doesn't appear to be anything special about the students who come to the program, nor is the effect of the program on student participants' health attitudes and practices outstanding. Nevertheless, qualitative data and personal experience support the notion that there *is* something special about HLTH 487 [AHDP] as an educational experience. The something 'special' has yet to be positively identified, or quantified in a substantial way" (1989, p. 102).

Farber (1983) was interested in determining whether the AHDP had a positive effect on reducing depression among Hispanic members. Using a randomized control experimental design, he found both a significant decrease in depression and an increase in morale.

CAMP REDISCOVERY

In 1983, Camp Rediscovery (formerly Camp AHDP), the first health and well-being camp designed specifically for the adult age 50 and older, was opened. Several camps have been conducted, and the health and well-being camp/resort model is envisioned as a means of earning funds to partially fund the campus and other AHDPs that may develop as part of a nationwide network. Evaluations are positive and alumni of the camp continue to return. The AHDP and Camp Rediscovery are seen as two sides of the same coin. Camp Rediscovery extended the theory and methods of the AHDP to the camp/resort environment using highly-trained staff to affect positively the health and well-being needs of older adults. Friendships develop along with trust. One sees people varying in age, health, culture, and socioeconomic level become friends who are truly interested in one another's lives and histories.

Send an Older Adult to Camp Project

During late August and early September, 1986, several corporations funded the first "Send an Older Adult to Camp Project." Corporations were asked to contrib-

ute $500 per camper, which paid for a one-week stay, transportation, and provided
$105 for the campus AHDP. The project has been continued because of its poten-
tial for benefiting a high-risk population and also raising funds for the AHDP.

As a result of that project, 21 low-income older adults spent a week at Camp
Rediscovery. Their evaluations were laudatory, but of greater significance was the
positive change in health behavior. Statistically significant improvement was found
in selected physical-fitness variables. Campers reported, "We don't have to eat
and watch television all day." Some subsequently enrolled in the University of
Maryland AHDP. Others reported that they have given up smoking, indicating that
the AHDP model has lasting effects on some participants. Other outcomes included people coming to see others as individuals, regardless of racial background
or economic status.

Case History

Learning from One Another

In another camp session, 15 people of low income, along with 10 or so middle-
class individuals, attended. On the first day, a White woman, obviously a member
of the latter group, drove up in her expensive car to the dining hall promptly at
noon for lunch. Her smile, indicative of her expectation of a good time and vaca-
tion, instantaneously changed to a frown when she saw a group, largely consisting
of elderly Black women, chatting amicably with one another. My wife, Susan,
welcomed her warmly and introduced her to her roommates—three other lively,
White, middle-class women.

The camp went very well. Everyone, campers and staffers, shared in such
activities as canoeing, exercise, the prebreakfast and after-dinner walks, square
dancing, a trip to Monticello in Virginia, campfires, sing-a-longs, health-education
hours, and the like. Campers and staffers told of their lives, roasted marshmal-
lows, and ate "s'mores." A close bond developed between staffers and campers,
and among the campers themselves.

During the last evening we had an "amateur" show. As the evening pro-
gressed, the leader of the group of the low-income attendees asked if she could talk
to the group. I handed her the microphone. She said she was not adept at making
speeches, yet she and her friends very much wished to convey their joy to the rest
of us. Would we allow them to entertain us for few minutes? For the next 30
minutes all of us were treated to a concert of Black spirituals beautifully rendered
by this group, whose average age was close to 75 years. It was a beautiful and
poignant moment.

Prior to her return home, the lady in the expensive car, packed and ready to
return, came up to my wife and me. "You know," she said, "I didn't think I would
make it when I first arrived. If you hadn't roomed me with such a wonderful group
of pals I know I would have left. They assuaged my apprehensions and said to give
it a few days. I want you know I've had the best time of my life. You don't know
how much I've learned from everyone, and how much confidence I've gained in
myself." She joined the others as they hugged, kissed, and said goodbye. She
subsequently returned to other camps.

Summative evaluations of campers indicated that more than 85% wished to
return to Camp Rediscovery, and perceived themselves to have benefited in terms

of improved health, sense of well-being, physical fitness, and health knowledge (Alessio & Leviton, 1988).

From a more subjective perspective, campers saw themselves as improved in health, risk-taking ability, and self-efficacy. The latter is the most germane to our topic, for *self-efficacy* refers to the perceived ability to produce results.

CONCLUSION

The AHDP concept is seen as an action approach to improving the quality of individual and global health. With its emphasis on friendship, the saliency of health, reinforcement of self-efficacy, health education, the ecological nature of health, and the need to preserve the quality of the future for children and grandchildren, the AHDP model has national implications. We call this the National Network Plan (NNP).

The NNP would develop cost-effective AHDPs at universities and colleges throughout the country, partially funded by local boards of directors and regional camp resorts run on AHDP principles. Everyone involved would gain. Students and others would be trained to understand health aspects of gerontology. Older adults would be served in an intergenerational, fun-oriented, meaningful environment with the goal of affecting health and well-being in a positive way. The universities would be fulfilling their classic missions of education, service, and research (as well as developing good public relations). Corporations would be involved in an effort to tighten the social fabric of the nation, and possibly the world.

A "building-blocks" approach is envisioned where the basic AHDP and camp/resort units are developed in a locale. Both units could be modified to suit community needs. For example, our first-stage model unit has always served the widowed, the caretakers for the chronically ill, the Hispanic elderly, the institutionalized, and non-Hispanic older adults living in the community. We have served individuals with early-stage Alzheimer's disease, multiple sclerosis, as well as the extremely healthy and vigorous. We have educated staffers from every academic discipline as well as volunteers from the community.

A second stage would develop an interdisciplinary community center for activity, aging, and health, where academic courses would be taught with the AHDP and Camp Rediscovery serving as both clinical focal points and real-world activity centers. As the NNP proliferated, a computer network would enhance the sharing of research and information regarding individual and community health.

A third stage would find the Children's Health and Developmental Clinic concept integrated into the NNP, providing a true intergenerational perspective.

Because of the AHDP's flexible nature, it could provide service, training, and research as community and global needs change. For example, it is obvious that businesspeople, educators, health-care professionals, politicians, and others will need to become increasingly knowledgeable about older adults, and proficient in their interaction with them as the older population grows. The AHDP is a viable, nonclinical, nonjudgmental, democratic way for people of different generations to learn about one another.

The AHDP concept has been presented by means of film and slides to groups in China, Israel, and representatives from Latin America, all of whom have received it well. In 1988 and 1989 the Japanese business community became supportive of the AHDP through financial contributions. (The AHDP is seen as being applicable to Japan with its increasing older population.) Eventually we hope to enroll Japanese students and faculty to be trained in AHDP theory and methods for eventual application in Japan.

The AHDP, used internationally, could have universal appeal that would do much to remove the "ugly American" stereotype, and might serve to bring all people together. That is the dream.

THEORIES OF CHILDREN'S LOVE AND PEACE BEHAVIORS

History and Philosophy

During the fall semester of 1975, I offered a health-education course called "Theories of Children's Love and Peace Behaviors" at the University of Maryland. My rationale was that health education should play a major role in bringing about the revolutionary change and adaptation necessary for survival on this planet. We need to be concerned with the attainment of *civilization*, that is, the condition of having humane laws, customs, and manners of restraints on total war and other destructive behaviors. *Improved human relations and the abolition of war and other destructive behaviors are noble and indeed necessary goals of health education* (Leviton, 1976). The quickest path to the accomplishment of this task is in the education of children, their parents, and teachers.

The overall goal of the course was to study love and peace behaviors in order to increase the probability of future generations becoming more loving and peaceful. The assumption was that the implementation of love and peace within ourselves and toward others has survival value, increases the probability of improved global health, and, therefore, is a health priority.

Practical Examples

One objective was to have students learn about the multidisciplinary subject matter and about practical examples of schools where love and peace behaviors are taught. Examples of the latter were schools modeled after Summerhill (Neill, 1960), selected Montessori schools, and both the Children' s Health and Development Clinic and the Adult Health and Development Program.

We had students ask for permission to observe, for significant lengths of time, families and elementary school classes where the emphasis was on establishing a loving and peaceful climate. Students were asked to analyze how and why such an environment developed. If children learn best through *reinforcement* and *modeling* by parents, peers, and teachers, we asked, what did those influential people do with their children? What were their attitudes and priorities? How much time was spent with their children? How much time was spent in play? How did the family and/or teacher serve as a buffer against the stresses of the outside world? How were love and peace behaviors taught, directly or indirectly, by means of modeling, or by means of reward? What was done to enhance the body image and self-concept of the child? Was the child able to feel, "Hey, I'm a unique and nice person?" Were play and physical education skills emphasized as well as intellectual and social skills? Too often, adults fail to realize the importance of play as a developmental necessity in all higher-level living organisms, especially children (Harlow, Gluck, & Suomi, 1972; Harlow, 1974; Johnson, Johnson, & Johnson, 1978; Sorokin, 1950).

The Subject Matter

The class met weekly for 14 weeks for 2½ hours. I led discussions until students had time to prepare their own research. That occurred by the 5th week. Then the students served as teachers, with the caveat that if the class became bored the "teachers" would forever be doomed to Dante's 14th ring of purgatory. By virtue of the fact that I had tenure, only I was permitted to be a bore. Thus students learned quickly about the abuse of power.

Session 1

During this introductory period terms such as peace, love, health, well-being, and parenting were defined. A *theoretical perspective* based on my version of psychosocial-environmental stress theory was explained. The development of the child into a peaceful, loving person was seen as a function of the influences and stresses he or she was subject to over time. These stresses could be positive (healthy) or negative (unhealthy). Examples of the former are love, play, stimulation, skin contact, and warm and nurturing human interaction.

Examples of the unhealthy stresses that could be direct or indirect were psychological or physical punishment and deprivation of basic needs such as food, clothing, warmth, and shelter. At another level were economic and social stresses and the structure and health of the family, community, nation state, and world. To make the point about negative stress, a headline in the *Washington Post* (February 16, 1989, p. A1) was presented: "13 shot in District [of Columbia] within 24 hours." This sort of community-social-environmental stress has an unhealthy and psychologically stunting affect on children (Rosenblatt, 1983; Townsend, 1980).

Session 2

Fortunately, videotapes, slides, and films are available to describe two programs that act to reinforce loving and peaceful behaviors: the Children's Health & Development Clinic and the Adult Health and Development Program. Students were encouraged to visit the programs to see them in action. The purpose was for students to see for themselves that love and peace theory and data could indeed be put into practice.

Session 3

Attitudes and socially sanctioned behaviors toward children vary historically. In earlier eras, children were seen as having little value until they survived to adolescence. Then they were perceived and expected to behave as "little adults." In Puritan America, they were regularly beaten to "drive out sin." Today, children are seen as developing human beings with special needs and desires (deMause, 1974). Still with all our knowledge, children are often brutalized and victimized worse than in any earlier era.

Session 4

This session was entitled, "The present and future danger in the nuclear age." Using videotapes concerned with the predicted effects of nuclear explosion (see Appendix A, this volume), and other forms of horrendous death, students became sensitized to the reality and actuality of multiple threats and the need for action. Special emphasis was given to the anxieties and fears of children concerning horrendous death from nuclear war.

Session 5

Students began their topical reports. The first concerned the research on children's attitudes toward horrendous death from war, homicide, holocaust, etc. (the student chose the topic). A second report was concerned with the behavior of children who lived in horrendous-death environments or survived forms of horrendous death.

At this point we turned to a positive approach of studying and applying the art and science of developing loving and peaceful relationships. The rationale was that while there are significant horrendous death threats to be eliminated, it is vital to look at the factors related to the development of a loving parent-child bond.

Session 6

This session was concerned with understanding the existing theory relating to love and peace behaviors and their opposites, such as aggression and violence. The works of Freud, Norman O. Brown, Wilhelm Reich, Abraham Maslow, James Prescott, Erik Erikson, and sociobiological theory were discussed and integrated into our special interest.

Session 7

The literature of loving and peaceable families was compared to that of unloving and violent ones.

A second report looked at correlates of love and peace, such as meaningful employment, socioeconomic and marital status, ethnic/racial background, and the like.

Session 8

An entire session was devoted to developmental play as a correlate of loving and peaceful behaviors, building on the pioneering work of Warren R. Johnson, the Founder of the Children's Health and Developmental Clinic (Fretz, 1974; Johnson & Cofer, 1974; Johnson et al., 1978). Play is a means to a child's developing a positive self-concept and appreciation and enjoyment of others. As a child comes to appreciate what he can do in terms of physical play and sports skills, the child comes to like him- or herself. This motor learning is always conducted in an atmosphere of fun in collaboration with the child's "student-clinician." Thus, the clinician, an older person, is perceived as "fun" and not merely the purveyor of rules, discipline, and punishment. I agree with Johnson and Cofer when they write that "play is the earliest and most basic of the infant's spontaneous, nondrive oriented behavior" (Johnson & Cofer, p. 390). Johnson always supported the critical-periods concept in the development of the individual. Among critical periods are the linkage of physical developmental events with subsequent psychosocial behavior (Johnson & Cofer, 1974, p. 392).

After this and other sessions culminated by asking students to teach the class a game or physical activity in which students would succeed and have fun (see Fluegelman, 1976).

Sessions 9 and 10

Because cultural structural factors are related to behavior, student reports focused on the relationship between the teaching and practice of organized *religion* and childrearing.

Two great taboo areas of human behavior for children are childhood sexuality and death. We examined how psychosexual and psychothanatological anxieties relate to the healthy development of people. One of the obvious payoffs was that the students themselves gained insight and felt at home with these taboo topics as they were matter-of-factly discussed in class.

Session 11

We again emphasized *action* by visiting schools which seemed to value the development of loving and peaceful behaviors in their curriculum, and in the selection and training of their teachers. In our area there were two schools which met the criteria and were visited for observation and discussions with teachers. One was based on the Summerhill approach of Neill (1960), and the other was a Montessori school with a particularly fine curriculum.

Sessions 12 and 13

One of the assignments was to interview parents or teachers whom students perceived as valuing loving and peaceful behaviors, according to our criteria. Of great interest was the method of resolving conflicts. It should be mentioned here that as part of nearly every session, students were asked to role-play the resolution of a given conflict.

Evaluations

Anonymous evaluations by students indicated that the materials were a combination of the new and the old, but packaged to give new insights into the profound responsibilities of parenting and teaching. Students also became sensitive to the need to be knowledgeable of and adept in the art and science of conflict resolution. For example, we played a "peace game," which required cooperation between sometimes hostile nuclear powers (the Soviet Union, China, Britain, France, and United States) to prevent another country (Pakistan) from developing its own nuclear weapons. Students gained an appreciation of the perception and anxieties of these countries toward one another. They also learned of the hard work necessary to come to compromise and agreement.

On the individual level, many reported that they never thought there were other approaches to rearing children other than how they were reared. For some it was a revelation that children do not need to be physically or psychologically punished to shape behavior. One afternoon during a repast at my house following the last class of the semester, the students met my children, at that time 5 and 10 years old. "Did you ever spank your kids," my wife and I were asked. "No," was the reply.

Throughout the evening, the kids were in and out of the room, into the food, into the conversation, into everything. At the end of the festivities and the close of the evening, one student, a good friend who had worked in the AHDP for years, remained. As he put on his coat and shook my hand, he good-naturedly commented, "Dan, you should have spanked them once!"

His indirect point was that parenting is hard work. There are times when filicide (child murder) appears quite reasonable. Kids, like anyone, can be a royal pain: inconsiderate, loud, nagging, selfish, cruel, and manipulative. But you keep "coaching" and teaching. Development is the key. Over time the emphasis on love and peace pays off. The little devils become decent adults . . . and there is fun to be had along the way.

My hope is that my children live long enough to be able to say, "I want my kids to live long and well."

REFERENCES

Alessio, H., & Leviton, D. (1988). Effects of health and well-being camp on the elderly. Final Report No. 1 R43 AG05018 01A2). Washington, DC: National Institute of Aging.

Cook, M. (1986). *Adult Health and Development Program: An assessment of organizational structure, channels of communication, and levels of responsibility.* Unpublished management project, University College, University of Maryland, College Park.

deMause, L. (Ed.). (1974). *The history of childhood.* New York: Psychohistory Press.

Dixon, M. (1989). *Successful caregiving experiences: Impact on health attitudes and practices.* Unpublished master's thesis, University of Maryland, College Park.

Faber, M. (1983). *The impact of the University of Maryland Adult Health and Development Program upon the perceived health and well-being of older Hispanic adults.* Unpublished master's thesis. University of Maryland, College Park.

Fluegelman, A. (1976). *The new games book.* Tiburon, CA: Headlands Press.

Fretz, B. (1974). Physical activity and developmental process. In W. Johnson & E. Buskirk (Eds.), *Science and medicine of exercise and sport* (pp. 287–305). New York: Harper & Row.

Fretz, B. (1979). College students and paraprofessionls with children and the aged. *American Journal of Community Psychology, 7,* 357–360.

Harlow, H. (1974). *Learning to love.* New York: Jason Aronson.

Harlow, H., Gluck, J., & Suomi, S. (1972). Generalization of behavioral data between nonhuman and human animals. *American Psychologist, 8,* 709–716.

Johnson, W., & Cofer C. (1974). Personality dynamics: Psychosocial implications. In W. Johnson & E. Burskirk (Eds.), *Science and medicine of exercise and sport* (pp. 379–402). New York: Harper & Row.

Johnson, W., Johnson, J., & Johnson, D. (1978). *A special time for parents and children.* College Park, MD: 3 J Education Enterprises.

Leviton, D. (1976). Education toward love and peace behaviors. *Journal of Clinical Child Psychology, 2,* 14–17.

Leviton, D., & Santa Maria, L. (1979). The Adult Health and Developmental Program: Descriptive and evaluative data. *19,* 534–543.

Maslow, A. (1968). *Toward a psychology of being* (2nd ed.). Princeton, NJ: Van Nostrand.

Montague, A. (1986). *Touching: The human significance of the skin* (3rd ed.). New York: Perennial Library.

Neill, H. (1960). *Summerhill.* New York: Hart.

One-to-one for fitness, friendship. (1989, February 21). *Prince George Journal,* p. 3.

Rosenblatt, R. (1983). *Children of war.* New York: Anchor Press.

Sorokin, P. (1950). *Explorations in altruistic love and behavior.* Boston: Beacon Press.

Townsend, P. (1980). *The smallest pawns.* Boston: Little, Brown.

III

Conclusion

12

Toward Rapid and Significant Action

Daniel Leviton
University of Maryland, College Park

INTRODUCTION

The precursor to this volume, *Horrendous Death, Health, and Well-Being* (Leviton, 1991), established that horrendous deaths, types I and II are deadly, unhealthy, and expensive, but can be eliminated if we put our will to the task.

On the other hand, this volume is concerned with action—what to do now to increase the probability of you and your children living long and well. If you fail to act in your own and loved one's best health interest after reading either or both volumes then the book's purpose remains unfulfilled.

Certainly there are other efforts than the ones cited here to improve the quality of global health. For example, the Worldwatch Institute functions to educate the public and policymakers, worldwide, on matters concerning the environment. Every month the subscriber receives the *Worldwatch Paper*, must reading for the health-educated person. This publication is unique in that it recommends strategies and tactics for overcoming problems. Two recent editions of *Worldwatch Paper*, "Slowing global warming: A worldwide strategy" (Flavin, 1989), and "Poverty and the environment: Reversing the downward spiral" (Durning, 1989) are examples of fascinating and original work. Their suggestions need to be analyzed, discussed, and implemented quickly.

How can the manufacture of ice cream improve the quality of global health? Ben & Jerry's Homemade Ice Cream produces a premium product in Waterbury, Vermont. Their business is the second largest tourist attraction in the state, drawing approximately 150,000 visitors per year (Kurtz, 1989). At the plant they are introduced to such exotic flavors as "Peace Pops" and "Rainforest Crunch," called by some a magnificent marketing strategy to sell the product as well as to sensitize the public to global health issues (Kurtz, 1989). Their financial contributions to worthwhile global health causes are significant.

Another example is the Educational Film & Video Project, a nonprofit national media resource center. It stocks film and videotapes that "foster greater public awareness and action to resolve the most critical national and global problems" (from their catalogue, *Preparing for the 21st century*, 1989).[1]

Brown University students took significant action in 1984, before the Cold War thawing. The students voted to have the campus health center stock cyanide pills so they could easily commit suicide in the event of a nuclear war ("Students to

---

[1] For information write to The Education Film & Video Project, 1529 Josephine St., Berkeley, CA 94703. Telephone: 415, 849-1649.

Vote on Stocking Cyanide Pills," 1984). The action caused many throughout the world, especially parents, to face the reality that nuclear war could kill their children.

So we can each act in ways suitable for us. Frankly, I fear that we are not acting quickly enough. As I write this in the last few months of 1990, we are in a lull in our unofficial wars with Iran, Libya, Nicaragua, and El Salvador, and readying for one with Iraq. President Bush hopes for a gentler and kinder nation, while the numbers of homeless on the streets and homicides in the nation's Capital sky-rocket.

The economic distresses of our imbalance of payments and our national debt portend an increase in morbidity and mortality. The economic threat is not solely national but global, and would certainly affect individual, national, and global health (*World Development Report*, 1988). The Worldwatch Institute predicts the next great "shock" (following the "oil shock" of the 1970s) affecting the global economy will be a shortage of grain and dramatically increased food prices (Rowan, 1989). And the ozone "hole" over Antarctica is not becoming smaller. In Ecuador the military capabilities of the drug lords are on par with the government.

I have the advantage of writing after the Worldwatch Institute's monograph was published. We are now facing the dilemma of another "oil shock" as well as war. The putrifying cancer, however, in the United States and much of the world, is racism and ethnicism and its correlates of poverty, undernutrition, economic deprivation, hatred between the races and ethnic groups, undereducation, and the like.

You chastise me for pessimism? Certainly lifegenic actions have occurred. President Mikhail Gorbachev has electrified the world with global health initiatives. Oligarchies and authoritarian governments are out and democracy is in. *Environment* is in. Corporate polluters now rank at the low end of the "most admired list" with drug suppliers and the arbitrage and leveraged buyout opportunists. Still, we, the concerned health-educated parents, grandparents, teachers, health professionals, and others have our work cut out for us. Improving the quality of global health is too important a matter to be left solely in the hands of politicians, corporate leaders, or others. I would have them join with us in concerted effort. Let me now address a means that would provide a firm base to increase citizen participation in health protective action. In this closing chapter I wish to respond to Albert Einstein's comment, made at the beginning of the nuclear age, that everything has changed but our way of thinking. Many of my comments were included in the conclusion of *Horrendous Death, Health, and Well-Being*.

First, I discuss a particular view of the world, and values that would be helpful for improving the quality of global health as defined in the Introduction to this volume. Next the focus shifts to implementation. While the Death As a Stimulus to Improve the Quality of Global Health project (DASIQGH) (see Introduction, this volume) is a means, the end is a system of democratic institutions designed to insure that health and well-being are attained by *all* human beings.

VIEWING THE WORLD FROM THE GLOBAL HEALTH PERSPECTIVE

In order to elicit change in the direction of global health the population needs to be informed, that is, health-educated. But knowledge is not enough to prevent horrendous-type death. A sense of responsibility, a global health ethic, and subsequent action must be developed through informal (by way of parenting, religious education, emphasizing sportsmanship in athletics, etc.) and formal health education. Although everyone ought to be health-educated, it is illusory to believe that action toward attaining global health will be universally supported. Unfortunately, too many of the world's population are preoccupied with attaining basic needs, even though they are as susceptible to horrendous-type death as anyone else. Others will be resistant for one reason or another. Some simply will not care. What is needed is a substantial segment of the population that is health-educated, action-oriented, and persevering to influence the domains of power toward the goal of improving global health and well-being.[2]

I suggest an integration of classic education and health and death education to produce a hegemony based on virtue in the Aristotelian sense of the word, that is, courage, integrity, a sense of altruism and mission to serve future generations. Children and adults need to study and emulate those who have acted to improve the lot of humankind even at risk to their own personal reputation and safety; people like Socrates, Einstein, Ghandi, Jesus and other prophets of the great religions. Martin Luther King, Ralph Nader, Paul Robeson, and Rachel Carson are other examples.

Leaders and the electorate, in order to live both long and well, will be well served by adapting a universal value system and way of looking at the world. Some of those values are discussed below.

Valuing the Individual and His or Her Culture

Individuals from different nation states and the nation states themselves need to be seen as fellow inhabitants of our planet and given the respect that we would give our family, friends, and neighbors. The stereotype, perhaps even, the word *enemy*, is best forgotten unless it refers to horrendous-type deaths, the enemy common to us all.

Some forms of horrendous-type deaths (preventable by definition) increase in probability as negative perceptions about people increase. Homicide, racism, political torture, and wars are examples. In the United States there is an widening division between the White and Black communities. On Black-oriented radio and television one hears of their fears of a formal plan of genocide conjured up by the White establishment, similar to that practiced by Nazi Germany upon Jews and other non-Aryans during World War II. It is a fear based on the more valid perception that Blacks are expendable victims—as soldiers in war, victims of homicide, victims of poverty, and victims of drugs. The fact that this perception of planned systematic genocide exists in the Black community should be of concern to everyone. Why? Two reactions to any threat are variations of flight and fight. Fight? One can expect increased race-related homicides, even race war in the future. Variations of flight are just as defeating. An individual or group can lose hope. An entire race can become a permanently demoralized underclass at best, or clinically depressed and/or suicidal at worst. In either case, the rich potential of the Black individual and culture to contribute to the health and well-being of the global

[2]The domains of global power were political institutions, the corporate sector, religion, philosophy, and education, science, the media, and the military.

community is lost. Thus, a view of the world that values the potential and worth of each human being and his or her culture is necessary.

That which encourages the elimination of stereotypes and labels is to be encouraged. Intermarriage and other forms of integration are one means. It is difficult to feel hostility toward someone of another race or ethnic background when one's own children are a member of that group. Alexander the Great was wise when he encouraged his soldiers to marry the women of his conquered land, learn their language, and live among them. Of course he had a great teacher in Aristotle.

Unless children and youths are valued and taught to respect and like themselves and others, the alternative is hatred of self and others. Today, in the United States, children shoot one another for staring, yes, looking at someone for over a second or two. Their behavior is similar to that of children raised in war-torn environments who become numbed to death. They get a "kick" out of killing. They have no conscience, no remorse, no humanity. Parents and governments in countries such as Iran, Iraq, Vietnam, and Cambodia have allowed their children to be used as killers. Deadly and dead children are now a social problem of increasing magnitude in the United States and other Western countries as well. The threat of class war looms larger each year. Imagine a nine-year-old murdering your nine-year-old. Impossible you say? Read the papers.

Concerned with the increasing scarcity of natural resources and their effect on survival, Richard Barnet's first principle for evolving a survival strategy is that "every person born has political and economic rights and has a vested right to a decent minimal share of world resources by virtue of having been born. The explicit purpose of a global resource system is to serve the world population, and that must mean everybody on earth" (Barnet, 1980, p. 310).

Parental, Social, and Institutional Support of the Developing Child to Instill a Positive Self-Concept

The birthright to a "decent minimal share of world resources by virtue of being born" is not enough. That birthright must include love and social support. If we wish people to be loving and peaceful human beings, to respect and value animal and human life and the ecosystem, they must have self-esteem while eliciting the respect and friendship of others. The key to this is in the love, education, support, and nurturance of the developing child provided by the (a) intact family; (b) community; (c) educational system; and (d) social institutions such as government, business, labor, religion, law, and the media.

For example, if the data clearly indicate that a child's development and well-being are related to the presence of a loving parent-child relationship, it follows that such behaviors should be reinforced by every means possible. A means to that end would be compulsory, formal, health education courses concerned with the art and science of parenting. Think of it. Any damn fool can hold two of the most profound occupations in the world without benefit of education or training: Parenthood and politics.

Barnet puts it another way. His second principle for evolving a survival strategy is the protection of communities. He writes, "A rational planning system should start with the goal of community health—physical, economic, and spiritual'' (Barnet, 1980, p. 311).

The minimum wage and income tax system need to be adjusted to allow parents to rear their children with a minimum of economic stresses. Certainly, the opportunity for upward mobility must be provided if we are to improve the health and well-being of people. Why are such recommendations made? To insure social stability, and individual and social health and well-being. It is worth the price.

The Values of Global Health and Futurity

The elimination of horrendous-type deaths, while enhancing lifegenic factors for the benefit of present and future generations, should be the top priority of all nation-states. Where does one place his or her priorities when it comes to life? Is it the acquisition of materials goods? Education? Travel? Children? One has to be alive in order to enjoy such pleasures. There also needs to be a future for us as well as our children. Thus we need to value the quality of life in the future. If we value children we need to think of leaving a legacy of a healthy planet. A planet without horrendous-type death.

Specifically, what forms of horrendous-type death would you eliminate first? Is the elimination or severe reduction of nuclear and conventional wars and their weapons number one? Or is it the elimination of the close relatives of war, such as homicide, genocide, holocaust, or terrorism? Is it the elimination of poverty and undernutrition? Is it the elimination of racism? Or is the elimination of threats to the environments number one? Do we need to place priorities? My view is that the elimination of horrendous-type deaths *as a class* is the priority. This view of the world considers present and future generations. Each person works in his or her own way to make the world a better place for children. Each person leaves a legacy of a healthy planet and its population.

In a new and valuable journal, *Peace Review*,[3] Wendell Barry, a noted American writer, is cited:

> *To what point . . . do we defend from foreign enemies a country that we are destroying ourselves? In spite of all our propagandists can do, the foreign threat inevitably seems diminished when our air is unsafe to breathe, when our drinking water is unsafe to drink, when our rivers carry tonnages of topsoil that make light of the freight they carry in boats, when our forests are dying from air pollution and acid rain, and when we ourselves are sick from poisons in the air. Who are the enemies of the country? (Renner, 1989a).*

As Pogo would say, 'The enemy is us!''

Causes and Symptoms

A view of the world is required that gives priority to the elimination of the causes of horrendous-type death as well as the symptoms or behaviors. Personally, I want the murderer off the street. I also want to eliminate the intrapsychic, social, and institutional causes of homicide so that there are fewer murderers, fewer jails, and the need for fewer police.

[3]For information write to *Peace Review Publications Inc.*, 2439 Birch St., Suite 8, Palo Alto, CA 94306.

Eschewing Greed, and Valuing Altruism and
Other Virtues

Viktor Frankl is an existential philosopher who found meaning in life while a prisoner of the Nazis in their hellish, horrible concentration camps. Writing on the value of altruism he said, "Only in the service of a cause higher than ourselves, and only through the love of a person other than ourselves do we become really human, and do we actualize our real selves" ("Viktor Frankl on Aging, Meaning, and Death," 1989, p. 7).

An example of what altruism is *not* was printed in the *Washington Post* ("Sudan Famine Relief Blocked," 1989, p. A-28). It tells of the blocking of food relief by Ethiopia to the Sudan endangering 100,000 lives. What decent motive could account for such behavior?

In the same edition of the *Washington Post*, Hobart Rowen writes of the irony that becomes obvious the Bush administration opposes a $4.55 minimum wage while Mike Milken, a Drexel Burnham junk bond salesman, earned $550 million dollars in 1987. A chief executive officer of Ralston Purina received $1 million in salary in 1988 and $12 million in stock-options profits (Rowen, 1989). How much money does one person need to live an enjoyable life? I argue that there is survival value in sharing the wealth and in narrowing the gap between haves and have nots. Would you steal to feed your starving child while abundant food was available to those who could afford it, and conspicuous consumption and greed were seen as virtuous and desirable? I would.

In order to eliminate forms of horrendous-type death trust has to exist between people. Apparently the American public casts a suspicious eye upon its leaders. It is taken for granted that our political, industrial, and educational leaders lie to their constituents. Think of that. Eisenhower lied about the U-2, Nixon about Watergate, and Reagan about the Iran-Contra affair. Presidents Kennedy and Johnson lied about Vietnam. A *Washington Post-ABC* poll found that 75% of Americans say that members of Congress will lie if the truth will hurt them politically (Morin & Balz, 1989).

Members of so-called noble professions fare little better in the public's view. Some scientists under pressure to show statistically significant results in order to obtain grants, and/or attain or maintain status, falsify data. According to one survey of 211 medical doctors, 33% "would mislead survivors if they knew their treatment error had contributed to the patient's death" (Van, 1989, p. A-7). As a member of the faculty at a large Eastern university for approximately 20 years, I've learned that not all academics, especially administrators, can be trusted.

When James E. Hansen, director of the Goddard Institute of Space Studies, starkly warned of the immediacy of the greenhouse effect and its ultimately deadly effects on the biosphere, his comments were altered, without his permission, by the White House (Peterson, 1989). Why was a scientist prevented from expressing his professional opinion concerning global health and well-being?

The United States is not alone. *Izvestia*, a Soviet newspaper, accused a government ministry of trying to cover-up accidents at nuclear plants. Apparently, increasing "nuclearphobia" in the Soviet Union after Chernobyl provoked the secrecy (Dobbs, 1989).

Plaintively, the columnist Haynes Johnson asks the Bush administration to provide presidential leadership in wisdom and honesty. He writes, "Wisdom and honesty: the very qualities Americans have yearned for in their presidents since the first George so long ago—and the same ones Bush will most need in the White House to lead America in the 1990s" (Johnson, 1989, p. A-7).

Shortly after the Johnson article, the Speaker of the U.S. House of Representatives and the Japanese Prime Minister were cashiered out of office for unethical behavior.

There is a price to be paid when we lose faith in our leaders. Whether in athletics, government, education or entertainment, kids need godlike figures and superheroes to emulate. Who should it be? A corporate raider? A drug or arms merchant? Or humanitarians like Mother Teresa, Dr. Albert Schweitzer, Dr. Albert Einstein, Dr. Martin Luther King, Jr., Ghandi, Mohammed, Confucius, and Jesus? These are people admired by the world's population year after year. They are the good ones. I believe they are the role models for many because of their altruism, their commitment to improve the health and well-being of present and future generations. Anything that reinforces altruism in the family, the schools, the community, and the world should be encouraged. Incorruptible and virtuous leaders and citizens are needed to serve as role models for the young.

Valuing Leadership By Example and Reward

It is a view of the world that realizes that the super military and economic powers—China, France, Great Britain, Japan, the Soviet Union, the United States—can best provide leadership in improving the quality of global health by good example and positive reinforcement rather than rhetoric and force. Does the United States wish Iraq to halt planned or actual production of chemical and biological weapons? Then the United States cannot continue production of binary and more exotic chemical weapons. How can we expect Pakistan or Brazil to refrain from producing nuclear weapons if we continue increasing our overkill capacity? If we wish nation states and their citizens to trust and value representative democracy then we cannot endorse and support brutal dictators like the late President Marcos of the Philippines or the late Shah of Iran simply because they wave the flag of anticommunism.

The underclass hearken to systems that provide health and well-being (e.g., food, employment, shelter, education, and health treatment) rather than rhetoric.

Valuing the Ecosystem

It is a view of the world that understands the interdependence of the constituent parts of the ecosystem on one another. Increasingly, nation states are dependent on one another economically and in trade. All one has to do is observe the United States' dependency on foreign oil and capital or the Soviet Union's need to trade for wheat.

Because the earth's natural resources are limited we will need to realize,

> In just 300 years a huge chunk of the geological capital of the ages was consumed as if it were an ever growing annuity guaranteed until the end of time. . . . The fundamental philosophical choice—can human beings dominate nature or are they limited by nature—now divides both capitalism and socialism. It may well be the issue on which a true "convergence" of the market economies and the centrally planned economies takes place. (Barnet, 1980, p. 301)

From the perspective of global health and well-being, maintaining the ecosystem and biosphere take priority over extraordinary and unnecessary consumption and luxurious living. Would you rather retain the ozone layer and reduce the probability of your loved ones dying of cancer or have hair sprays propelled by chlorofluorocarbons? Desire nuclear power? What will you do with its waste products?

Valuing Animal and Human Life

Preserving human life of one's tribe is a universal value of all culture except under certain conditions (e.g., warfare, self-defense, etc.). The law, thou shall not kill, was extended by religious and social prohibitions beyond kinfolk and tribal members to all human beings. We need to return to valuing not only human life, but also animal life.

Two world wars and the Nazi Holocaust imprinted mass murder upon the public's consciousness. Although generally accepted by civilized people as an abomination, the collective conscious of the Allies during the early part of World War II was numbed by the huge numbers of murders and the efficiency of the gas chambers and lethal injections. If the German citizenry denied such mass death even as boxcars of prisons rumbled past their towns and the odor of burning flesh permeated the air, so did religious institutions (the Catholic church) and governments (e.g., the United States) within and outside of Germany.

If humans are noted for their adaptability it may be said, as we prepare to enter the 21st century, that we have adapted to the ubiquitous quality of horrendous-type death. However, there remains an ethical and psychological schism between the accepted social contract (thou shall not kill) and the reality of horrendous-type death. The result of this conflict between our "good" and "dark" sides is individual and group anxiety.

How did this come to be? Barnet (1980) makes an interesting and, to my way of thinking, valid observation. He writes,

> *The three traditional impulses for protecting human life have been deadened by progress. One is religious. The obligation to respect the individual is derived from a duty to a supreme being or supernatural source. There is a transcendent value to each soul. . . . The religious commandments in the Old and New Testaments that worshipping God requires ministering to the poor and the helpless have lost much of their force. (Barnet, 1980, p. 304)*

One does not have to be religious in a formal sense to appreciate and see the necessity of the values derived from religion for getting on well with our global neighbors. The two icons of the Christian-Judaic religions, "Love thy neighbor" and "Do unto others as you would have them do unto you" serve well as a basis for civil behavior among people. Why not add, "Serve well those who will inherit the earth"?

A second "impulse for valuing life is a sense of community . . . the traditional obligations to family and village" where each individual has a duty to protect the other members of the community (Barnet, 1980, p. 304). David Broder, in his column, cited a survey by pollster Peter D. Hart, entitled "Democracy's Next Generation" (Broder, 1989, p. A-27). Hart's survey involved 1,000 young Americans between the ages of 15–24 years with supplemental information from 405 social studies teachers. Hart found his sample placed priority on personal happiness, freedom, and license "almost to the complete exclusion of service or participation." Sixty percent were not involved in any type of community service. Only one third foresaw a time when they "might join the military or work as a volunteer in a political campaign." Hart emphasized that parents, teachers, families, and schools are far more important in shaping "the values that underlie active democratic citizenship than distant politicians." The social studies teachers were alarmed at what they saw in the classroom. That is, "the emphasis on self-fulfillment which is obviously a natural quality of that stage of life, is increasingly crowding out a sense of involvement within the community and nation." Broder concluded his article by writing that "One way or another, we have to find a way to teach this generation the other half of democracy's story: the experience of civic involvement and citizenship obligation." On the other hand, I see many high school and college students engaging in voluntary, altruistic endeavors that would not have occurred to me or to the sports-oriented group to which I belonged as a young man. In some high schools and colleges community service is required or strongly encouraged. There is no doubt that an ethic of community service would be helpful toward achieving our goals.

We need to develop a sense of community, a sense of the commons in which the protection of children from violence is everyone's responsibility. The studies of children who grow up in violent environments indicate that they become numbed to the value of life because their lives are meaningless. Thus, any plan to eliminate horrendous-type deaths and enhance global health and well-being should develop a strong sense of religious values and community—emphasizing the healthy nurturing of children.

A community is not inherently warlike. Johan Galtung, one of the pioneers in the relatively new field of peace research,[4] feels that peace and war are not part of human nature but influenced greatly by culture and structure (Galtung, 1987). Certain religious cultures such as Buddhism and some aspects of Hinduism are very peace- and love-oriented, while others, such as Christianity and Islam, are known to be friendly to the sword depending on the circumstances. In terms of structure, nomadic social structures such as the Eskimo, compared to sedentary groups, tend to be peaceful. To paraphrase Galtung, we need more Buddhist Eskimos if we wish peace. On the other hand, we can emphasize and teach the religious values of ahism, shalom, brotherhood, peace, and love in our social structures (family, schools, community, government, business, military, etc.) regardless of one's personal, formal religion.

Anything that denigrates life and numbs us to suffering does not contribute to our scheme of global health and well-being. A mark of a highly civilized society is the care and nurturing provided the weak: Children, the aged, the impoverished, and animals.

A word about the latter. The legitimization and institutionalization of hunting and fishing contribute to a devaluing of life. It is easy to become inured to the suffering and death of the hunted deer, the baited bear, the "fighting dog." Ani-

---

[4]The peace research movement started in the late 1950s as a result of the devastation and horrendous death caused by World War II. One of the first organized efforts was the Norwegian International Peace Research Institute in 1959.

mals should never be considered "pets"; a more civilized terminology and way of thinking would be "companion animal."

As a former athletic coach and participant I have always felt that hunting and fishing were never "sport." The term applies equal opportunity for each participant to "win" the contest. When was the last time a doe killed a hunter, or a trout hooked a fisherperson?

You might say that hunting is one thing, but society would never condone the brutal killing of fellow human beings, except soldiers killing enemy soldiers in times of war, or killing one another in self-defense. The Nazi Holocaust and the other state-sponsored programs of genocide under Stalin, Pol Pot, Idi Amin, and our own disgraceful behavior in My Lai, ended the myth that civilized people are beyond inflicting mass death on their fellow humans. It is easy to abandon the veneer of civil and civilized behavior. We need to modify culture and provide structures that value life, not death. How would civilization suffer if hunting were to become extinct?

PREVENTIVE INTERVENTION

In any policy concerning horrendous-type death, prevention is the only sensible strategy. Before discussing modification of the DASIQGH project as a means of preventive intervention, some assumptions need to be stated. The first is that democracy is preferred over more authoritarian forms of government even in an emergency. Second, that a sound education focusing on global health and well-being is the *sine qua non* to the high efficiency and effectiveness of a democracy. Third, that reform in the global economic system is related to global health and well-being.

Preference for Democratic Institutions

In the long run democratic institutions are preferred over authoritarian ones. As the threat of horrendous-type death increases the pressure to turn to authoritarian rule and simplistic answers while abandoning democratic processes and institutions increases.

For example, during World War II Japanese-American citizens were indiscriminately placed in concentration camps in violation of their constitutional rights. Why? Anyone of Japanese descent was thought to be a collaborator or spy. If the war fever between Iraq and the United States and others increases, one would predict unwarranted persecution of Arab-Americans.

Another example: In order to reduce the incidence of homicides and drug traffic in Washington, DC, a curfew for teenagers was put forth, but was ultimately found unconstitutional by the courts.

The phrase "McCarthyism" refers to socially stigmatizing an individual or group by associating it with a "life-threatening" menace (i.e., Communism). Citizens were accused of being Communists or Communist sympathizers without the right to face their accusers, and other forms of due process. Consequently jobs were lost, many were blacklisted for years, and reputations were ruined. No wonder McCarthyism was equated with witch hunting.

It is tempting to disregard constitutional liberties and rights when threatened by the "hordes of Nippon" during World War II, Iran or Iraq today, homicide in

Washington, DC, or the specter of Communism. Society is better served dealing with the real or perceived threat using established institutions. The risk is great that once individual liberties and freedoms are removed they will be difficult to restore. Guardians of the freedoms guaranteed by the Bill of Rights (e.g., the American Civil Liberties Union) are to be valued.

Democracy is often a slow acting process. Considering the *immediate* threats to life and limb posed by horrendous-type deaths wouldn't we be better off opting for a benevolent, enlightened despot or oligarchy? No doubt speed of action is a characteristic of authoritarian rule.

However, mechanisms exist in a democratic system that allow the government to act immediately. It took only hours to declare war on the axis powers after the United States was attacked on December 7, 1941. In 1990 military forces acted, defensively, to insure that Iraq would not invade Saudi Arabia. In time of natural disaster, rescue operations are activated almost minutes after the event. We should and can react expeditiously to horrendous-type death. If necessary the system can be modified and improved.

In a representative democracy the will of the people is supposedly carried out by its elected representatives. Many feel this notion to be more fancy than fact. There is reason for such a jaundiced view. Too often it is the vested interest, the political action committee, which influences elected officials. In a *Washington Post-ABC* poll cited earlier, 75% of Americans believe House and Senate members favor special interests over the needs of the average citizen (Morin & Balz, 1989). Too often the members of the electorate see themselves as ineffectual in influencing their elected officials and, consequently, public policy. Perhaps that is one reason why approximately only 50% of those eligible to vote in the United States do so.

Even considering the stresses on and shortcomings of representative democracy, it is to be preferred because of its inherent system of checks and balances, debate over issues, accountability, and ability to gain the consent (as opposed to coercion) of a large population toward a common effort.

Education and Democracy

Education is central to any effort to insure the best possible representative government and policies. Historically, seventeenth century Americans were involved in their government. They were knowledgeable. Newspapers and journals of the day were read voraciously and issues debated. Although few citizens were college educated, they were literate thanks to the influence of the Protestant ethic: Every person should be able to read God's word in the Bible independent of a pastor or anyone else (Beard, Beard, & Beard, 1960). Thus, self-taught education and intellectualism provided the basis for quality self-government during the early history of the United States. If the ultimate goal of all institutions is to improve the quality of global health and well-being, then the prerequisite is, again, education. Unfortunately, the formal education necessary for democracy to flourish envisioned by Aristotle, Jefferson, Franklin, and others has decreased in quality as have the family, religion, and other institutions also responsible for education of the young.

Harking back to Barnet's traditional impulses for protecting life I would emphasize education toward the health and well-being of the individual, family community, nation, and globe as an interdependent system. Interwoven would be themes of ethics, economics, responsibility toward others, and responsibility toward the future. Community service would, at the very least, be on par with varsity sports and less costly.

Education as a Means of Escaping Poverty and the Underclass

In the 17th century, Robert Coram, a brave seaman during the War of the Revolution and an intellectual, called for the training of all children as a way of "assuring personal independence and overcoming the poverty which belied civilization" (Beard, Beard, & Beard, p. 154). Considering that poverty is an insidious and pervasive form of horrendous-type death, Coram's declaration still rings true today.

How does one educate toward wisdom while, at the same time, develop the specialists necessary to manage our increasing complex technology? Any answer to the problem would be complex and multifaceted and suggests the need for a worldwide mobilization of intellectual and economic resources similar to the Manhattan Project during World War II.

Education to improve economic status and security must involve governments and global corporations for they control global economics, that is, markets and marketing, labor, and capital. Governments and global corporations need to understand how their own existence, and global health and well-being are adversely affected by unemployment, poverty, and the resulting social instability. The theme of job security needs to be balanced with the need for profit and maintaining a healthy ecosystem. The traditional *raison d'etre* of the corporation is profit in return for production of goods and services. It, too, needs to be expanded to include global responsibility for health and well-being. One way is to involve the local community in development of corporate policies. Policies concerning traditional corporate matters such as cutbacks and internationalization of labor, plant safety, environmental responsibility and the like are a community as well as a corporate matter. Barnet and Muller suggest that "public directors" be added to the boards of large public corporations elected by shareholders or appointed by management (Barnet & Muller, 1974, p. 382). My suggestion would be appointment of "advocates of global health" to corporate boards.

If education is a lifetime process the "retired," experienced, and knowledgeable older adult, serving as teacher or mentor, needs to be utilized and viewed as a valued resource. The older adult would be well-served by engaging in purposeful and meaningful work in a period often characterized as one full of despair and lacking in meaning. Certainly the younger student would gain from the knowledge and experience of his or her teacher—experiences that probably include coping with a work environment subject to change.

Education and Saliency of Horrendous-Type Death

A third value of education is it can serve as a means to raise the issues concerning horrendous-type death and the action necessary to preserve global health and well-being. This book is one example of an effort to educate the public about horrendous-type death. Media, film, and books are increasingly educating their audience toward the threat of horrendous-type death.

The effects of a health-educated electorate can be profound. In Europe, the Greens have become a legitimate political party. Its constituency is concerned with improving the quality of global health and well-being with special reference to the environment.

Apparently 80% of the American public are health-educated enough to favor discussion between NATO allies and the Soviet Union to reduce short-range nuclear weapons (Morin & Balz, 1989), an attitude sure to influence leaders of both groups.[5] President Gorbachev must have sensed the anathema toward horrendous-type death by all people prior to his grand peace initiatives in 1989.

The Content of Education

If education is viewed as a lifetime process I would recommend a combination of classical education, health education, and death education. *Classical education* refers to the study of "Great Books" as defined by Robert Maynard Hutchins (1968). The value of the classics is its emphasis on wisdom more than merely the acquisition of facts. It underscores the responsibility we have to one another to improve health and well-being. Classical literature is about relationships—the relationships of people to one another and their universe. It is the bedrock of democratic institutions. It includes the study of civics, geography, history, human relations, philosophy, the role of institutions, ethics, morality, virtue, and the universal problems of life. To that I would add the study of cultures, or cultural anthropology, as a means to understanding the great and rich diversity of people the world over. It is also a valuable means to reducing ethnocentrism. That which promotes affection and understanding between cultures and people is to be encouraged. Thus education should encourage student exchanges, overseas study programs, and programs such as the Peace Corps and ACTION.

If the Great Books utilize the wisdom of the past to resolving the problems of today, health and death education are concerned about the problems relating to living long and well today and tomorrow. They are reality oriented.

Health and Death Education

What should be the subject matter of health education? Much of it should be similar to the content of this book, and its earlier companion, *Horrendous Death, Health, and Well-Being.*[6] If "health" is the Yin, so the study of death is the Yang. Each is one side of the same coin. It should enhance the value of life and living by describing the fragility and interdependence of all life.

It would only partially resemble the formal health education found in schools and colleges today. Present day, formal school health education is primarily con-

[5]As this is written (September 1990), President Bush and President Gorbachev have collaborated on beneficial initiatives that may portend a new era of global health.

[6]Should the book become a required textbook for every student in the world the royalties would be mind-boggling. The reader has my word that a significant percentage of my share would go to support the Adult Health & Development Program, the Association for Death Education and Counseling, and the St. Francis Center in Washington, DC.

cerned with prevention of disease. The emphasis is on prevention of AIDS and other venereal diseases, coronary heart disease, diabetes, kidney disease, and others diseases by modification of health behaviors such as exercise, diet, smoking, and stress. Unfortunately, general or "required" health education, especially at the university level, is theory and data oriented. Missing is the personal-affective domain that affects learning. My guess is that professional health educators or their classes rarely interact with a person with AIDS or one recovering from a disease. We rarely carry on a dialogue with an impoverished or chronically unemployed person, nor do we consider it an appropriate topic for health education. I think health education should be concerned with more than disease prevention.

Health Education as Hedonism

Another problem with my profession is in its emphasis on health hedonism, that is, where the ultimate good is personal pleasure by way of health activities (e.g., exercise, nutrition, etc.). Like any other type of hedonism it is egocentric in that it causes one to focus on "every fluctuation of his or her navel." The ear is tuned, almost exclusively, to one's own self-interest and sense of well-being.

At the 1989 American Alliance for Health, Physical Education, Recreation, and Dance (AAHPERD) conference in Boston, during a session sponsored by the health education section, the featured speaker (its scholar of the year) declared that the ultimate goal of health education was pleasure, that is, "feeling good." Nothing was said about the value of "feeling good" resulting from actions to improve the pleasure and well-being of others, here and now, and in the future. Hedonistic health education is somewhat analogous to masturbation. Certainly one feels good during the process but most people would prefer lovemaking with a partner. There is a joy and satisfaction in giving pleasure. There is nothing wrong with masturbation or "self-pleasuring." There is nothing wrong with traditional health education, health promotion, and "feeling good." It is the focus on health hedonism that is troublesome. Pursuing the analogy, contemporary formal health education might emphasize "feeling good" as a result of altruistic more so than egocentric actions (read, self-centered). Both provide individual gratification. However, altruistic health behavior has survival value of the planet.

I suspect that much of our efforts toward improving health, that is, preventing disease and feeling good, is motivated by fear of old age and dying. We live healthily to retard aging and postpone dying. We exercise, stop smoking, diet, eat oats to reduce high cholesterol, and apply Aloe and vitamin-laden creams to our faces to eliminate wrinkles. I see nothing wrong with that, except it should be understood that death always wins. Now altruistic health behavior, too, cannot promise eternal youth, but it can provide meaning and purpose to life. What better feeling could one have as death draws near then to be able to say I did what I could to make the world a better place for my children and grandchildren?

Health Education and Personal Control of Health

Another icon of the school and college health education establishment is what is called health locus of control, with emphasis on "internality." *Internal* health locus of control refers to the belief that the individual controls his or her own health. Thus, the individual who exercises regularly, follows a proper diet, works and lives in an environment in which psychosocial stress is low, has an optimistic view of the world, and sleeps soundly eight hours each night will live long and well. Now there is some truth to that especially if one's parents are long-lived. One problem is that *external* factors such as death as a result of murder, war, poverty, loss of one's job, or accident are almost totally ignored by professional health education organizations such as the American School Health Association (ASHA), and to a lesser degree, The American Alliance for Health, Physical Education, Recreation, and Dance (AAHPERD). Neither in the journals or at national conferences of the organizations has there been any significant mention of horrendous-type death as a health risk, although AAHPERD shows promise. Teaching universities responsible for the education of the professional health educator do not fare better. I think formal health education and its institutions should serve as means to eliminate external causes of poor health, that is, horrendous-type death. How? Through health education's traditional means of education, service, and research. A fourth means should be added: advocacy toward the goal of global health and well-being.

Economic-Political Organization Germane to Global Health and Well-Being

Earlier it was stated that reforms were needed in our educational and economic systems if global health and well-being are to be attained; a word about economic reform.

One question is how will national and international global health and well-being initiatives and programs be funded?

Funding

I give top priority to health and well-being, that is, eliminating horrendous-type death while increasing the probability of lifegenic factors. At what expense? The two great entities controlling wealth in the world are governments and national and global corporations. Within government the military sector is most ripe for reform because of over pricing, waste, fraud, and scandal. President Eisenhower called this cabal of defense-related industries, ancillary professions, and their contacts in government the "Military-Industrial Complex." They share, in common, huge profits that result from an expensive war economy. Let's look at some data.

Military Expenditures and Cutbacks

Using Ruth Sivard's data (Sivard, 1987), the Gross National Product per capita (GNP/C) for the *developed countries* is $9795.00 (for the United States it is $15,541.00).

Now recall this contrast cited in the Introduction to this volume. The public expenditure per *soldier* for developed countries is $58,882.00 (in the United States it is $105,638.00). Contrast those figures with the public expenditures per person for *education and health*. For the developed countries, the expenditure per person on *education* is $497.00 (in the United States it is $771.00). For *health*, the expenditure per person in developed countries is $469.00 (in the United States it is $674.00). As suggested in the Introduction to this volume, our priorities should be reversed.

To that end I would reduce military spending in the United States from approximately 6–7% to 1% of GNP over a 5-year period. Translated into dollars, the GNP of the United States is over 3.6 trillion dollars (Sivard, 1987). A goal of 1% would leave the military with a budget of approximately $36 billion after 5 years. It would free more than $200 billion (or over $40 billion the first year alone) to repair the physical and social infrastructure of the country. Is this too radical? One percent of the GNP is exactly what Japan, one of the wealthiest countries of the world, spends on its military.

From a world perspective, approximately $825 billion was spent on the military out of a global GNP of close to $14 trillion. A limit of 1% would make available for civilian use throughout the world $685 billion ($825 billion − $140 billion) (Sivard, 1987).

Conversion from a military to a civilian-based economy would be a problem perhaps, not as great as the military-industrial complex would have us think. More jobs would be available in a civilian- than a military-based economy. One reason that military spending creates fewer jobs is because it is capital rather than labor intensive. As complexity of weapons increase there is a greater demand for higher technology and highly trained technicians and engineers, and less so for unskilled and other types of labor (Cassidy, 1989). A study by the U.S. Congressional Budget Office found that for every billion dollars spent in military contracting, the same billion would create 4,000 more jobs, on the average, when spent in the civilian sector (Cassidy, 1989). Another study conducted by the International Association of Machinists (IAM), one of the two major unions involved in military work, found that IAM members suffered a net loss of job opportunities when military spending was high (Cassidy, 1989).

To the end of economic conversion, a bill sponsored by U.S. Representative Ted Weiss (D-NY) would create an institutional framework for national conversion planning, mandate the formation of local alternative-use committees in every military base, plant or laboratory, and provide for occupational retraining for the civilian sector of managers, engineers, and workers (Renner, 1989). Most developed countries involved in World War II gained experience in economic conversion. Within a few years the United States transferred 30% of its GNP to civilian goods and services following the close of the war (Renner, 1989).

Just to give an idea of how the newly available funds might be allocated, consider that the estimated cost of cleaning up the nuclear wastes in the 560-square-mile Hanford nuclear reservation is approximately $50 billion dollars ("Cleanup Pact Signed for Nuclear Site," 1989, p. A3). Some other tradeoffs are found in Table 1.

These tradeoffs only partially indicate the need to improve the quality of global health. I would make the trade.

Fiscal Responsibility of Global and National Corporations

Richard Barnet and Ronald Muller, in their study of global corporations, introduce the reader to their tremendous influence and power: "The men who run the global corporations are the first in history with the organization, technology, money, and ideology to make a credible try at managing the world as an integrated unit" (Barnet & Muller, 1974, p. 13). The growth rate of global corporations has been phenomenal. If the 1973 GNP of the countries and the annual sales of certain countries are compared, General Motors is richer than Switzerland, Pakistan, and

Table 1 Some of the Tradeoffs Necessary to Improve the Quality of Global Health

Military priority	Cost	Social/Environmental priority
Trident II submarine and F-16 jet fighter program	$100,000,000,000	Estimated clean-up cost for the 3,000 hazardous waste dumps in the United States.
Stealth bomber program	68,000,000,000	Two-thirds of estimated costs to meet U.S. clean water goals by 2000
Approximately 4 days of global military spending	8,000,000,000	Action plan over 5 years to save the world's tropical forests
2 months of Ethiopian military spending	50,000,000	Annual cost of proposed U.N. antidesertification plan for Ethiopia

Source: Renner, 1989, pp. 48–49.

South Africa: Royal Dutch Shell is richer than Iran, Venezuela and Turkey; and, Goodyear Tire is richer than Saudi Arabia (Barnet & Muller, 1974, p. 15). When Barnet's and Muller's book was published in 1974, global corporations were basically an American phenomenon. An example is the oil giant, Standard Oil of New Jersey (Esso), which dropped the local appellation, New Jersey, for the more general but global, Exxon. Today, the United States has been joined by Japan, Britain, France, West Germany, and other countries in the development of the global corporation.

Their power, according to Barnet and Muller (1974), comes from their ability to create wealth on a global scale. Their scope is so large that their everyday decisions have more impact "than most sovereign governments on where people live, what work, if any, they will do; what they will eat, drink, and wear; what sorts of knowledge schools and universities will encourage; and what kind of society their children will inherit" (Barnet & Muller, 1974, p. 15). Unfortunately, the "community" has little input into these decisions. While the representatives of global corporations see themselves as apostles of social change and peace, the evidence indicates that the drive for acquisition of world markets, cheap labor, and profits remains their primary goal.

From our perspective there are two needs:

1. Because the wealth of the global corporations is so immense and because of their ability to avoid being taxed, means should be developed to return to nation states life-sustaining capital. One suggestion would be to develop international agreements regarding taxation, minimum wage, and the like. Concerning the latter, an international agreement on a minimum wage would do much to prevent one of the great causes of unemployment, that is, shopping for that cheapest labor pool regardless of where it is located, and the subsequent loss of jobs in the "abandoned" country.

2. The global corporation, like the nation state and other institutions, needs to take the lead in improving the quality of health and well-being. As indicated in the introductory chapter, no one can escape horrendous-type death, including chief executive officers of corporations. What good are huge profits if one's children, grandchildren, and oneself are dead?

Thus, revenues from cutting back military expenditures, and tax revenues from global and nation-state corporations are two ways of rechanneling capital into the constructive path of improving global health and well-being. Undoubtedly there are others.

ORGANIZATION TOWARD ACTION

The shift toward global health and well-being involves two dimensions: One is the elimination of horrendous-type death; the other is to maximize lifegenic factors. In his discussion of the *structure of peace*, Galtung (1987) lists six conditions:

1. *Symbiosis.* Nation states have to be mutually useful to one another.
2. *Symmetry.* They have to be about equally useful to one another.
3. *Diversity.* They must complement one another.
4. *More than two parties.* Polarization is mitigated when more than two parties are involved.
5. *More than one issue.* Having more than one issue on the table allows for greater latitude in negotiation.
6. *Supranational organization.* As the family is superordinate to its members, so the supranational organization is superordinate to nation states.

The Supranational Organization

I would like to discuss the last, the supranational organization, as a means toward global health and well-being. From the League of Nations, which followed the great war to end all wars, and the United Nations, which followed the second great war to end all wars, people of good faith have put forth the idea of a supranational institution to which all nation states would be bound to support and obey in its efforts to maintain peace and promote the general welfare. A network of local and regional organizations feeding information into a supranational organization is necessary to prevent horrendous-type death, while promoting lifegenic factors.

One group that has consistently championed world peace through world law is the World Association for World Federation (its journal is *The Federalist*).[7] It is "based upon the principles of federalism, on the rejection of any exclusive concept of the nation and on the hypothesis that the supranational era of the history of mankind has begun. The primary value *The Federalist* aims to serve is peace" (*The Federalist*, 1988). While it remains steadfast in its goal of world peace

[7]Strong links exist between the Union of European Federalists, the American counterpart, and the World Association for World Federation.

The subscription for the European Community is $25; other countries is $35. European residents should send their payment to EDIF, via Porta, Pertusi 6, I-27100 Pavia, Italy. United Kingdom residents should mail their payment to Federal Trust, Whitehall Place 1A, London SW1A 2HA, Great Britain. U.S. and Canadian residents should send their payment to AUD, PO Box 75920, Washington, DC 20013.

through world law, it is studying options "to bring the ultimate ideal down from the lofty pinnacle of perfect dreams where it is unsullied by any trace of reality, to the level of the most practical proposition for realizing what is essential in it" ("Concretizing the Path Toward World Government," 1988, p. 219).

The guiding concept of "partial world government" was first formulated by Albert Einstein. In a sense this process has already begun. Cooperative agreements exist between Europe, Japan, and North America. Considering the Bush-Gorbachev disarmament initiatives, and the democratization of the U.S.S.R., the ideal relationship between northern hemisphere countries such as the United States, Canada, Soviet Union, Europe, and Japan is coming to fruition.

Ira Straus, writing in *The Federalist*, observed that international unification does not proceed in discrete steps from the regional (European), intercontinental (Atlantic, Trilateral), and finally, to the global level. Rather it should be seen as simultaneous movement along three staircases ("Concretizing the Path Toward World Government," 1988). Movement up the European stairway has been rapid, accepted by governments and their citizens as their destiny. One hears talk of an eventual European federal government. On the other hand, the path up the Atlantic/Trilateral staircase has been slow, and advancing the goal of global inte-gration has been slowest. The thread binding each political unit to one another is primarily economic. A stronger bind would be mutually beneficial cooperation toward economic goals *and* global health and well-being.

An institution or institutions should be developed at the nation state, regional, and global levels to serve the cause of *insuring* global health and well-being. We need, at the nation state level, an organization like the Federal Reserve Board in the United States to act (by controlling interest rates) to prevent inflation or de-pression. Why not develop within nation states, and at regional and the global levels, Health Action Boards with at least four functions?

1. Serve as a barometer or "watchdog" to *predict* and pinpoint threats of horrendous-type death.

2. Coordinate strategies, tactics, and action to *prevent* horrendous-type deaths from occurring.

3. Coordinate strategies, tactics, and action to *eliminate* horrendous-type death.

4. Coordinate strategies, tactics, and action to *maximize* health and well-being to benefit all members of the community served by the Board.

The entire supranational organization would be vested with political and eco-nomic authority, and the right to "give orders to nation states and other parties involved in international relations" ("Nation States and a New International Sys-tem, 1988, p. 210). The supranational organization would coordinate and cooper-ate with its subordinate organizations as well as with governments, the business community with special reference to the global business community, and the other members of the spheres of influence described in chapter one.

A "conational" system, as suggested by Tibor Palankai, would provide the supranational organization working *in cooperation* with nation-states ("Nation States and a New International System," 1988). The theme of *cooperation* and *democratic procedures* at the nation state, regional, and international levels needs to be stressed. Fear of loss of autonomy, power, and wealth is one reason why supraorganizations have not been as successful as they might have been. Nation states need to be assured of retaining their autonomy and unique culture.

Galtung's (1987) work is helpful here. His alternative security system for nation states would emphasize:

1. Defensive rather than offensive capabilities, because they reduce the threat of attack. Examples of defensive weapons are land mines, fixed air defense systems, anti-armor missiles, and fighter interceptor aircraft (See Fisher & Bloomgarden, 1989). Switzerland, Sweden, Malaysia, Yugoslavia, Austria, and Finland are examples of countries whose military posture is primarily defensive.

2. Less dependence on super weapons.

3. Greater economic and political self-reliance.

4. Greater cooperation with nation states that have different ideologies and values.

I would add "greater cooperation to enhance health and well-being." If invasion (and implied death) by an enemy is seen as a national security program, than so are the forms of horrendous-type death. Elimination of horrendous-type death would add to the security of any nation state, as would the elimination of a deadly enemy.

The Death as a Stimulus to Improve the Quality of Global Health Project as Process

The Death as a Stimulus to Improve the Quality of Global Health project (DASIQGH) (see Introduction to this volume) is seen as one viable means to get the varied gatekeepers of power to the negotiating table. It capitalizes on the fact that fear of the possibility of horrendous-type death for oneself and loved ones is a stark means of getting people to focus and remain focused on developing a global policy on health and well-being. The DASIQGH is the means to developing the conational system of governing necessary to our goals presented in this book. It is also a means to arouse the public to action and supplements the examples of action described in this book.

If the DASIQGH or a variation were to come to fruition some lessons learned from the study of death (thanatology) and health might be helpful.

RANDOM THOUGHTS

Values

The strength of the DASIQGH lies in its focus on its participants' fear of horrendous death as a stimulus to action. The study of death can affect one's values. Try this exercise: Say to yourself, "I may die tomorrow." What would you do? How does that knowledge affect your daily routine? Your job? Your love relationships? What would you do now that you realize your life is limited? Late in the 16th century the French philosopher Montaigne wrote, "The value of life is not in its extension, but in its use. It is not the number of years that determine whether you have lived enough. . . . I enjoy life twice as much as others do. . . . Now that I see my life limited in time, I want to extend it in weight. I want to arrest the speed of its flight by the speed of my grasp and by the vigor of my use to compensate for the haste of its flow. To the extent that the possession of life is short, I have to make it the more profound and full" (Choron, 1963, p. 101). Eliminating horrendous-type death is one way life can be rendered "the more profound and full." It should be everyone's *raison d'etre*.

Play

Another value often derived from facing the reality of limited mortality is that of play. The essence of fun and enjoyment of life is play. It is a powerful means to develop friendship and trust. Play is a spice and necessity of life. I try to say yes to the play requests of my kids. In fact they have learned of my Achilles Heel; "Dad," my son will say, "will you practice football with me?" "I can't—I have to work on this book," I reply. "But you know I might die tomorrow," is Matt's response (accompanied by a far-away, crestfallen look and a sigh). "Get the ball, Matt." My beautiful, intelligent daughter, Leslie, prefers to play at Martha's Vineyard in New England. Sometimes requests cannot always be accommodated.

We need to play more with friends, family, and even perceived enemies. I recommend that world leaders come together to play. Kicking a soccer ball, jumping on a trampoline, or simply "horsing around" and having fun may be a valid and unique means to negotiation and resolution of world problems.

Social Constraints

Global society needs to agree upon and accept a set of commonly shared values such as improving the quality of global health. Contemplated or actual violations by nation states, institutions, or individuals should be met by social constraints such as disapproval, ostracism, shame, and boycott, accompanied by education and persuasion. Ostracism is a form of social death. Those who would encourage and wage war, murder, violate the environment, engage in racism, exploit others and so forth, would be viewed and treated by the world community, to paraphrase Ibsen, as "an enemy of the people," a social pariah. Why? Because the violator will kill our children unless prevented from doing so. Violation of the common good should be considered unacceptable behavior akin to treason in time of war. In fact, if an enemy is a psychological necessity enabling individuals and nation states to integrate and coalesce toward common purpose, let the enemy be the prevention of horrendous-type deaths.

However, the approach should be Ghandian whenever possible. The great danger is a swing to fanaticism focused on health and well-being. The process needs to be thought through, else it lead to form of health fundamentalism in which diverse opinion and dialogue are not tolerated.

Thus, thanatology should teach one to enjoy and value life, present and future. A story illustrates the point. Ethan Allen, the Revolutionary War hero, while lying on his death bed, was told by his parson that the angels were waiting. "Waiting are they? Waiting are they? Well, God damn 'em, let 'em wait!" (Feifel, 1959, p. 126). We need to tell political, corporate and other leaders whether in the United

States, the Soviet Union, Iran, Ireland, Great Britain, and other countries that horrendous-type deaths will not be tolerated. We need to tell our angels of horrendous death that they *can* wait!

Do the authors and yourself a favor. Before, during or after reading this book go out and act to eliminate horrendous death. Write your political representatives concerning a related issue. Donate money to a organization like the United Nations, Greenpeace, SANE, the National Association for the Advancement of Colored People, or the Sierra Club. Join the organization. Demonstrate at the White House or Pentagon. Take a class designed to improve the quality of global health and well-being. Teach such a class if you have the skills and knowledge. Write a letter to your newspaper. Eschew furs. Help wildlife live. Help the poor live. Feed the hungry human or animal. Recycle trash, plant a tree, throw your Uzi or AK47 away, get your friend to throw his or hers away, run for elective office on a peace and global health platform (you may lose, so try again), learn a foreign language, talk to a person from a foreign country, become friendly with someone you aren't quite sure of (e.g., if Jewish or Christian invite an Arab to your home, if an Arab, invite a Jew or Christian). Play with your mate and kids. Above all become a health-educated advocate to preserve the health and well-being of all kids.

We, the authors, wish our children, grandchildren, and other loved ones to live long *and* well—don't you? Then why don't you act!

REFERENCES

Barnet, R., & Muller, R. (1974). *Global reach: The power of the multinational corporations.* New York: Simon & Schuster.

Barnet, R. (1980). *The lean years: Politics in the age of scarcity.* New York: Simon & Schuster.

Beard, C., Beard, M., & Beard, W. (1960). *The Beard's history of the United States.* Garden City, NY: Doubleday & Co.

Broder, D. (1989, November 29). Young America's civic failings, *The Washington Post,* p. A-27.

Cassidy, K. (1989). Arms control and the home front: Planning for the conversion of military production facilities to civilian manufacturing. *Peace & Change, 14,* 46–64.

Choron, J. (1963). *Death and Western thought.* New York: Collier Books.

Cleanup pact signed for nuclear site. (1989, May 16). *The Washington Post,* p. A-3.

Concretizing the path toward world government. (1988). *The Federalist, 30,* 218–226.

Dobbs, M. (1989, April 27). Izvestia hits secrecy on A-accidents. *The Washington Post,* p. A-1.

Durning, A. (1989). Poverty and the environment: Reversing the downward spiral. *Worldwatch Paper 92,* Washington, DC: The Worldwatch Institute.

Feifel, H. (1959). *The meaning of death.* New York: McGraw-Hill.

Flavin, C. (1989). Slowing global warming: A worldwide strategy. *Worldwatch Paper 91,* Washington, DC: The Worldwatch Institute.

Fisher, D., & Bloomgarden, A. (1989). Non offensive defense. *Peace Review, 1*(2), 7–11.

The Federalist. (1988). *30*(3), p. 157.

Galtung, J. (1984). *There are alternatives: Four roads to peace and security.* Chester Springs, PA: Dufour Editions.

Grobman, A., & Landes, D. (1983). *Genocide: Critical issues of the holocaust.* Los Angeles: Simon Wiesenthal Center.

Hutchins, R. (1968). *The learning society.* New York: New American Library.

Johnson, H. (1989, Jan. 2). *The Washington Post,* p. A-1.

Kurtz, H. (1989, November 29). Ben & Jerry: Premium ice cream sprinkled with liberal ideology. *The Washington Post,* p. A-3.

Leviton, D. (Ed.) (1991). *Horrendous death, health, and well-being,* Washington: Hemisphere.

Morin, D., & Balz, D. (1989, May 26). Majority in poll criticize Congress. *The Washington Post,* p. A-8.

Nation states and a new international system. (1988). *The Federalist, 30,* 208–217.

Peterson, C. (1989, May 9). Experts, OMB spar on global warming. *The Washington Post,* p. A-1.

Renner, M. (1989). *National security: The economic and environmental dimensions* (Worldwatch paper 89). Washington, DC: Worldwatch Institute.

Renner, M. (1989a). Who are the enemies? *Peace Review, 1*(2), 22–26.

Rowen, H. (1989, April 27). Minimum wages, maximum greed. *The Washington Post,* p. A-23.

Sudan famine relief blocked. (1989, April 27). *The Washington Post,* p. A-28.

Sivard, R. (1987). *World military and social expenditures, 1987–88.* Washington, DC: World Priorities, Box 25140, Washington, DC 20007.

Students to vote on stocking cyanide pills. (1984, October 4). *The Washington Post,* p. A-33.

There are alternatives. (1987) Videotape produced by NRK-TV, Norway. Distributed by The Educational Film & Video Project, 5332 College Ave., Suite 101, Oakland, CA 94618.

Van, J. (1989, May 27). Most doctors willing to lie, study suggests. *The Washington Post,* p. A-7.

Viktor Frankel on aging, meaning, and death. (1989). *The Aging Connection, 10*(3), 7.

World development report. (1988). New York: Oxford University Press.

Appendix A

Resource For Action: But What Can I Do?—A Self Survey

Individuals entering the world-affairs field need to assess their strengths to determine where and how their efforts can help. The following questions can help you clarify your own situation.

I. Who am I?

Name: _____

Address: _____

City: _____ State: _____ Zip: _____

Educational level: _____ Occupation: _____

Religious, political, professional or other organizations to which you belong:

_____

Major peace activities: _____

Work preferences: (check one or more)

leadership role?	nuts and bolts?
help others?	execution?
conceptualization?	meeting new people?
planning?	research?

Groups I enjoy working with (check one or more)

children?	conservative?
young adults?	liberal?
religious?	secular?
professional?	nonvocational
avant garde?	consensus building?

II. In what war/peace, environment, etc., field am I interested? (check one or more)

_____ the U.N., International Organization, and growth toward world law

_____ hunger, world economic development, and social development

_____ building human rights conceptions and enforcement procedures

_____ the arms race, arms control, and general and complete disarmament

_____ conscience and war: the moral issues and value choices involved

_____ current crisis problems: the Middle East, energy, hunger, Southeast Asia, the B-1 bomber, the law of the sea. . .

_____ building understanding across ideological, regional, religious, and ethnic barriers

_____ nonviolent methods of forcing change or conducting conflict
others:_____
_____ I need more information deciding

III.   What do I believe?
        In a word, how do I describe myself?
        _____ world federalist?   _____ pacifist?
        _____ personalist   _____ internationalist?
        _____ deterrence advocate?   _____ next step foreign policy?
        _____ concerned but confused?   _____ other

IV.   What special skills or talents do I have?
        _____ public speaking   _____ persuading others
        _____ discussion leader   _____ motivating others
        _____ office management   _____ organizing groups
        _____ identifying unifying factors _____ raising money
        _____ layout and design   _____ research

V.   How much time can I give?
        _____ full time   _____ one or two days a week
        _____ an hour a day   _____ a few hours a month

VI.   What type of work experience do I need to continue?
        _____ Uncritical acceptance of every peace activity
        _____ Work based on a thoughtful analysis of the reality of conflict
              purposes and power enters in world politics
        _____ Immediate results
        _____ A sense of accomplishment
        _____ A recognition that the work is badly needed

VII.   Where should I work?
        _____ Professional organization (psychiatrists, doctors, lawyers. . .)
        _____ Religious organization (church, synagogue, temple, mosque. . .)
        _____ Business association
        _____ Labor union
        _____ Teacher
        _____ Opinion leaders
        _____ Idea center
        _____ Major institution (school, library, business. . .)
        _____ News media
        _____ University
        _____ Coalition

VIII.   What type of activity makes most sense?
        _____ Developing a film library
        _____ Work with elected officials
        _____ Making visible, intelligent publications in the field
        _____ Protest and demonstration activity
        _____ Campaigns, petitioning, letter writing

_____ Public meetings
_____ Research and idea development
_____ Symbolic witness
_____ Engaging new organizations
_____ Improving the work of old organizations
_____ Building a transnational constituency
_____ Reaching the mass media
_____ Gaining opinion leader support
_____ Educating

IX.   What will I actually do?

The need for serious and specific community work is clear. The variety of possibilities is almost endless. The trick is to match your skills, time, and interest with a task that is both challenging and feasible.

BUT WHAT CAN I DO?—TWENTY-FIVE ANSWERS

Here are twenty-five examples, written in the first person because they are summaries of actual individual experiences.

Work with Decisionmakers

1. We believe in a time of crisis. The best way is to go directly to the decision-makers themselves. If you do not have access directly, find out who does and get them to go. During the Cuban missile crisis I[*] called key Soviet scientists and key American scientists. They in turn reached government officials. An informal channel of communication was opened to the very top leaders. I think we averted World War III that way. I am worried about the next crisis and have continued to build contacts across the ideological divides in the world. I'm grateful for others who have gathered scientists, opinion leaders, members of nongovernmental organizations, even if the concrete results are meager.

2. What ever work is done, in this country or elsewhere, pays off in Washington. Therefore, I have helped work with members of Congress to organize them. We meet periodically to plan strategy in Congress, to work out approaches to specific issues, and to connect work on issues to long-term strategy.

Work on a Transnational Constituency

3. My emphasis has been on transnational relationships. All the focus on this country and on decision-makers in Washington seems to me to be beside the point. We need to develop a transnational constituency for the goals and ideas needed to build a world order. I have thus aided the Institute for World Order in World Order Models Projects. Through this a transnational academic constituency has developed. Soon it may be possible to form a transnational political party. It is an oddity of American politics that the connections to political organizations in other countries are almost nonexistent. Given an interdependent world, we need political

[*] "I" refers to Dr. Robert Woito, author of this survey.

officials willing to run for office on platforms designed to address the new scope of foreign policy.

Enlarging the Knowledge Base

4. When I was young, I knew how to end war. This world is full of surprises. I have turned to an academic career seeking to increase the amount of validated knowledge available to diplomats. There is a large network of peace researchers working in every corner of the world. During the next decade I plan to test out a simulation of the international system developed through a team effort in this country. We will test the simulation in other cultural and ideological settings to eliminate bias.

Direct Involvement

5. Enough now is known to work on the problem of war. What is needed is to apply what we know. I, therefore, gather peace researchers and diplomats in conferences to discuss what is relevant to decision-makers. We have also worked with the nongovernmental International Peace Academy, which trains people for U.N. peacekeeping roles and to her mediation efforts. We are interested in new efforts to form nonviolent "armies" of people willing to act as mediators, even when the parties at war do not ask for mediation. "Seeding" individuals with nonviolent conflict mediation skills in crisis areas may be the best way to build local contacts prior to the time when a crisis erupts. They will then be positioned to mediate.

6. My skills are more administrative than academic. I am working to develop the structure of a government-sponsored Peace Institute designed to teach people conflict-resolution skills. I call it the West Point of the peace movement. I have gone to the U.N. University in Tokyo to study how they have worked out curriculum, relationships between contending perspectives, and the support system needed. Setting up such an institution will be an enormous challenge.

The World-Affairs Field

7. I have worked full time in this field for over thirty years. The field is an imbroglio of organizations. Nearly every new issue that comes along leads to the creation of a new organization. After six months they are usually gone. Those that survive carry an idea, conduct a function, create an arena, or serve a specialized constituency. Almost no one looks at the whole field. My task is to gather and link these organizations, to develop functional relationships among them, to create a mosaic of organizations that can work jointly to make this country a competent actor in world politics.

8. You rarely encounter thoughtful discussions of world affairs. I was curious, at first, why this was so. It now appears that the field is particularly susceptible to conspiracy theories—much of the decision making is done in secret and by elites. I discovered that there is a special role for elites because only a few people are willing to take the time to become experts on an issue or crisis area. Thus, I try to get organizations to sponsor programs that cut beneath the surface questions of issues to the values or the goals involved; then individuals who are not specialists

can become experts on ends and means. In the arenas created as a result, no one point of view carries the day. Many points of view are encountered and each must clarify its values. The point is to map out areas of agreement and disagreement so that possibly, just possibly, we can regain a sense of direction.

Education

9. I'm a social studies teacher. In my field the problem is to keep up with the outpouring of literature from a variety of curriculum development centers, and then to get teachers to use it. School boards, curriculum development centers, research institutes, social studies organizations—all of these are places where critical decisions are being made daily to prepare children for the world they will face. I work in each area to improve the resources available to teachers and to focus attention on nonmilitary alternatives to war as the means to resolve international conflict.

10. I work in curriculum development. We have tried to break out of the national focus into a global perspective. The nation state is still the critical actor but the interaction between states, the problems that no state can solve alone, provide the challenge to us. Some of the new curricula are very imaginative. Students at each grade level participate in creating connections between people and places, change and continuity, cultural differences and underlying uniformities. Because we are continually meeting people from new cultures, ideologies, religions, and various walks of life, it is essential to prepare students first to appreciate and to understand their own values, then comfortably meet and relate to people with different values. That way we can increase the chances that the inevitable conflicts in world politics will be handled without violence, because misperceptions resulting from misunderstandings can be reduced, and perhaps institutions can be created for resolving real conflicts that remain.

Mass Media

11. I'm a writer and a TV producer. Using the skill and channels now open to me obviously makes the most sense. The media is the major "shaper" of ideas and attitudes in this society. I'm always on the lookout for intelligent programming that helps clarify how international conflict can be conducted and resolved without violence and which then increases our understanding of others; all of this aids in promoting constructive change. Sometimes this means connecting a resource person with a talk show host; sometimes it means developing a script into a TV series; sometimes it means writing a script from scratch.

12. I have two small children and spend much of the day at home. I have done editing for world affairs organizations that engage in publishing or preparing news releases and grant proposals. In addition, I keep track of all the radio and TV talk shows, the kind of ideas they focus on, and how people who care about world affairs can be heard.

Peace Education with Children

13. I believe it is important to work with children. I have, therefore, done a survey of available curricula for churches and temples and found much of it is of

real value. We have set up workshops for religious leaders to sort through the available curricula, picking those that are open-ended because they have more than one outcome. We have also used intergenerational and intercultural curricula and projects for families and for religious institutions as a means of preparing children for an interdependent world.

Reach Opinion Leaders

14. There is in my region of the country a select number of people whose judgment really has weight. The important thing is to get them to put world affairs high among their priorities and to nurture them so they can offer wise leadership. I have a list of fifteen people whom I regularly inform of key decisions and another ten in my profession with whom I maintain regular correspondence.

Work Through World Affairs Educational Organizations

15. I have been very skeptical of organizations in the world-affairs field. For the most part, they are so one-sided in their portrayal of the virtues and vices of the various actors in the field, so selective in their presentation of facts, so focused in what they want, that I avoid them. Instead, I've joined the World Affairs Council and the Foreign Policy Association. They offer balanced programs and do a sophisticated job of education on the realities of world politics. Each year we study the Great Decisions booklet, and form opinions on a variety of world affairs issues. These opinions are then tabulated and passed on to decision-makers. In that way, an informed public opinion can be achieved and it can have an impact on those now responsible for policy.

16. I've found that world affairs organizations rarely challenge the prevailing views in the Department of State. What they do, an important task to be sure, is to create an informed dialogue within the framework of assumptions and beliefs in government. I think far more of our efforts should go into making the United Nations a viable, effective keeper of the peace. I, therefore, focus my energies on the United Nations Association.

Choose an Issue

17. I like to focus all my energy on one issue. Whether it is a new weapons system or one of a whole series of economic issues or a human rights question or some crisis, I work on what is current. I try to become an instant expert by reading a number of different periodicals, consulting with specialists, reading the newspapers, and by meeting with organizational leaders. Then, I can write letters to the editor, form or join an ad hoc organization, visit my representative or write the President.

Conscience and War

18. My church was deeply divided by the draft in the 1960s. Some people did draft counseling that was little different from a resource for people wanting to

avoid military service. A group of us in the church challenged this approach, indicating that it was advocating dishonesty. We then studied questions of conscience and war and formulated guidelines for a counseling center. We insisted that the center honestly present information, that counseling be done that challenged people to think carefully about the contending bodies of thought related to war. Some of those we counseled filed for conscientious objector status. Others joined the army. Still others acted out of their judgment by refusing to register. I think most of the people we counseled were aware of the shortcomings of any position offered in answer to the question: Are you a conscientious objector toward? A few, whatever they decided at the time, have continued to work to develop nonmilitary ways to conduct and resolve international conflict.

Become an Expert in a Specific Program Area

19. I've become an expert on good war/peace films. I've seen most of them. I developed a rating system to aid people conducting programs in schools, religious institutions, or world affairs organizations. The ratings, plus annotations of what is in the films, together with ordering information makes the film resource list I developed a hot item. It is hard to turn the feelings and ideas engendered by most war/peace films into constructive programs, so resources to aid in that endeavor have been and are being developed.

Religious Institutions

20. My institution has been skeptical about its appropriate role in the world-affairs field. At first we let the small group that cared passionately about issues use a few of our resources. They did not, however, deeply influence the religious instruction, the sermons, or the adult education classes. Then we thought through what should be the institution's response to these issues. To do so required discussion with people with very different perspectives. Out of that discussion came a framework of belief most agreed upon and which then enabled us to engage the institution in a consideration of how its values ought to be applied to world affairs.

People-to-People

21. I've always felt that we miss a great opportunity to influence world affairs when we ignore the visitors in our midst. I was amazed at the number of students, visiting officials, business people, diplomats, newspaper correspondents, and others I have met from other countries. I have worked with exchange students. Some of these relationships have continued over the years.

Symbolic Acts

22. I'm impatient with those approaches that counsel caution. Education is fine, but the major issues of our time are moral questions. Surely these eternal meetings miss the point—the point is to act. I've helped organize a walk across the United States and Europe, from Seattle to Moscow. We plan to talk to everyone we meet urging concern about the threats to our survival.

23. The most important thing you can do is say no. To say no forcefully re-

quires that you put your body on the line. I've learned the techniques of civil disobedience and have organized a mass protest. We plan to encircle the Pentagon, the Soviet embassy, and the embassy of any country at war at that time.

Support a Professional

24. I've been impressed by the quality of people working sacrificially in the world-affairs field. I am, therefore, making a regular pledge to a world affairs organization. It was hard to decide which one to support. I requested the organizational leaflets of the twenty-five which interested me most, then went to visit the five that seemed particularly well-conceived.

Be a Professional

25. I've decided to work full time in a world affairs organization. It is a challenging choice. We have yet to secure a funding base, so financial sacrifice is the reality. But the challenge of developing ideas, organizations, and resources makes it worthwhile.

ACTING WITHIN AN ORGANIZATION

An Organizational International Human Rights Quotient and an Assessment Tool

We know that the question of peace and the question of human rights are closely related.
Without recognition of human rights, we shall never have peace.
It is only within the framework of peace that human rights can be fully developed.
Dag Hammarskjold

The Assessment

First, your own perspective: A concern for international human rights is now an important element in U.S. foreign policy. What is your reaction?

In answering the following questions, try to assess both your national organization's and your local organization's work in the field of international human rights.

I. International Human Rights and Your Organization: Facts

1. In your judgment, should advancing international human rights have a prominent place on your organization's agenda?
   a. Does it now?
   b. If it does, are there formal guidelines or policy statements to direct the organization's international human rights work? How valuable are these?
2. What kinds of international human rights violations have been the objects of your organization's concerns?
3. What countries' human rights practices have received your organization's attention in the past five years?
   a. How has that attention been expressed?

4. Is there a committee and/or staff person assigned responsibility for international human rights work in your organization?

nationally   _____ committee _____ staff person
locally   _____ committee _____ staff person

II. International Human Rights and Your Organization: Concepts

These questions are to help you assess your organization's ideas on international human rights (or, if not developed), what they should be.

Standards

5. In developing its human rights concepts, does your organization assert that there are universal human rights, fundamental rights of all people, which constitute moral standards to which we can appeal in making judgments about countries with traditions different from our own?

6. The world being as it is, human rights violations are legion. Limitations of time and energy require choosing those cases of human rights violations to which your organization will respond. Is your organization clear on what it considers "persistent patterns of gross violations of human rights," requiring an expenditure of organizational energy and resources?

a. Is there a statement in writing of how your organization makes that judgment?

7. Is your organization's human rights activity vulnerable to charges of being suspiciously selective, directed toward Chile, South Korea, and Iran, but not Cuba, Vietnam, and Mozambique (or vice versa)?

a. Because no organization can work on everything, most develop a pattern of response or activity in the human rights field. If your organization has, is that pattern desirable and appropriate to the organization? Is it vulnerable to a charge of "double standard"?

8. Should there be a single standard, or are there other values and goals in our foreign policy that, in some cases, should take priority over our human rights concerns? If so, what are they?

Balance

9. There are societies committed to and working on a broad range of human rights, societies which are open to scrutiny and criticism. There are also societies in which gross violations of human rights are a matter of state policy, and reporting these is difficult because information is rigidly controlled.

In between these two extremes are a variety of intermediate arrangements. Does your organization understand this situation and deal with it wisely?

Intervention

10. What is your reaction to this statement: "The U.S. Government should not interfere in the internal affairs of other countries." ?

11. If you think there are situations in which the United States should intervene, what means should be used?

12. Do you think that the human rights situation in the United States today is such that this country can legitimately seek to forward human rights internationally?

Scope

13. Here are two statements:

The language and concepts of human rights cannot be restricted to the traditional North Atlantic civil and political liberties, nor to the question of government in its relationship to individuals. Human rights must include those fundamental claims to food, work, medical care, education, and culture that are primary requisites of a human life.

The language and concepts of human rights should be reserved to the arena of political and civil liberties. Other language and concepts will serve us better in seeking to meet other basic human needs. This is because there is a difference between the essential goals of any enlightened political community, and identifying those goals as entitlements to be delivered primarily by governments under the rubric of human rights. Government may not be the best way to reach those goals, and the price of giving government this power may be a serious encroachment on the civil and political liberties that define a democratic society.

    a. Which of these statements most accurately reflects your approach to human rights?
    b. Which of these statements most accurately reflects your organization's approach to human rights?

Rationale

14. Much of the current discussion of international human rights invokes ethical or legal concepts. Are there practical reasons that our country should give a high priority for advancing international human rights?

III. International Human Rights and Your Organization: Action

We're approaching this from the point of view of a member of an American nongovernmental organization (NGO).

You are asked first to outline your organization's international human rights work at various levels, and then to survey your attitude toward the range of human rights programming available to a U.S. NGO.

Check the levels of your organization that presently conduct international human rights activities and, where possible, give an example.

Examples

15. _____ for its local members
16. _____ for the local community
17. _____ as a national organization
18. _____ in relation to the U.S. government

19. _____ in relation to the U.N. and its agencies
20. _____ with the international NGO to which your organization relates
21. _____ with other international NGOs and

Elements of a Developed International Human Rights Program for an American NGO. Circle appropriate category.
A. Would welcome my organization doing this.
B. We're doing it nationally.
C. We're doing it here locally.

22.   Publications: Do you publish materials that
draw on your organization's tradition,
discipline, or function to set out your role
in the international human rights field?   A.   B.   C.

23.   Newspaper, newsletter, or other
information services: Regular reporting on
international human rights problems?   A.   B.   C.

24.   Statements: By your organization's
leader(s) on U.S. international human
rights policy?   A.   B.   C.

25.   Statements: By your organization's
leader(s) on international human rights as a
program focus on your organization?   A.   B.   C.

26.   Leadership training: Are there
opportunities for those wanting to take
responsibility in this field to learn the
business—ideas, perspectives, other
organizations, government actors and
agencies, program-funding strategies, etc.?   A.   B.   C.

27.   Education programs for your membership:
a. for adults?   A.   B.   C.
b. for young people?   A.   B.   C.
c. for children?   A.   B.   C.

28.   Programs for the local community:
a. arena-setting events?   A.   B.   C.
b. media visibility   A.   B.   C.

29.   Legislative information: Does your
organization keep abreast of current
Congressional action that bears on U.S.
international human rights policy?   A.   B.   C.

30.   Congressional and executive action:
             Response to or attempts to encourage
             action (by the Congress, the President, the
             State Department, or other federal
             agencies) your organization thinks is
             necessary?   A.   B.   C.

31.   Advocacy: Petitions, boycotts, issue
             campaigns, etc.?   A.   B.   C.

32.   Action in relation to the international NGO
             to which you are linked: Joining its
             international human rights activities in both
             substance and program; catalyzing needed
             action?   A.   B.   C.

33.   Action in relation to the U.N. and its
             affiliate agencies: Monitoring action and
             resolutions; formulating positions in
             relation to theirs; acting through NGO
             channels in New York and Geneva.   A.   B.   C.

34.   Symbolic events? public witness activity:
             Special services or days designed to
             highlight and remind your organization and
             the wider community of the fundamental
             commitments from which all this activity
             arises.   A.   B.   C.

35.   Mass media activity: Press releases, press
             conferences, etc.?   A.   B.   C.

36.   Direct action in support of victims in
             human rights violations abroad: Aiding in
             visibility, funding, and support before
             relevant governments and/or U.N. agencies   A.   B.   C.

IV. International Human Rights and Your Organization: Problems and Countries

On which of these problems is your organization currently working (either in a human rights context or as a means of meeting basic human needs and aspirations)?

	Concern of my organization	Understood and worked on in a "human rights" context.

37. adequate medical care (physical and mental health)
38. adequate standard of living (food, clothing, housing)
39. arbitrary arrest and detention
40. benefits of authorship or intervention
41. emigration
42. employment
43. equal pay for equal work
44. equal status before the law
45. ethnic language and culture
46. form and maintain a family
47. free assembly
48. free press
49. free speech
50. free and compulsory primary education
51. freedom of conscience, thought, and religion
52. genocide
53. leisure time
54. participation in cultural life
55. racial discrimination
56. safe working conditions
57. self-determination
58. sex discrimination
59. social security
60. torture
61. other:

Which of these countries is presently the focus of your organization's international human rights concern and action? (The list is not exhaustive, feel free to add others.)

_____ 62. Argentina
_____ 63. Bangladesh
_____ 64. Brazil
_____ 65. Burma
_____ 66. Central African Empire
_____ 67. Chile
_____ 68. China (PRC)
_____ 69. China (Taiwan)
_____ 70. Cuba
_____ 71. Ethiopia
_____ 72. India
_____ 73. Indonesia
_____ 74. Iran
_____ 75. Northern Ireland
_____ 76. Israel
_____ 77. Kampuchea
_____ 78. North Korea

_____ 79. South Korea
_____ 80. Libya
_____ 81. Mexico
_____ 82. Mozambique
_____ 83. Namibia
_____ 84. Pakistan
_____ 85. Philippines
_____ 86. Poland
_____ 87. Romania
_____ 88. Saudi Arabia
_____ 89. South Africa
_____ 90. Syria
_____ 91. Uganda
_____ 92. U.S.S.R.
_____ 93. Vietnam
_____ 94. Zimbabwe
_____ 95. Other

V. International Human Rights and Your Organization: The Quality of the Endeavor

In short, as you look at the full range of your organization's international human rights thought and activity, not quantitatively but qualitatively, is it an expression of the best in your tradition and values?

1	2	3	4	5	6	7	8	9	10

unclear, thoughtless,   lots of problems   speaks from the
confused, hypocritical   but basically on the   very best of our
                                 right track   roots and addresses
                                                            these issues wisely
                                                            and effectively

SPECIALIZING IN A SUBJECT AREA: AN EXAMPLE

Most of the material in this book is intended to give you a general overview of the world-affairs field. As you become familiar with the ideas and problems in the field, you may want to deepen your knowledge of some section of it which is of special interest to you. Whether the subject is disarmament or development, the Middle East or South Africa, ethics and war, or transnational corporations, there is a need for specialized knowledge plus an understanding of how a particular problem area relates to the overall problem of progress toward an end to war. What does the latter require? Using the disarmament area as an example, to develop a specialist's understanding, you should come to know:

1. The crucial periodicals that deal regularly with issues of arms control and disarmament (e.g., *Foreign Affairs, Foreign Policy, The Bulletin of Atomic Scientists,* etc.). You probably already follow arms control and disarmament issues in the general circulation magazines and newspapers. It is important that you also familiarize yourself with the relevant specialists and scholarly journals, and become acquainted with general circulation periodicals that present a range of political perspectives on arms control problems.

2. The best introductory pamphlets, books, and research center reports dealing with disarmament problems.

3. The government agencies, congressional committees, and staffs of the executive branch who are responsible for arms control and disarmament policy.

You should know: who on the President's staff is influential on arms control and disarmament questions, who in the National Security Council, the Pentagon, the State Department, and the CIA is responsible for arms control and disarmament matters, who heads the U.S. Arms Control and Disarmament Agency and what staff officers are most helpful, who chairs the relevant Congressional committees and who are the key staff? Are you on their mailing lists?

4. The staff and members of committees and sections of the United Nations that deal with disarmament questions; the specialized international agencies involved.

Does the U.N. General Assembly have disarmament questions on its agenda for this year? What issues are being discussed? Is another Special Session on Disarmament planned? Is the Committee on Disarmament meeting? What is the Secretary-General doing to promote disarmament negotiations and agreements? What is the U.N. Centre for Disarmament doing? Who in the U.S. delegation to the U.N. is especially concerned with disarmament questions?

5. What specific arms control and disarmament issues will confront the President, Congress, the United Nations, bilateral and multilateral negotiators, and the American public this year? What new technological developments are shaping the course of the nuclear and conventional arms races? When will this year's arms control impact statements be issued? What new weapons systems will require Congressional authorization? What disarmament legislation is pending before Congress? What other issues will be discussed in public media—nuclear proliferation, zonal disarmament, nuclear strategy, international supervision and inspection, conventional disarmament, arms embargoes?

6. The international and national nongovernmental organizations and thought centers that do educational, political and research work on arms control and disarmament issues; the positions they have taken on specific issues. What coalitions or interorganizational policy approaches have been adopted? What policies have been discussed by representatives and people from proliferation ideological camps?

7. The individuals articulating the major distinct approaches to arms control and disarmament problems, their arguments and responses to their critics' arguments. As the debate over an issue takes shape, it is important to know the contending schools of thought. As you follow the discussion in general circulation and scholarly journals, you will probably notice that within each school of thought most spokespersons defer to the arguments of a particular scholar or expert. You should know who these experts are and be familiar with their perspectives.

8. Educational resources in the field: bibliographies, films, tapes, reports, article reprints, speakers available locally and nationally, and program materials prepared for work at both levels.

There is a wealth of educational materials available, but you need to know how to evaluate them, what they are useful for, and where they can be obtained.

9. Your own context, standards, values, goals, and conceptions of what you are doing. This is a reminder that although you may acquire much specialized knowledge, you will be working on only one part of the problem of war. How does work on disarmament relate to problems of world law, economic development, and building a sense of world community? How might the goals, which you pursue in the areas of arms control and disarmament, be aided by international agreements in other areas?

10. What specific peace initiatives by one country could demonstrate a willingness to move beyond arms control toward disarmament? Is its initiative simply to reduce its own level of threat or does it combine such reduction with efforts to gain reciprocal reductions by others?

This is the essential task and one "payoff" for a specialist. It is rarely done well. When you take policy proposals that are offered throughout the literature and turn them into specific acts one country (or other international actor) can take which initiate process toward disarmament goals (and others), then you are working within the context recommended by the book, *To End War*. All of these may sound too much for one person to handle; but a minimal filing system, a relationship with one of the good world affairs organizations in your subject area, links to a few important centers of thought nationally, and a sustained intention to build your own understanding will soon enable you to make a significant contribution to the policy decision-making process.

Passion and ignorance are too frequently combined in the world-affairs field. It is essential that you do your homework on your part of the field. You'll be a valuable resource person in your community or organization if you do.

Appendix B

Nuclear Weapons and Nuclear War: An Annotated Mediagraphy

Richard A. Pacholski
Millikin University, Decatur, Illinois

For many years nations have had in place the means of wiping all human civilization from the face of the globe. Yet nations persist to this day in expending billions of dollars developing the wherewithal to perform that global scouring many times over. The nuclear weapons race thus adversely affects the global quality of life in its massive diversion of material wealth and human energy from perennial human problems of poverty, hunger, and disease. And in individual lives all over the globe, growing fears of annihilation of both the self and humankind are having as yet untold effects.

Teachers, discussion leaders, counselors, and others wanting to explore the history and impact of the nuclear arms race, the effects of nuclear war, and the means (if there are any) of securing the future for generations to come may choose from hundreds of audiovisual programs. Presented here is a carefully annotated, highly selective short list of what I consider the best, most recent (produced after 1982) nuclear audiovisuals. They are grouped into the following categories to facilitate intelligent selection: (a) introductions to basic issues—audiovisuals covering a wide range of topics, suitable for structured classroom learning; (b) surveys of special topics—programs for audiences already familiar with the basics, exploring particular issues in some depth; (c) consciousness raisers—programs not so much structured or academic in their approach as attention-getting and aiming to make general audiences aware of the importance of nuclear issues ("calls to action" are included here); and (d) feature films.

For further information on older media dealing with nuclear issues, consult these sources:

War. Peace. Film Guide (188 pages, 1980) describes and evaluates more than 285 films, program aids, and other materials. Available for $5.75 from World Without War Publications, Suite 1417, 67 East Madison, Chicago, IL 60603.

Guide to Disarmament Media (May 1982) describes 26 films, videotapes, and slideshows especially appropriate for educational purposes; lists guidebooks and other sources of information; and offers advice on program planning. An *Update* (October 1983) lists 50 additional titles. Available for $1.00 each from Media Network, 208 West 13th Street, New York, NY 10011.

"How to Run a Film Series on the Nuclear Arms Race and Nuclear War," by John Dowling, provides brief reviews, descriptions, and availability information on what Dowling calls "the eleven best" or classic films on these topics produced from 1965 to 1982. Published in *Bulletin of the Atomic Scientists, 38*(6), 51–52.

1984 National Directory of A-V Resources on Nuclear War and the Arms Race (57 pages), edited by Karen Sayer and John Dowling, is a massive, richly annotated mediagraphy providing thorough coverage of materials produced before 1984, giving content summaries, and evaluating the materials; the detailed subject index will facilitate programming decisions. Available for $4.00 from the University of Michigan Media Resources Center, 400 Fourth Street, Ann Arbor, MI 48103.

Landers' Film Reviews, Media and Methods, Library Journal, Choice, and *Booklist* are the best periodical sources of detailed information about and capsule reviews of new audiovisual releases. Be sure to keep in touch with your reference librarian or media specialist; audiovisuals on nuclear war and nuclear weapons are being produced apace.

INTRODUCTION TO BASIC ISSUES

Aptly titled, *A Place to Begin: An Approach to Nuclear Education* presents an instructional model for teachers who want to become involved in nuclear issues education. The film describes a high school short course, emphasizing the rationale, instructional methodology, and subject matter content of such a course. Handled responsibly, nuclear issues instruction can enhance students' basic skills—critical thinking and oral and written communication—while at the same time fostering responsible citizenship through heightened awareness of essential human values.

As for subject matter content, nuclear issues education is quintessentially multidisciplinary, affecting literally every field of human knowledge. *A Place to Begin* depicts a month-long course exploring these basic questions:

1. Who are the "experts" who define the issues for the rest of us? On what terms?

2. What techniques do the experts use? That is, what is "propaganda" and how does it work?

3. What are the existing types of nuclear weapons and weapons systems?

4. Who has them? How many? How are they deployed and controlled?

5. How and why has the arms race developed since World War II?

6. Who are the Russians? Why do we relate to them as we do?

7. Where is the nuclear situation taking us? What options do we have? How can individuals become involved in determining the collective future of the human race?

Other issues might be covered, such as the legality and morality of nuclear war planning, the merits of civil defense, nuclear winter, and the capability of the health care delivery system to deal with the aftermath of a nuclear attack. Content can be tailored to the particular interests and strengths of the teacher or the sponsoring academic department. Of course, instructional units can never examine every relevant topic; nor need they. What is important is that the subject is broached and that students be taught how to explore it intelligently, to understand its relevance to human life, and to *act* upon the imperatives of their knowledge and understanding.

With scenes of actual classroom interchange, *A Place to Begin* illustrates how a well-prepared teacher fosters thinking, speaking, and listening skills—as well as good citizenship—during discussion of nuclear issues. (Videotape, all formats, color, 30 min, 1985; available from Educators for Social Responsibility, 23 Garden Street, Cambridge, MA 02138; telephone 617-492-1764.)

Nuclear Strategy for Beginners, originally presented on the public television *Nova* series, surveys the historical background of present-day nuclear policies and provides helpful definitions and explanations of many key concepts (strategic bombing, counterforce and countervalue targets, flexible response, mutual assured destruction [MAD], and so on). Informative film clips, illustrations, and interviews with various authorities make this a very fine introductory survey. (Videotape, all formats, color, 60 min, 1983; available from Time Life Video, 100 Eisenhower Drive, Paramus, NJ 07652.)

A more recent filmstrip/audiocassette program, *Nuclear Weapons: Concepts and Controversies,* covers the same historical ground as it describes the evolution of current nuclear war fighting strategy and related foreign policy, and defines relevant terminology. President Reagan's proposed Strategic Defense Initiative (SDI), the "Star Wars" missile defense system, is discussed at length; equal time is given to both sides of that controversial program. (Two color filmstrips and audiocassettes, 15 min each; also available in VHS videocassette format, 1985; available from Human Relations Media, 175 Tompkins Avenue, Pleasantville, NY 10570.)

Notes on Nuclear War is a useful film introduction to many related topics—the history and development of the arms race; the political attitudes and doctrines that have fueled superpower relations; and the various military strategies preferred over time as the best ways to assert national preeminence, to compete with and to best rivals, and to "guarantee" victory (whether military or political) in changing situations. For example, governmental attitudes toward the "survivability" of "limited" nuclear war, various "civil defense" proposals (whether of whole populations or leadership cadres), and the intimate interrelationships between the military and the industrial sectors are surveyed and analyzed. Other topics are covered too, such as early bomb testing methods and programs, the effects of the Hiroshima and Nagasaki bombs, and the comparable effects on people and property in the event of explosions of modern nuclear devices. This award-winning program (Blue Ribbon Award, American Film Festival, 1986) would be especially useful for general adult and community audiences, as well as for senior high and college groups. (Color film and videocassette, 60 min, 1986; available from Films Incorporated, 5547 North Ravenswood Avenue, Chicago, IL 60640.)

Several programs focus on the nuclear arms race and efforts to halt or limit it. *Disarmament: The Quest for Lasting Peace* will help its audience put the various test-ban treaties, SALT (strategic arms limitations) treaties, and START (strategic arms reduction) talks—all the disarmament and weapons-freeze proposals of recent years—into historical context. Specifically, the current world political situation and efforts to normalize superpower relationships are traced to their roots prior to World War I. Emphasis is given, of course, to developments since 1945. The positions of various administration arms control negotiators, and those of several experts who disagree, are presented in detail. Throughout, well-chosen visuals (e.g., photographs, art work, political cartoons, and illustrative graphics) and different narrator voices maintain interest and enhance instruction. Difficult concepts are highlighted and repeated. (Four color filmstrips and audiocassettes, 15 min each, also available in VHS videocassette format, 1983; available from Human Relations Media, 175 Tompkins Avenue, Pleasantville, NY 10570.)

Another filmstrip/audiocassette program surveying all sides of the arms control debate is *Arms Control: Contemporary Issues.* The divergent views of many authorities are presented: Roger Mollander, of the antinuclear group Ground Zero; David Trachtenburg, of the Committee on the Present Danger; and Ronald Lehman, of the U.S. Department of Defense, among others. Topics discussed include the effects of nuclear war, nuclear arms proliferation, recent arms control efforts, and the implications of growing public concern about these issues. Produced by the *Encyclopedia Britannica.* (Color, 20 min, 1984; available from Social Studies School Service, 10200 Jefferson Boulevard, P.O. Box 802, Culver City, CA 90232-0802; telephone 800-421-4246, in California call collect, 213-839-2436.)

The arms race and what to do about it are also the topic of *The Freeze,* a film that presents the differing views of many people: private citizens, political and military leaders, workers in nuclear weapons facilities, and scientists. Intercut with these interviews are scenes of the Hiroshima–Nagasaki bombings, clips from several other award-winning films on nuclear issues, diagrams of patterns of destruction were a nuclear bomb to be exploded over San Francisco, and arguments that there can be no such things as "civil defense" or "surviving" in an all-out nuclear war. The only thing to do, the film concludes, is to freeze nuclear weapons production. It is a well-made film, suitable for intermediate grades through adult audiences. (Color film or videotape, 25 min, 1983; available from Direct Cinema Limited, P.O. Box 69799, Los Angeles, CA 90069-9976; telephone 213-652-8000.)

For a balanced introduction to both sides of the nuclear freeze debate and an analysis of its implications, teachers may also consider *Issue: The Nuclear Freeze Controversy.* Produced by the *New York Times,* this filmstrip/audiocassette program covers the history of the debate, outlines the roles played by government agencies on the one hand and by freeze proponents (chiefly grass roots movements) on the other, and gives a chronology of key events shaping the debate over the years. The growing importance of the issue in public opinion and its possible impact on political developments in the next few years in the United States and elsewhere are also explained. (Color, 17 min, 1984; available from Social Studies School Service, 10200 Jefferson Boulevard, P.O. Box 802, Culver City, CA 90232-0802; telephone 800-421-4246, in California call collect 213-839-2436.)

Addressing a key element in our ongoing arms control negotiations with the Soviet Union, a test ban treaty, *A Step Away from War* argues that such a treaty is workable and safe and that it would represent a major step both in reducing dependence on nuclear arms and in normalizing relationships among the superpowers. Produced by the Center for Defense Information (CDI), this program features archival film footage and interviews with Glenn Seaborg (former member of the Atomic Energy Commission), Congressmen Jim Leach and Jim Wright, geophysicist Jack Evernden, and Admiral Gene LaRoque (retired), Director of CDI. (Color videocassette, 28 min, 1986; available from Aylmer Press, 930 Spring Street, Madison, WI 53705.)

Though the greatest danger to world peace seems to lie in the arms race between the United States and the Soviet Union, many experts claim that war, if it comes, will be precipitated by smaller countries or terrorists. A recent documentary, *The Other Nuclear Arms Race,* describes the "proliferation" of nuclear weapons and weapons-building technology to other countries, many of them politically unstable and at odds with their neighbors. Efforts to limit proliferation through treaty and technology control are discussed by experts involved in those efforts: Kenneth Adelman, Joseph P. Nye, James Schlesinger, and Brent Scowcroft. (Videocassette, all formats, color, 30 min, 1986; available from Social Studies School Service, 10200 Jefferson Boulevard, P.O. Box 802, Culver City, CA 90232-0802; telephone 800-421-4246, in California call collect, 213-839-2436.)

Discussions of war and peace in the nuclear age inevitably lead to questions about the Russians. They are the reason we must be ready to go to war, we have been told. They have been the aggressors. Can they be trusted to share the world in peace now? An informative film, *What About the Russians?,* analyzes such questions and the preconceptions of those who ask them. The approach here is to examine current U.S. military/nuclear policies in light of how we interpret Russian attitudes, motives, and plans. Are they really "ahead"? Can they be trusted? How are they responding to NATO deployment of Pershing II missiles? And why? Authorities like Robert McNamara, Paul Warnke, Mark Hatfield, and George Kennan offer penetrating insights into the nature of American thinking, and "misthinking," about our major world adversary, and suggest ways out of the present nuclear impasse. (Color film or videotape, 26 min, 1983; available from Educational Film and Video Project, 1725 Seabright Avenue, Santa Cruz, CA 95062.)

Another film, *US versus USSR: Who's Ahead?,* focuses tightly on the one question basic to those annual debates fought out so vigorously in Congress over the size of our "defense" budget. Actor Martin Sheen narrates a careful analysis of the topic, presenting the views and approaches of Pentagon officials, appropriations experts from the Central Intelligence Agency, and other military spending specialists. The key question is subdivided: What does "ahead" mean? "Ahead" in what categories of weapons? To what degree of readiness? In what geographical contexts? Does "military superiority" really *mean* anything transferable into dollar and ruble equivalents? Basic assumptions about the arms race and its costs come in for vigorous debate in this well-made film. (Videocassette, color, 29 min, 1983; available from Ideal Communications, P.O. Box 53398, Washington, DC 20003; telephone 202-543-7777.)

Finally, consider a pair of films offering concise presentations of opposing viewpoints on the nature of the current world political situation and on related military and other solutions to the nuclear predicament. These two programs would be most useful if presented to audiences in tandem; together they present a full range of alternative visions for the future of humanity. *Countdown for America* makes the best case for the "peace through strength" position. That is, peace can be attained only by taking the hardest line toward the Soviets, by developing every possible weapons system, by modernizing our military forces on an ongoing basis, and by spending whatever is necessary to achieve and retain military superiority over the Russians. (16-mm film or 3/4-inch videocassette, color, 27 min, 1983; available from American Security Council Foundation, Reston, VA 22713; telephone 703-825-1776.) The title of the other film, *War Without Winners,* is indicative of its assumptions. While proponents of the "peace through strength" position are given time to make their arguments that nuclear war can be won, the thrust of

War Without Winners is to argue the folly of planning for nuclear war and to question the assumptions made by various administrations with regard to Russian intentions and capabilities. What must be done, this film suggests, is to work to normalize relationships with the communist bloc and eventually to "outlaw all nuclear weapons." (16-mm film, color, 28 min, discussion guide included, 1982; available from Center for Defense Information, 303 Capitol Gallery West, 600 Maryland Avenue, SW, Washington, DC 20024.) Again, showing both of these hard-hitting films will generate vigorous and valuable discussion of the full range of nuclear war–nuclear weapons issues, particularly at the beginning of an instructional unit or course.

In the spring of 1989, Public Broadcasting Service (PBS) aired a new 13-program series, *War and Peace in the Nuclear Age*. Produced by WBGH in Boston and Central Independent Television in Great Britain in association with NHK in Japan, this series was designed originally as a college-credit course, of primary interest to students of history and political science. Accompanying print materials (a reader, study guide, and trade book) have been published by Alfred A. Knopf. The series provides coverage of all Nuclear Age topics from the 1930s to the present. In 13 hr, of course, time is available for in-depth exploration of material that is only surveyed in most other audiovisuals. Included are extended retrospective interviews with scientists and politicians, many of them European and Russian, who have not been seen in other audiovisuals and also much archival film footage not seen elsewhere. Topics include the earliest nuclear research efforts, the Manhattan Project, the origins of the Cold War, the significance of Sputnik, NATO and European nuclear weapons, the era of McNamara and Kissinger, Nonproliferation and SALT treaties, Star Wars, and prospects for the future. The series of 13 programs is available for $350; each program sells for $29.95—seemingly, a bargain. (Available from Annenberg Project, P.O. Box 4069, Santa Barbara, CA 93140-4069; telephone 800-532-7637.)

SURVEYS OF SPECIAL TOPICS

Several informative films explore the historical and political backgrounds of contemporary nuclear realities in great detail, rather than simply introducing a variety of basic issues and concepts. Thus the following audiovisuals are best shown to audiences prepared to benefit fully from them.

Hiroshima and Nagasaki

Recent research has called into question some basic dogmas of our nuclear history and nuclear thinking, for example, that we had to develop atomic weapons before our Nazi and other enemies did and that we had to drop atomic bombs on two Japanese cities to bring World War II to a successful conclusion. This new research is reported in *Hiroshima and Nagasaki: Was Truman's Decision to Use the Bomb Justified?* Apparently President Truman had several other military, as well as political and diplomatic, alternatives for ending the war, all of which he rejected. Truman's rationale for choosing the course he did is analyzed critically, and arguments on many sides of the issue are examined. This new program thus provides rich background on the wartime development of the atomic bomb as it reviews the staggering devastation in Hiroshima and Nagasaki. Included are clips of recently released Japanese and other archival footage. (Color and B/W video-cassette, 20 min, study guide included, 1989; available from Social Studies School Service, 10200 Jefferson Boulevard, P.O. Box 802, Culver City, CA 90232-0802; telephone 800-421-4246, in California call collect 213-839-2436.)

Prophecy is one of three films describing the effects of the Hiroshima–Nagasaki atomic blasts from the Japanese perspective. Using clips of film taken by Japanese cameramen (released here for the first time in the United States), *Prophecy* records the immediate destruction in the two cities and documents the thousands upon thousands of deaths from both the blast itself and subsequent radiation poisoning. Highlights from "nuclear history"—weapons tests around the world, for example, and "improvements" in the nuclear arsenals of the superpowers—are intercut with scenes showing the disabilities, the scars, and the continuing medical treatment of many Hiroshima–Nagasaki survivors. In summary, the Japanese say to us: "It's your future. It's your choice" (Red Ribbon Award winner, American Film Festival, 1983). (Color film or videocassette, 45 min, 1983; available from Films, Incorporated, 1144 Wilmette Avenue, Wilmette, IL 60091).

Survivors focuses on a little-publicized group of Japanese Americans who, trapped in Japan at the start of the war, happened to be in Hiroshima or Nagasaki when the atomic bombs fell. Now living again in the United States, these survivors tell about their blast- and radiation-induced injuries, their lingering illnesses, their fears of having children—the countless ways, large and small, The Bomb has affected their lives. This moving film helps its audience make a crucial imaginative leap: from knowing the effects of two primitive atomic weapons on some 30 people, to conceiving the sort of future promised to the survivors, if any there are, of even a "limited" exchange of modern weapons. (16-mm film, color, 58 min, 1983; First Run Features, 153 Waverly Place, New York, NY 10014.)

A more personal view of what it means to be a survivor of an atomic bomb explosion, and how that experience continues to affect one's life, is presented in *Hellfire: A Journey from Hiroshima.* Two Japanese artists who were under the Hiroshima bomb have portrayed vividly, in their murals, what they saw then and what they continue to see and feel. Their paintings, reproduced effectively in this film, are striking, as are their quietly uttered comments about war and violence. Users of this stimulating film will receive a printed guide to the artwork. A companion book of illustrations called *The Hiroshima Murals* (published by Kodansha International, 1985) is also available. (Color film or videocassette, 58 min, 1986; available from First Run Features, 153 Waverly Place, New York, NY 10014.)

The Early Days of the Atomic Age

When the United States was losing its nuclear monopoly after World War II, the attitudes of the American people to The Bomb took some bizarre twists, largely as the result of government propaganda efforts at calming people's objections and fears. The film *No Place to Hide* reviews some of the propaganda films of the 1950s (e.g., *Self-Preservation in an Atomic Attack, You Can Beat the A-Bomb,* and *Duck and Cover*) designed to convince Americans that they could survive an atomic bomb blast by ducking under furniture and then soaping off the radiation. The community fallout shelter projects of the 1960s, proffered by the government with a bit more subtlety, are then recalled, juxtaposed with telling commentary that reminds us we have no such "civil defense" plans in place today; the carefully stockpiled food in those shelters is rotting away. Questions are forcefully raised: Who has been lying to us? Why? Can anyone survive? What can we know about nuclear weapons and the realities of nuclear war? An award-winning film (American Film Festival, 1982), it is an excellent stimulus for class discussion. (16-mm film or videocassette, color, 29 min, 1982; available from Direct Cinema Limited, P.O. Box 69799, Los Angeles, CA 90069-9976; telephone 213-662-8000.)

The Atomic Cafe covers some of the same territory, the 1940s and 1950s, in a different way. Without narration, it juxtaposes carefully edited documentary film footage; Army atomic battlefield training films; and clips from television shows, newsreels, and those mindless "duck and cover" educational musicals for school children. Thus through visual images, interspersed with hit tunes, gospel music, and hymns of the era, the attitudes of people and the government to nuclear issues are revealed. Included are excerpts from the Nixon–Hiss tapes and accounts of the Rosenberg executions, to suggest the nature of the rabid anticommunism that has fueled the arms race from the beginning. (Videocassette, color and B/W, 92 min; 1982, available from Social Studies School Service, 10200 Jefferson Boulevard, P.O. Box 802, Culver City, CA 90232-0802; telephone 800-421-4246, in California call collect 213-839-2436.)

Radio Bikini is a new film report on the early tests of the hydrogen bomb at Bikini Atoll in the Pacific. At the time, the United States was both confident of its burgeoning scientific and military power and ignorant of the actual effects and implications of massive nuclear explosions. Bikini Atoll, its native people, and U.S. servicemen are still experiencing the tragic effects of those explosions today. The "media circus" surrounding the Bikini tests is documented in this film; much of this newly released footage was classified soon after it was taken. Thus *Radio Bikini* nicely captures the irony "of a government-orchestrated media blitz for a bomb that turned out to be much more dangerous than expected." (Color and B/W videocassette, 56 min, 1988; available from Social Studies School Service, 10200 Jefferson Boulevard, P.O. Box 802, Culver City, CA 90232-0802; telephone 800-421-4246; in California call collect 213-839-2436.)

The Arms Race

Three films offer fascinating background on the nuclear arms race between the superpowers. *How Much is Enough?: Decision Making in the Nuclear Age* explains in some detail just how and why key nuclear arms decisions were made in the past 20 years. Some of these decisions, simply arbitrary or crassly political, are both surprising and disturbing. For example, John Kennedy campaigned for the presidency claiming that he would counter Russian superiority in nuclear missiles. Not only were the Russians *not* ahead in the numbers game, but Kennedy, once elected, approved deployment of 1,000 missiles (Eisenhower had budgeted but 200) for no other reason than that "1000 is a good, round number in our culture," in the words of one advisor. The film also backgrounds our triadic military–nuclear structure (bombs on land, on sea, and in the air) and its growth from turf struggles of the three military services. Also discussed are the development of MIRVs (multiple-warhead missiles), the effects of the SALT I treaty, and the impact of French and British nuclear capability on Russian policies. The thinking of the Committee on the Present Danger, a strong advocate of continued nuclear arms buildup to counter what it sees as the Russian threat, is covered at some length (significantly so, because Ronald Reagan and many of his advisors and arms control negotiators were members of that committee). Interviews with past and present policymakers and stimulating graphics to illustrate complex information make this film an excellent tool for understanding our present nuclear situation. It is a winner of several awards, including first prize at the United States Film and Video Festival. (Color film or videocassette, 59 min, 1982; available from Docu-America Films, P.O. Box 985, Vallejo, CA 94590.)

No First Use: Preventing Nuclear War raises questions about the nuclear arms race and current policies by examining a particular aspect of the present-day standoff between the two superpowers: the "defense" of Western Europe. The United States, its NATO allies, and the Soviet Union are perhaps closest to a nuclear exchange in Europe. This film explains why, examining the postwar history of the area and the gradual buildup of armed forces on both sides in response to one another's growing arsenals. Because of Soviet superiority in manpower and conventional weaponry, NATO depends heavily on its nuclear strength. While recent political changes in the Soviet Union and Eastern Europe promise a lessening of military tensions, plans are still in place for the use of "tactical" nuclear weapons to respond to a Russian invasion. The United States and its NATO allies remain unwilling to adopt a "no-first-use" policy. Thus the tension, thus the danger. The film presents interviews with military and national leaders responsible for current policies. An alternative proposal offered by the Union of Concerned Scientists (the producers of this film)—building up NATO's conventional forces so that both sides would be less likely to resort to the nuclear option—is then presented and analyzed. A balanced yet moving presentation of crucial issues, this film was a finalist at the 1983 American Film Festival. (Color film or videocassette, 30 min, 1983; available from University of California Extension Media Center, 2176 Shattuck Avenue, Berkeley, CA 94704; telephone 415-642-0460.)

The third film in this group reminds us that, after all, arms control is not simply a matter of getting two superpowers to cut their nuclear arsenals. *The Last Empire: Intervention and Nuclear War* demonstrates how the United States, for example, has used its nuclear leverage for years to influence the outcome of "conventional" wars, disagreements, and even the day-to-day behavior of governments around the world. Likewise, nuclear proliferation to countries beyond the superpowers' spheres of influence complicates attempts at disarmament simply because governments large and small relish the power they can wield by brandishing their nuclear weapons. Historians, nuclear theorists and peace advocates, for example, Daniel Ellsberg, Noam Chomsky, Howard Zinn, Ronald Dellums, and Helen Caldicott, comment on the significance of these complex realities. (16-mm film or videocassette, color, 30 min, 1986; available from Cambridge Documentary Films, P.O. Box 385, Cambridge, MA 02139.)

Any discussion of arms control efforts among the superpowers is complicated in these days by current U.S. policy regarding SDI, or "Star Wars." The Bush administration seems as committed to moving ahead on this proposed antiballistic missile defense system as the Reagan administration was, despite its provocative nature, its astronomical cost, and its dubious functional value. SDI is debated vigorously in *Reliability and Risk: Computers and Nuclear War.* Produced by a group called Computer Professionals for Social Responsibility, this program calls into serious question the essential feasibility and putative reliability of SDI. The argument is made by professionals in the computer field that SDI simply cannot do what its proponents claim: identify, track, and destroy, by means of computerized surveillance and weapons systems, enemy missiles aimed at the United States. People on both sides of the "Star Wars" issue need to come to terms with these arguments and to understand how the SDI proposal, no matter its inherent merits, is affecting arms control negotiations today as well as our ongoing relationships with the Soviet Union. (Color videocassette, 34 min, 1986; available from Aylmer Press, 930 Spring Street, Madison, WI 53705.)

Nuclear War: Medical Effects

Advanced students of nuclear issues will want to tackle this gruesome topic. Indeed, teachers and discussion leaders should be certain that audiences of a vivid film on the short- and long-term effects of nuclear blast, thermal pulse, and radiation, *The Last Epidemic,* are properly prepared for what they will see and are carefully debriefed afterwards. A context must be provided, out of respect for the feelings of the audience. And in that context the teacher or leader might well explore the ironies implicit in his or her so caring in the abstract, in a classroom situation, while political leaders, in reality, are setting the stage for such human suffering on apocalyptic levels. (16-mm film or videocassette, 36 min, 1981; available from Educational Film and Video Project, 1725 Seabright Avenue, Santa Cruz, CA 95062.)

The Impact of Nuclear Reality on Children and Adolescents

The psychological and emotional effects of present-day nuclear realities on people, and in particular on children, are just now being explored. Several audiovisuals deal with these topics. Of special interest to classroom teachers is *Growing Up with the Bomb,* a 17-min videotaped interview (a segment of ABC's news program *20/20)* with two Harvard child psychiatrists, William Beardslee and John E. Mack. Focusing on children ages 10 to 18, these authorities argue that fear of nuclear holocaust is widespread and significant. Children typically have fewer defenses against such fears than do adults, so parents, teachers, and counselors must try to channel and alleviate those fears. Beardslee and Mack explain what can be done. (Color film or videotape, 17 min, 1982; Social Studies School Service, 10200 Jefferson Boulevard, P.O. Box 802, Culver City, CA 90232-0802; telephone 800-421-4246, in California call collect 213-839-2436.)

Professor Mack is also featured on a more recent program, *In the Nuclear Shadow: What Can the Children Tell Us?* He and psychiatrist–author Robert Jay Lifton open the film with background commentary. Mack introduces a questionnaire on nuclear issues he devised for children, and then children ranging in age from 7 to 17 tell their feelings. Their comments are both very moving and thoughtful. As they describe their fears and their nightmares, their frustrations and anger at what adults have done, they argue the necessity of immediate action. The world is worth saving, and the children believe there is hope. Film consultant Karen Sayer says, "If you could show only one film about the impact on children of the threat of nuclear war, *In the Nuclear Shadow* should be it." (Color film or videotape, 26 min, 1983; available from Educational Film and Video Project, 1725 Seabright Avenue, Santa Cruz, CA 95062.)

Similar insights into the fears (and the great wisdom) of children as they attempt to deal with nuclear realities is offered in another recent film, *Bombs Will Make the Rainbow Break.* Children are interviewed as they play. They tell about their drawings of explosions and fireballs and horrible dying. The film concludes with footage of a recent children's march on the White House protesting the arms race; letters from children all over the country were read aloud during the rally. The point is that much *can* be done. A very polished, carefully produced film, it is the winner of the 1983 CINE Golden Eagle Award. (Color film or videotape, 26 min, 1983; available from Films, Incorporated, 1144 Wilmette Avenue, Wilmette, IL 60091.)

Older students and their attitudes toward nuclear issues are the topic of *The Nuclear Nightmare: A Forum for Teen Expression.* Through carefully structured discussions, interviews, and individual presentations, a group of young people, their schoolteachers, and national and international experts on nuclear issues provide the audiences of this program with a forum: the opportunity to hear their fears and concerns expressed, to acquire basic knowledge about this complex topic, and to learn what can be done about the nuclear predicament. Keyed to these well-organized presentations, leader's guide suggestions for writing and discussion enable viewers to come to grips with their own feelings, to know that those feelings are widely shared, and to explore ways of bringing about meaningful action and change. The production values of the film are first-rate; the commentators uniformly articulate, intelligent, and stimulating. While high school social studies, English, and science courses would provide the most appropriate venues for this program and its related study, discussion, and writing activities, general adult audiences (e.g., church, community, library, club, and Parent–Teacher Association groups) will find the *The Nuclear Nightmare* worthwhile. (Color videocassette, 40 min, 1986; available from United Learning, 6633 West Howard Street, Niles, IL 60648.)

The group International Physicians for the Prevention of Nuclear War has been conducting classroom discussions at various grade levels, exploring the thoughts and opinions children have about nuclear weapons and nuclear war. Conducted by "nondirective" leaders, these discussions have been videotaped and edited into several separate programs. A 21-min overview of the whole project, *There's A Nuclear War Going On Inside Me,* includes an introduction and rationale presented by discussion leaders Dr. Eric Chivian and Roberta Snow; it then offers selections from student comments recorded in first-, third-, fifth-, seventh-, and ninth-grade classrooms. Separate *edited* tapes made at grades 3 (35 min), 5 (13 min), and 9 (24 min), called *Third [Fifth, Ninth] Graders Discuss Nuclear Issues,* are available, as are *unedited* tapes (60 min long) of discussions in grades 1, 3, 5 and 9. (Color videotape, 1983; available from Educators for Social Responsibility, 23 Garden Street, Cambridge, MA 02138; telephone 617- 492-1764.)

A good discussion trigger for high school or general audiences concerned with issues of nuclear weapons and nuclear fear is *Safe Harbor.* This is a simple but well-acted story about a young man, an aimless and unmotivated beach bum living hand to mouth, who one day has to dive into the ocean to escape a thug collecting his gambling debts. He's picked up by a couple of people fishing, an elderly Japanese American survivor of the Hiroshima bomb and his granddaughter. Our hero, now patched up and fed, confides in the young lady that he has frequent nightmares about nuclear explosions, so he's convinced life is to be lived for pleasure and for self. If the civil defense sirens ever signal a real attack he's just going to get stoned. He resists his benefactors' rebuttals that it's hope that turns caterpillars into butterflies and fish into nets; that if enough people make peace with their own fears, we may just be able to make peace in the world; and that to heal fear one must work, and live, and love. A couple of plot twists later, after another run-in with erstwhile buddies, our hero is ready to reconsider. *Safe Harbor* is not as trite as it may seem. The action is exciting in several places. Conflicts— physical, psychological and intellectual—maintain interest. And good acting carries the day. After viewing the film, teachers and group leaders can generate useful discussion of meaningful alternatives to solipsistic thinking, and thus help young people get at their fears and feelings of insecurity. (Color film or videocassette, 27 min, 1984; available from The Media Guild, Suite E, 11722 Sorrento Valley Road, San Diego, CA 92121; telephone 619-755-9191.)

Audiences interested in ongoing effects of nuclear reality on young people ought to consider those effects on Soviet youth as well. There is cause for hope in knowing that Soviet young people are at the forefront of critical thinking about nuclear reality in their country. And—need we be reminded—the Soviets are human, too. In their basic human values and hopes, in their expressed concern for the future of human civilization, we may see our own reflected. A fine film will demonstrate. *What Soviet Children Are Saying About Nuclear Weapons* consists of a series of responses by Soviet children to questions put to them by American psychiatric researchers. To get at some of the prejudices American audiences feel against the Soviets, users of this film should write down *their* answers to the questions before they view the Soviet children responding, then watch the film, and listen. (Videotape, all formats, color, 20 min, 1983; available from Educators for Social Responsibility, 23 Garden Street, Cambridge, MA 02138; telephone 617-492-1764.)

CONSCIOUSNESS RAISERS

Films in this category best serve particular audiences: school and general adult groups not necessarily participating in organized classroom or workshop activities on nuclear issues, but rather gathered together on an ad hoc basis to be introduced or exposed to the subject. To say that these programs raise consciousness through theatrical techniques, visual shock tactics, or other emotional appeals is not to condemn them. One must begin somewhere, somehow. Let it be with vigor and interest!

If You Love This Planet: Dr. Helen Caldicott on Nuclear War is the famous Canadian film that the U.S. government called "propaganda" and tried to censor upon its release in 1982; it subsequently won an Academy Award for its quality. Basically a filmed lecture by Dr. Caldicott, the film outlines the consequences of a single 20-megaton bomb explosion. Dr. Caldicott's analyses are supplemented with film clips and photographs of the damage done to the cities of Hiroshima and Nagasaki, and the sufferings of survivors. As is well known, Dr. Caldicott is an activist in the antinuclear movement; she urges her audience to direct action (protest marches, civil disobedience, and the like). Whether or not we agree with her methods, we must come to grips with the frightening data and insights Dr. Caldicott gives us. (Color film or videotape, 26 min, 1982; available from Direct Cinema Limited, P.O. Box 69799, Los Angeles, CA 90069-9976; telephone 213-652-8000.)

Nuclear War: A Guide to Armageddon takes a similar approach to documenting the effects of a nuclear blast, in this instance in a primarily British context. The narrator postulates the detonation of a 1-megaton bomb over St. Paul's Cathedral in central London, and then describes the death and destruction to follow. Effective animation and film clips of the Hiroshima bombing illustrate the presentation. The narrator concludes by questioning the value of fallout shelters, arguing that "survivors" of atomic warfare would have no civilization to return to. Our only hope is to reduce the likelihood of nuclear conflict *now*. It was a finalist at the 1983 American Film Festival. (Color film or videotape, 25 min, 1983; available from Films, Incorporated, 1144 Wilmette Avenue, Wilmette, IL 60091.)

In 1982, 150 residents of Stafford, Vermont, produced a "pageant" about nuclear destruction in their town. *Button, Button: A Dream of Nuclear War* is a 14-min film outline of that event. Employing the costumes and conventions of mime, theater, and dance, and with background music ranging from Verdi's "Requiem" to folk, the people present scenes from daily life intercut with gathering armies and growing arsenals. Politicians exchange their blather, generals posture, and the red phones are brought out. Finally, buttons are pushed and nuclear holocaust occurs. People "dance" wildly in panic and pain as the film—now in slow motion and overexposed—records the barrenness of the aftermath. This highly recommended film can both stimulate discussion of nuclear issues and demonstrate, under a discussion leader's guidance, the great evocative power of the theater. (Color film or videotape, 14 min, 1982; available from Cantomedia, P.O. Box 315, Franklin Lakes, NJ 07417.)

Changing the Silence is another theater piece, conceived and performed by high school students in Boston at the end of a short course on nuclear issues. As one method of putting into action the lessons they learned, the students used song, dance, pantomime, and poetry to express their fears and hopes. The film comes with a packet of information on the short course that inspired this production, and suggestions for using *Changing the Silence* in other contexts. (Color videocassette, two versions: 19 and 36 min, 1985; available from STOP Nuclear War, 636 Beacon Street, #203, Boston, MA 02215.)

A similar sort of production is *If the World Goes Away, Where Will the Children Play?* Like *Changing the Silence* it would be effectively used with school-age audiences. The theatrical interest is strong: James Earl Jones serves as narrator, and professional musicians perform the score, as, in allegory, a mime forms children into a "circle of peace" depicting the story of the creation. Then the world is shattered by atomic explosions. Child survivors of Hiroshima and Nagasaki tell, and show, their wounds, and the children of the circle begin to throw balloon "missiles" at each other in their anger. Shocked, the mime has dancers depict the "uncreation" of nuclear holocaust, and the children throw away their weapons and join hands once more. A fascinating, well-made production. (Color film or videocassette, 45 min, 1985; available from Mass Media Ministries, 2116 North Charles Street, Baltimore, MD 21218.)

Ghosts of Hiroshima also combines theater with showing and telling, but in a different way. The film's title is actually the title of a play by Debra Lubar that is videotaped here in performance. Then, using well the resources of the film medium, the director intersperses throughout the photographs and spoken testimony of the Hiroshima and Nagasaki atomic bomb survivors whose stories had provided Lubar with the raw material for her play. The original drama and this videotape are

especially effective in ironically juxtaposing official government claims that nuclear war is survivable (e.g., the mails will be running again in a few days) with
eyewitness testimony of the horrendous destructiveness of the primitive, miniscule
atomic explosions of World War II. This film will give one pause! (Color videotape, 30 minutes, 1983; available from Filmakers Library, 133 East 58th Street,
New York, NY 10022.)

The Game Room, a play made for television, is a story with a difference. The
initially routine shopping-center arcade setting of this film story takes on an arrest-
ingly symbolic aura when a barefoot self-declared "Earth Mother" walks in, looking for her "lost children." She finds them, many similarly barefoot and tattered,
in the arcade's back room, tensely watching a high-stakes war game. The players
are two presidents, their game board a map of the world studded with nuclear
weapons "pieces" deployed in thick clusters. Earth Mother watches the presidents' aides give the game room manager IOUs for more and more "pieces"; she
is aghast as tension mounts and the players threaten cataclysmic confrontation.
Earth Mother pleads with the Presidents to stop the game. They don't really want
to kill people, she tells them. Everyone is family. Besides, the game is using up the
world's resources, and because of their war game the children are starving. At the
very last moment, the two leaders hear her and agree to talk. This imaginative
little story, with its polished acting is an excellent trigger for discussion of the
complex problems of world peace; the economic, social, and psychological costs
of weapons' proliferation; and the growing danger of global nuclear war. High
school and general adult audiences will find the program provocative. (16-mm
film and videocassette, color, 27 min, 1986; available from The Media Guild,
Suite E, 11722 Sorrento Valley Road, San Diego, CA 92121; telephone 615-755-
9191.)

Finally, a number of excellent film programs combine vividly presented information on various nuclear war issues with calls to action of various kinds. Audiences are urged to act upon their new awareness, for the individual can make a
difference. A particularly effective film to stimulate classroom discussion, *One
Million Hiroshimas,* highlights the presentations made by a number of physicians,
scientists, military people, and others at the Second Congress of International
Physicians for the Prevention of Nuclear War in Cambridge, England, 1982. The
overall thesis is that the nuclear arms race threatens humankind with extinction,
but that much can still be done to lessen the risks. Among the participants are Carl
Sagan, Helen Caldicott, Jonas Salk, Bernard Lown, and two retired military
leaders—a Russian general and an American admiral—who agree in a conversation
that nuclear arsenals on both sides must be reduced. This film was a finalist at the
1983 American Film Festival. (Color film or videotape, 28 min, 1982; available
from Resource Center for Nonviolence, P.O. Box 2324, Santa Cruz, CA 95060.)

Sponsored by another activist physicians group, Physicians for Social Responsibility, *Race to Oblivion* carefully combines an interview of a badly disfigured
survivor of the Hiroshima bomb with footage of nuclear explosions, scenes of
devastation, and statements of arms control activists calling for a freeze in weapons production. This meaningful combination of the theoretical, the actual, and the
personal, together with moving scenes of children singing "If there's ever to be
peace on earth, it's up to you and me," results in a powerful film, especially
recommended for general audiences. (Color film or videotape, 49 min, 1982;

available from Physicians for Social Responsibility, P.O. Box 35385, Los Angeles, CA 90035.)

Several fine films focus on various antinuclear activists and activities, emphasizing that much is being done and much *can be done* to halt the spread of nuclear weapons. *Gods of Metal* comments at length on current budget priorities that allocate billions for weapons and precious little to alleviate hunger and disease. People are interviewed who have protested against militarism in various ways, for example, refusing to pay the "defense" share of their taxes and protesting at munitions plants. The film ends with scenes of mass antinuclear protest marches and calls on its audience to act in similar fashion. It was nominated for an Academy Award (best short documentary) in 1982. (Color, 27 min, 1982; available from Icarus Films, Incorporated, Room 1319, 200 Park Avenue South, New York, NY 10003.)

The Time Has Come stresses the international character of growing activism against nuclear weapons, presenting footage of protest marches in Europe and in Japan, as well as in many cities in the United States. Individuals representing many religious, ethnic, and national groups are interviewed and filmed as they work together in various antinuclear activities. A well-made film, suitable for all school and general adult audiences (intermediate grades and up), it was a finalist at the 1983 American Film Festival. (Color film or videotape, 27 min, 1983; available from NARMIC/American Friends Service Committee, 1501 Cherry Street, Philadelphia, PA 19012.)

How to Prevent a Nuclear War covers the same ground, making the same point even more forcefully, through its refreshingly upbeat approach and readily demonstrable thesis—that each of us can make our voice heard; each of us can do something to lessen the threat of war. The structure of this new program is simple. It consists of 15 vignettes describing the efforts of peace activists of all types: a suburban housewife who stuffs pamphlets in the pockets of fellow skiers while riding the ski lift; another housewife who ran for school board because of her concern for educating for peace; a retired librarian who now devotes her "working" days to disarmament activities; a clergyman who uses his pulpit to educate his congregation; the founder of an inner city gospel choir who conducts a Concert for Peace; and a union leader, shipyard worker, flight attendant, professor, and high school student who, in various ways in their own communities, are doing what they can. Musical performances enhance the entertainment value of this film, and thus its impact. Included are a cabaret performance of Tom Lehrer's song, "We'll All Go Together When We Go" and clips of the Vernon Jones Gospel Singers in concert. This well-made program, which was a finalist at the American Film and Video Festival in 1988, is especially appropriate for showing to any number of general student and adult audiences, in high schools, public libraries, churches, clubs and other community organizations. (Color 16-mm film and videocassette, 50 min, 1988; available from New Day Films, Suite 1210, 853 Broadway, New York, NY 10003; telephone 212-477-4604.)

Anyone who studies the various peace movements and leading peace activists in the country these days is struck by the prominent leadership role played by women. *Women—For America, For the World* focuses on the work of several women as they raise questions about our current economic, political, and military policies and practices as they relate to the arms race in general and "Star Wars" in particular. Key assertions are that the world's nuclear stockpiles are far too large for basic deterrent needs, that the "Star Wars" antiballistic missile defense system threatens peaceful relations with the Soviet Union at the same time it is extravagantly wasteful of scientific and human resources (to say nothing of its shocking dollar cost), that attitudes toward erstwhile "enemies" have got to be normalized, and that massive money commitments to the military must be redirected to solving social and economic problems both at home and in Third World countries. The point is that individual people can bring about changes in governmental policies, and women are admirably suited to lead those efforts. This Oscar Award-winning film (best short documentary, 1986) features interviews with Joanne Woodward (actress), Randall Forsberg (director of the Institute for Defense and Disarmament Studies), Alice Tepper-Marlin (executive director of the Council on Economic Priorities), Dorothy Reddings (League of Women Voters), Patricia Schroeder (House of Representatives), and Mary Dent Crisp (co-chair of the Republican National Committee). (Color 16-mm film and videocassette, 29 min, 1986; Aylmer Press, 930 Spring Street, Madison, WI 53705.)

A man who has seen the globe in its entirety, Apollo 9 astronaut Russell Schweikart has said that "there are no frames. There are no boundaries." Beginning with Schweikart's insights, the film *No Frames, No Boundaries* reminds us that nuclear weapons and nuclear war *will* reach across national and indeed continental boundaries to wreak their havoc. Historically, the film explains, nations could go to war with some assurance that their walls would protect them and that their efforts at destruction would have a self-contained result. The folly behind today's nuclear buildup is that people still believe they can go on warring as they always have and still live on as a state and a race. Better, this film argues, to work toward disarmament, toward the breaking down of frames and boundaries, building a new world upon the commonalities of human experience and ideals as revealed, for example, in all religious faiths. Some may see such ideas as simplistic, but this well-made film (a finalist at the 1983 American Film Festival) will, in any case, stimulate thought and discussion. (Color film or videotape, 21 min, 1982; available from Creative Initiative Foundation, 222 High Street, Palo Alto, CA 94301.)

FEATURE FILMS

Many feature films over the years have turned nuclear themes into theatrical entertainment for the masses. Although pressure to turn a profit at the box office often results in oversimplification or trivialization of complex issues, feature films, because of their entertainment value, can be powerful teaching tools. Their length, of course, may make scheduling difficult, and their artistic complexity may complicate teaching. But for those willing and able to make the effort, here are a few fine films from which to choose, films praised for their artistic value and for their stimulating presentations of nuclear issues.

On the Beach, based on the novel by Nevil Shute, portrays a group of Australians awaiting the aftereffects of a nuclear war that has destroyed the rest of the world. Directed by Stanley Kramer and starring Gregory Peck, Ava Gardner, and Fred Astaire. (Color, 133 min, 1959; available for rental from United Artists 16, 729 Seventh Avenue, New York, NY 10019; or for purchase on videotape from Direct Cinema Limited, P.O. Box 69799, Los Angeles, CA 90069-9976, telephone 213-652-8000.)

Dr. Strangelove, Or How I Learned to Stop Worrying and Love the Bomb is a very funny and very frightening look at the dangers of nuclear war, focusing on the sort of very imperfect human beings likely to be in charge. Fine performances by Peter Sellers, George C. Scott, and Slim Pickens. (B/W, 93 min, 1964; available for rental from Swank Motion Pictures, 201 South Jefferson Avenue, St. Louis, MO 63166, or for purchase on videotape from Social Studies School Service, 10200 Jefferson Boulevard, P.O. Box 802, Culver City, CA 90232-0802; telephone 800-421-4246, in California call collect 213-839-2436.)

Fail Safe demonstrates the inevitable, fatal flaws in our vaunted technology. A computer error launches a nuclear attack on Moscow that cannot be called back. The harrowing conclusion depicts the fruitless efforts of world leaders to forestall retaliation and universal annihilation. Henry Fonda and Walter Matthau give brilliant performances. (Color, 111 min, 1964; available for rental from Budget Films, 4590 Santa Monica Boulevard, Los Angeles, CA 90029, or for purchase on videotape from Direct Cinema Limited, P.O. Box 69799, Los Angeles, CA 90069-9976, telephone 213-652-8000.)

In *Seven Days in May,* a five-star general plans a military coup against a U.S. president who has signed a nuclear disarmament pact with Russia. The film makes one wonder about who, in our democracy, really runs things. Directed by John Frankenheimer, with fine performances by Burt Lancaster, Kirk Douglas, Fredric March, and Ava Gardner. (B/W, 118 min, 1964; film version available for rental or purchase from Films, Incorporated, 1144 Wilmette Avenue, Wilmette, IL 60091; videotape may be purchased from Social Studies School Service, 10200 Jefferson Boulevard, P.O. Box 802, Culver City, CA 90232-0802; telephone 800-421-4246, in California call collect 213-839-2436.)

Three more recent feature-length films worth considering are *The Day After, Testament,* and *Wargames.* Broadcast on the ABC television network in 1983, *The Day After* depicts the horrible, destructive aftermath of nuclear bombs dropped on Kansas City and, by suggestion, elsewhere around the globe. Thus, the film questions the wisdom of nuclear "deterrence," mutual assured destruction (MAD), and other moral issues of the arms race. (Color videotape [purchase only], 150 min, 1983; available from Social Studies School Service, 10200 Jefferson Boulevard, P.O. Box 802, Culver City, CA 90232-0802; telephone 800-421-4246; in California call collect 213-839-2436.)

Testament begins with a similar premise, that a major city (San Francisco) has been bombed, but concentrates on the human responses within a surviving but dying family. This focus on the personal—in a very understated manner at that—proves ultimately more moving and more convincing than many films that recreate fireballs, crushed buildings, and mass death. *Testament* can affect one at deeper levels than *The Day After,* and is in every other way a superior work of film art. (Color videotape [purchase only], 90 min, 1983; available from Social Studies School Service, 10200 Jefferson Boulevard, P.O. Box 802, Culver City, CA 90232-0802; telephone 800-421-4246; in California call collect 213-839-2436.)

Wargames modernizes the premise of the 1964 film *Fail Safe,* reminding us of the fallibility of our "superior" technology. In this story, a precocious young computer hacker unwittingly breaks into super-secret Defense Department files and, thinking he's playing a war game, sets in motion the irreversible countdown to World War III. (Color videotape [purchase only], 114 min, 1983; available from Social Studies School Service, 10200 Jefferson Blvd., P.O. Box 802, Culver City, CA 90232-0802; telephone 800-421-4246; in California call collect 213-839-2436.)

INDEX